T0210477

Lecture Notes in Business Information Processing

198

Series Editors

Wil van der Aalst
Eindhoven Technical University, Eindhoven, The Netherlands
John Mylopoulos
University of Trento, Povo, Italy
Michael Rosemann
Queensland University of Technology, Brisbane, QLD, Australia
Michael J. Shaw
University of Illinois, Urbana-Champaign, IL, USA
Clemens Szyperski
Microsoft Research, Redmond, WA, USA

More information about this series at http://www.springer.com/series/7911

Darshana Sedera · Norbert Gronau
Mary Sumner (Eds.)

Enterprise Systems

Strategic, Organizational, and Technological Dimensions

International Workshops
Pre-ICIS 2010, St. Louis, MO, USA, December 12, 2010
Pre-ICIS 2011, Shanghai, China, December 4, 2011
and Pre-ICIS 2012, Orlando, FL, USA,
December 16, 2012
Revised Selected Papers

 Springer

Editors
Darshana Sedera
Queensland University of Technology
Brisbane, QLD
Australia

Mary Sumner
Southern Illinois University
Edwardsville, IL
USA

Norbert Gronau
Universität Potsdam
Potsdam
Germany

ISSN 1865-1348   ISSN 1865-1356   (electronic)
Lecture Notes in Business Information Processing
ISBN 978-3-319-17586-7   ISBN 978-3-319-17587-4   (eBook)
DOI 10.1007/978-3-319-17587-4

Library of Congress Control Number: 2015937956

Springer Cham Heidelberg New York Dordrecht London
© Springer International Publishing Switzerland 2015

Printed on acid-free paper

Springer International Publishing AG Switzerland is part of Springer Science+Business Media
(www.springer.com)

Preface

Enterprise Systems are large-scale, real-time, integrated application-software packages that use the computational, data storage, and data transmission power of modern information technology to support processes, information flows, reporting, and business analytics within and between complex organizations (Seddon, Calvert, and Young 2010). Enterprise Systems seem to impound deep knowledge of new ways of designing and executing organizational processes, and that they can cause considerable assimilation difficulties for client organizations (Robey et al. 2002). There are several terms used in academia, *enterprise system* and *ERP* being the most commonly used refer to all large organization-wide packaged applications including enterprise resource planning (ERP), customer relationship management (CRM), supply chain management (SCM), data warehousing, and any application components of the software platforms on which these applications are built (e.g., SAP's NetWeaver and Oracle's Fusion) (Seddon, Calvert, and Young 2010). Further, there is a new frontier of applications being developed in the Enterprise Systems domain, with the enablement of cloud and mobile computing. Such technologies will provide greater innovation potential, as well as computerization to small- and medium-sized organizations (Elragal and Kommos 2012). A survey by the Gartner group on the future of corporate-wide systems adoption has found that 47% of the firms planned to move cloud-based systems within the next 5 years and the majority of those were from SMEs (Rayner 2014).

In 2006, the Special Interest Group for Enterprise Systems (SIG-ES) held their first Pre-ICIS workshop at Milwaukee, Wisconsin, USA, with Prof. Peter Seddon as the keynote speaker and Chaired by Dr. Darshana Sedera. Since then, the Enterprise Systems Pre-ICIS workshop has attracted much attention from senior and early-career academic colleagues. The papers included in this edited book represent a peer-reviewed, small sample of contemporary research that attempts to document and advance the research on diverse topics related to Enterprise Systems.

The contributory papers in this edited book are multidisciplinary in scope and cover strategic, organizational, and technological dimensions. They range from purely conceptual to literature reviews to papers on teaching-related aspects. Taken together, these papers provide a snapshot of the critical concerns and developments in the Enterprise Systems research domain. The 17 papers in this edited book were predominantly selected from workshops held in the years of 2010, 2011, and 2012. The papers are arranged in such a way that they provide a holistic value to the reader, commencing by introducing the key characteristics, next discussing the implementation, followed by the nuances of Enterprise System Use. The last few chapters discuss specific solutions like CRM and SCM application, while the concluding chapter provides the future direction of Enterprise Systems.

January 2015

Darshana Sedera
Norbert Gronau
Mary Sumner

Contents

Characteristics of Enterprise Software

Alexandra Kees[✉]

Department of Computer Science, Hochschule Bonn-Rhein-Sieg,
Grantham-Allee 20, 53757 Sankt Augustin, Germany
alexandra.kees@h-brs.de

Abstract. Enterprise software is very complex and has an enormous impact on the competitiveness of enterprises. Many stakeholder groups are affected by enterprise software. To standardise and improve the communication within and among these stakeholder groups, a 'morphological box for enterprise software' was designed. Several iterations have been tried, the current version 5.0 is being released in this work. It comprises 5 feature groups with 19 features and 103 characteristics which were all derived from related work and/or feasibility, pilot and case studies conducted for this purpose. The morphological box is then applied to two ERP-software systems. This paper demonstrates that this approach is easy to apply, flexible to adapt to different needs and helpful to visualise the nature of enterprise software. The approach therefore enhances the description, classification and pre-selection of enterprise software. Future work should focus on deriving an improved range of characteristics for specific features.

Keywords: Enterprise software · Enterprise system · Business software · Business system · ERP-software · ERP-system · Taxonomy · Morphological scheme · Morphological box

1 Introduction

Enterprise software systems provide interdivisional support for the business processes of an enterprise and use master data to improve the cooperation between the different departments [1–3]. There are different types of enterprise software [4, 5], e.g.:

- Customer relationship management software (CRM-software),
- Enterprise resource planning software (ERP-software),
- Supply chain management software (SCM-software),
- Business intelligence software (BI-software),
- Business process modeling software (BPM-software),
- Enterprise content management software (ECM-software),
- Document/knowledge management software,
- Workflow management software etc.

These software systems are used by software developers, software vendors, software users, consultants, researchers and in training. In all these fields, people need to be able to describe or classify enterprise software systems. Unfortunately, there is hardly any

D. Sedera et al. (Eds.): Pre-ICIS 2010-2012, LNBIP 198, pp. 1–18, 2015.
DOI: 10.1007/978-3-319-17587-4_1

standardisation of how enterprise software should be described or classified. Furthermore, existing market guides would benefit from using a method to visualise the characteristics of enterprise software systems [6–11]. This would make it easier to compare the different enterprise software systems in the pre-selection phase of a software selection project.

This work aims to bridge this gap. The following section provides an overview of the morphological method based upon which a morphological scheme is derived to describe, classify and pre-select the most important features and characteristics of enterprise software. The underlying logic has been confirmed by related work and/or feasibility, pilot and case studies which have been conducted for this purpose. This leads to a morphological box for enterprise software. The morphologic box is then applied to two enterprise software systems. Finally, the findings and the contribution of this work are discussed.

2 Approach

The morphological method based upon Zwicky is an established method to describe and classify objects. The term morphology comes from the Greek words *morphé* (shape, form) und *lógos* (word, teaching, reason) and stands for the science of form and shape. Johann Wolfgang von Goethe originally developed the morphological method as a purely descriptive logic to describe natural phenomena [13] while today it is also being used for describing the features of research objects [14, 15]. Zwicky established the morphological method as a creative way of problem-solving [16, 17] while it has also been utilised for standardisation and classification purposes [18].

The morphological method is based on the identification of the particular features of objects and the definition of all the possible characteristics which each feature could take on. Its application requires consideration of the following aspects:

- identification of the *relevant* features applicable to the specific inquiry;
- *suitable* definition of the characteristics of the features in generic terms with defined ranges of values because
  - many features can have a significant number of characteristics (e.g. the feature 'number of users' can have characteristics 0, 1, 2, … 100.000, 100.001, etc.) and
  - the number of characteristics varies according to each feature;
- *independence* to the greatest possible extent (mindful of the fact that complete independence is only rarely possible)
  - between the characteristics of each distinguishing feature and
  - between the characteristics of different distinguishing features.

The logic of the morphological classification of features will be referred to as a morphological scheme and illustrated in the form of a morphological box. The lines of connection between the characteristics of the features of an object are termed pathways [16].

The aim of this approach is to provide a clear description of the enterprise software through its features and characteristics. The possibility of using the morphological scheme for classifying and pre-selecting enterprise software is thereby provided (e.g. by comparing the pathways of different objects). The features and their characteristics are

- derived from existing taxonomies and/or
- feasibility and pilot studies conducted for this purpose [19, 20], and/or
- case studies conducted in cooperation with a consultancy specialising in enterprise software selection (IT-Matchmaker database) [21].

Zwicky implies the definition of the characteristics of a feature, so that when describing an object only one characteristic of each feature applies. This is in order to avoid any horizontal sections in the pathways between characteristics [16, 17]. Later works withdrew this position [6, 14], and it will not be applied in in this work either, to make some features more user-friendly.

3 Morphological Scheme for Enterprise Software

As confirmed in a number of feasibility, pilot and case studies conducted in the course of this research, the following five groups of features need to be considered when describing, classifying and pre-selecting enterprise software [19–23]:

(1) maturity, as defined by
- version
- edition
- year of origin
  (The combination of the name of the software, its version number and its edition designation make it possible to clearly identify the software and assign a complete software name (thus complete software name = name of the software + version number + edition designation)).
(2) target group, as defined by
- scope
- target industry sector
- target enterprise size
- target economy
(3) technology, as defined by
- delivery mode
- server operating system
- client operating system
- database
- programming language
(4) dissemination, as defined by
- number of customers
- number of reference customers
- number of installations
- number of users
- number of partnering enterprises

(5) contracting, as defined by
- license
- contracting partner.

The individual features will be described below. For each feature, a suitable number of characteristics will be derived.

3.1 Version

The version number indicates the development stage that a software has reached. It often consists of a sequence of numbers divided by full stops (numerical version number, e.g. webERP 4.07.8). In some cases the enterprise software possesses a version number based on the year in which the version was released (date based version number, e.g. AvERP 2012.02). The numbers of pre-versions and/or unreleased versions are normally extended by the suffix

- 'α': pre-version of a software that requires testing,
- 'β': pre-version of a software that has already gone through the α-stage but is still not fully approved and requires further testing or
- RC (Release Candidate): pre-version of a software that has gone through the α-and β-stages and is deemed to be bug-free and stable – it is therefore considered to be ready for release for the software's users but still should undergo final testing.

This results in alphanumerical version numbers. Version numbers beginning with '0' are usually α-, β- or RC-versions of a software to which no version has ever been released before.

When considering the nature of the feature 'version', the following clusters have been identified in the feasibility, pilot and case studies [19–21]:

- non-released pre-version: unreleased version of a software to which no version has ever been released before (version number usually follows the pattern 0.*)
- non-released version: unreleased version of a software that still requires testing (version number is usually extended by 'α', 'β' or 'RC')
- first released version: the first version of a software that has been released (version number is usually 1.0)
- lower version: comparably 'young' version of a software (usually with a version number between 1.0 and 3.0)
- improved version: software version which has already been revised numerous times (version number usually between 3.0 and 5.0)
- often revised version: software version which has been frequently revised (version number usually between 5.0 and 10.0)
- very often revised version: software version which has been very frequently revised (version number usually above 10.0).

In the morphological box for enterprise software, the feature 'version' is thus represented as shown in Fig. 1.

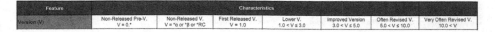

Feature	Characteristics						
Version (V)	Non-Released Pre-V. V = 0.*	Non-Released V. V = *α or *β or *RC	First Released V. V = 1.0	Lower V. 1.0 < V ≤ 3.0	Improved Version 3.0 < V ≤ 5.0	Often Revised V. 5.0 < V ≤ 10.0	Very Often Revised V. 10.0 < V

Fig. 1. Characteristics of the feature 'version'

3.2 Edition

An edition is a pre-configuration of software modules for a specific application of the software. The pre-configuration is usually associated with the performance capacity of the software (e.g. differentiating between 'basic edition', 'standard edition' and 'professional edition') or refers to a particular target group (e.g. various lines such as 'automotive edition', 'chemical edition').

It is important to know how many and which editions of the software are available. Within the feasibility, pilot and case studies, it is noted that the majority of enterprise software systems are available in a maximum of three different editions, but in some cases four (or even more) editions are available [19]. In relation to the definition of the characteristics of the features, the following distinctions should be noted:

- There is one edition of the software.
- There are two editions of the software.
- There are three editions of the software.
- There are four editions of the software.
- There are five or more editions of the software.

This leads to the following representation of the feature 'edition' (Fig. 2):

Feature	Characteristics						
Edition (E)	E = 1	E = 2	E = 3	E = 4	5 ≤ E	...	...

Fig. 2. Characteristics of the feature 'edition'

3.3 Year of Origin

The year of origin refers to the year that the source code for the software was developed (or the development started). Depending upon the complexity of an enterprise software, sometimes the time span for the programming process is used rather than a specific year (e.g. 'the beginning of the 1990s' or '2002–2004').

When describing, classifying or pre-selecting enterprise software it is sufficient to specify the decade in which it was programmed because this can often suggest the programming mode used (procedural, object-oriented, etc.). As enterprise software was first introduced on the business arena in the 1970s, a grouping of the possible features starting with the 1970s suffices [21].

This leads to the following extension of the morphological box (Fig. 3):

Fig. 3. Characteristics of the feature 'year of origin'

3.4 Scope

The scope of a software describes which departments of an enterprise are supported and what range of functionality can be expected. The granularity of the characteristics of this feature aligns to the functionality of the software modules supplied. Since there is no established standardisation either in content or terminology the description of the scope of enterprise software is derived from the IT-Matchmaker database [21]:

- Production planning and control (PPC)/supply chain management (SCM).
- Finance/accounting/controlling/business intelligence (BI).
- Human resources.
- Purchase/inventory/logistics/customer relationship management (CRM).
- Product development/manufacturing/production.
- Service/maintenance/information technology (IT).
- Other: none of the characteristics listed above applies.

Figure 4 shows the characteristics of the feature 'scope'.

Fig. 4. Characteristics of the feature 'scope'

3.5 Target Industry Sector

An industry sector is defined as a branch of the economy and represents a variety of businesses with similar activities and fields of output, both real and intangible. There are a number of enterprise software systems that are designed to serve the requirements of particular 'target industry sectors' (e.g. automobile industry, pharmaceutical industry, insurance, etc.).

A standardisation of the description of industry sectors has advanced so much in the past years that the European definition of industrial sectors NACE (nomenclature statistique des activités économiques dans la communauté européenne) is largely in agreement with the international standard ISIC (International Standard Industrial Classification of all Economic Activities) [24, 25] Both standards name 21 sectors at the highest descriptive level. For the purposes of the morphological scheme, this level of description has been compressed to the following [19, 20]:

- none: the enterprise software is not designed for any specific industry sector
- craft: the enterprise software is designed for craftsmen

- trade: the enterprise software is designed for trade
- banking and insurance: the enterprise software is designed for banking and insurances
- manufacturing: the enterprise software is designed for manufacturing enterprises
- other: none of the characteristics listed above applies.

The respective representation in the morphological box is shown in Fig. 5:

Feature	Characteristics						
Target Industry Sector	None	Craft	Trade	Bank / Insurance	Manufacturing	Other	---

Fig. 5. Characteristics of the feature 'target industry sector'

3.6 Target Enterprise Size

Many enterprise software systems are designed to serve enterprises of a certain size ('target enterprise size'). The enterprise's size is defined according to the annual average number of full time equivalent employees and either the annual turnover or the total equity as detailed in the balance sheet [26] (Fig. 6).

Enterprise Size	No. of Employees (E) (Annual Work Units)		Turnover (T) in mio €		Balance Sheet Total (B) in mio €
Very Small Enterprise	$E < 10$	and	$T \leq 2$	or	$B \leq 2$
Small Enterprise	$10 \leq E < 50$	and	$2 \leq T < 10$	or	$2 \leq B < 10$
Medium-Sized Enterprise	$50 \leq E < 250$	and	$10 \leq T < 50$	or	$10 \leq B < 43$
Large Enterprise	$250 \leq E$	and	$50 \leq T$	or	$43 \leq B$

Fig. 6. Classification of enterprise sizes of the European Commission [26]

It should be noted that the description of an enterprise's size is primarily determined by the number of full time equivalent employees. If either the annual turnover or the balance sheet total is within the range specified for the number of employees then the other variable is not significant for the selection.

This leads directly to the characteristics of the feature 'target enterprise size' (Fig. 7).

3.7 Target Economy

Some enterprise software systems focus on particular countries or regions. These systems apply the respective legal requirements (e.g. in relation to tax law) or interface in the language spoken in the region. The feature 'target economy' addresses these cases.

Feature	Characteristics						
Target Enterprise Size	Very Small Enterprise	Small Enterprise	Medium Sized Enterprise	Large Enterprise	---	---	---

Fig. 7. Characteristics of the feature 'target enterprise size'

Because the definition of characteristics based upon countries would exceed the framework of a morphological scheme, the following classification as defined in the feasibility, pilot and case studies was found to be workable [19–21]:

- national: only one target economy (e.g. a country)
- regional: the software focusses upon a region (e.g. D/A/CH = Germany, Austria, Switzerland)
- international: the software is applied internationally
- mixed: the software is applied in several countries and/or regions but not internationally
- other: none of the characteristics listed above applies.

The morphological box is therefore to be extended as follows (Fig. 8).

Feature	Characteristics						
Target Economy	National	Regional	International	Mixed	Other	--	--

Fig. 8. Characteristics of the feature 'target economy'

3.8 Delivery Mode

The description of the varying ways of delivering enterprise software can be summarized as follows [19–21]:

- on-premises: The software is installed on-site and is operated with access supplied via the enterprise's own network.
- cloud computing: The software is provided by an external IT service-provider and used via the internet.
  - application service providing (ASP): The enterprise software provided is used by one enterprise (1 : 1).
  - software-as-a-service (SaaS): The enterprise software provided can be used by many enterprises (1 : M).
- other: none of the characteristics listed above applies.

The representation of the feature 'delivery mode' is shown in Fig. 9.

Feature	Characteristics						
Edition (E)	$E = 1$	$E = 2$	$E = 3$	$E = 4$	$5 \le E$	--	--

Fig. 9. Characteristics of the feature 'delivery mode'

3.9 Server Operating System

Because there is a large number of operating systems which would add unwanted complexity to the morphological box, the characteristics of the feature 'server operating system' were grouped on the basis of case studies and the IT-Matchmaker database [21] as follows:

- Windows
- Mac OS
- Unix
- Linux
- other: none of the characteristics listed above applies.

The morphological scheme can therefore be extended as shown in Fig. 10.

Feature	Characteristics						
Server Operating System	Windows	Mac OS	Unix	Linux	Other	---	---

Fig. 10. Characteristics of the feature 'server operating system'

3.10 Client Operating System

The characteristics expected of the server operating system are basically also expected of the client operating system, albeit with one difference: Many enterprise software systems are installed so that the client's access is through a web-based platform – either by inter- or intranet – and therefore the software runs independently of the client's operating system. Because of this the data of the case studies [21] incorporates the following characteristics:

- Windows
- Mac OS
- Unix
- Linux
- platform-independent (local)
- platform-independent (web-based)
- other: none of the characteristics listed above applies.

Figure 11 shows the characteristics of the feature 'client operating system'.

Feature	Characteristics						
Client Operating System	Windows	Mac OS	Unix	Linux	Platform-Independent (local)	Platform-Independent (web-based)	Other

Fig. 11. Characteristics of the feature 'client operating system'

3.11 Database

The characteristics of the feature 'database' are also derived from the IT-Matchmaker references data collection for enterprise software [21] as:

- Oracle
- PostgreSQL
- mySQL

- SQL-Server
- database-independent
- other: none of the characteristics listed above applies.

The resulting characteristics are represented in Fig. 12.

Feature	Characteristics						
Database	Oracle	PostgreSQL	mySQL	SQL-Server	Database-Independent	Other	--

Fig. 12. Characteristics of the feature 'database'

3.12 Programming Language

The feature 'programming language' is also described according to the data provided by the IT-Matchmaker in relation to enterprise software systems. The listing of the most current programming languages [21] is:

- Java
- Delphi
- PHP
- Python
- Perl
- C/C ++
- other: none of the characteristics listed above applies.

The respective extension of the morphological box is comprised in Fig. 13.

Feature	Characteristics						
Programming Language	Java	Delphi	PHP	Python	Perl	C / C++	Other

Fig. 13. Characteristics of the feature 'programming language'

3.13 Number of Customers

A customer is defined here either as a human being or a legal entity (in the form of a firm or organisation) who undertakes a contract with a software developer or a partnering enterprise to use the software. For enterprise software the customer is usually an enterprise. The customer in this context should not be confused with the user referred to in the feature 'number of users'.

According to the results of the feasibility, pilot and case studies for the purposes of this research project, the following definitions for the characteristic 'number of customers' has proven its worth [19–21]:

- no customers
- very few customers: less than five customers
- a few customers: between five and ten customers
- some customers: between ten and 50 customers

- many customers: between 50 and 100 customers
- very many customers: more than 100 customers.

In the morphological box, this leads to the following representation (Fig. 14):

Feature	Characteristics						
Number of Customers (C)	C = 0	1 ≤ C < 5	5 ≤ C < 10	10 ≤ C < 50	50 ≤ C < 100	100 ≤ C	—

Fig. 14. Characteristics of the feature 'number of customers'

3.14 Number of Reference Customers

A reference customer is a customer that uses the software and has agreed to be listed as a referee for the software so that other potential customer enterprises can contact them to obtain information on their experiences with the software in question. The number of reference customers officially published in the form of a reference list can give an indication of the dissemination rate of the software.

The following classification is drawn from the findings of the feasibility, pilot and case studies within the framework of this research, drawing on the experience gained in the classification of the feature 'number of customers' to classify the feature 'number of reference customers' by using the same parameters [19–21]:

- no reference customers
- very few reference customers: less than five reference customers
- few reference customers: between five and ten reference customers
- some reference customers: between ten and 50 reference customers
- many reference customers: between 50 and 100 reference customers
- very many reference customers: more than 100 reference customers

This leads to the characteristics in Fig. 15:

Feature	Characteristics						
Number of Reference Customers (R)	R = 0	1 ≤ R < 5	5 ≤ R < 10	10 ≤ R < 50	50 ≤ R < 100	100 ≤ R	—

Fig. 15. Characteristics of the feature 'number of reference customers'

3.15 Number of Installations

Depending on the number of locations from which an enterprise operates it may be necessary to install the same software on several sites. The number of installations of the enterprise software is therefore different to the number of customers. One customer could install the software at several sites. This is described under the feature 'number of installations'.

The following classifications are drawn from the findings of the feasibility, pilot and case studies within the framework of this research, drawing on the experience gained in the classification of the feature 'number of customers' to classify 'number of installations' using the same parameters [19–21]:

- no installations
- very few installations: less than five installations
- a few installations: between five and ten installations
- some installations: between ten and 50 installations
- many installations: between 50 and 100 installations
- very many installations: more than 100 installations.

Therefore, the morphological box can be extended as follows (Fig. 16):

Feature	Characteristics							
Number of Installations (I)	I = 0	1 ≤ I < 5	5 ≤ R < 10	10 ≤ I < 50	50 ≤ I < 100	100 ≤ I	---	

Fig. 16. Characteristics of the feature 'number of installations'

3.16 Number of Users

A user is a human being using the software. The number of users of the enterprise software is the number of people (normally staff members of the customer enterprises) working with the software. This usually denotes the number of named users (i.e. the number of users administered by the software), which is different to the number of concurrent users (i.e. the number of users who can use the software at the same time).

The following classification is drawn from the findings of the feasibility, pilot and case studies within the framework of this line of research [19–21]:

- no users
- very few users: less than 10 users
- few users: between 10 and 50 users
- some users: between 50 and 250 users
- many users: between 250 and 5 000 users
- very many users: more than 5 000 users.

Figure 17 shows the respective feature and its characteristics in the morphological box for enterprise software.

Feature	Characteristics						
Edition (E)	E = 1	E = 2	E = 3	E = 4	5 ≤ E	---	---

Fig. 17. Characteristics of the feature 'number of users'

3.17 Number of Partnering Enterprises

A partnering enterprise is an enterprise which offers services related to the software and/ or actively (using their own staff) or passively (through means such as advertisements or sponsorships) promotes the software. The names and contact data of the partnering enterprises are normally published in the internet in the form of a list can therefore easily be counted. The number of partnering enterprises can give an indication of the dissemination of the software. In this context the following clustering was derived [19–21]:

- no partnering enterprise
- one partnering enterprise
- few partnering enterprises: between 2 and 5 partnering enterprises
- some partnering enterprises: between 5 and 10 partnering enterprises
- many partnering enterprises: between 10 and 20 partnering enterprises
- very many partnering enterprises: more than 20 partnering enterprises.

Figure 18 visualises the characteristics of 'number of partnering enterprises'.

Feature	Characteristics						
Number of Partnering Enterprises (P)	P = 0	P = 1	2 ≤ P < 5	5 ≤ P < 10	10 ≤ P < 20	20 ≤ P	...

Fig. 18. Characteristics of the feature 'number of partnering enterprises'

3.18 License

Commercial software is usually distributed under a closed source license which does not give any permission to modify, (re-)distribute or sell the software without the explicit consent of the originator (copyright). Open source licenses allow access to the software source code, and permit the modification and (re-)distribution of the original and/or modified code.

A software is defined as open source software if the license under which it is being distributed has been approved by the Open Source Initiative (OSI) [27]. There are different types of open source licenses (e.g. no copyleft, weak copyleft, strong copyleft). For the purpose of describing, classifying and pre-selecting enterprise software, the mere distinction between open and closed source enterprise software has proved to be adequate [19–21]:

- open source: The license under which the sofware is being (re-)distributed has been approved by the OSI.
- closed source: The license under which the sofware is being (re-)distributed has not been approved by the OSI.

This leads to the following extension of the morphological box (Fig. 19):

Feature	Characteristics						
License	Closed Source	Open Source	...	...	...	...	...

Fig. 19. Characteristics of the feature 'license'

3.19 Contracting Partner

An enterprise which intends to use a software product usually enters into a contract for the use of the license and/or the maintenance of the software with a so called 'contracting partner'. The contracting partner can either be the enterprise developing the respective software or a partnering enterprise (see above). The feature 'contracting partner' thus has the following characteristics [19–21]:

- software developer: enterprise which actively develops a software
- partnering enterprise: enterprise which offers services related to the software and/or actively (using their own staff) or passively (through means such as advertisements or sponsorships) promotes the software
- other: none of the characteristics listed above applies.

This results in the following representation of the feature 'contracting partner'in the morphological box (Fig. 20):

Feature	Characteristics						
Contractual Partner	Software Developer	Partnering Enterprise	Other	---	---	---	---

Fig. 20. Characteristics of the feature 'contracting partner'

3.20 Morphological Box for Enterprise Software

Using the above logic the morphological scheme is formed with five feature groups, 19 features and 103 characteristics. The respective morphological box is described in Fig. 21. The morphological box for enterprise software has been revised and expanded numerous times in the course of the underpinning research and currently stands at version 5.0.

	Feature	Characteristics						
Maturity	Version (V)	Non-Released Pre-V. V = 0.*	Non-Released V. V = *α or *β or *RC	First Released V. V = 1.0	Lower V. 1.0 < V ≤ 3.0	Improved Version 3.0 < V ≤ 5.0	Often Revised V. 5.0 < V ≤ 10.0	Very Often Revised V. 10.0 < V
	Edition (E)	E = 1	E = 2	E = 3	E = 4	5 ≤ E	---	---
	Year of Origin	≤ 1970ies	1980ies	1990ies	2000s	2010s	---	---
Target Group	Scope	PPC / SCM	Finance / Accounting Controlling / BI	Human Resources	Purchase / Inventory / Logistics / CRM	Product Development / Manufact. / Product.	Service / Maintenance / IT	Other
	Target Industry Sector	None	Craft	Trade	Bank / Insurance	Manufacturing	Other	---
	Target Enterprise Size	Very Small Enterprise	Small Enterprise	Medium Sized Enterprise	Large Enterprise	---	---	---
	Target Economy	National	Regional	International	Mixed	Other	---	---
Technology	Delivery Mode	On-Premises	Application Service Providing (ASP)	Software-as-a-Service (SaaS)	Other	---	---	---
	Server Operating System	Windows	Mac OS	Unix	Linux	Other	---	---
	Client Operating System	Windows	Mac OS	Unix	Linux	Platform-Independent (local)	Platform-Independent (web-based)	Other
	Database	Oracle	PostgreSQL	mySQL	SQL-Server	Database-Independent	Other	---
	Programming Language	Java	Delphi	PHP	Python	Perl	C / C++	Other
Dissemination	Number of Customers (C)	C = 0	1 ≤ C < 5	5 ≤ C < 10	10 ≤ C < 50	50 ≤ C < 100	100 ≤ C	---
	Number of Reference Customers (R)	R = 0	1 ≤ R < 5	5 ≤ R < 10	10 ≤ R < 50	50 ≤ R < 100	100 ≤ R	---
	Number of Installations (I)	I = 0	1 ≤ I < 5	5 ≤ R < 10	10 ≤ I < 50	50 ≤ I < 100	100 ≤ I	---
	Number of Users (U)	U = 0	U < 10	10 ≤ U < 50	50 ≤ U < 250	250 ≤ U < 5 000	5 000 ≤ U	---
	Number of Partnering Enterprises (P)	P = 0	P = 1	2 ≤ P < 5	5 ≤ P < 10	10 ≤ P < 20	20 ≤ P	---
Contracting	License	Closed Source	Open Source	---	---	---	---	---
	Contractual Partner	Software Developer	Partnering Enterprise	Other	---	---	---	---

Fig. 21. Morphological box for enterprise software 5.0

4   Application of the Morphological Box

ERP software is held to be of the highest significance to an enterprise because these software systems are used throughout the entire enterprise. While conducting the feasibility, pilot and case studies referred to above, the current morphological scheme was applied to all the different practice-oriented open source ERP-software systems that were available on the market [28].

Below, the morphological box is applied to the following ERP-software systems:

- SAP ERP – most popular enterprise software by the market leader SAP AG [29] (Fig. 22) and
- Odoo (former OpenERP) – most popular among all practice-oriented open source ERP-software systems [28, 30] (Fig. 23).

Feature	Characteristics						
Maturity							
Version (V)	Non-Released Pre-V. V = 0.*	Non-Released V. V = *α or *β or *RC	First Released V. V = 1.0	Lower V. 1.0 < V ≤ 3.0	Improved Version 3.0 < V ≤ 5.0	Often Revised V. 5.0 < V ≤ 10.0	Very Often Revised V. 10.0 < V
Edition (E)	E = 1	E = 2	E = 3	E = 4	5 ≤ E	---	---
Year of Origin	≤ 1970ies	1980ies	1990ies	2000s	2010s	---	---
Target Group							
Scope	PPC / SCM	Finance / Accounting Controlling / BI	Human Resource	Purchase / Inventory / Logistics / CRM	Product Development / Manufact. / Product.	Service / Maintenance / IT	Other
Target Industry Sector	None	Craft	Trade	Bank / Insurance	Manufacturing	Other	---
Target Enterprise Size	Very Small Enterprise	Small Enterprise	Medium Sized Enterprise	Large Enterprise	---	---	---
Target Economy	National	Regional	International	Mixed	Other	---	---
Technology							
Delivery Mode	On-Premises	Application Service Providing (ASP)	Software-as-a-Service (SaaS)	Other	---	---	---
Server Operating System	Windows	Mac OS	Unix	Linux	Other	---	---
Client Operating System	Windows	Mac OS	Unix	Linux	Platform-Independent (local)	Platform-Independent (web-based)	Other
Database	Oracle	PostgreSQL	mySQL	SQL-Server	Database-Independent	Other	---
Programming Language	Java	Delphi	PHP	Python	Perl	C / C++	Other
Dissemination							
Number of Customers (C)	C = 0	1 ≤ C < 5	5 ≤ C < 10	10 ≤ C < 50	50 ≤ C < 100	100 ≤ C	---
Number of Reference Customers (R)	R = 0	1 ≤ R < 5	5 ≤ R < 10	10 ≤ R < 50	50 ≤ R < 100	100 ≤ R	---
Number of Installations (I)	I = 0	1 ≤ I < 5	5 ≤ R < 10	10 ≤ I < 50	50 ≤ I < 100	100 ≤ I	---
Number of Users (U)	U = 0	U < 10	10 ≤ U < 50	50 ≤ U < 250	250 ≤ U < 5 000	5 000 ≤ U	---
Number of Partnering Enterprises (P)	P = 0	P = 1	2 ≤ P < 5	5 ≤ P < 10	10 ≤ P < 20	20 ≤ P	---
Contracting							
License	Closed Source	Open Source	---	---	---	---	---
Contractual Partner	Software Developer	Partnering Enterprise	Other	---	---	---	---

Fig. 22. Morphological box 5.0 for SAP ERP

5   Evaluation and Contribution

The following weaknesses have been identified when applying the morphological scheme to existing enterprise software:

- The characteristics of the features 'scope' and 'industry sector' still show potential for improvement.
- The dissemination of a software system is a very important issue when describing and classifying enterprise software. Unfortunately, it is very difficult to obtain reliable information on the features of the feature group 'dissemination'. This problem is

Feature	Characteristics						
Maturity							
Version (V)	Non-Released Pre-V. $V = 0.*$	Non-Released V. $V = *\alpha$ or $*\beta$ or $*RC$	First Released V. $V = 1.0$	Lower V. $1.0 < V \leq 3.0$	Improved Version $3.0 < V \leq 5.0$	Often Revised V. $5.0 < V \leq 10.0$	Very Often Revised V. $10.0 < V$
Edition (E)	$E = 1$	$E = 2$	$E = 3$	$E = 4$	$5 \leq E$	--	--
Year of Origin	≤ 1970ies	1980ies	1990ies	2000s	2010s	--	--
Target Group							
Scope	PPC / SCM	Finance / Accounting Controlling / BI	Human Resources	Purchase / Inventory / Logistics / CRM	Product Development / Manufact. / Product.	Service / Maintenance / IT	Other
Target Industry Sector	None	Craft	Trade	Bank / Insurance	Manufacturing	Other	--
Target Enterprise Size	Very Small Enterprise	Small Enterprise	Medium Sized Enterprise	Large Enterprise	--	--	--
Target Economy	National	Regional	International	Mixed	Other	--	--
Technology							
Delivery Mode	On-Premises	Application Service Providing (ASP)	Software-as-a-Service (SaaS)	Other	--	--	--
Server Operating System	Windows	Mac OS	Unix	Linux	Other	--	--
Client Operating System	Windows	Mac OS	Unix	Linux	Platform-Independent (local)	Platform-Independent (web-based)	Other
Database	Oracle	PostgreSQL	mySQL	SQL-Server	Database-Independent	Other	--
Programming Language	Java	Delphi	PHP	Python	Perl	C / C++	Other
Dissemination							
Number of Customers (C)	$C = 0$	$1 \leq C < 5$	$5 \leq C < 10$	$10 \leq C < 50$	$50 \leq C < 100$	$100 \leq C$	--
Number of Reference Customers (R)	$R = 0$	$1 \leq R < 5$	$5 \leq R < 10$	$10 \leq R < 50$	$50 \leq R < 100$	$100 \leq R$	--
Number of Installations (I)	$I = 0$	$1 \leq I < 5$	$5 \leq R < 10$	$10 \leq I < 50$	$50 \leq I < 100$	$100 \leq I$	--
Number of Users (U)	$U = 0$	$U < 10$	$10 \leq U < 50$	$50 \leq U < 250$	$250 \leq U < 5\,000$	$5\,000 \leq U$	--
Number of Partnering Enterprises (P)	$P = 0$	$P = 1$	$2 \leq P < 5$	$5 \leq P < 10$	$10 \leq P < 20$	$20 \leq P$	--
Contracting							
License	Closed Source	Open Source	--	--	--	--	--
Contractual Partner	Software Developer	Partnering Enterprise	Other	--	--	--	--

Fig. 23. Morphological box 5.0 for Odoo (former OpenERP)

present for both open and closed source enterprise software. The reason for this with closed source software is because the software developers/partnering enterprises do not communicate this data to outside bodies (sometimes even the limited communicated data may be of doubtful reliability). With open source software the number of operative installations cannot be tracked because the software is normally provided cost-free via internet download and the software dissemination is not monitored. In both cases the lack of dissemination data does not lie in the concept of the morphological scheme.

Despite these limitations the developed morphological scheme provides a list of the most important characteristics that describe enterprise software and can therefore be regarded as a basis for standardising the description of enterprise software. This approach leads to a quicker and more systematic communication amongst the different interest groups.

The representation of the evaluation in form of a morphological box assists visualising the characteristics much easier than merely listing the values. The morphological box enhances the comparison of enterprise software systems. This is particularly beneficial in the pre-selection phase of a new enterprise software system. Furthermore, the grouped values that comprise the characteristics of the different features already form a basis for a classification. The classification could even be extended by applying pattern recognition methods in order to determine at which point in the software lifecycle the respective enterprise software system is lies (e.g. based upon the maturity characteristics and/or the technology characteristics).

Due to the high degree of modularity in both the vertical (features) and horizontal (characteristics) dimension, the morphological scheme for enterprise software can easily be extended and/or adapted to other developing fields of interest (e.g. to the specifics of open source enterprise software [28]).

6   Summary and Outlook

The different types of enterprise software systems are very complex and have an enormous impact on the competitiveness of enterprises. A number stakeholder groups such as software developers, software vendors, software users, researchers and staff in training are affected by enterprise software and need to be able to communicate about them. To standardise and improve the communication within and among these stakeholder groups, a 'morphological box for enterprise software' was designed.

Several iterations of the morphological box have been tried, the current version 5.0 of the 'morphological box for enterprise software' is being released in this work. It comprises 5 feature groups with 19 features and 103 characteristics which were all derived from related work and/or feasibility, pilot and case studies conducted for this purpose. In this paper, this morphological box is applied to two well-known ERP-software systems. It is shown that it provides an approach which is easy to apply by staff members with different backgrounds, flexible to adapt to different needs and helpful to visualise the nature of the different enterprise software systems. It therefore enhances the description, classification and pre-selection of enterprise software. Nevertheless, there is still potential for improvement of the 'scope' and 'industry sector' features and it is recommended that future work focus on deriving an improved range of characteristics for these features. Apart from this, future work should also provide a pattern-based method for classifying the pathways of objects described by a morphological box.

Acknowledgments.   The author would like to thank Trovarit AG for their support of the case studies as well as Scott Cawley and Prof. Christine Bruce for their helpful comments related to the ideas of this paper

References

1. Klaus, H., Rosemann, M., Gable, G.: What is ERP? Inf. Syst. Front. **2**(2), 141–162 (2002)
2. Gronau, N.: Enterprise Resource Planning. Architektur, Funktionen und Management von ERP-Systemen, 2nd edn. Oldenbourg Wissenschaftsverlag, Munich (2010)
3. Kees, A., Gadatsch, A.: Von Enterprise Resource Planning zu Enterprise Resource Management. ERP-Manage. **10**(3), 61–63 (2014)
4. Strong, D.M., Volkoff, O.: Understanding organization – enterprise system fit: a path to theorizing the information technology artifact. MIS Q. **34**(4), 731–756 (2010)
5. Seddon, P., Calvert, C., Yang, S.: A multi-project model of key factors affecting organizational benefits from enterprise systems. MIS Q. **34**(2), 305–325 (2010)
6. Schuh, G.; Stich, V. (ed.): Marktspiegel Business Software - ERP/PPS 2011/2012. Forschungsinstitut für Rationalisierung (FIR) e. V., Aachen (D) (2011)
7. Schwetz, W.: Marktspiegel Business Software – CRM 2011. 19th edn. (2011)
8. Böhn, M., Burkhardt, A., Gantner, M.: Prozessmodellierungswerkzeuge – Systeme für Dokumentation, Entwurf. Simulation und Analyse. BARC GmbH, Würzburg (D) (2010)

9. Eggert, S., Meier, J.: ERP-Marktüberblick – 107 Systeme im Vergleich. ERP-Manage. **6**(3), 48–55 (2010)

10. Mussbach-Winter, U., Wochinger, T., Kipp, R.: Marktspiegel Business Software – MES/ Fertigungssteuerung 2010/2011, 3rd edn. (2010)

11. Böhn, M., Schiklang, M., Gantner, M.: Enterprise Content Management. BARC GmbH, Würzburg (D) (2009)

12. Becker, J. (ed.): Marktspiegel Business Software – Warenwirtschaft 2008/2009. Trovarit AG, Aachen (D) (2008)

13. N. N. (ed.): Johann Wolfgang von Goethe, Naturwissenschaftliche Schriften 1, vol. 13. Hamburger Ausgabe, Munich (D) (2000)

14. Rosemann, M.: Komplexitätsmanagement in Prozessmodellen. Methodenspezifische Gestaltungsempfehlungen für die Informationsmodellierung. Gabler Verlag, Wiesbaden (D) (1996)

15. Wöhe, G., Döring, U.: Einführung in die Allgemeine Betriebswirtschaftslehre, 24th edn. Franz Vahlen Verlag, Munich (D) (2013)

16. Zwicky, F.: Entdecken, Erfinden. Forschen im Morphologischen Weltbild. Knaur Verlag, Zurich (CH) (1966)

17. Zwicky, F.: Morphologische Forschung, 2nd edn. Verlag Baeschlin, Glarus (1989)

18. Schuh, G.: Produktionsplanung und -steuerung. Grundlagen, Gestaltung und Konzepte, 3rd edn. Springer, Heidelberg (D) (2006)

19. Kees, A. (ed.): Marktspiegel Free and Open Source Software für Betriebliche Anwendungssysteme, 3rd edn. Feasibility study, Hochschule Bonn-Rhein-Sieg, Sankt Augustin (D) (2010)

20. Kees, A. (ed.): Free and Open Source ERP-Systeme. Pilot study, Hochschule Bonn-Rhein-Sieg, Sankt Augustin (D) (2011)

21. Trovarit, A.G., (ed.): IT-Matchmaker. http://www.trovarit.com/it-matchmaker/software-projekte-mit-dem-it-matchmaker.html. Accessed 1 Mar 2012

22. Benlian, A., Hess, T.: Comparing the relative importance of evaluation criteria in proprietary and open-source enterprise application software selection. Inf. Syst. J. (ISJ) **21**(6), 503–525 (2010)

23. Mayer, M., Ahlemann, F.: Management Software Systems. Requirements, Selection Process and Products, 6th edn. BARC GmbH, Würzburg (D) (2011)

24. Eurostat (ed.): NACE Rev. 2. Statistische Systematik der Wirtschaftszweige in der Europäischen Gemeinschaft. European Community, Luxemburg (LUX) (2008). http://epp.eurostat.ec.europa.eu/cache/ITY_OFFPUB/KS-RA-07-015/DE/KS-RA-07-015-DE.PDF. Accessed 1 Mar 2012

25. United Nations Statistics Devision (ed.): International Standard Industrial Classification of All Economic Acitivities (ISIC). Revision 4. United Nations Publication, New York (USA) (2008). http://unstats.un.org/unsd/cr/registry/isic-4.asp.(1 April, 2012)

26. European Commission (ed.): The New SME Definition. European Commission, Brussels (B) (2006). http://ec.europa.eu/enterprise/policies/sme/files/sme_definition/sme_user_guide_en.pdf. Accessed 1 Mar 2012

27. Open Source Initiative (OSI) (ed.): The Open Source Definition. http://opensource.org/docs/osd. Accessed 1 Mar 2012

28. Kees, A.: Open Source Enterprise Software. Springer, Heidelberg (2015)

29. SAP AG (ed.): SAP. http://www.sap.com

30. OpenERP s.a. (ed.): OpenERP. Open Source Business Applications. http://www.openerp.com. Accessed 24 Oct 2014

EMR Implementation: Lessons Learned from ERP

Mary Sumner[⊠]

Department of Computer Management and Information Systems,
School of Business, Southern Illinois University Edwardsville,
Edwardsville, IL 62026, USA
msumner@siue.edu

Abstract. The adoption of electronic medical records is a strategy for improving health care in the United States, and there are national efforts to provide funding for the initial purchase of EMR systems. The use of IT in making clinical health care more efficient and effective is well known. But recent articles in the healthcare domain indicate that 20 to 30 % of electronic medical record (EMR) systems fail within a year of implementation [11]. This study examines the implementation of EMR systems and compares these practices, issues, lessons learned, and critical success factors with what we have learned from implementing ERP systems. The findings identify the similarities between ERP and EMR systems projects and offer insights into applying the lessons learned in the past to the current challenges in EMR implementation.

Keywords: Electronic medical record implementation · Project management

1 Motivation and Importance of the Research

"Those who do not learn from history are doomed to repeat it," is a well-known quote by George Santayana. The current wave of electronic medical records system projects is similar in many respects to the enterprise systems implementation projects of the past 10–15 years. Electronic medical records systems are enterprise systems in that they are implemented to enable data integration, efficiency, and cross-functional process integration [3, 14]. The integration of data and processes requires that the enterprise system be aligned with the best practices that the system is designed to support.

When enterprise systems are introduced into an organization, there is often a "misfit" between the best practices supported by the software and the existing processes of the organization. In order for enterprise systems to be successful, the organization can re-engineer its processes to "fit" the best practices supported by the ERP or EMR software. In general, re-engineering or "tight coupling" is needed to achieve the benefits of integration and control that is associated with ERP/EMR implementation [12, 36, 37].

However, the "gaps" between the best practices of the ERP/EMR software and existing organizational practices can be quite great [35]. To address these gaps, one alternative is to customize the software to support existing organizational processes. Another alternative is for end-users to do "work-around's" or improvisations which

D. Sedera et al. (Eds.): Pre-ICIS 2010-2012, LNBIP 198, pp. 19–44, 2015.
DOI: 10.1007/978-3-319-17587-4_2

lead to "drift." That is, providers continue to conduct their practices outside the system [6, 35, 43].

A number of researchers have examined settings where enterprise systems have been implemented with "work-arounds." This is known as "loose coupling." "Loose coupling" involves the timing and performance of activities different from the expectations of the system [31, 35, 43]. In a university setting, administrative staff enabled faculty to work-around procurement processes supported by a new enterprise system [31, 43]. In a healthcare organization, nurses handled patient scheduling processes outside the system, only to reconcile them later [35]. Researchers in a pharmaceutical company captured data on paper during working hours rather than entering it into the enterprise system. The problem with "loose coupling" is that the benefits of process and data integration that should result from ERP/EMR implementation are compromised.

2 Research Objectives

1. To conduct an in-depth case study of EMR implementations to develop a grounded theory of why, when, and how IT innovation occurs and the impact of change.
2. To compare the best practices and critical success factors for EMR implementation with the best practices and critical success factors for ERP implementation.
3. To identify the similarities in best practices and critical success factors between EMR and ERP implementation.
4. To identify unique challenges in implementing EMR systems.

3 Related Literature: ERP Implementation Studies

ERP systems are adopted by organizations to provide an integrated, packaged solution to their information needs. In most cases, ERP packages replace aging legacy systems which no longer meet business needs or have become too difficult and expensive to maintain. Despite ERPs promise, these software solutions have proven "expensive and difficult to implement, often imposing their own logic on a company's strategy and existing culture" [23, 32] cite ERP failure rates to be as high as 50 %. Brown and Vessey [10] observe, "Although failures to deliver projects on time and within budgets were an old IT story, enterprise systems held even higher risks – they could be a 'bet-our-company' type of failure."

A number of research studies have addressed the best practices and critical success factors for successful ERP projects. As in all large-scale IT projects, top management support, presence of a champion, good communication with stakeholders, and effective project management, are critical success factors in ERP projects. Factors which are unique to ERP implementation include re-engineering business processes, understanding corporate cultural change, and using business analysts on the project team [39]. Management support of the project team, a project team with the appropriate balance of technical/business skills, and commitment to change by all the stakeholders are all of paramount importance [29].

CSF 1. Business Justification for ERP. It is important to make the business case and to establish measurable benefits at the outset of an ERP project, so that these results can be assessed [33].

CSF 2. Vanilla ERP Implementation. Re-engineering business processes to support the best practices supported by the ERP software is linked with on-time, on-budget ERP implementation [19]. Vanilla ERP implementation and business process re-engineering affords the organization the greatest possible return on investment through streamlined operations [9]. Minimal customization is a key factor in successful ERP projects [29].

CSF 3. ERP Project Team has Business Experts. Business experts should be assigned to the project on a full-time basis [9, 10, 21]. The project team should include members representing the business functions to be affected by the ERP implementation [21].

CSF 4. ERP Project Leadership. Project leadership is a very important issue, and project leaders need to have a proven track record [10]. One of the lessons learned in case studies of ERP projects is that a strong project leader needs to keep the project on track, even when changes require following contingency plans [34]. A disciplined approach to project management which includes project scope, time, and cost management is important [42]. A project manager must prevent scope creep and must monitor project activities through tracking milestones, dates, and costs [26].

CSF 5. Effective Training. User training is critical to ERP success, because people's jobs will change. User training should focus on business processes, not just technical training on how to use the software [45]. Umble et al. [42] cite education/training as the most widely recognized critical success factor. Researchers have found a relationship between user satisfaction with training and user satisfaction with the ERP system. Training should enable managers to use query and reporting tools to generate needed reports [33].

CSF 6. Use of External Consultants. Effective management of external consultants is important for the success of an ERP project, because they can offer valuable expertise in analyzing cross-functional business processes and in configuring application specific modules [10]. Organizations should use consultants, but take advantage of opportunities to develop internal knowledge [45].

CSF 7. CEO Involvement. The involvement of senior executives is a common characteristic of ERP projects that finish on-time and on-budget [19, 25, 29]. Top management needs to promote ERP as a top priority [10, 22]. Bradford and Florin [8] found in a survey of SAP users that top management support is related to perceived organizational performance and user satisfaction.

CSF 8. Project Champion. A project champion is essential to project success [25, 29, 45]. Bowen et al. [7] found both statistical and qualitative support to the proposition that higher levels of involvement of project champions are associated with IT project implementation success. Beyond this, project team members need to have the authority to make decisions on behalf of their functional area [10].

CSF 9. Reducing Resistance to Change. In implementing ERP, companies often fail to address resistance to change, especially resistance to changes in job design. Since ERP implementation entails changes in business processes, change management is essential [10, 22, 25]. A review of 43 articles published in 20 IT and IT-related journals over the last 25 years found that user resistance is treated as a key implementation issue. An organizational culture which fosters open communications is important to avoid resistance to change [34].

CSF 10. Steering Committee Meets on a Regular Basis. A steering committee with executive leadership is one of the strategies used in successful ERP projects, as measured by on-time and on-budget implementation [10].

4   Related Literature: EMR Implementation Studies

As background, the gap between actual EMR adoption and target goals is still great. In a survey of 1,000 hospitals in 2002, 80.7 % of the hospitals surveyed were not using EMR/Computerized Physician Order Entry (CPOE) systems. The gap existed because of environmental factors (information safety, cost), organizational factors (significant investment in time and cost, resistance to change), personal factors (perspective that new technologies detract from patient care), and technical factors (systems integration challenges between hospital records and office-based records). Physicians are more likely to adopt EMR systems in a hospital based setting because of organizational support [1].

A number of studies have addressed the issue of how the use of EMR affects the quality, timeliness and effectiveness of patient care. A meta-analysis and synthesis of 63 papers relevant to EMR implementation reported that EMR systems increased the time it took to enter initial patient information, but that the use of standardized forms enabled nurses to be more efficient. One trade-off is that the increased time it takes to enter documentation takes time away from patient care, but information in the record is more complete. The outcome is increased quality of patient care [30].

Getting physicians on-board to using EMR systems is a challenge, so it is important to understand factors associated with adoption. The research on adoption of EMR systems includes studies of office-based use of EMR and hospital-based use of EMR. When physicians were interviewed as part of the National Ambulatory Care Survey (NAMCS, 2006), conducted by the Center for Disease Control, 29.2 percent of the office-based physicians surveyed claimed to use EMR systems. The survey used a representative sample of 3350 office-based physicians. While this represented a 22 percent increase in EMR use over 2005, the full functionality of EMR systems were not being used. Among physicians with full EMR systems, 63.7 % said that their systems had reminders for guideline-based interventions, or screening tests, but only one-half of those physicians send prescriptions electronically. Even though EMR systems are becoming more widespread in physicians' practices, continued efforts are needed to increase adoption [16].

In terms of office-based use of EMR, several studies have used interviews, observations, and archival data to study office-based use of EMR systems. While the goal of EMR implementation was to streamline front-desk operations such as patient check-in and appointment scheduling, one study indicated that the EMR system increased the time it took to conduct these procedures—largely because system functions forced employees to collect specific information before moving forward [46]. This study raises the issue of re-engineering processes to align with the best practices of the EMR software system.

EMR use by physicians in a hospital setting has also been studied. One of the most high-profile cases in EMR implementation occurred at Cedars-Sinai Medical Center—where physicians forced the system implementation to be cancelled. Physicians did not see CPOE as beneficial to patient care and therefore didn't view it as positive change for the patient [5]. Physicians were ambivalent about whether tools would help them do their job and even thought that the system might negatively affect their job performance. Since they viewed CPOE as being "forced upon them," most of them viewed its implementation negatively.

Successful adoption of CPOE requires adoption by the hospital system and by physicians themselves. Physicians dislike the extra time it takes to use a CPOE, but they value their ability to enter orders (e.g. tests, medication) from any location and the ability to use pre-set orders for common conditions [13]. Successful CPOE implementation requires top management leadership, extensive training, involvement of key stakeholders, and commitment to resources.

Some attention has been paid to the impact of social influence factors on EMR use. By promoting an EMR system, senior physicians can influence junior physicians to use a system. Champions can also influence physician adoption of EMR systems [41]. Other factors influencing physician use of EMR systems are learning costs and economic costs. The researchers considered factors influencing indirect system use (having an assistant enter data for them) vs. direct system use (personally using the system). Higher learning costs increased the likelihood that physicians would choose indirect system use, whereas higher economic cost increased the likelihood that physicians would choose direct system use [41]. In either case, it is important for physicians to be convinced of the value of using the EMR system.

In another study of influence tactics, Ilie found that using hard tactics (direct pressure, demands, reminders) created resistance to change while simply using soft tactics (encouragement) created compliance but not commitment. Since the goal is to gain commitment, strategies such as needs assessment, implementation support, and end-user involvement are more effective in facilitating adoption [17].

Clearly, change management is critical to successful EMR implementation. In the high-pressure, high-stress healthcare environment, managing change is difficult because changing work methods and processes is threatening. One of the most effective ways of overcoming resistance to change is to enable those affected by the change to take ownership over the change. Finding out what the needs are, and providing healthcare workers with tools and processes to do their job(s) more effectively is important to information systems success [18].

5 Research Design and Methodology

The research uses the grounded theory approach [15] to understand the success factors in EMR implementation. In the grounded theory approach, qualitative data is gathered and used to guide the theory-building process. The data collection phase involves interviews and observations in the context of EMR implementation. The first round of interviews was designed to identify EMR implementation practices and to develop core categories for organizing the data. The results of the first round of interviews were reported in a working paper [38]. The second round of interviews applied the concepts gathered from the first round of interviews to depict best practices and success factors for EMR implementation from the vantage point of the clinicians themselves.

6 The Case Studies

The study used a case study design. The case studies are based on EMR implementation at a major hospital system between 2007 and 2010. The project justification for EMR implementation included: improved workflow, systems integration, and operational cost reduction. The implementation of common processes and an integrated common database assured quality patient care by reducing the number of repeat procedures, reducing errors, and providing better information for clinical decision-making. The systems benefits included access to a common medical record, use of on-line tools to place orders for medications and tests, and availability of decision support tools, including best practice alerts and medication reconciliation alerts.

7 The Sample

The respondents were clinicians at a major hospital system in the St. Louis area. Seventy-five clinicians were invited to participate in the survey via an email message explaining the objectives of the survey. Of these 75, 15 clinicians accepted the invitation to participate in an interview. Of these 15 possible respondents, 10 participated in the actual interview process. The other five could not be reached on a timely basis because of other commitments.

8 Interviews

The data were collected using structured interviews. The preliminary interviews used the project retrospective instrument (Nelson, 2005) as a basis for obtaining data on project characteristics, project management organization, project timeline, impact of the system, and project success factors. Additional questions relevant to the impacts of EMR systems and EMR system use were added to the structured interview form. The data were collected using phone interviews. Respondents completed the structured interview form as well.

The focus of the interviews included:

1. Motivations for the project, including project justification and management expectations.
2. Project team leadership and composition, including the role of clinicians, IT professionals, external consultants, project managers, and super-users.
3. Project characteristics, including project timeline and costs.
4. The impact of the system on health care quality, patient safety, communication among clinicians, interactions with patients, efficiency, and documentation.
5. EMR system use, including the impact of the system on work processes, how workflow issues were resolved, and the extent of customization.
6. Problems arising in system implementation and factors important to project success.
7. Critical success factors for project success, including project manager expertise, the role of super-users, the effectiveness of training, the involvement of top management support, the role of the project champion, the effectiveness of change management, and steering committee leadership.
8. Issues of acceptance, from the perspective of the end-users (providers, medical staff).

See Appendix A for the structured interview form.

9   Case Studies of EMR Implementation

The interviewees participating in the project were healthcare professionals with roles in the design and implementation of EMR and CPOE systems. With clinical backgrounds, they transitioned into roles as "super-users," with responsibility for process re-design, testing, training, and support. Their job title, role in EMR project implementation, and the systems being implemented are summarized in Table 1. Most of the projects were EMR systems implementation projects supported by commercial off-the-shelf software, including Metavision, Sunrise Clinical Manager, Horizon, McKesson, and Cerner. The hospital system used a "best-of-breed" approach, whereby different systems are acquired and implemented based upon the extent to which they met requirements.

10   Project Need

Project justification included upgrading from legacy systems, better documentation, standardization, error-reduction, integration with billing systems, and improved safety. These findings are summarized in Table 2.

11   Project Characteristics: Project Teams and Project Schedule

The project teams consisted of information technology (IT) professionals, clinicians, consultants, project managers, and specialized health information technology coordinators. Table 3 summarizes these roles across the projects, along with the project schedules,

Table 1. Case studies of EMR implementation

Job title of interviewee	Role in project	System
Health information coordinator	Information management	Metavision/Surgical information system/compass
Lab technical coordinator	Testing, validation	Horizon lab
Nurse practice specialist	Workload assessment	Sunrise clinical manager-CPOE
	Advocate (for nursing professionals)	
	Consultant—best practices	
Clinical director— informatics	Clinical (physician) "lead"	MetaVision
Process consultant	Process consultant—IT	Horizon clinicals
Testing coordinator	Test planning and testing	Clinical manager (Eclipsis)
Coordinator	Project manager	McKesson med admin
		Cerner eclipsis
Senior analyst—RN	Team lead	Surgical information system (SIS)
Operating room IS team		Metavision
Senior analyst–IT	Configuration, process re-design	Cerner
	Education	McKesson
	Troubleshooting, help desk	
	System maintenance	
	Data mining	
Periop IS resource nurse	Teaching, support	Surgical information system (SIS)

including start dates, expected completion dates, and actual completion dates. As you can see, most of the projects were on-schedule.

12 System Impacts

The assessment of system impacts is central to the effectiveness of EMR systems. These impacts included improving the quality of patient care, patient safety, improving the communications among clinicians, improving interaction with patients, improving overall efficiency, and improving documentation. These effects were assessed on a scale of 1 to 5, with 5 = met to a great extent, 3 = met to a moderate extent, and 1 = not met. The comments relevant to these impacts are equally relevant to the quantified measures. Tables 4, 5, and 6 provide the data on these system impacts.

Table 2. Project need

System	System type	Reason for implementation
Metavision/SIS	CPOE	Operating room documentation
	Nursing documentation	Decreased medical errors
		Improved patient safety
		Upgrade outdated system
Horizon lab	Lab system	Upgrade system
Sunrise clinical manager	Medical barcoding	Upgrade outdated system
	CPOE	Provide single place for documentation
		Provide audit for safety and compliance
		Standardize orders
		Provide timely access to orders from multiple locations
		Decrease transcription errors
		Improve patient safety
		Track medications for billing
MetaVision	EMR anesthesia	Improved billing throughput
		Improved quality of documentation
		Improved patient safety
		Robust research database
Horizon clinicals	EMR	Standardize EMR across hospitals
Clinical manager (eclipsis)	EMR	Common system
	CPOE	
McKesson medical admin	EMR	Improved processes
Cerner eclipsis	CPOE	Enhanced technology
		Competitive advantage
Surgical information system (SIS)	EMR	Upgrade old system
Metavision	CPOE	Ability to track patient orders (lab, radiology)
McKesson	EMR	Improve patient safety
Cerner	CPOE	Reduce errors
		Improve reporting
		Improve interdepartmental communications
		Upgrade outdated system
		Prepare for government stimulus package
Surgical information system (SIS)	EMR	Upgrade outdated system

Table 3. Project characteristics

Project	Project roles[a]				Project schedule		
	Clin	IT	Con	PM	Start	Exp	Actual
Metavision/SIS	x	x	x	x	Multiple phases	Multiple phases	Multiple phases
Horizon lab	x	x	x	x	2002	2004	2004
Sunrise clinical manager	x	x	x	x	Late 2007		2009
MetaVision	x	x	x	X	Jan 2008	July 2009	Oct 2009
Horizon clinicals	x	x		x	Nov 2009	Dec 2010	Oct 2010
Clinical manager (eclipsis)	x	x	x	x	Sept 2008	Dec 2009	Dec 2009
McKesson medical	x	x	x	x	Not reported		
Surgical information system (SIS)	x	x	x	x	Various dates		
McKesson Cerner	x	x	x	x	Ongoing	Ongoing	Ongoing
Surgical information system (SIS)	x	x	x	x	Jan 2009	Apr 2009	Apr 2009

[a] Clin: Clinician. IT: Information Technology. Con: Consultant. PM: Project Manager.

13 System Impacts: Quality and Safety

In terms of system impacts on quality (Table 4), the respondents noted that transcription errors were reduced and that accountability was increased. Error-reduction and system-generated warnings led to greater safety.

14 System Impacts: Communication and Patient Interactions

In terms of the impact of the systems on communications among clinicians (Table 5), the theme of better documentation was re-iterated. Shared documentation meant that the medical record was accessible to everyone on the multi-disciplinary team, which enhanced coordination and communication. The increased focus on documentation did impact patient interactions, and some respondents noted that the technology-focus actually reduced time for interaction with patients (see Table 5).

15 System Impact: Efficiency and Documentation

EMR systems also have an impact on efficiency and documentation. One clinician noted, "efficiency will grow along with the learning curve in using the system," but that initially it took more time to enter the documentation into the medical record (See Table 6).

Table 4. System impact (quality and safety)

System	Quality		Safety	
Metavision/SIS		5		5
Horizon lab	Great improvement	5	Reduction in errors	5
Sunrise clinical manager	Reduced transcription errors	4	Better access to medical information	3
	Better documentation		Fewer transcription errors	
	Multi-disciplinary care		Orders distributed to correct department	
MetaVision	Improved communication	5	Probably, but no data to support	
	Better decision support			
	Improved legibility			
Horizon clinicals	Benefits not achieved yet	3	Expectation	5
Clinical manager (eclipsis)		4		4
McKesson medical admin		3	Better warnings (e.g. dosage)	3
Cerner eclipsis				
Surgical information system (SIS)	Will monitor	3	Will monitor	3
Metavision				
McKesson	Better accountability	5	Reduced medication errors through bar code scanning	5
Cerner				
Surgical information system (SIS)		4		4
Average		**4.10**		**4.11**

Scale: 5 = met to great extent; 3 = met to moderate extent; 1 = not met

The availability of more accurate, more legible, and more complete documentation would facilitate better information retrieval and reporting (Table 6). Yet, at the initial stages, entering all of this information was cumbersome. One clinician noted that the patient data consisted largely of "checkboxes," rather than clinical opinion—a shortcoming that would need to be addressed by better design of the system itself.

16 System Impacts

The assessment of system impacts reflect the trade-off's between systems objectives and the implementation learning curve. Respondents rated the impact of the system on quality, safety, and documentation relatively higher than the impact of the system on

Table 5. System impact (communications among clinicians, patient interactions)

System	Communication among clinicians		Patient interactions	
Metavision/SIS		5		5
Horizon lab	Real-time posting of lab results	5	Patients feel better	5
Sunrise clinical manager	Multiple access to medical records	4	Better access to information, but takes time away from bedside	3
MetaVision	More legible documentation	5	Using a computer and talking to patient difficult	3
Horizon clinicals	To be expected	5	To be expected	5
Clinical manager (eclipsis)		5		
McKesson medical cerner eclipsis	Encourages communications; fixes broken processes	4	Changes focus to the technology, not the patient and family	2
Surgical information system (SIS) Metavision	Will monitor	3	Will monitor	3
McKesson Cerner	Provides better documentation; difficulty retrieving information	3	Easily printed patient instructions	5
Surgical information system (SIS)		3		4
Average		**3.90**		**3.89**

Scale: 5 = met to great extent; 3 = met to moderate extent; 1 = not met

communications, patient interaction, and overall efficiency. The learning curve and time associated with inputting documentation evidently has a perceived impact upon communications and patient interaction. Several respondents reported that computer-time took away from time with patients and family. This may be a learning curve phenomenon and could be diminished as system use becomes more familiar and widespread (Table 7).

17   Impact of EMR on Work Processes

One of the most important issues addressed in this study is the impact of the EMR system on work processes, the resulting changes in workflow, and the resolution of these issues—by adapting to new processes, by creating workaround's, or by customizing the

Table 6. System impact (efficiency, documentation)

System	Efficiency		Documentation	
Metavision/SIS		5		5
Horizon lab	Reduction in errors	5	Provides audit trail	5
Sunrise clinical manager	Efficient documentation (but time-consuming)	3	Better organized information (but cumbersome workflow)	4
MetaVision	Supports existing anesthesia clinical workflow	5	More legible, complete documentation	5
	Improved backoffice billing			
	Improved research data			
Horizon clinicals	Expected	5	Expected	5
Clinical manager (eclipsis)		3	Ability to read documentation	4
McKesson medical cerner eclipsis	Better efficiency (wish to go back to old methods)	3	More legible documentation / Improved completeness	4
Surgical information system (SIS)	Faster	4	Needs to be clearer	4
Metavision				
McKesson	Efficiency will grow	3	Better documentation,	3
Cerner	Paradigm shift		But checkboxes, not narrative with thoughts/ opinions	
Surgical information system (SIS)		3		4
Average		**3.90**		**4.40**

Scale: 5 = met to great extent; 3 = met to moderate extent; 1 = not met

software to "fit" existing processes. These issues are core to the implementation of off-the-shelf enterprise systems, including EMR systems.

This study confirmed what earlier research on the impact of enterprise systems implementation on work processes says. The benefits of EMR implementation are the ability to improve processes, re-engineer processes to "fit" the best practices supported by the software, and derive a better audit trail. However, the issues of "fit" did occur. In one case, the anesthesiology physicians on the design team tailored the new system to "fit" their existing, preferred processes. The use of dual systems—a byproduct of the "best-of-breed" approach, required users to re-key information from a physician documentation system to a clinical management system. Both of these issues illustrate the

Table 7. System impacts

Response	Quality	Safety	Comm	Patient	Efficiency	Document	Resistance
1	5	5	5	5	5	5	
2	5	5	5	5	5	5	4
3	4	3	4	3	3	4	6
4	5		5	3	5	5	6
5	3	5	5	5	5	5	6
6	4	4	2		3	5	6
7	3	3	4	2	3	4	10
8	3	3	3	3	4	4	8
9	5	5	3	5	3	3	7
10	4	4	3	4	3	4	4
Average	**4.10**	**4.11**	**3.90**	**3.89**	**3.90**	**4.40**	**6.33**

Table 8. Impact of EMR on work processes

System	Work processes—Plus's	Work processes—Minus's
Metavision/SIS	Improved work processes	Creates interaction issues with pharmacy and the hospital
	Consistency	
	Meets regulatory requirements	
	Easier to customize physician orders	
	Improved testing results	
	Faster to change electronic forms than paper	
Horizon lab	New processes safer for the patient	New processes difficult for the nurses
		Time-consuming to access patient data
		Complaints from the beginning
Sunrise clinical manager	Orders go directly to appropriate department	Lengthens patient discharge time
	Improved order tracking	Resulted in dual systems for documentation (nurses must re-key documentation from physician system to clinical management system)
MetaVision	Increased use of data repository	Physicians didn't like system processes for charting
	Improved access to information to physicians for pre-op	
	Improved workflow	
	Tailored "build" to match preferred processes	

(*Continued*)

Table 8. (*Continued*)

System	Work processes—Plus's	Work processes—Minus's
Horizon clinicals	Impact on clinical workflow	
	Impact on medication administration	
Clinical manager (eclipsis)	Physicians do order-entry	Creates issues:
		Physicians enter incorrect information
		"System is a tool"—it doesn't practice medicine
		Difficult to get physicians' buy-in
		Too much reliance on the system rather than talking to each other
McKesson medical admin	Impacts all processes	Users create workarounds
Cerner eclipsis	Users "re-pave" the cow paths	Workarounds not always negative
Surgical information system (SIS)	Configured system to mimic current processes	Change upsets routines
Mctavision		Difficult to customize because it affects regulatory compliance
		Concerns about information security
McKesson	Real-time charting a big change for clinicians	Lack of readiness—end-users with little computer experience
Cerner	Looking to see how EMR impacts health care	Resistance to change
		Software not meeting expectations
		End-users are skeptical
Surgical information system (SIS)	Big change in documenting healthcare plans	Customizing system processes and reports a problem

challenge of trying to make the new system accommodate the processes of the legacy environment—with negative productivity impacts. There are constant trade-off's between re-engineering work processes to "fit" the software vs. trying to customize the software to "fit" existing practices. See Table 8 for details.

Workflow issues (the difference between the workflow supported by the systems and the workflow preferred by the clinicians and physicians) were addressed in numerous ways. Strategies included adapting to the new processes, configuring the software to "fit" current practices, and deploying workarounds (Table 9). To gain support for new processes, the respondents recommended training, support, the involvement of super-users, and leadership. One clinician pointed out that continuously trying to customize the software to "fit" current practices would create upgrade issues because customizations could not be migrated to the next versions. Better participation in the design process was key to resolving these issues and gaining the buy-in of the

Table 9. How workflow issues were addressed

System	How Workflow Issues were Addressed
Metavision/SIS	Staff and physician buy-in, participation on teams
	Time-off work to participate on teams
	Effective training
Horizon lab	Some workarounds
	Adapted to new processes for the most part
Sunrise clinical manager	Discharge process evaluated for "fixes"
	Trying to link to systems to prevent re-keying
MetaVision	Application very customizable
	Very few user workarounds
	Some processes cannot be modified
	Less computer-savvy users write
Horizon clinicals	Not known yet
Clinical manager (eclipsis)	Peer leadership resolves issues
	Super-users assist older physicians
McKesson medical admin	Education, individualized training
Cerner eclipsis	Strong leadership
	Best not to customize
Surgical information system (Metavision	Education
McKesson	Education
Cerner	
Surgical information system (SIS)	Involve key players in planning, testing, teaching, implementation

end-users, particularly the physicians. End-user involvement in requirements definition in advance of systems acquisition would also help bridge the gap between user preferences and the processes supported by the system.

18   Systems Implementation: Problems and Success Factors

Many of the challenges of EMR systems implementation were highlighted when respondents were asked to describe major problems. Some of these problems were the tendency for users to do workarounds, the time it took to learn the new system, excessive workload from having to learn the new system while doing normal duties, poor end-user support, and physician resistance (Table 10). The success factors recommended by the respondents addressed these issues and included: obtaining top management buy-in, obtaining end-user involvement, supporting new workflow and standardized processes, and using clinicians as champions. Education, training, testing, and communications were all key to successful implementation. In the section dealing with Critical Success Factors in system implementation, we will go into each of these factors in greater detail.

Table 10. Systems implementation: problems and success factors

System	Problems implementing	How to make an EMR project a success
Metavision/SIS	Contractors making changes at the users request—not going through process (through committees)	Stick to the plan
	Turnover of project design staff	Written policies and procedures
	Difficulty recruiting staff	Buy-in of top management
	Super-users enabling un-intended uses of system	
	Hardware issues, printing issues	
	Reporting issues	
	Changes in super-users	
Horizon lab	Excessive workload (trained 150 users in 6 weeks)	End-user involvement
	Learning curve (learning other systems)	End-user help in overcoming resistance
	Excessive support calls	
Sunrise clinical manager	All-at-once implementation	Achieve goals without negative impact to patient safety
	Providing 24-hour support a challenge	Achieve goals without increasing nursing workload
	Physicians did not attend training	
	Champions had to provide users' training	
	Learning process increased workload	
	Increased time to enter orders	
	System more complex	
	System time-consuming to learn	
	System use takes time away from bedside–may negatively affect patient care	
MetaVision	Some great ideas not implemented	Need clinician champions
	Post "go-live" support poor	"Go-live" needs to go smoothly
	Hospital help desk had no application expertise	Workflow needs to be well-understood
	Hospital helpdesk had to page vendor	Need to stay true to new workflow
		Use vendor-supported help desk
Horizon clinicals		Understand that process workflow will change

(Continued)

Table 10. (*Continued*)

System	Problems implementing	How to make an EMR project a success
		Standardize processes
		Provide training early
		Provide refresher training
		Skilled project management
Clinical manager (eclipsis)	Problems with user adoption of system	Communications
McKesson medical admin	Technology issues—connectivity, lack of hardware	Top management backing
		Planning with input from all disciplines
Cerner eclipsis	User resistance—system avoidance	Education and training
	Cost more than planned	Communications of changes
		Sufficient hardware and on-site support
Surgical information system (SIS)	Staff resistance	Buy-in of staff
Metavision		End-user involvement
		Keep administration aware of issues
		Maintain momentum
McKesson	Staff have little computer experience	Education
Cerner		
Surgical information system (SIS)	Vendors promising too much	Take time to practice
	Distrust of system	Scenarios are helpful
	Distrust of IT and vendor	Need to practice before using system in patient care

19   Critical Success Factors in Systems Implementation

The final section of this study deals with the critical success factors in systems implementation. First, we will look at the critical role of the super-users. The super-users were clinicians who were responsible for application design, training, implementation support, and testing. Many of the super-users participated in these interviews and were on the "front lines" of systems implementation.

Two other critical success factors were effective training and top management commitment. Training was at best "adequate," and at worst "weak," according to the respondents. Many "learned on the fly," and relied on vendor training. One respondent noted that "cheat sheets" were far more beneficial than a 500-page reference manual. In most cases, vendor training was the primary source of training and was adequate.

Top management commitment was essential. Top management provided vision, leadership, budget, and support. They were responsible for major approvals—scope, time, and budget—as well as scope changes. At times, they were responsible for expediting the project by anticipating issues and providing problem resolution.

Each project was governed by a steering committee which was composed of clinical leaders, including physicians, management, and nursing professionals. The responsibilities of the steering committee were making design decisions, supporting standardized processes, and making systems implementation decisions. Steering committee members were responsible for managing upgrades, including mandating testing before an upgrade went into production.

Finally, the role of the champion was critical to the success of the projects studied. The champions were physicians, clinicians, nursing professionals, and super-users representing the end-user constituencies. In most projects, there were multiple champions, including physicians, nursing professionals, and super-users representing various functional units. Table 11 summarizes the critical success factors mentioned by the respondents in each of the EMR implementation projects:

Table 11. Critical success factors in EMR systems implementation

Project	Super-users	Training	Top Mgmt	Steering Comm	Champion
Metavision/SIS	x	x	x	x	x
Horizon lab	x	x	x	x	x
Sunrise vlinical	x	x	x	x	x
MetaVision	x	x	x	x	x
Horizon clinical	x	x	x	x	x
Clinical (Eclipsis)	x	x	x	x	x
McKesson Med	x	x	x	x	x
Metavision/SIS	x	x	x	x	x
Cerner, McKesson	x	x	x	x	x
Surgical I/S	x	x	x	x	x

20 Resistance to Change

Resistance to change was a factor. On a scale of 1 to 10, with 10 being the highest level of resistance, the overall average resistance reported by the respondents was **6.3.** Strategies for managing resistance to change were: communications, top management commitment, end-user involvement, education, and implementation support. As noted by one super-user, many of the older physicians were resistant to the new system and training/hand-holding/support were key to success (Table 12).

Table 12. Managing resistance to change

Project	Level resist	Strategies to manage resistance
Metavision/SIS	n/a	Address technical problems
Horizon lab	4	Keep staff in the loop
Sunrise llinical	6	Early communications (goals, system justification)
MetaVision	6	Top management commitment, end-user buy-in
Horizon clinical	6	Communications, training, practice, collaboration
Clinical (eclipsis)	6	Super-users working one-on-one with end-users
McKesson Med	10	Administration backing, education
Metavision/SIS	8	Discussions with staff
Cerner, McKesson	7	Give end-users ownership, provide support
Surgical I/S	4	Little resistance (replacing a system)
Overall	6.3	

21   Systems Implementation: Open-Ended Comments

Open-ended comments by the respondents confirmed many of the issues mentioned earlier. First, many of the respondents believed that the new systems being implemented provided benefits, including data integration across areas, more timely reporting, improved efficiency, reduced medical transcription errors, order tracking, and improve patient safety. Overall, they welcomed the benefits of the new systems.

Yet, the learning curve and the time it took to enter data, particularly on the part of the physicians themselves, detracted from patient interaction. Double-entry of data into multiple systems also created time-consuming bottlenecks, largely because the hospital system pursued a "best-of-breed" approach, compared with a fully integrated "common" system.

The open ended-comments also confirmed several of the critical success factors which were mentioned previously. These included "pushing" for more end-user participation and following standard processes, as opposed to making workarounds and changes.

22   ERP and ERP: Similarities

The issue raised by the title of this paper is: EMR implementation: What lessons have been learned from ERP implementation? From these case studies in EMR implementation, several preliminary observations can be made. First, the critical success factors for EMR implementation are remarkably similar to the critical success factors in ERP implementation. These CSF's include the participation of super-users (e.g. functional area healthcare professionals) on project teams, the importance of training, the importance of top management support, the role of the steering committee, and the role of the champion.

Second, the issue of re-engineering vs. customization was continuously addressed. While clinicians and other healthcare professionals wanted to implement workarounds and customizations, project team members were vividly aware of the importance of re-engineering existing processes and workflow to conform with the best practices supported by the enterprise-wide software.

23 Summary and Conclusions

A telling comment by one of the clinicians was that EMR systems implementation was a continuous process requiring continuous process improvement, ongoing application upgrades, ongoing fixes, and continuous testing. Continuous systems implementation was largely being justified in terms of improving patient care through better information, better reporting, better documentation, error-reduction, and an audit trail.

However, systems implementation was dependent upon the emerging, important role of the clinicians themselves who participated in this survey. These clinicians are the super-users who are responsible on an ongoing basis for providing training, support, and design. Their knowledge of clinical processes, and their ability to understand and support the new systems and their processes, is critical to realizing systems outcomes—in terms of safety, quality, and patient care.

Without a doubt, the greatest take-away from this research was their commitment to leadership and their invaluable role in project success. If there is any lesson to be learned from these data, it is that the people (the super-users, top management, team members, steering committee members) are critical to systems success. All of these people are healthcare professionals who are transitioning to individuals responsible for the design, implementation, testing, deployment, and maintenance of information systems. Their role is unique because it combines a clinical background with responsibility for information systems design and implementation.

Appendix A: Project Interview Form

Organization Name _____

Contact Person: Phone: _____ **Email:** _____

Job Title: _____ **Department:** _____

Part 1: EHR Project Information

1. What information system have you been involved in implementing?

   o   Name of system _____

   o   System type (EHR, Lab system, etc.)
   _____

   o   What was the reason for acquiring the system?
   _____

2. Who is involved in the project? (check all that apply)

    ___   Clinicians
    ___   IT professionals
    ___   External consultants
    ___   Project managers
    ___   Other
    What is your role in the project? _____

Part 2: Project Timeline

    o   Start date _____
    o   Expected completion date _____
    o   Actual completion date (if complete) _____

Part 3: Impact of the System

1. On a scale of 1 to 5, with 5 being the highest, please assess the extent to which each of these systems objectives were met:
    5 = met to a great extent
    3 = met to a moderate extent
    1 = not met
    NA = not applicable

    _____   Quality: improving the quality of patient care.
               Comment: _____

5 = met to a great extent
3 = met to a moderate extent
1 = not met
NA = not applicable

_____   Patient Safety: reducing medication errors.
           Comment: _____

_____   Communication: improving communications among clinicians.
           Comment: _____

_____   Patient Interactions: improving interactions with patients.
           Comment: _____

_____   Efficiency: improving efficiency.
           Comment: _____

_____   Documentation: improving documentation.
           Comment: _____

Other benefits:

_____

Part 4: EHR System Use

1. What was the impact of the system on work processes? What aspects of workflow changed?

   _____

   _____

2. How were these issues resolved? (users adapted to new processes, users created workaround's, software was customized).

   _____

   _____

3. What were some of the problems arising in implementing the system?

   _____

   _____

4. In your opinion, what needs to happen to make the project a success?

   _____

   _____

Part 5: Evaluation of EHR Project Success Factors

1. How was the project managed? Was it managed by healthcare professionals or was it an IT project?

   _____

2. What role did the "super-users" play a role in system implementation?

   _____

3. How do you feel about the training? Did you receive enough training?

   _____

4. What is top management's involvement?

   _____

5. Is there a champion?

   _____

6. On a scale of 1 to 10, with 10 being the highest, what was the level of resistance to change? _____
   What methods were used to reduce resistance to change?

_____

7. Is there a project steering committee? _____

Other notes:

_____

References

1. Ash, J., Bates, D.: Factors and forces affecting EHR system adoption: report of a 2004 ACMI discussion. J. Am. Med. Inf. Assoc. **12**(1), 229 (2005)
2. Bancroft, N., Seip, H., Sprengel, A.: Implementing SAP R/3, 2nd edn. Manning Publications, Greenwich (1998)
3. Barki, H., Pinsonneault, A.: A model of organizational integration, implementation effort, and performance. Organ. Sci. **16**(2), 165–179 (2005)
4. Baron, R.J., Fabens, E.L., Schiffman, M., Wolff, E.: Electronic health records: just around the corner? or over the cliff. Ann. Intern. Med. **143**(3), 222–226 (2005)
5. Bhattacherjee, A., Davis, C., Hikmet, N., Kayhan,V.: User reactions to information technology: evidence from the healthcare sector. In: Twenty Ninth International Conference on Information Systems (2008)
6. Boudreau, M.C., Robey, D.: Enacting integrated information technology: a human agency perspective. Organ. Sci. **16**(1), 3–18 (2005)
7. Bowen, P.L., Cheung, M.-Y.D., Rohde, F.: Enhancing IT governance practices: a model and case study of an organization's efforts. Int. J. Acc. Inf. Syst. **8**, 191–221 (2007)
8. Bradford, M., Florin, J.: Examining the role of innovation diffusion factors on the implementation success of enterprise resource planning systems. Int. J. Acc. Inf. Syst. **4**, 205–225 (2003)
9. Brady, C., Gargeya, V.: Success and failure factors of adopting SAP in ERP system implementation. Bus. Process Manag. J. **11**(5), 501–516 (2005)
10. Brown, C., Vessey, I.: Managing the next wave of enterprise systems: leveraging lessons from ERP. MIS Q. Executive **2**(2), 65–77 (2003)
11. Chin, T.: Avoiding EMR meltdown: how to get your money's worth. In: American Medical News (2006)
12. Ciborra, C.: From Control to Drift: The Dynamics of Corporate Information Infrastructures. Oxford University Press, Oxford (2000)
13. Doolan, D., Bates, D.: Computerized Physician Order Entry Systems in Hospitals: Mandates and Incentives. Project HOPE-The People-to-People Health Foundation Inc, Millwood (2002)
14. Gattiker, T.F., Goodhue, D.L.: What happens after ERP implementation: understanding the impact of inter-dependence and differentiation of plant-level outcomes. MIS Q. **29**(3), 559–585 (2005)
15. Glaser, B.G., Strauss, A.: The Discovery of Grounded Theory. Aldine, Chicago (1967)

16. Hing, E.S., Burt, C., Woodwell, D.: Electronic Medical Record Use by Office-Based Physicians and Their Practices: United States, 2006. Advance Data from Vital and Health Statistics, Hyattsville (2007). Number 393
17. Ilie, V.: How to influence physicians to use electronic medical records (EMR)? social influence tactics and their effects on EMR implementation effectiveness. In: Thirtieth International Conference on Information Systems (2009)
18. Lorenzi, N., Riley, R.: Managing change. J. Med. Inf. Assoc. **7**, 116–124 (2000)
19. Mabert, V.A., Soni, A., Venkataramanan, M.A.: Enterprise resource planning: managing the implementation process. Eur. J. Oper. Res. **146**(2), 302–314 (2003)
20. Markus, M.L., Axline, S., Petrie, D., Tanis, C.: Learning from adopters' experiences with ERP: problems encountered and successes achieved. J. Inf. Technol. **15**, 245–265 (2000)
21. Motwani, J., Mirchandanai, D., Madan, M., Gunasekaran, A.: Successful implementation of ERP projects, evidence from two case studies. Int. J. Prod. Econ. **75**(1–2), 83–94 (2002)
22. Motwani, J., Subramanian, R., Gopalakrishna, P.: Critical factors for successful ERP implementation: exploratory findings from four case studies. Comput. Ind. **56**, 529–544 (2005)
23. Muscatello, J.R., Parente, D.H.: Enterprise resource planning (ERP): a postimplementation cross-case analysis. Inf. Resour. Manag. J. **19**(3), 61–80 (2006)
24. Muscatello, J.R., Small, M.H., Chen, I.J.: Implementing enterprise resource planning (ERP) systems in small and midsize manufacturing firms. Int. J. Oper. Prod. Manag. **23**(7/8), 850–871 (2003)
25. Nah, F.F.-H., Delgado, S.: Critical success factors for enterprise resource planning implementation and upgrade. J. Comput. Inf. Syst. **46**(5), 99–113 (2006)
26. Nah, F.F.-H., Lau, J.L.-S., Kuang, J.: Critical factors for successful implementation of enterprise systems. Bus. Process Manag. J. **7**(3), 285–296 (2001)
27. Nelson, R.Ryan: Project retrospectives: evaluating project success, failure, and everything in between. MIS Q. Executive **4**(3), 361–373 (2005)
28. Parr, A.N., Shanks, G., Darke, P.: Identification of necessary factors for successful implementation of ERP systems. In: Ngwerryama, O., Introna, L., Myers, M., DeGross, J. (eds.) New Information Technologies in Organizational Processes, pp. 99–119. Kluwer Academic Publishers, Boston (1999)
29. Parr, A., Shanks, G.: A model of ERP project implementation. J. Inf. Technol. **15**, 289–303 (2000)
30. Poissant, L., Pereira, J., Tamblyn, R., Kawasumi, Y.: The impact of electronic health records on time efficiency of physicians and nurses: a systematic review. J. Am. Med. Inf. Assoc. **12**(5), 505–516 (2005)
31. Pollack, N., Cornford, J.: ERP systems and the university as a 'unique' organization. Inf. Technol. People **17**(1), 31–52 (2004)
32. Pozzebon, M.: Combining a structuration approach with a behavioral-based model to investigate ERP usage. Paper Presented at Americas Conference on Information Systems 2000, Long Beach (2000)
33. Ross, J., Vitale, M., Willcocks, L.: The continuing ERP revolution: Sustainable lessons, new modes of delivery. In: Shanks, G., Seddon, P., Willcocks, L. (eds.) Second-Wave Enterprise Resource Planning Systems. Cambridge University Press, Cambridge (2003)
34. Scott, J., Vessey, I.: Managing risks in enterprise systems implementations. Commun. ACM **45**(4), 74–81 (2002)
35. Soh, C., Sia, K., et al.: Misalignments in ERP implementation: a dialectic perspective. Int. J. Human-Comput. Interact. **16**(10), 81–100 (2003)
36. Srivardhana, T., Pawlowski, S.D.: ERP systems as an enabler of sustained business process innovation: a knowledge-based view. J. Strateg. Inf. Syst. **16**(1), 51–69 (2007)

37. Sumner, M.: Risk factors in managing enterprise-wide ERP projects. J. Inf. Technol. **15**, 317–327 (2002)
38. Sumner, M.: Critical success factors in EMR implementation. Working Paper, The McDowell Research Center for Global Information Technology Management, University of North Carolina Greensboro, October 12, 2009 (2009)
39. Sumner, M.: Risk factors in managing enterprise-wide/ERP projects. J. Inf. Technol. **15**(4), 317–327 (2002)
40. Tong, Y., Teo, H.-H., Tan, C.-H.: Direct and indirect use of information systems in organizations: an empirical investigation of system usage in a public hospital. In: Twenty Ninth International Conference on Information Systems (2008)
41. Tong, Y., Teo, H.-H.: Migrating to integrated electronic medical record: an empirical investigation of physicians' use preference. In: 30th International Conference on Information Systems (2009)
42. Umble, E.J., Haft, R., Umble, M.M.: ERP: implementation procedures and critical success factors. Eur. J. Oper. Res. **146**, 241–257 (2003)
43. Wagner, E.L., Newell, S.: Best for whom? the tension between 'best practice' ERP packages and diverse epistemic cultures in a university context. J. Strateg. Inf. Syst. **13**(4), 305–328 (2004)
44. Wilcox, A., Bowes, W.A., Thornton, S., Narus, S.: Physician use of outpatient electronic health records to improve care. In: Columbia University, New York Presbyterian Hospital, Intermountain Healthcare, Department of Biomedical Informatics, University of Utah, American Medical Informatics Association (AMIA) 2008 Symposium Proceedings, pp. 809–813 (2008)
45. Willcocks, L.P., Sykes, R.: The role of the CIO and the IT function in ERP. Commun. ACM **43**(4), 22–28 (2000)
46. Yeow, A., Faraj, S.: Marrying work within the healthcare organization: a narrative network perspective on IT innovation-mediated organization change. J. Assoc. Inf. Syst. (2008)
47. Zandieh, S., Mills, S., Yoon-Flannery, K., Kuperman, G., Kaushal, R.: Provider' expectations of ambulatory electronic health records (EHR's). In: American Medical Informatics Association (AMIA) 2008 Symposium Proceedings, 1191. Weill Cornell Medical College, New York, New York-Presbyterian Hospital, New York, Columbia University, New York (2008)

Critical Success Factors for ERP System Implementation Projects: An Update of Literature Reviews

Christian Leyh[✉] and Pauline Sander

Chair of Information Systems, esp. IS in Manufacturing and Commerce,
Technische Universität Dresden, 01062 Dresden, Germany
christian.leyh@tu-dresden.de

Abstract. The aim of our study was to gain insight into the research field of critical success factors (CSF) of enterprise resource planning (ERP) system implementation projects. Therefore, we conducted two literature reviews, more specifically systematic reviews of relevant articles in five different databases and among several international conference proceedings. Ultimately, we identified 320 relevant papers (144 single or multiple case studies, 118 surveys, and 58 literature reviews or articles from which CSFs can be derived). From these existing studies, we discovered 31 different CSFs for ERP system implementation projects. The top three factors identified are Top management support and involvement, Project management, and User training. However, most of the relevant papers focus on large enterprises. Only 37 papers explicitly focus on smaller and medium-sized enterprises (SMEs), which is clearly a research gap in this field.

Keywords: ERP systems · Critical success factors · CSF · Literature review · Small and medium-sized companies · SME

1 Motivation

Today's enterprises are faced with the globalization of markets and fast changes in the economy. In order to be able to cope with these conditions, the use of information and communication systems as well as technology is almost mandatory. Specifically, the adoption of enterprise resource planning (ERP) systems as standardized systems that encompass the activities of whole enterprises has become an important factor in today's business [1]. Therefore, during the last decades, the segment of ERP systems was one of the fastest growing segments in the software market, and these systems are one of the most important developments in information technology. The demand for ERP applications arises from several sources, for example, competitive pressures to become a low-cost producer, expectations of revenue growth, and the desire to re-engineer the business to respond to market challenges. There are several benefits of a properly selected and implemented ERP system such as considerable reductions in inventory costs, raw material costs, lead time for customers, production time, and production costs [2].

© Springer International Publishing Switzerland 2015
D. Sedera et al. (Eds.): Pre-ICIS 2010-2012, LNBIP 198, pp. 45–67, 2015.
DOI: 10.1007/978-3-319-17587-4_3

Due to the saturation of ERP markets targeting large-scaled enterprises, ERP system manufacturers today are also concentrating on the growing market of small and medium-sized enterprises (SMEs) [3, 4]. This has resulted in a highly fragmented ERP market and a great diffusion of ERP systems throughout enterprises of nearly every industry and every size [5–7].

Due to the strong demand and the high fragmentation of the market, there are many ERP systems with different technologies and philosophies available on the market. This multitude of software manufacturers, vendors, and systems implies that enterprises that use or want to use ERP systems must strive to find the "right" software as well as to be aware of the factors that influence the success of the implementation project. The implementation of an information system (e.g., an ERP system) is a complex and time-consuming project during which companies face great opportunities, but at the same time face enormous risks. To take advantage of the potential, rather than getting caught by the risks of these implementation projects, it is essential to the study / to focus on those factors that support a successful implementation of an information system [8, 9]. If aware of these factors, a company can positively influence the success of the implementation project and effectively minimize the project`s risks [8]. Recalling these so-called critical success factors (CSFs) is of high importance whenever a new system is to be adopted and implemented or whenever a running system needs to be upgraded or replaced. Errors during the selection, implementation, or maintenance of ERP systems; wrong implementation approaches; or ERP systems that do not fit the requirements of the enterprise can all cause financial disadvantages or disasters, perhaps even leading to insolvency. Several examples of such negative scenarios can be found in the literature (e.g., [10, 11]). SMEs especially must be aware of the CSFs since they lack the financial, material, and personnel resources of larger companies [12]. Thus, they are under greater pressure to implement and run ERP systems without failure and as smoothly as possible.

In order to identify the factors that affect the success or failure of ERP system implementation projects, several case studies, surveys, and literature reviews have already been conducted by different researchers (e.g., [13–15]). Most of these literature reviews cannot be reproduced, because descriptions of the review methods and procedures are lacking. Thus, some researchers clearly point out the drawbacks of the current literature review articles. Specifically, critics note the lack of methodological rigor [16]. Therefore, in order to update the existing reviews by including current ERP literature, we conducted two literature reviews (the first one in 2010, the second one in 2013). More specifically, these were two systematic reviews of articles from five different databases and from several international conference proceedings. The CSFs reported in this paper were derived from 320 papers identified as relevant, and the frequency of the occurrence of each CSF was counted. The aggregated results of these reviews will be presented in this paper. Additionally, we will focus on CSFs specifically for SMEs within the identified papers.

Therefore, the paper is structured as follows. The next section presents a short overview of our data collection methodology in order to make our review reproducible. Afterwards, in section 3 the critical success factors that were focused on during the review will be explained in detail. The fourth section deals with the results of the literature review. We will point out which factors are the most important and which factors seem to have little influence on ERP project success. Finally, the paper concludes with a summary of the results as well as a critical acclaim of the conducted literature review.

2   Data Collection Methodology – Literature Review

The literature review to identify the CSFs was performed in several steps similar to the approach suggested by Webster & Watson [17]. In general, it was a database-driven review with an additional search in the proceedings of several IS conferences. To make our review reproducible, we listed tables with the databases and search terms in the Appendix (see Tables 4 and 5).

Here, we conducted two separate literature reviews according to the same search procedure and steps. The first one was done in the mid-2010 (see also [5, 18]). Since we identified 20 papers or more published each year it is essential for us to update this review every two or three years. Therefore, we conducted the second review in the mid-2013.

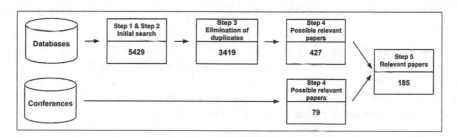

Fig. 1. Progress of the literature review from 2010

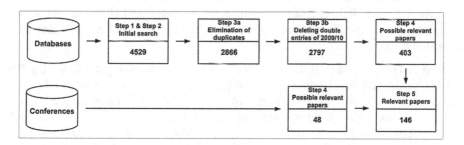

Fig. 2. Progress of the literature review from 2013

The steps of our review procedure are presented in the following paragraphs. An overview is given in Fig. 1 and Fig. 2 with regard to the numbers of papers identified or remaining during/after each step. With each step, the number of papers was reduced according to the assembly of different criteria.

Step 1: The first step was to define the sources for the literature review. Therefore, several databases and conference proceedings were identified (see Appendix - Table 4).

Step 2: Within this step, we had to define the search terms for the database-driven review. Keywords selected for this search were mostly derived from the keywords supplied and used by the authors of some of the relevant articles identified in a preliminary literature review. The search terms that we used are listed in Table 5. Since the WISO database also provides German papers, we additionally used the German translation of most of the search terms. For the conference papers, only inappropriate search fields were provided. Hence, we decided to review the abstracts and titles of the papers in this step manually.

Step 3: During step 3 we performed the initial search according to step 1 and step 2 and then eliminated duplicates.

- Review 1: The initial search provided 5,429 papers from the databases. After eliminating the duplicates, 3,419 articles remained. From the conference search, 79 papers remained. Altogether, 3,498 papers were identified during the initial search step.
- Review 2: During the initial search step, 4,529 articles were found. After deleting the duplicates (step 3a) and deleting double entries resulting from papers from review 1 (step 3b), 2,797 papers remained. From the conferences, 48 papers remained. Therefore, altogether a total of 2,845 papers were found during these steps.

Step 4: Step 4 included the identification of irrelevant papers. During the initial search, we did not apply any restrictions. The search was not limited to the research field of IS; therefore, papers from other research fields were included in the results, too. Thus, these papers had to be excluded. This was done by reviewing the abstracts of the papers and if necessary by examining the paper content.

- Review 1: Of the papers, 427 stemming from the database search and all 79 conference papers remained. Altogether, this review yielded 506 papers potentially relevant to the field of CSFs for ERP system implementations (see Fig. 1).
- Review 2: Here, 403 papers resulting from the databases and all conference papers remained as potentially relevant. Altogether, 451 had to be read in depth according to step 5 (see Fig. 2).

Step 5: The fifth and final step consisted of a detailed analysis of the remaining 506 and 451 papers and the identification of the CSFs. Therefore, the content of all papers was reviewed in depth for the purpose of categorization of the identified success factors. Emphasis was placed not only on the wording of these factors but on their meaning. Following this step, 185 relevant papers that suggested, discussed or mentioned CSFs remained from review 1 and 146 articles remained from review 2.

Step 6: Additionally, while conducting review 2, we added a sixth step. Within this step, we cross-checked papers from the same authors or with similar author composition from review 1 and review 2 regarding their content (despite the duplicates check of steps 3a and 3b). Since often papers which are published at conferences are subsequently published as extended versions in journals, these papers should not be counted twice within the reviews. We identified eleven papers which were such extended journal versions. So these relevant papers were deleted, too. This led to a final sum of 320 relevant papers. The results of the analysis of these papers that mentioned CSFs are described in the following sections.

3 Critical Success Factors of ERP Implementation Success

A critical success factor for ERP projects is defined according to Finney and Corbett [14] as reference to any condition or element that was seen necessary in order for the ERP implementation to be successful. The goal of the performed literature review is to gain an in-depth understanding of the different CSFs already identified by other researchers. The identified papers consist of papers that present single or multiple case studies, conducted surveys, literature reviews or articles where CSFs are derived from chosen literature. Within these papers, the following 31 CSFs were identified:

- Available resources (e.g., budget and employees)
- Balanced project team

- Business process reengineering
- Change management
- Clear goals and objectives (e.g., vision and business plan)
- Communication
- Company's strategy/strategy fit

- Data accuracy (e.g., data analysis and conversion)
- Environment (e.g., national culture and language)
- ERP system acceptance/resistance

- ERP system configuration
- ERP system tests
- External consultants
- Interdepartmental cooperation
- Involvement of end-users and stakeholders

- IT structure and legacy systems

- Knowledge management
- Monitoring and performance measurement
- Organizational culture
- Organizational fit of the ERP system
- Organizational structure

- Project champion
- Project team leadership/empowered decision makers
- Project management

- Skills, knowledge, and expertise

- Top management support and involvement
- Troubleshooting
- Use of a steering committee
- User training
- Vendor relationship and support
- Vendor's tools and implementation methods

Available Resources (e.g., budget, employees, etc.): ERP implementation projects require a lot of resources such as money, time and employees. These requirements need to be determined early in the project or even before the project starts [19]. It is very difficult to secure resource commitment in advance [20] to ensure the success of the implementation project. An appropriate budget is the basis for a solid execution of projects. If the budget allocated is too small other success factors can be affected negatively [21].

Balanced Project Team: In general, a project team consists of at least two persons working together for a common goal whereby each team member has defined responsibilities and functions [22]. The characteristics of the team members should complement each other, on their experience, their knowledge as well as their soft skills [23]. For an ERP implementation it is important to have a solid, core implementation team that is comprised of the organization's best and brightest individuals [14]. These team members should be assigned to the project on a fulltime basis. Only then they can fully concentrate on the project and are not disturbed or distracted with their daily business [24].

Business Process Reengineering: Business process reengineering (BPR) is a crucial project phase in ERP projects although it often leads to delays in ERP implementations [25]. During ERP projects companies have to review their business processes and explore new ways of doing things relatively to the best practices embedded in the ERP system. The deeper and more detailed this review is, the better the outcome of the BPR will be [26, 27]. Changing activities and workflows in business processes before, during or after the ERP implementation may lead to a different and maybe minimized level of ERP system configuration [19]. It is advisable to minimize the extent of the ERP system modification. This reduces errors and the company can more easily take advantage of newer versions and releases. Therefore, the project team or the top management should decide to what extent the company has to change their business processes to fit the ERP system [28].

Change Management: Change management involves early participation of all persons affected by a change process in order to reduce resistance against these changes. An important component is adequate training especially of the IT-department as well as an early communication of the changes to provide employees with an opportunity to react [29]. Change management strategies are responsible for handling the enterprise-wide cultural and structural changes. Therefore, it is necessary to train and educate the employees in various ways. Thereby, change management not only aims towards preventing rejection and supporting acceptance. Moreover, its goal is making employees understand and want the changes. Integrating the employees early in the planning and implementation process is important to achieve this understanding. Also, during the user training sessions a support team should be available in order to clarify and answer questions regarding the new processes and function. Furthermore, an additional evaluation with the end users should be accomplished after the "go live" to uncover problems and to avoid discords [30].

Clear Goals and Objectives (e.g., vision, business plan, etc.): Clear goals and objectives are seen as CSF by many researchers (e.g., [2, 13, 31]). This requires formulating a business vision, calculating a business case, identifying and communicating clear goals and objectives regarding the ERP implementation, and providing a clear link between business goals and the company's IS strategy [14, 32]. This is needed to steer the direction of the project throughout the whole ERP implementation. Therefore, a good business plan that outlines proposed strategic and tangible benefits includes resources, calculates costs and risks as well as specifies a clear timeline that is critical to an ERP project. These instruments can be very helpful to maintain the focus on project benefits and outcomes [30].

Communication: The CSF communication is one of the most difficult and most challenging tasks during the implementation of an ERP system. The existence of a clear concept addressing communication, which contains a communication strategy as well as the respective communication channels and methods, is very important. This strategy should match with the goals and requirements of the ERP project and should enable open and free communication by providing an adequate communication platform [32]. Expectations at every level need to be communicated [30]. The communication between the management, the project team and the employees should be clear on a regular basis. Detailed information about the project status, achieved results or decisions made by the management is as essential as the direct discussion, for example, of fears and conflicts.

Company's Strategy / Strategy Fit: To ensure the success of an ERP implementation, the changes caused by the ERP system have to be linked with the company's longtime strategic goals. The ERP system should support this strategy or even be one of the important factors for the strategy's success. The implementation project as part of the enterprise-wide strategy (e.g., the implementation as a method of strategic goal achievement) is mandatory [33].

Data Accuracy (e.g., data analysis and conversion): A fundamental requirement for the effectiveness and the success of ERP systems is the availability of accurate data. Problems concerning data can cause heavy implementation delays. Therefore, the management of data migration represents a critical factor throughout the whole implementation [2, 34]. Identifying which data has to be loaded into the system and which is extraneous as well as converting all disparate data structures into a single, consistent format is an important challenge. The conversion process is often underestimated. In addition, interfaces with other internal and external systems (between departments such as accounting and production, data warehouses, etc.) have to be considered, too [2].

Environment (e.g., national culture, language, etc.): The effects and the relevance of national cultures to the ERP implementation are pointed out in several studies (e.g., [35, 36]). Basic values, beliefs and norms in different countries are factors that influence the organizational culture, and in turn, affect the practices of professional activities including ERP implementation [35]. Cultural differences can cause problems during an ERP project such as different beliefs in providing access to information, miscommunication due to language difficulties or problems in reengineering organizational processes [37].

ERP System Acceptance / Resistance: Every person and department should be responsible and accountable for the whole ERP system and the key users from different departments have to be committed to the implementation project on a fulltime basis [38]. Therefore, a lack of user and stakeholder inputs and acceptance may reduce the chance of a successful implementation [39]. In case employees are not psychologically ready for change and do not accept the new ERP system, their attitudes and behaviors will hinder them from working and resolving conflicts with consultants, as well as from acquiring the necessary ERP knowledge [40]. Accordingly, a higher user and stakeholder support should positively affect the communication and conflict resolution in the ERP consulting process [41].

ERP System Configuration: Since the initial ERP system version is based on best practices, a configuration or adaption of the system according to business processes is necessary in every ERP implementation project. Hence, as far as possible, the company should try to adopt the processes and options built into the ERP, rather than seek to modify the ERP [13]. Following Hong & Kim [42], the more strongly the original ERP software is modified (e.g., even beyond the "normal" configuration) the smaller the chance is for a successful implementation project. Hence, a good business vision is helpful because it reduces the effort of capturing the functionality of the ERP business model and therefore minimizes the effort needed for the configuration [13]. Again, extensive system modifications will not only cause implementation problems, but also harm system maintenance. Therefore, fewer adjustments reduce the effort of integrating new versions, releases or updates [30].

ERP System Tests: In ERP implementation, "go live" on the system without adequate and planned system testing may lead to an organizational disaster. Tests and validation of an ERP system is necessary to ensure that the system works technically correct and that the business process configurations were done in the right way [43]. Therefore testing and simulation exercises for both, the whole system and separate parts / functions, have to be performed during and in the final stages of the implementation process [14, 32].

External Consultants: The use of external consultants depends on the internal know-how and experience at the moment of the project initiation [13]. Many organizations use consultants to facilitate the implementation process. Consultants are experienced in specific industries, have comprehensive knowledge about certain modules and may be better able to determine what will work best for a given company [44]. Consultants are often involved in all stages of the implementation: performing requirements analysis, recommending a suitable solution and managing the implementation [2]. Therefore, it is necessary to determine the number of consultants, how and when to use them as well as their responsibilities within the implementation project [13].

Interdepartmental Cooperation: To successfully implement an ERP system it is necessary that all departments cooperate at the same level of intensity and engagement since an ERP system affects all business units and business processes across functional and departmental boundaries. This requires the sharing of common goals instead of emphasizing individual pursuits. Also, to share information within a company and between different companies requires cooperation between partners, employees, managers and corporations based on trust and the willingness to cooperate. Issues such as prestige, job security and control feelings or departmental politics are also involved and have to be considered and managed [2, 45].

Involvement of End-Users and Stakeholders: This factor is one of the most frequently cited CSFs [46]. Users and stakeholders must perceive the system as being important and necessary to their work [47]. Therefore, end-user involvement and participation during the ERP project and the involvement of all stakeholders that are affected by the ERP implementation is mandatory and will result in a better fit of user requirements achieving better system quality, use and acceptance [13]. It is important to get users and stakeholders involved during the system implementation and to make use of their knowledge in areas where the project team lacks expertise and knowledge [26]. According to Ghosh [48], this involvement in the project, from start to finish, is just as crucial as the involvement of top management.

IT Structure and Legacy Systems: It is critical to assess the IT readiness of the company including the IT architecture and skills of the employees [2, 14]. If necessary, infrastructure might need to be upgraded or changed considering the requirements of the ERP system [49, 50]. Also, the current legacy systems need attention. It is important that an organization approaches the transition of a legacy system carefully and develops a comprehensive plan. Within ERP projects, the existing legacy systems have to be exactly reviewed, defined and evaluated to encounter possible problems and hindrances during the ERP implementation [31, 32, 51].

Knowledge Management: Knowledge management during ERP implementation projects is an important factor. Sharing knowledge is somewhat unique since ERP projects redefine jobs and blur traditional intra-organizational boundaries [52]. It is crucial to exchange knowledge and problems within the organization. Employees possess a base of knowledge that is indispensable to the company [26]. During ERP implementation knowledge must be shared among departments and functional and divisional boundaries [53]. Thus, a knowledge management process has to be established to ensure that information will be correctly exchanged within the project team and with all other involved people of the ERP project (e.g., external consultants or employees of the ERP vendor). In addition, the organization must ensure the transfer of as much knowledge as possible from consultants or ERP vendors in order to be able to use the new ERP system autonomously [26].

Monitoring and Performance Measurement: In the context of project management mechanisms for performance measurement have to be established. Measuring and evaluating performance is a critical factor for ensuring the success of any business organization [32]. Constant measurement and monitoring of the progress enables early discovery of errors and gaps as well as their removal or correction [29].

Organizational Culture: Organizational culture is embedded within the national culture and therefore it is a critical factor affecting ERP system implementation. Every company has its own, unique organizational culture, which may or may not be strong and enduring, and which may be reflected in either openness for changes or the opposite [38]. An organization that implements an ERP system has to change its business processes to achieve a better fit with the ERP best-practice processes. These changes both impact the organization's culture and are constrained by it [35, 38]. Some researchers argue that a successful technological innovation requires that either the technology be designed to fit the organization's current structure and culture or that the organization's structure and culture has to be redesigned and changed to fit the new technology [54, 55].

Organizational Fit of the ERP System: The fact that the organizational fit of an ERP system should be examined and considered comprehensively before its implementation sounds logical. Nevertheless, ERP vendors tend to set up blind confidence in their ERP package even if it is obvious that the organizational fit is low. Hong & Kim [42] empirically examined to what extent the implementation success of an ERP system depends on the fit between company and ERP system and found out that the adaptation and configuration effort negatively correlates with the implementation success. Therefore, it is essential to select an ERP system carefully by considering its specific organizational fit such as company size or industry sector. Thus, the right ERP system selection is an important factor to ensure the fit between the company and the ERP system.

Organizational Structure: Organizational structure is a determining factor concerning ERP system implementations. Since ERP systems are designed according to the principle of "best practice," they aim towards a fit for the greatest possible number of companies. Therefore, the configuration becomes essential to map the functions of the systems with the structure of the company [56]. So, the company's structure should enable the implementation and use of ERP systems as well as other IT systems. Nevertheless, BPR can also become mandatory, since not all of the company's structure can be mapped with the ERP system and so the structure has to be adapted. Many organizations underestimate the lack of alignment between the ERP system and their organizational structure, and thus the effort required for system configuration or BPR during the implementation [26].

Project Champion: A project champion can be seen as an imperturbable advocate of the respective ERP implementation project – necessary in order to enable better and faster agreements within the project and to oversee the entire processes and the whole project life cycle. The main tasks of the project champion are to be the first contact person for any issues concerning the ERP project and to ensure the project progress within the enterprise. Therefore with having a project champion resistances and conflicts can be solved promptly and in a slighter manner as he also serves as a mediator [30]. In many ERP implementations the leader of the ERP project takes the position of project champion, but this is not the only solution. Also some other member of the senior management, who is not a direct project team member, can act as project champion, too.

Project Leadership / Empowered Decision Makers: The project leader should be a strong and charismatic person with experience in project management and expertise in directing employees. He has to manage the project according to the project plan and react on problems that can arise during an ERP implementation. Therefore, the project leader can take the role as project champion as well. In general, project team leaders have to be empowered to make quick decisions, which reduce delays during implementation. This is important since even small delays can heavily impact such a long-term project like ERP implementations [13]. With empowered decision makers and a strong project leadership, effective timing with respect to the implementation is enhanced [14, 24, 57].

Project Management: Project management refers to the ongoing management of the implementation plan [14]. The implementation of an ERP system is a unique procedure that requires an enterprise-wide project management. Therefore, it involves the planning stages, the allocating of responsibilities, the definition of milestones and critical paths, training and human resource planning, and the determination of measures of success [29, 31]. This enables a better organized approach to decision making and it guarantees that these are made by the most suitable company members. Furthermore, a continuous project management makes it possible to focus on the important aspects of the ERP implementation and ensures timeliness and that schedules are met [29]. Within project management, a comprehensive documentation of the tasks, responsibilities and goals is indispensable for the success of ERP implementations [58].

Skills, Knowledge and Expertise: The existing knowledge and the experiences of the companies' employees play a central role while implementing an ERP system. Better knowledge, experience and education as well as personal skills can improve the ERP project's accomplishment and enable an easier handling of the implementation. This factor is often influenced and affected by the companies' strategy as well as by the financial budget. The acceptance of and the readiness for changes is substantially higher in enterprises, where a philosophy of constant improvement and knowledge enhancement prevails [21].

Top Management Support and Involvement: Top management support and involvement is one of the most important success factors for an ERP implementation [21]. A committed leadership at the top management level is the basis for the continuous accomplishment of every project [14]. Thus, innovations, in particular new technologies, are better accepted by employees if they are promoted by top management. Before the project starts, top management has to identify the peculiarities and challenges of the planned ERP implementation. Since many decisions that have to be made during the project affect the whole enterprise, they will need the acceptance and the commitment of the senior managers and often can only be made by them [59]. Commitment of top management is important in order to allocate necessary resources, to make quick and effective decisions, solve conflicts that need enterprise-wide acceptance and to reach and support a co-operation of all different departments [32].

Troubleshooting: Troubleshooting is essential and starts at the shakedown phase. This factor is related to the problem and risk areas of ERP projects [13, 30]. Quick responses, patience, perseverance and problem solving capabilities are important during an ERP system implementation [28]. There should be an implementation plan that includes various troubleshooting mechanisms. Two important critical "moments" are the migration of old data as well as the "go live" [13].

Use of a Steering Committee: To make ERP projects succeed, it is necessary to form a steering committee. A steering committee enables the senior management to directly monitor the project team's decision making, thereby ensuring adequate control mechanisms. Therefore, this committee should consist of members of the senior management (from different departments or corporate functions), representatives from the project management and end users (as well as from different departments). Such a composition will guarantee appropriate involvement across the whole company [2, 60].

User Training: Often, missing or lacking end user training is a reason for the failure during the implementation of new software. The main goal of end user training is to provide an effective understanding of the new business processes and applications as well as the new workflows that result from the ERP implementation. Therefore, it is important to set up a suitable plan for the training and education of the employees [32]. Furthermore, during such an extensive project it has to be determined which employee fits best for which position or for which application of the new software. This depends strongly on his/her knowledge already acquired and/or for which employee additional training courses are necessary [61].

Vendor Relationship and Support: ERP systems may be a lifelong commitment for many companies. There will always be new modules and versions to install, bug fixes to be rolled out and changes to achieve a better fit between business and system. Therefore, good vendor support (technical assistance, emergency maintenance and updates) is an important factor. Accordingly, the relationship/partnership with the vendor is vitally important to successful ERP projects. This relationship should be strategic in nature with the ERP provider enhancing an organization's competitiveness and efficiency [2, 62].

Vendor's Tools and Implementation Methods: Implementation technologies, programs and methods provided by the vendors can significantly reduce the cost and time of deploying ERP systems [2]. Depending on the chosen implementation and roll-out method (e.g., big bang strategy, satellite strategy, etc.) there are advantages and risks that have to be considered. Also, not every strategy is applicable in every ERP project or company. Hence, the choice has to be made carefully. An additional goal of implementation tools is the knowledge transfer of using the software, understanding the business processes within the organization and recognizing industry best practices [2].

4 Literature Review – Results

As stated above, 320 papers (single- or multiple-case studies, surveys, literature reviews, etc.) were identified that referred to critical success factors of ERP implementation projects. These papers were reviewed again in-depth in order to determine the different concepts of CSFs. Overall, 31 factors (as described above) were identified. In most previous literature reviews, the CSFs were grouped more coarsely so that a lower number of CSFs was used (e.g., [2, 14, 30]). The grouping was not done within our review. With 31 factors, we used a larger number than earlier researchers had because we expected the resulting distribution to be more insightful. If wider definitions of some CSFs might be needed later on, a further aggregation is still possible.

ACADEMIC SOURCE COMPLETE								
ID	YEAR	FORMS OF DATA COLLECTION	NUMBER OF COMPANIES & COMPANY SIZE	ERP SYSTEM CONFIGURATION	BALANCED PROJECT TEAM	PROJECT MANAGEMENT	EXTERNAL CONSULTANTS	USER TRAINING
1936.	2008	Literature-based, survey	91 responses from companies which have implemented ERP systems	X			X	X
1685.	2008	Literature-based, survey	281 responses		X	X	X	X
1777.	2003	Literature review, survey	54 responses from CIOs of companies which have implemented ERP systems		X	X		
1733.	2007	CSFs derived from literature and proven by field studies / survey	48 Mexican companies		X	X	X	X
1785.	2004	Case studies	5 large companies		X		X	X
1659.	1999	Literature review & case studies	8 large companies	X		X		
1977.	2008	Survey	130 responses, SME	X				X

Fig. 3. Snapshot of the CSF results

Table 1. Paper distribution

Year	Papers	Year	Papers
2013	30	2005	15
2012	31	2004	20
2011	39	2003	11
2010	37	2002	11
2009	42	2001	5
2008	22	2000	5
2007	24	1999	3
2006	24	1998	1

After identifying the relevant papers as well as the factors stated within them, we developed a table to match the factors with the papers for the analysis. Figure 3 shows a snapshot of this CSF table. As it is shown for each paper the CSFs were captured as well as the year, the type of data collection used within, and additionally the number and size of companies from which the CSFs were derived.

All 320 papers were published between the years 1998 and 2013. Table 1 shows the distribution of the articles per year. Most of the papers were published between 2013 and 2006. Since 2004, around 20 papers were published each year. Since 2009 around 30 papers were published each year or even more papers were published about CSFs. Therefore, it can be argued that a review every two or three years is reasonable in order to update the results of previous literature reviews, especially considering evolving technology and the changing system availability like the "Software-as-a-Service" concept and ERP systems provided in the cloud.

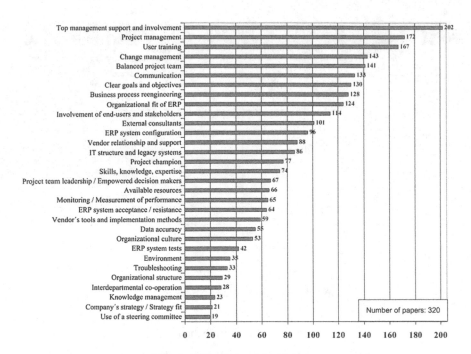

Fig. 4 CSFs Ordered by Frequency

It has to be emphasized that we conducted review 2 in mid-2013. Therefore, not all papers published in 2013 were part of this review. Additionally, some databases provide access to some journal articles only if they are older than 12 months. Thus, such articles were not included in our review nor those presented at ICIS 2013, since that conference had not taken place until the date of our review.

Figure 4 shows the results of our review: the identified CSFs and their total numbers. The figure shows that *Top management support and involvement*, *Project management* and *User training* are the three most named factors, numbering around and above 160. The factor *Top management support and involvement* ranked number one, having been referred to in more than 200 papers.

Comparing these results with other literature reviews, such as Finney and Corbett's [14], it became obvious that the top five factors were similar while only the ranks differed. Due to our large literature base, our total numbers are much higher (see Table 2).

Regarding the form of data collection, it has to be stated that the papers consisted of 144 single- or multiple-case studies, 118 surveys and 58 literature reviews or articles where CSFs were derived from chosen literature.

To categorize critical success factors, Esteves-Sousa & Pastor-Collado [13] suggested a matrix scheme. Here, they consider the tactical or strategic direction of the CSFs and divide them into organizational and technological factors. Thus, tactical CSFs tend to relate to short-term aspects and goals of the system implementation whereby strategic factors aim for long-term impacts of activities with strong connections to the

Table 2. Literature review comparison

	Finney & Corbett [14]		Our review	
	Factor	Number of instances	Factor	Number of instances
Rank #1	Top management commitment and support	25	Top management support and involvement	202
Rank #2	Change management	25	Project management	172
Rank #3	BPR and software configuration	23	User training	167
Rank #4	Training and job redesign	23	Change management	143
Rank #5	Project team: the best and brightest	21	Balanced project team	141

development of the organization in relation to mission, vision and core competencies of the business activity. Considering the technological and organizational character of the CSFs – the specificity and significance of technological factors strongly depend on the ERP systems themselves, whereas organizational factors focus on corporate culture and its environment with its specific processes and structures [13, 19, 63].

Table 3 gives an overview of the categorization of the CSFs identified in our literature review with a focus on their ranking and the incidence in the literature. It is shown that only a few CSFs (6 out of 31) are technological factors whereas more than 50% of the factors (17 out of 31) are organizational factors with a strategic characteristic. Also, most of the top 10 factors belong to the organizational category. Only one of the top 10 factors (*Organizational fit of the ERP system*) is part of the technological category. Therefore, enterprises and ERP manufacturers should especially consider organizational aspects when implementing an ERP system.

Considering the different years in which the identified papers were published, we have analyzed four different time spans (1998–2003, 2004–2007, 2008–2010 and 2011–2013) to identify changes in the CSF ranking. The results of this analysis with the respective top five factors of each time span are shown in Fig. 5.

As shown, *Top management support and involvement* is again the most frequently named factor, ranking number one in each time span. Additionally, *Project management* and *User training* are always in the top five positions throughout the different time spans. However, the CSF *Business process reengineering* has gained more importance whereas others have lost some importance throughout the years (e.g., *Clear goals and objectives* and *Monitoring and performance measurement*). *Business process reengineering* has even gained a rank in the top five in time span 2011–2013. Reasons for this can be seen in the highly fragmented ERP system market as well as in the increasing multitude of software manufacturers and ERP systems. Enterprises are facing more and more difficulties to identify the best fitting ERP system. Therefore, more emphasis is laid on the reengineering of business structures to use the whole functionality of the ERP systems in efficient and effective way.

Table 3. Categorization of CSFs (Model Adapted from [13, 19, 63])

Perspectives		Critical Success Factors	Rank	Number of instances in literature
Organizational	Strategic	Top management support and involvement	1	202
		Change management	4	143
		Balanced project team	5	141
		Clear goals and objectives	7	130
		Business process reengineering	8	128
		Involvement of end-users and stakeholders	10	114
		Vendor relationship and support	13	88
		Project champion	15	77
		Project team leadership / Empowered decision makers	17	67
		Available resources	18	66
		ERP system acceptance / resistance	20	64
		Organizational culture	23	53
		Environment	25	35
		Organizational structure	27	29
		Knowledge management	29	23
		Company's strategy / Strategy fit	30	21
		Use of a steering committee	31	19
	Tactical	Project management	2	172
		User training	3	167
		Communication	6	133
		External consultants	11	101
		Skills, knowledge and expertise	16	74
		Monitoring / Measurement of performance	19	65
		Troubleshooting	26	33
		Interdepartmental co-operation	28	28
Technological	Strategic	Organizational fit of the ERP system	9	124
		ERP system configuration	12	96

(Continued)

Table 3. (*Continued*)

Perspectives		Critical Success Factors	Rank	Number of instances in literature
	Tactical	IT structure and legacy systems	14	77
		Vendor´s tools and implementation methods	21	59
		Data accuracy	22	55
		ERP system tests	24	42

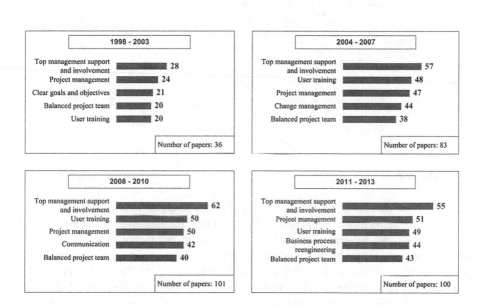

Fig. 5. Time span analysis of the CSFs

Concerning the company size during review 1, only 12 papers explicitly focus on small and medium-sized enterprises (SMEs), and there mostly within single- or multiple-case studies. Within review 2, 25 articles deal with SMEs explicitly.

In some surveys SMEs are included and analyzed as well, but they are a minority in these surveys. Therefore, deriving CSFs which are important for SMEs is difficult. As is shown by Fig. 6, *Top management support and involvement*, *Project management* as well as *User training* are again the most frequently named factors for ERP projects in smaller enterprises.

However, the differences in the CSF frequencies are only minimal and may be related to the small number of identified papers. Therefore, deriving CSFs that are important for SMEs is difficult due to the small number of studies focusing solely on them. This clearly is a research gap in the ERP CSF research area.

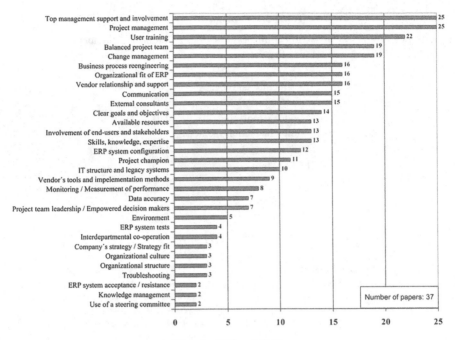

Fig. 6. CSFs of SMEs

5 Conclusion

The aim of our study was to gain an insight into the research field of critical success factors in ERP implementation projects. Research on ERP implementation and critical success factors can be seen as a valuable step toward enhancing chances of implementation success [14]. Our study reveals that there are several papers – case studies, surveys as well as literature reviews – that are focusing on CSFs. All in all, we identified 320 relevant papers. From these existing studies, we derived 31 different CSFs. We identified the following top three CSFs: *Top management support and involvement, Project management* and *User training.*

This ranking is similar to the ranking of other literature reviews (e.g., [2, 14]). Compared to these other reviews, the number of papers included in our study exceeds their numbers. One reason that these reviews included fewer papers is simply that they were conducted earlier than ours. As shown in Table 1, every year since 2004 at least 20 CSF papers have been published. This is not surprising considering the fast evolving technologies and the changes throughout the ERP market. Thus, one conclusion is that it is advisable to renew literature reviews on ERP system CSFs every two or three years in order to update the results as we did by conducting review 2 as an update for our first review. Another conclusion is related to the size of the companies. Most of the identified papers and studies focus on large companies. Small and medium-sized enterprises are – if included at all – usually underrepresented in quantitative studies. Studies exclusively focusing on SMEs are rare. We identified 37 out of the 320 articles with an explicit SME focus. These are just less than 12% of all published papers with CSF focus. Even if research focusing on CSFs in smaller companies is recommended in the research community for several years (e.g., [58, 64]), our reviews reveal that SMEs are still not the primarily focus of CSF research. Therefore, SMEs still can be seen as in need of further research.

Regarding our literature review procedure, there are limitations that have to be mentioned, too. We are aware that we cannot be certain to have identified all relevant papers published in journals and conferences, since we made a selection of five databases and five international conferences. Therefore, journals not included in our databases and proceedings of other conferences might also comprise relevant articles. Another limitation is the coding of the CSFs. We tried to reduce this subjectivity by formulating coding rules and by discussing the coding of the CSFs among three independent researchers. Hence, other researchers may code the CSFs in another way.

Appendix

Table 4. Sources for the literature review

Databases	Conferences
Academic Search Complete	AMCIS
Business Source Complete	ECIS
Science Direct	HICCS
SpringerLink	ICIS
WISO	Wirtschaftsinformatik

Table 5. Search fields and search terms

Database + Search fields	Search terms / Keywords
Academics Search Complete: "TI Title" or "AB Abstract or Author Supplied Abstract"	ERP + success* ERP + failure ERP + crit* ERP + CSF
Business Source Complete: "TI Title" or "AB Abstract or Author Supplied Abstract"	ERP + CFF ERP + fact* "Enterprise system*" + success*
Science Direct: "Abstract, Title, Keywords"	"Enterprise system*" + failure "Enterprise system*" + crit*
SpringerLink: "Title" or "Abstract"	"Enterprise system*" + CSF "Enterprise system*" + CFF
WISO: "General Search Field"	"Enterprise system*" + fact*

References

1. Gronau, N.: Industrielle Standardsoftware: Auswahl und Einführung. Oldenbourg Verlag, Muenchen, Germany (2001)
2. Somers, T.M., Nelson, K.: The impact of critical success factors across the stages of enterprise resource planning implementations. In: Proceedings of the 34th Hawaii International Conference on System Sciences (HICSS 2001), January 3-6, Hawaii, USA (2001)
3. Deep, A., Guttridge, P., Dani, S., Burns, N.: Investigating factors affecting ERP selection in the made-to-order SME sector. Journal of Manufacturing Technology Management 19(4), 430–446 (2008)
4. Koh, S.C.L., Simpson, M.: Change and uncertainty in SME manufacturing environments using ERP. Journal of Manufacturing Technology Management 16(6), 629–653 (2005)
5. Leyh, C.: Critical Success Factors for ERP System Implementation Projects: A Literature Review. In: Møller, C., Chaudhry, S. (eds.) Advances in Enterprise Information Systems II, pp. 45–56. CRC Press/Balkema, Leiden, The Netherlands (2012)
6. Winkelmann, A., Klose, K.: Experiences while selecting, adapting and implementing ERP systems in SMEs: a case study. In: Proceedings of the 14th Americas Conference on Information Systems (AMCIS 2008), August 14-17, Paper 257. Toronto, Ontario, Canada (2008)
7. Winkelmann, A., Leyh, C.: Teaching ERP systems: A multi-perspective view on the ERP system market. Journal of Information Systems Education 21(2), 233–240 (2010)
8. Jones, A., Robinson, J., O'Toole, B., Webb, D.: Implementing a bespoke supply chain management system to deliver tangible benefits. International Journal of Advanced Manufacturing Technology 30(9/10), 927–937 (2006)
9. Ngai, E.W.T., Cheng, T.C.E., Ho, S.S.M.: Critical success factors of web-based supply-chain management systems: an exploratory study. Production Planning & Control 15(6), 622–630 (2004)
10. Barker, T., Frolick, M.N.: ERP Implementation Failure: a case study. Information Systems Management 20(4), 43–49 (2003)
11. Hsu, K., Sylvestre, J., Sayed, E.N.: Avoiding ERP Pitfalls. The Journal of Corporate Accounting & Finance 17(4), 67–74 (2006)
12. Welsh, J.-A., White, J.-F.: A small business is not a little big business. Harvard Business Review 59(4), 18–32 (1981)
13. Esteves-Sousa, J., Pastor-Collado, J.: Towards the unification of critical success factors for ERP implementations. In: Proceedings of the 10th Annual Business Information Technology Conference (BIT 2000). Manchester, UK (2000)
14. Finney, S., Corbett, M.: ERP implementation: A compilation and analysis of critical success factors. Business Process Management Journal 13(3), 329–347 (2007)
15. Nah, F.F-H., Zuckweiler, K.M., Lau, J.L-S.: ERP implementation: Chief information officers' perceptions of critical success factors. International Journal of Human-Computer Interaction, vol. 16, no. 1, pp. 5-22 (2003)
16. Vom Brocke, J., Simons, A., Niehaves, B., Riemer, K., Plattfaut, R., Cleven, A.: Reconstructing the giant: On the importance of rigour in documenting the literature search process. In: Proceedings of the 17th European Conference on Information Systems (ECIS 2009), June 8-10. Verona, Italy (2009)
17. Webster, J., Watson, R.T.: Analyzing the past, preparing the future: Writing a literature review. MIS Quarterly 26(2), 13–23 (2002)

18. Leyh, C.: Critical Success Factors for ERP System Selection, Implementation and Post-Implementation. In: Léger, P.-M., Pellerin, R., Babin, G. (eds.) Readings on Enterprise Resource Planning, Chapter 5. ERPsim Lab, HEC Montreal, Montreal (2011)

19. Remus, U.: Critical Success Factors for Implementing Enterprise Portals: A Comparison with ERP Implementations. Business Process Management Journal 13(4), 538–552 (2007)

20. Reel, J.S.: Critical Success Factors in Software Projects. IEEE Software 16(3), 18–23 (1999)

21. Achanga, P., Nelde, G., Roy, R., Shehab, E.: Critical success factors for lean implementation within SMEs. Journal of Manufacturing Technology Management 17(4), 460–471 (2006)

22. Humphrey, W.S.: Introduction to the team software process. Addison-Wesley, Amsterdam (1999)

23. Hesseler, M., Goertz, M.: Basiswissen ERP-Systeme – Auswahl, Einführung & Einsatz betriebswirtschaftlicher Standardsoftware.W3 l, Witten, Germany (2007)

24. Shanks, G., Parr, A.: A model of ERP project implementation. Journal of Information Technology 15(4), 289–303 (2000)

25. Kumar, V., Maheshwari, B., Kumar, U.: An Investigation of Critical Management Issues in ERP Implementation: Empirical Evidence from Canadian Organizations. Technovation 23 (10), 793–807 (2003)

26. Francoise, O., Bourgault, M., Pellerin, R.: ERP Implementation by Critical Success Factor Management. Business Process Management Journal 15(3), 371–394 (2009)

27. Rajagopal, P.: An Innovation-Diffusion View of Implementation of Enterprise Resource Planning (ERP) Systems and Development of a Research Model. Information and Management 40(2), 87–114 (2002)

28. Rosario, J.G.: On the Leading Edge: Critical Success Factors in ERP Implementation Projects. Business World, May, pp. 15–29 (2000)

29. Al-Mashari, M., Al-Mudimigh, A.: ERP Implementation: Lessons from a Case Study. Information Technology & People 16(1), 21–33 (2003)

30. Loh, T.C., Koh, S.C.L.: Critical Elements for a Successful Enterprise Resource Planning Implementation in Small-and Medium-Sized Enterprises. International Journal of Production Research 42(17), 3433–3455 (2004)

31. Nah, F.F-H., Lau, J.L-S., Kuang, J.: Critical Factors for Successful Implementation of Enterprise Systems. Business Process Management Journal, vol. 7, no. 3, pp. 285-296 (2001)

32. Al-Mashari, M., Al-Mudimigh, A., Zairi, M.: Enterprise Resource Planning: A Taxonomy of Critical Factors. European Journal of Operational Research 146(2), 352–364 (2003)

33. Soja, P.: Success Factors across ERP Implementation Phases: Learning from Practice. In: Wojtkowski, W., Wojtkowski, W.G., Zupancic, J., Magyar, G., Knapp, G. (eds.) Advances in Information Systems Development: New Methods and Practice for the Networked Society, pp. 275–286. Springer, New York (2007)

34. Umble, E.J., Haft, R.R., Umble, M.M.: Enterprise Resource Planning: Implementation Procedures and Critical Success Factors. European Journal of Operational Research 146(2), 241–257 (2003)

35. Krumbholz, M., Maiden, N.: The Implementation of Enterprise Resource Planning Packages in Different Organizational and National Cultures. Information Systems 26(3), 185–204 (2001)

36. Zhang, L., Lee, M.K.O., Zhang, Z., Banerjee, P.: Critical Success Factors of Enterprise Resource Planning Systems Implementation Success in China. In: Proceedings of the 36th Hawaii International Conference on System Sciences (HICSS 2003), January 6-9, Hawaii, USA (2003)

37. Xue, Y., Liang, H., Boulton, W.R., Snyder, C.A.: ERP Implementation Failures in China: Case Studies with Implications for ERP Vendors. International Journal of Production Economics 97(3), 279–295 (2005)

38. Zhang, Z., Lee, M.K.O., Huang, P., Zhang, L., Huang, X.: A Framework of ERP Systems Implementation Success in China: An Empirical Study. International Journal of Production Economics 98(1), 56–80 (2005)

39. Soh, C., Sia, S.K., Tay-Yap, J.: Cultural Fits and Misfits: Is ERP a Universal Solution. Communications of the ACM 43(4), 47–51 (2000)

40. McLachlin, R.D.: Factors for Consulting Engagement Success. Management Decision 37(5), 394–402 (1999)

41. Wang, E.T.G., Chen, J.H.F.: Effects of Internal Support and Consultant Quality on the Consulting Process and ERP System Quality. Decision Support Systems 42(2), 1029–1041 (2006)

42. Hong, K.-K., Kim, Y.-G.: The Critical Success Factors for ERP Implementation: An Organizational Fit Perspective. Information and Management 40(1), 25–40 (2002)

43. Appelrath, H., Ritter, J.: SAP R/3 Implementation: Method and Tools. Springer, Berlin, Germany (2000)

44. Piturro, M.: How Midsize Companies Are Buying ERP. Journal of Accountancy 188(3), 41–48 (1999)

45. Stefanou, C.: Supply Chain Management and Organizational Key Factors for Successful Implementation of Enterprise Resource Planning (ERP) Systems. In: Proceeding of the Americas Conference on Information Systems (AMCIS 1999), August 13-15, Milwaukee, WI, USA (1999)

46. Esteves, J., Pastor, J., Casanovas, J.: A Goal/Question/Metric Research Proposal to Monitor User Involvement and Participation in ERP Implementation Projects. Paper presented at the Information Resources Management Association Conference (IRMA), Philadelphia, USA, May (2003)

47. Barki, H., Hartwick, J.: User Participation and User Involvement in Information System Development. In: Proceedings of the 24th Annual Hawaii International Conference on System Sciences, January, Kauai, Hawaii, IEEE Computer Society, vol.4, pp. 487-492 (1991)

48. Ghosh, S.: Challenges on a Global Implementation of ERP Software. In: Proceedings of the IEEE International Engineering Management Conference, Cambridge, August 18-20, IEEE International, vol. 1, pp. 101-106 (2002)

49. Kumar, V., Maheshwari, B., Kumar, U.: ERP Systems Implementation: Best Practices in Canadian Government Organizations. Government Information Quarterly 19(2), 147–172 (2002)

50. Palaniswamy, R., Frank, T.G.: Oracle ERP and Network Computing Architecture: Implementation and Performance. Information Systems Management 19(2), 53–69 (2002)

51. Holland, C., Light, B.: A Critical Success Factors Model for ERP Implementation. IEEE Software 6(3), 30–36 (1999)

52. Jones, M.C., Price, L.R.: Organizational Knowledge Sharing in ERP implementation: Lessons from Industry. Journal of Organizational and End User Computing 16(1), 21–40 (2004)

53. Baskerville, R., Pawlowski, S., McLean, E.: Enterprise Resource Planning and Organizational Knowledge: Patterns of Convergence and Divergence. In: Proceedings of the 21st International Conference on Information Systems (ICIS), December 10-13, pp. 396-406, Brisbane, Australia (2000)

54. Cabrera, A., Cabrera, E.F., Barajas, S.: The Key Role of Organizational Culture in a Multi-System View of Technology Driven Change. International Journal of Information Management **21**(3), 245–261 (2001)
55. Yusuf, Y., Gunasekaran, A., Abthorpe, M.K.: Enterprise Information Systems Project Implementation: A Case Study of ERP in Rolls-Royce. International Journal of Production Economics **87**(3), 251–266 (2004)
56. Soffer, P., Golany, B., Dori, D.: Aligning an ERP System with Enterprise Requirements: An Object-Process-Based Approach. Computers in Industry **56**(6), 639–662 (2005)
57. Gupta, A.: Enterprise Resource Planning: The Emerging Organizational Value Systems. Industrial Management & Data Systems **100**(3), 114–188 (2000)
58. Snider, B., da Silveira, G.J.C., Balakrishnan, J.: ERP implementation at SMEs: Analysis of five Canadian cases. International Journal of Operations & Production Management **29**(1), 4–29 (2009)
59. Becker, J., Vering, O., Winkelmann, A.: Softwareauswahl und –einführung in Industrie und Handel – Vorgehen bei und Erfahrungen mit ERP- und Warenwirtschaftssystemen. Springer, Berlin (2007)
60. Sumner, M.: Critical Success Factors in Enterprise Wide Information Management Systems. In: Proceedings of the Americas Conference on Information Systems (AMCIS 1999), August 13-15, pp. 232-234, Milwaukee, WI, USA (1999)
61. Teich, I., Kolbenschlag, W., Reiners, W.: Der richtige Weg zur Softwareauswahl. Springer, Berlin (2008)
62. Willcocks, L.P., Sykes, R.: The Role of the CIO and IT Function in ERP. Communications of the ACM **43**(4), 32–38 (2000)
63. Esteves-Sousa, J.: Definition and Analysis of Critical Success Factors for ERP Implementation Projects. Barcelona, Spain (2004)
64. Sun, A.Y.T., Yazdani, A., Overend, J.D.: Achievement assessment for enterprise resource planning (ERP) system implementations based on critical success factors (CSFs). International Journal of Production Economics **98**(2), 189–203 (2005)

Impediments to Enterprise System Implementation Across the System Lifecycle: Understanding the Role of Country Economic Development

Piotr Soja[✉] and Grażyna Paliwoda-Pękosz

Cracow University of Economics, Kraków, Poland
eisoja@cyf-kr.edu.pl
paliwodg@uek.krakow.pl

Abstract. This chapter's goal is to investigate impediments to successful enterprise system (ES) implementation across the system lifecycle. Drawing from the opinions of 82 ES practitioners and building on the authors' previous work on source problems in ES adoption, this study performs the further data analysis incorporating the ES lifecycle. The analysis employs the Cooper and Zmud's six-stage model of IT diffusion and investigates how the difficulties change along the ES lifecycle. Our findings suggest that Adaptation phase, which is the main implementation stage, is the most challenging period of the ES adoption project. The results also indicate that problems with employees are the most significant impediments to ES adoption success. The findings imply that difficulties during later stages of the ES adoption can be minimized by an appropriate system choice, a good training schedule, and the preparation of a suitable IT infrastructure and database needed by the new system. The comparison of findings with prior literature suggests that ES adoption considerations change from system- to business-related issues along the level of country's economic development.

Keywords: Enterprise system · ERP · Adoption · Implementation · Lifecycle · Problem · Poland

1 Introduction

Enterprise systems (ES) are complex application software packages that contain mechanisms supporting the management of the whole enterprise and integrate all areas of its functioning (Davenport 1998, p. 121). ES adoption is a multistage and usually lengthy process during which the company may experience many problems and impediments to project success (e.g. Kim, Lee and Gosain 2005, Kremers and van Dissel 2000, Markus et al. 2000, Themistocleous and Irani 2001, Themistocleous et al. 2001, Wright and Wright 2002).

The multistage nature of the ES adoption results in the situation where considerations experienced by implementation projects depend on the actual phase of the project (Markus et al. 2000, Soja 2007). Further, prior literature reports various problems which represent diverse levels of generality and some of them, such as lack of benefits

© Springer International Publishing Switzerland 2015
D. Sedera et al. (Eds.): Pre-ICIS 2010-2012, LNBIP 198, pp. 68–84, 2015.
DOI: 10.1007/978-3-319-17587-4_4

(O'Leary 2000), generally seem to be the consequence of other difficulties that appear during the implementation process. Other reported problems, in turn, appear to cause further problems, such as system drawbacks or lack of business problem reengineering (Kim et al. 2005, Kremers and van Dissel 2000, Wright and Wright 2002).

Prior research suggests that ES adoption considerations might differ depending on the level of national economy development (Bingi et al. 2000; Huang and Palvia 2001). This also applies to transition economies, i.e. countries in transition from a communist style central planning system to a free market system (Roztocki and Weistroffer 2008b). In particular, as suggested by prior research, ES adoption projects in transition economies are strongly affected by financial and people-related problems and may go through a different system lifecycle (Soja 2008, 2011a; Themistocleous et al. 2011). Taking into consideration the scarcity of ES-related research in transition economies (Roztocki and Weistroffer 2011b) it seems worthy to investigate how impediments to ES adoption occur over the system lifecycle in transition economies and compare the findings with the experience of developed countries.

This chapter seeks to address the above mentioned issues and tries to investigate source problems in ES adoption projects across the ES lifecycle phases on the basis of research conducted among ES practitioners in Poland, a transition economy from Central and Eastern Europe. The particular research questions involved in this study can be formulated as follows:

- What are the source problems in ES adoption over the system lifecycle?
- How do the occurrences of problems across the system lifecycle differ depending on the level of national economy development?

The chapter is organized as follows. Next section gives an overview of previous research that concern impediments to an enterprise system implementation. Then, the methodology of research conducted among Polish practitioners is described and results of this research are presented, discussed, and compared with similar research conducted in developed economies. Finally, the implications for researchers and practitioners are discussed and directions for future research are outlined.

2   Literature Review

Prior literature includes several studies that are dealing with difficulties in ES implementation and are based on empirical research conducted among ES practitioners. The enquired respondents include adopters (e.g. Kim et al. 2005, Kremers and van Dissel 2000, Themistocleous et al. 2001), experts representing system suppliers or consulting companies (e.g. Soja 2008, Wright and Wright 2002), and representatives of both system providers and adopters (Markus et al. 2000). The prior studies report issues having various meaning and use varied categorizations which makes comparing their findings difficult.

Different categorizations of problems used by prior studies illustrate the complexity and pervasiveness of ES adoption projects. In particular, Kim et al. (2005) use the categorization into so called areas that include: human resources and capabilities management, cross-functional coordination, ERP software configuration and features, systems development and project management, change management, and organizational leadership. Themistocleous et al. (2001) employs the categorization into managerial and technical problems. Finally, Soja (2008) uses the classification of problems into economic, technical, organizational, and social difficulties.

Table 1 summarizes the most important difficulties reported by prior research in developed countries. The prior studies recognize mainly organizational problems connected with time overruns and the alignment of organizational structure with ES. They also acknowledge system deficiencies and lack of users' involvement as the most important impediments during ES implementation. Other important difficulties cover mostly organizational issues connected with inter-departmental conflicts, change management, and trainings. The extant research also indicates technical problems with integration and system customization, point to impediments connected with costs, and highlight problems related to user resistance.

Table 1. The most important difficulties to ES adoption reported by prior studies in developed economies

Difficulties	Study
Time over-run	Kremers & van Dissel (2000), Themistocleous et al. (2001)
Business processes not redesigned	Kim et al. (2005), Wright & Wright (2002)
System drawbacks	Kremers & van Dissel (2000), Wright & Wright (2002)
Users not involved	Kim et al. (2005), Wright & Wright (2002)
Inter-departmental conflicts	Kim et al. (2005)
Organizational change expertise	Kim et al. (2005)
Inadequate training	Wright & Wright (2002)
Integration	Themistocleous et al. (2001)
Problems with customization	Themistocleous et al. (2001)
Cost over-run	Themistocleous et al. (2001)
User resistance	Kim et al. (2005)

Different research approach was applied in the study by Soja and Paliwoda-Pękosz (2009) that investigates the causal relationships between problems and seeks to discover the source problems in ES adoption, i.e. those impediments whose occurrences cause other problems. It reveals the following source problems of ES implementation: knowledge of employees holding various positions in the adopter organizations' hierarchy, changes in the enterprise occurring during ES adoption, finance, enterprise structure, IT infrastructure, data import and legacy systems, and training schedule.

Among the above mentioned prior research works dealing with difficulties in ES adoption, only the study by Markus et al. (2000) incorporated the system lifecycle into the research approach. Their categorization includes the following four ES implementation stages (Markus and Tanis 2000):

- Project chartering – making a key business decisions concerning the scope of the project, budgeting, choosing system vendor, etc.
- The project – the main implementation phase with the purpose of getting system and users "up and running",
- Shakedown – stabilizing and incorporating ES in everyday operations,
- Onward and upward – deriving benefits from ES implementation.

It should be noted that the ES lifecycle has also other definitions in prior research works (Soja 2011b, Themistocleous et al. 2011). In particular, Parr and Shanks (2000) divide implementation process into 3 general phases: Planning, Project, and Enhancement. Within the Project phase, they distinguish 5 sub-phases: Set up, Reengineering, Design, Configuration and testing, and Installation. Ross and Vitale (2000) suggest 5 adoption stages: design, implementation, stabilization, continuous improvement, and transformation. The most comprehensive understanding of the ES lifecycle is defined by Somers and Nelson (2004) who distinguish 6 implementation phases grounding their approach in the six-stage model of IT diffusion (Cooper and Zmud 1990). The proposed stages of ES implementation are as follows (e.g. Themistocleous et al. 2011):

- Initiation – a company justifies the need for adopting an ES system, chooses the actual enterprise system, and defines business needs and goals,
- Adoption – during which the definition of the project takes place, the solution design is created and project participants are selected,
- Adaptation – the main implementation stage where the project team translates the solution design into reality,
- Acceptance – with the main purpose to deliver and run the system,
- Routinization – part of the post-implementation stage during which usage of ES is encouraged as a normal activity,
- Infusion – part of the post-implementation period where the company experiences the full potential of the ES operation.

The Somers and Nelson model's strength consists in two last stages representing post-adoption behavior. The presence of clearly articulated post-implementation stages helps in capturing the whole complexity of ES adoption and prevents overlooking important considerations of events happening after the system roll-out. Due to these advantages the Somers and Nelson's lifecycle model has been employed by this study.

Much of the literature dealing with ES implementations originates from and describes application contexts in North America and Western Europe where most ES developers are located and most implementations have occurred (Davison 2002; Soh et al. 2000). In consequence, the existing literature mostly builds on the experience of developed countries. However, prior research suggest that ES adoptions in transition economies experience specific considerations which might be connected with various environmental factors such as fast changing laws and regulations, strong governmental control, low and rising salaries, high demand for highly qualified workers, and continuous and fast economic growth (Roztocki and Weistroffer 2011b). ES adoptions in transition economies, as compared to developed countries, seem to be affected to a greater extent by financial and people-related problems (Soja 2008; 2011a). Also, ES adopters in transition economies appeared to place greater emphasis on phased ES deployments and expected higher levels of external support (Bernroider et al. 2011). In addition, ES adoption projects may go through a different system lifecycle and might require different roles of the project participants, as compared to developed countries (Themistocleous et al. 2011). Hence, it would be interesting to compare the difficulties experienced by Polish practitioners over the ES lifecycle with experiences of companies from developed economies.

3   Methodology

In general, the authors' intention was to work out the comprehensive list of impediments to ES adoption success on the basis of information gathered from people located at the source of issues investigated. To this end, the authors turned to practitioners who participated in ES adoptions and hence experienced various difficulties during their adoption projects. In order to meet the research goals and assumptions, a qualitative research approach based on grounded theory proposed by Glaser and Strauss (1967) was adopted with interviews employed as a data-gathering method.

The researchers decided to use open-ended questions, rather than employing a predefined list of possible benefits developed from the prior literature. This was done in order not to suggest the answers and to allow the respondents to express their opinions in an unconstrained way. The respondents were asked to specify the most important problems that occur during their ES adoption projects and express their opinions regarding the causes of each problem enumerated. For each discussed issue, the respondents were asked to point the phase of the ES lifecycle during which the problem occurred.

Data have been gathered from 82 ES practitioners from Poland who represented companies of various sizes, operating in a variety of industries, and implementing a wide range of ES systems. The data was interpreted and classified by the authors who performed their own open and axial coding (Corbin and Strauss 1990). The researchers adopted a 'bottom-up' approach to coding data and developed coding schemes inductively, grounding the examination of emerging issues in the data. In particular, in the process of open coding, statements given by the respondents were compared and analyzed in the search of similarities and differences, and were assigned labels. During this process the basic categorization of impediments emerged and tentative categories and subcategories were created. Next, in the process of axial coding, categories and subcategories were inspected and verified, categories were related to their subcategories, and the relationships were tested against data.

In order to discover the source problems, in the first step, a causal map of interrelations among problem categories has been worked out on the basis of the respondents' declarations as regards problems and their possible causes. In the next step, potential source problems have been selected following the rule that a potential problem (represented by a problem subcategory) was not reported as the consequence of other problems outside the category. In the last step, building on the two abovementioned rules, the list of source problems has been proposed. For more details regarding the applied analytical procedure see (Soja and Paliwoda-Pękosz 2009).

The distribution of problems cross the system lifecycle in Polish companies was compared with the study of Markus et al. (2000) who analyzed this issue in companies that operate in developed economies. On the basis of this comparison some conclusions were drawn concerning the influence of the level of a country economic development on the nature of problems and their distribution across the ES lifecycle.

4 Data Analysis and Discussion

4.1 Problem Categories

As a result of data analysis, 45 problems have been identified. These problems are represented by subcategories and have been categorized into 9 problem categories. The discovered problem categories are as follows:

- Employees – problems connected with employees' skills and negative attitudes such as fear, reluctance, lack of system acceptance, habits, and not sufficient knowledge,
- Enterprise – difficulties related to changes in the adopting company, its financial condition, organizational structure, experience, preparation for the project, and cooperation with a vendor,
- System – problems connected with the enterprise system solution, its errors, efficiency, level of complexity, and communications across modules,
- IT infrastructure – difficulties related to network and hardware infrastructure needed by the enterprise system, and incompatibility of IT infrastructure with the implemented system,
- System misfit – problems with lack of fit between the company and the enterprise system, its customization and functional deficiency,
- System replacement – difficulties related to existing legacy systems and data import,
- Training – problems connected with trainings' scope and schedule and cooperation with the vendor,
- Implementation process – difficulties related to the project definition, duration time, and involved participants,
- System vendor – problems with the vendor's lack of sufficient resources and problems with implementation consultants.

4.2 Problems Across the ES Lifecycle

The distribution of problems across the enterprise system lifecycle is presented in Table 2. The bars in the table depict problem occurrences in appropriate phases as declared by the respondents.

Table 2. Problem categories across the enterprise system lifecycle

Group\Phase	Initiation	Adoption	Adaptation	Acceptance	Routinization	Infusion
Employees						
Enterprise						
System						
IT Infrastructure						
System Misfit						
System Replacement						
Training						
Implementation Process						
System Vendor						
All						

The largest number of problems was reported during Adaptation phase and during Initiation. Overall, in all phases, the most recognizable problems seem to be connected with employees, either directly or indirectly, such as through the category Training. Problems connected with the general enterprise condition were especially visible during Initiation and Routinization. Issues connected with the system were the most recognizable during Adoption and Infusion. Problems connected with IT infrastructure were noticeable in all phases with the stronger visibility during phases: Acceptance, Initiation, and Adaptation. System misfit revealed itself mostly during Adaptation and Infusion. Finally, issues connected with the system replacement, trainings, and implementation process were mostly visible during Adaptation phase. The distribution of problems and problem categories across the ES lifecycle is presented in Table 3. The subcategory [general], which appears in categories System Misfit and Training, encompasses problems that were formulated by the respondents in a general way, not referring to any individual items but only addressing the broader category of impediments. Examples of such opinions include "*Bad system fit to the company needs*" and "*Problems with trainings*".

Table 3. Problems and problem categories across the enterprise system lifecycle

Group\Phase	Initiation	Adoption	Adaptation	Acceptance	Routinization	Infusion
Employees						
fear	●	○	●		◐	○
reluctance	◐	◐	●	○	○	◐
computer skills	○	○	◐	◐	○	◐
habits	○	○	◐	○	◐	◐
knowledge	◐	○	○	○	○	○
skills		○	○	◐	○	○
lack of system acceptance		○	○		○	
Enterprise						
changes	○	○	◐	◐		○
project	●	○	○		○	
finance	○	○	○	○	○	
preparation	◐	○	○		○	
structure		○			○	
cooperation with vendor				○	○	
System						
errors	◐		●	◐	◐	●
communications across modules		○	○	◐	○	
IT infrastructure						
network infrastructure	◐	◐	◐	●	◐	◐
inadequate hardware	◐	○	◐	○	○	○
incompatibility	◐	○	◐	○		
System Misfit						
[general]	◐	○	●	◐	◐	◐
functional deficiency		○	◐		○	●
customization	◐	○	○	○	○	○
System Replacement						
data import	◐		●	◐	○	
smooth replacement	○		○	○	○	
legacy systems	○		◐			
Training						
schedule	◐	○	●	○	○	○
[general]	○	○	◐	○	○	○
cooperation with vendor					○	○
scope			○			
Implementation Process						
duration time		○	◐	○		
employees	◐	○	○			
project definition	○		○			
project manager	○					
System Vendor						
lack of time	○	○			○	○
consultants			◐			

Note: Bullets represent the level of problem occurrence reported by the respondents: ● – high, ◐ - medium ○–low

In the problem category connected with employees, the most frequently listed are those connected with fear and reluctance towards a new system and towards changes caused by the new system. These problems were visible mostly in Initiation and Adaptation phases. Problems with skills manifested themselves mainly in Acceptance phase.

In the problem category related to the enterprise, difficulties connected with conducting necessary changes in the company were the most visible with a special emphasis on Adaptation and Acceptance phases. During Initiation phase, the implementation design played the most significant role. Financial problems appeared in all phases with the exception of Infusion phase. The problems connected with the adjustment of the company structure to the new system requirements revealed themselves during Adoption and Routinization phases.

Problems connected directly with the new system errors were visible at all stages except for Adoption phase. Further, problems with communication between system modules revealed themselves mostly during Acceptance phase.

Network infrastructure seemed to be the most identifiable problem in the IT infrastructure problem group. Interestingly, network-related problems were assigned to all phases, whereas hardware incompatibility was mostly noticeable during Initiation and Adaptation phases.

Among problems with the system misfit, the most evident were general problems connected with the lack of system fit to the enterprise needs and these difficulties were mostly recognizable during Adaptation phase. Lack of system functionality was visible mostly during Infusion, while problems with customization ran though all phases; nonetheless, they seemed to be noticeable to a lesser extent.

4.3   Source Problems Across the ES Lifecycle

As a result of data analysis, from among 45 problems discovered, 20 difficulties have been elicited as candidates for source problems, i.e. those being the causes of other impediments. Table 4 presents the distribution of these source problems across the enterprise system lifecycle phases.

Among the source problems, the most significant category of difficulties is connected with the system and denotes system errors and too high level of system complexity. These impediments revealed themselves during all phases of the system lifecycle except for Adoption phase and are the most strongly noticeable during Adaptation and Infusion. The problems connected with the system are followed by the difficulties connected with employees (fear, habits, knowledge) that appeared in all phases with the special emphasis on Initiation and Adaptation. Network infrastructure and inadequate hardware manifested themselves in all phases and were the most visible during Acceptance. Difficulties with data import, other problems connected with legacy systems, inadequate training schedule, and limited finance revealed themselves mainly during Adaptation phase.

Table 4. Source problems across the enterprise system lifecycle

Group\Phase	Initiation	Adoption	Adaptation	Acceptance	Routinization	Infusion
System						
errors	◐		●	◐	◐	●
too complicated	○		○			
Employees						
fear	●	○	●	○	◐	○
habits	○	○	◐	○	◐	◐
knowledge	◐	○	○	○	○	○
IT infrastructure						
network infrastructure	◐	◐	◐	●	◐	◐
inadequate hardware	◐	○	◐	○	○	○
Enterprise						
changes	○	○	◐	◐		○
finance	○	○	○	○	○	
structure			○		○	
cooperation with vendor				○	○	
lack of experience	○		○			
needs				○	○	
System Replacement						
data import	◐		●	◐	○	
legacy systems	○		◐			
Training						
schedule	◐	○	●	○	○	○
System Misfit						
customization	◐	○	○	○	○	○
System Vendor						
lack of sufficient resources			○		○	
Implementation Process						
project definition	○		○			

Note: Bullets represent the level of problem occurrence reported by the respondents: ● – high, ◐ - medium ○–low

4.4   Comparison with Prior Research in Developed Economies

In order to perform the comparison of the current study's results with prior research conducted in developed economies the study by Markus et al. (2000) was chosen. However, since the Markus et al. study was based on a different classification of ES lifecycle stages, the mapping of the two employed lifecycle models was needed. The mapping is presented in Table 5.

Table 5. Mapping of ES lifecycle phases

Lifecycle stages proposed by Cooper and Zmud (1990)	ES lifecycle stages proposed by Markus et al. (2000)
Initiation Adoption	Project chartering
Adaptation Acceptance	The project
Routinization	Shakedown
Infusion	Onward and upward

In Table 6 the results of comparison are summarized. The bullets denote different levels of problem occurrences across the ES lifecycle, while the examined phases of the lifecycle are listed in columns. Additionally, sub columns marked with PL concern Polish respondents and sub columns marked with Dev relate to respondents from developed economies.

The findings illustrate the similarity of problem perception in the chartering phase as regards factors: culture resistant to change, lack of result orientation in the business, and lack of top management support. In the project phase, the similarly perceived problems are mainly connected with system integration, cutting end-user training, data quality, consultants, reports, and business process reengineering (BRP). Problems with fragile human capital were perceived by both Polish and developed economies-based practitioners in project and onward phases; however, their intensity varied. It is also noticeable that in Polish companies the human capital-related problems were spread throughout the whole lifecycle.

The majority of problems which were significant for practitioners from developed economies but were not perceived in Polish companies accumulated in the project stage. This group of problems included inadequate testing, personnel turnover, cutting scope of the project, and problems connected with software modifications. Problems specific to industrialized countries that occurred in shakedown phase concern decreased performance of business processes. For the last onward phase, the developed economies-specific problems include disappointing business results, migration problems and unknown business results.

Table 6. Mapping problems reported by polish ES practitioners onto difficulties in developed economies (based on Soja and Paliwoda-Pękosz (2013b))

Problem \ Phase	Chartering		Project		Shakedown		Onward	
	PL	Dev	PL	Dev	PL	Dev	PL	Dev
lack of results orientation in the business	◑	●						
culture resistant to change	●	●	●		◑		◑	
lack of top management support	○	●						
system integration	◑		●	●	○		○	
implementation consultants	○		○	●	○		○	
cutting end-user training	◑		●	●	○		○	
inadequate testing				●				
BPR (not first improving business processes where this needs doing)	○		○	●	○			
data quality	◑		◑	●	○			
reports			○	●			○	
software modification				●				
personnel turnover				●				
emphasis on functional perspective				●				
inappropriately project scope cutting				●				
system performance	○		●		○	●	◑	
decreased performance of business processes						●		
disappointing business results								●
fragile human capital	●		●	○	◑		◑	●
migration problems				○				●
unknown business results								●
IT infrastructure	◑		●		○		○	
system-misfit	◑		●		◑		◑	
company financial and organizational condition	○		◑		○		○	
legacy systems replacement	○		◑					
problems with implementation process (duration time, participants, project definition)	◑		◑		○			
trainings scope and schedule	○		○		○		○	
legal regulation and situation in industry	○		○					

Note: Bullets represent the level of problem occurrence reported by the respondents: ● – high, ◑ - medium ○ –low

It should be noticed that some problems reported in developed economies only in one phase were spread across the whole lifecycle in Polish companies. This group of problems mainly includes culture resistant to change, problems with system integration, consultants, and cutting end-user training.

It is noticeable that Polish respondents tended to focus on the system-related issues, which was manifested in unique reporting of problems with IT infrastructure, system-misfit, and legacy systems replacement. They were also concerned about financial and organizational condition of their companies and adequate training throughout the whole ES implementation lifecycle. The group of difficulties uniquely reported by the Polish respondents is complemented by problems having their roots in the company's environment and connected with changing legal regulations and situation in industry.

To sum up, practitioners from developed economies seem to focus on business-related issues as opposed to Polish companies that were influenced mostly by system-related problems. Problems in companies based in Poland tended to spread over the whole lifecycle and affect companies to a greater extent than in developed economies. Specifically, the results illustrate that constant care is required as regards to cooperation with the system vendor. This finding supports the results of Themistocleous et al. (2011) suggesting that in transition economies different rules of collaboration between ES adopters and providers may exist.

The current study results suggest that special attention should be paid to group of problems connected with system migration, such as migration problems and legacy system replacement. These problems are most visible in project phase. Both analyzed groups of respondents reported these problems but they seem to have different background depending on country-related context. Polish companies migrate mainly from legacy systems to enterprise systems whereas companies in developed economies update an enterprise system to the newest version or migrate to another brand of the system. This corroborates the prior research findings suggesting that companies in transition economies were in the first wave of ES adoption whereas companies from developed economies experienced second or even third wave of ES adoption (Lukman et al. 2011; Shanks et al. 2003; Stein and Hawking 2003).

5 Implications

The results of this study have several implications for practitioners dealing with ES implementations. The particular beneficiaries of this study's outcome are managers running the ES adoption projects or planning to implement an enterprise system. The implications for practitioners are formulated in the following.

- Practitioners should pay special attention to Adaptation as this phase appears to be the most difficult stage of the project. Nonetheless, the results suggest that practitioners should be watchful during the whole system lifecycle, even during the very last phases of the project when they might have expected less difficulties as the new system exploitation should reach its full potential at this stage.
- Managers should be aware that the right system choice is crucial for the whole implementation process. Although the system errors reveal themselves most frequently only in Infusion phase, the system should be thoroughly tested before the

final decision about the particular system choice is made. By following this rule the managers would have possibility to opt for another system solution in case of serious system-related problems.

- Special attention should be paid to employees' training, starting from the very beginning of the implementation project in order to minimize the employees' fear of the new system and to change systematically their habits. The trainings should involve appropriate participants and training schedule should be prepared carefully.
- The necessity of adjusting IT infrastructure to the new system needs may cause problems not only during Initiation but also during other phases, with a special emphasis on Acceptance phase. This illustrates the necessity to carefully consider the technical details of ES implementation during Initiation phase.
- Managers should be prepared for problems connected with data import from legacy systems in Adaptation phase. In order to minimize these problems, the process of transferring data from legacy system should be carefully prepared in advance, presumably in Initiation phase.
- It might be anticipated that the nature of problems and their distribution over the ES lifecycle may change in Polish companies as the economic environment in Poland is shifting towards the more developed market. The predicted change refers first and foremost to an expected greater emphasize placed on business-related issues instead of system-related considerations.

On the basis of conducted research we may also formulate some implications for researchers conducting studies in enterprise systems domain. The main implications for ES researchers are formulated in the following.

- There is a necessity to incorporate the system lifecycle into ES research in order to gain a full insight into ES adoption considerations. As illustrated by the current study, such an approach might be beneficial to a comprehensive analysis of enterprise system adoption problems.
- It is important to adopt a research framework which fits the research context. The current study illustrates that by the application of an adequate research approach the investigators might avoid the risk of overlooking important considerations of ES adoptions.

6   Limitations and Future Research

The main limitation of this study's findings refers to their transferability, which is connected with the fact that the research data concerned only Polish enterprises. Therefore, the generalization of findings should be done with caution. Poland is a transition economy, i.e. an economy which is experiencing fast changes from centrally planned economic system to a market driven system (Roztocki and Weistroffer 2008a, 2011a). In consequence, this study's findings might possibly be applied to the countries that are undergoing economic transformation and belong to the same geographical region, i.e. Central and Eastern Europe. This limitation indicates a promising avenue for future research which might be connected with expanding the research sample and performing a cross-country analysis.

In the recent years a change in approach to enterprise system modeling and enterprise system design has been noticed and is particularly connected with Service Oriented Architecture (SOA), Software as a Service (SaaS) model, and cloud computing (Demirkan et al. 2010, Linthicum 2009). Researchers have started to explore potential benefits of these new paradigms (e.g., Spillner et al. 2013, Wang and Xu 2013) and companies have begun to apply them (Miranda 2013). Nonetheless, these innovative models bring new challenges to enterprise system adoption and it would be interesting to explore which considerations of enterprise system adoption will remain important and which will lose significance. However, enterprise system solutions that follow SaaS and SOA are still in the early stages of development, especially in Poland where new information technologies are usually adopted later than in developed countries (Soja 2011a, Soja and Paliwoda-Pękosz 2013b). For this reason, investigating SaaS- and SOA-based enterprise system adoptions in less developed economies seems an interesting path for future research.

7 Conclusions

The chapter analyzed the impediments across the system lifecycle in Polish companies and compares them with distribution of problems in companies that operate in developed economies. To this end, the Cooper and Zmud's six-stage model of IT diffusion has been employed and classification of problems developed previously by the authors. The main findings suggest that Adaptation phase seems to be the most difficult with the highest number of impediments perceived by the respondents. Among these difficulties, problems connected with employees appeared the most significant. The analysis of source problems occurrence over the lifecycle yielded valuable implications for managers who, firstly, should be aware of the crucial role of choosing the right, error-free system solution which should have been thoroughly tested during the initial phase of the project. Second, managers should be aware of the need for preparing appropriate training schedule in order to minimize future problems connected with employees. The third important issue resulting from this study relates to the necessity of careful preparation of the IT infrastructure adjustment and data import from legacy systems during Initiation phase in order to minimize potential problems in subsequent stages.

The comparison of problems reported by Polish practitioners with difficulties experienced in developed economies revealed some similarities in problem perception, mainly during the first organizational stage of ES implementation, concerning lack of result orientation in the business and lack of top management support. Nonetheless, the achieved results suggest that differences are more significant. Firstly, in companies that operate in developed economies, a shift from system-related problems to business-related problems was noticeable over time, whereas companies in a transition economy tended to struggle mainly with system-related issues throughout the whole system lifecycle. Secondly, people-related problems were visible mostly during the chartering phase in both studies; however, they were also recognized during other phases of ES implementation by Polish practitioners. Similarly, training problems recognized mostly in the project phase were also noticeable in other phases in Poland. Finally, there appeared problems specific for Polish companies, e.g. difficulties connected with financial and organizational condition, mostly visible during the project phase, and problems with the implementation project management emphasized greatly in the chartering phase.

Acknowledgments. This research has been financed by the funds granted to the Faculty of Management, Cracow University of Economics, within the subsidy for maintaining research potential.

References

Bernroider, E.W.N., Sudzina, F., Pucihar, A.: Contrasting ERP absorption between transition and developed economies from central and eastern europe (CEE). Inf. Syst. Manage. **28**(3), 240–257 (2011)

Bingi, P., Leff, L.G., Shipchandler, Z.E., Rao, S.: Critical IT implementation issues in developed and developing countries. Inf. Strategy Executive's J. **16**(2), 25–34 (2000)

Cooper, R., Zmud, R.: Information technology implementation research: a technological diffusion approach. Manage. Sci. **36**(2), 123–139 (1990)

Corbin, J., Strauss, A.: Grounded theory research procedures, canons, and evaluative criteria. Qual. Sociol. **13**(1), 3–21 (1990)

Davenport, T.H.: Putting the enterprise into the enterprise system. Harvard Bus. Rev. **76**(4), 121–131 (1998)

Davison, R.: Cultural complications of ERP. Commun. ACM **45**(7), 109–111 (2002)

Demirkan, H., Cheng, H.K., Bandyopadhyay, S.: Coordination strategies in an SaaS supply chain. J. Manage. Inf. Syst. **26**(4), 119–143 (2010)

Glaser, B., Strauss, A.L.: Discovery of Grounded Theory: Strategies for Qualitative Research. Aldine, Chicago (1967)

Huang, Z., Palvia, P.: ERP implementation issues in advanced and developing countries. Bus. Process Manage. J. **7**(3), 276–284 (2001)

Kim, Y., Lee, Z., Gosain, S.: Impediments to successful ERP implementation process. Bus. Process Manage. J. **11**(2), 158–170 (2005)

Kremers, M., van Dissel, H.: ERP system migrations. Commun. ACM **43**(4), 53–56 (2000)

Linthicum, D.S.: Cloud Computing and SOA Convergence in Your Enterprise: A Step-by-step Guide. Addison-Wesley Professional, Reading (2009)

Lukman, T., Hackney, R., Popovic, A., Jaklic, J., Irani, Z.: Business intelligence maturity: the economic transitional context within Slovenia. Inf. Syst. Manage. **28**(3), 211–222 (2011)

Markus, M.L., Axline, S., Petrie, D., Tanis, C.: Learning from adopters' experiences with ERP: problems encountered and success achieved. J. Inf. Technol. **15**(4), 245–266 (2000)

Markus, M.L., Tanis, C.: The enterprise systems experience – from adoption to success. In: Zmud, R.W. (ed.) Framing the Domains of IT Research: Glimpsing the Future Through the Past, pp. 173–207. Pinnaex Educational Resources, Cincinnati (2000)

Miranda, S.: ERP in the cloud: CFOs see the value of running enterprise applications as a service. Fin. Executive **29**(1), 65–66 (2013)

O'Leary, D.: Enterprise Resource Planning Systems. Cambridge University Press, Cambridge (2000)

Parr, A., Shanks, G.: A model of erp project implementation. J. Inf. Technol. **1**, 289–303 (2000)

Ross, J.W., Vitale, M.R.: The ERP revolution: surviving vs thriving. Inf. Syst. Front. **2**(2), 233–241 (2000)

Roztocki, N., Weistroffer, H.R.: Information technology in transition economies. J. Glob. Inf. Technol. Manage. **11**(4), 1–9 (2008a)

Roztocki, N., Weistroffer, H.R.: Information technology investments in emerging economies. Inf. Technol. Dev. **14**(1), 1–10 (2008b)

Roztocki, N., Weistroffer, H.R.: From the special issue editors: information technology in transition economies. Inf. Syst. Manage. **28**(3), 188–191 (2011a)

Roztocki, N., Weistroffer, H.R.: Information technology success factors and models in developing and emerging economies. Inf. Technol. Dev. **17**(3), 163–167 (2011b)

Shanks, G., Seddon, P.B., Willcocks, L. (eds.): Second-Wave Enterprise Resource Planning Systems: Implementing for Effectiveness. Cambridge University Press, Cambridge (2003)

Soh, C., Kien, S.S., Tay-Yap, J.: Cultural Fits and Misfits: Is ERP a Universal Solution? Commun. ACM **41**(4), 47–51 (2000)

Soja, P.: Success factors across ERP implementation phases: learning from practice. In: Wojtkowski, W., Wojtkowski, W.G., Zupancic, J., Magyar, G., Knapp, G. (eds.) Advances in Information Systems Development. New Methods and Practice for the Networked Society, vol. 2, pp. 275–286. Springer Science + Business Media, LLC, New York (2007)

Soja, P.: Difficulties in enterprise system implementation in emerging economies: insights from an exploratory field study in Poland. Inf. Technol. Dev. **14**(1), 31–51 (2008)

Soja, P.: Examining determinants of enterprise system adoptions in transition economies: insights from polish adopters. Inf. Syst. Manage. **28**(3), 192–210 (2011a)

Soja, P.: The role of implementation strategy in enterprise system adoption. In: Pokorny, J., Repa, V., Richta, K., Wojtkowski, W., Linger, H., Barry, C., Lang, M. (eds.) Information Systems Development, pp. 709–719. Springer Science + Business Media, LLC, New York (2011b)

Soja, P., Paliwoda-Pękosz, G.: What are real problems in enterprise system adoption? Ind. Manage. Data Syst. **109**(5), 610–627 (2009)

Soja, P., Paliwoda-Pękosz, G.: Comparing benefits from enterprise system adoption in transition and developed economies: an ontology-based approach. Inf. Syst. Manage. **30**(3), 198–217 (2013a)

Soja, P., Paliwoda-Pękosz, G.: Impediments to enterprise system implementation over the system lifecycle: contrasting transition and developed economies. Electron. J. Inf. Syst. Dev. Countries **57**(1), 1–13 (2013b)

Somers, T.M., Nelson, K.: A taxonomy of players and activities across the ERP project life cycle. Inf. Manag. **41**, 257–278 (2004)

Spillner, J., Muller, J., Schill, A.: Creating optimal cloud storage systems. Future Gener. Comput. Syst. **29**, 1062–1072 (2013)

Stein, A., Hawking, P.: The second wave ERP market: an Australian viewpoint. In: Grant, G.G. (ed.) ERP & Data Warehousing in Organizations: Issues and Challenges, pp. 72–88. IGI Global, Hershey (2003)

Themistocleous, M., Irani, Z.: Benchmarking the benefits and barriers of application integration. Benchmarking Int. J. **8**(4), 317–331 (2001)

Themistocleous, M., Irani, Z., O'Keefe R.M., Paul, R.: ERP problems and application integration issues: an empirical survey. In: Proceedings of the 34th Hawaii International Conference on System Sciences (2001)

Themistocleous, M., Soja, P., Cunha, P.R.: The same, but different: enterprise systems adoption lifecycles in transition economies. Inf. Syst. Manage. **28**(3), 223–239 (2011)

Wang, X.V., Xu, X.W.: An interoperable solution for cloud manufacturing. Robot. Comput.-Integr. Manuf. **29**(4), 232–247 (2013)

Wright, S., Wright, A.M.: Information system assurance for enterprise resource planning systems: unique risk considerations. J. Inf. Syst. **16**(suppl.), 99–113 (2002)

Offshoring ERP Implementations: Critical Success Factors in European Perspective

Rajneesh Chauhan[✉]

FORE School of Management, Qutab Institutional Area,
New Delhi 110 016, India
rajneesh@fsm.ac.in

Abstract. Information Technology (IT) offshoring is changing the way IT departments are run and organized by organizations. Enterprise Resource Planning (ERP) applications are changing the way organizations run their businesses. Both are seminal trends which bring along with their associated benefits to organizations. However, both IT offshoring and ERP implementations are loaded with risks. When IT offshoring and ERP implementations happen together, the risks get compounded. This paper presents the critical success factors of offshoring ERP implementations. The study is an exploratory and qualitative study that starts with in depth interviews and concludes with a focus group discussion. The findings reveal that six factors are critical in offshoring of ERP implementations, namely communication & culture, offshoring partner, organization change management, project management, team skills and work & team distribution. The scope of the study was restricted to offshoring happening from Europe to India and the focus was on large offshoring engagements.

Keywords: Enterprise resource planning · Implementations · Offshoring · Europe · Critical success factors

1 Introduction

Information Technology (IT) offshoring and Enterprise Resource Planning (ERP) applications are two technology related trends that started around the same time during the 1980's. Both these trends hold potential for tremendous benefits. With IT offshoring the value chain that delivered IT services got transformed and became global. IT offshoring has tremendous benefits and has become an industry changer. However, offshoring has its share of risks and uncertainties. ERP systems integrate the various business processes across the organization. ERP holds a lot of allure as they bring efficiencies in businesses processes, better decision making and also provide a platform for business innovation. However, even after decades of existence, ERP implementations are still fraught with risks and failures. Against this background, there are organizations that are trying to combine IT offshoring and ERP implementations by offshoring parts of ERP implementations. This opens up immense possibilities of gains but at the same time risks get pronounced as both ERP implementations and offshoring are fraught with uncertainties. In the past, various studies were carried out on critical success factors of IT offshoring

© Springer International Publishing Switzerland 2015
D. Sedera et al. (Eds.): Pre-ICIS 2010-2012, LNBIP 198, pp. 85–94, 2015.
DOI: 10.1007/978-3-319-17587-4_5

and likewise multiple studies were conducted on critical success factors of ERP implementations, separately. This paper focuses specifically on the cusp of IT offshoring and ERP implementations, It is in this context that this study has been conducted on critical success factors for offshoring of ERP implementations from Europe to India.

2 Foundation and Related Research

Offshoring is defined as provision of organizational products and services from locations in other countries, whether they are actually overseas or not [11]. Offshoring is not something new. It has its roots in the outsourcing waves triggered by industrial revolution [10]. Offshoring started in manufacturing but soon spread to services. With the advent of digitization, there were certain services that could be digitized and electronically sent over distances, and this led to offshoring of services in the area of IT.

Advantages of IT offshoring range from cost benefits, to accessibility to a larger talent pool, to focus on core competency etc. However, advantages apart, IT offshoring is risky [39], and hence studies have been undertaken to understand IT offshoring better. Studies have been undertaken that have helped develop frameworks and models around offshoring [36, 40, 48], viewpoints on the role of trust in outsourcing [1], the mindset changes needed [2] and very detailed studies that help understand offshoring better [5, 15, 21, 38]. Offshoring brings along with issues & impediments [23], risks and co-ordination problems [28]. Offshoring is a decision that will be taken by the senior management, but the middle management that has to make it happen, will not share the same vision and enthusiasm for offshoring [25]. Offshoring is fraught with uncertainty [8]. To reduce uncertainties, some organizations try taking the middle path where offshoring is done but not outsourcing [27, 31]. In offshoring, there could be factors like culture, time zone, knowledge, language, infrastructure, offshoring backlash etc. that could jeopardize offshoring [16, 26]. There are studies focused on studying the critical success factors of offshoring like customer interaction skills, business process skills, ERP package skills etc. [32]. And as IT offshoring matured, organizations are going in for offshoring of more and more complex IT services. What started as offshoring of low end coding work has come a long way and today, in spite of the inherent risks of offshoring, we see parts of ERP implementations also getting offshored.

Like IT offshoring, ERP also has generated a lot of interest as ERP too bring both benefits and risks. ERP is defined as a technology strategy that integrates a set of business functions like finance, human resources, purchasing and operational aspects, such as manufacturing or distribution, through tight linkages from operational business transactions to financial records. An ERP can also provide analytic applications based on the transactional data set that is generated by the functionality contained within the suite. Most ERP solutions enable the flow of information across the organization, in end-to-end business processes, through a comprehensive set of interconnected modules [18].

ERP applications have advantages and bring to the organization not only the benefits of integration, operational efficiencies, better decisions but also gives organizations an opportunity to relook, and transform their business process [32]. ERP systems are expected to reduce costs by improving efficiencies through computerization and enhance decision-making by providing accurate and timely enterprise-wide information [30]. They reflect an innovative business strategy, as ERP adoption involves business process improvement, best practices implementation, intra enterprise integration and inter-enterprise coupling [20]. The lure of these benefits is such that more and more organizations are leaving custom built applications and going for readymade and configurable ERP applications. However, ERP packages are complex to implement. The failure rates are high and not many organizations are able to deploy them successfully. Various studies have been conducted and though the exact percentage might differ but almost fifty per cent of ERP implementations do not deliver the results expected from them. In the Gioia [14] survey, 51 per cent viewed their ERP implementations as unsuccessful. The Conference Board Survey interviewed executives in 117 companies that attempted ERP implementations and 40 per cent of the projects failed to achieve their business case within one year of going live [9]. Given the challenges and failures in ERP implementations, critical success factors for ERP implementations have been an object of research over the decades. Early research on ERP implementations looked upon the critical success factors from the perspective of their being strategic or tactical [19]. Study has also been done to find out the success factors that are more relevant to ERP projects as compared to a regular IT projects or general projects. In this study it was found that for ERP projects, critical success factors are cultural changes, business changes, managing consultants, managing conflicts and staff retention [35]. Some of the studies have specifically focused on singular dimensions of critical success factors like importance of change management in ERP implementation [47] and expound on how change management is the key. Geography centric researches have been done to capture the impact of local factors. For ERP implementations in China, critical success factors were identified explicitly [17, 50]. Likewise, there have been similar studies done for ERP implementations in Mexico [13] and India [45]. Further studies of critical success factors have been done against a backdrop of classical management theory as well [4]. Over the years for ERP IMPLEMENTATIONS various dimensions like the barriers [29], organization structures [12], quality issues [24], communication effects [49], consultant selection [43], software selection [41], leadership [34], planning and control [42] etc. have been the object of research. In all these studies there is a bevy of critical success factors that come into play starting from top management support, goal, objective, vision, user knowledge & training, project management to inter departmental conflicts etc. [3, 6, 7, 22, 32, 37, 44, 46, 50].

So it can be aptly concluded that both ERP and offshoring are two seminal, business relevant trends and their importance cannot be underestimated. Against this backdrop, there are organizations that are trying to marry ERP implementations and offshoring. This opens up immense possibilities of gains but at the same time risks get compounded as both ERP implementations and offshoring are fraught with uncertainties. It is in this context that this study has been conducted on critical success factors for offshoring of ERP implementations.

3 Research Approach

This study takes a qualitative and exploratory approach that entails in-depth, semi structured interviews with "ERP and offshoring experts" to elicit the success factors in offshoring of ERP implementations. These "ERP and offshoring experts" were ERP program managers who had played a key leadership role in ERP implementations involving offshoring. Thirty such ERP and offshoring experts were interviewed as a part of this study. Since the scope of study is Europe, and India being a prominent offshoring location, hence the scope has been restricted to ERP implementations in Europe, with the offshoring location being India. Further given the prominence of "offshored outsourced" scenarios vis-a vis "offshored insourced" scenarios, scope has been restricted to "offshored outsourced" scenarios and not "offshored insourced" scenarios. Also, ERP is a generic name that sometimes gets loosely defined to include small business packages as well. Hence the scope of study has been restricted to include the traditional ERP offerings from the stable of SAP and Oracle. These two companies are the major ERP product players and between them control more than 50 per cent of the market. Lastly, the focus has been on large ERP offshoring engagements that have an offshoring team of at least 100 personnel.

The questions were open-ended and followed a flow which started with "introductory questions" to introduce the objective of study, and also to bring to the fore, background of the interviewee. This was followed by the "transition questions" which moved the interview into the broad scope of study. Next were the "key questions" that drove deep into details and elicited insights and perspectives. Finally it was the "ending questions" which were used to summarize and bring closure to the discussion.

Semi structured interviews were recorded. Subsequently the recordings were analyzed and researcher coded the data. Further the coded data was analyzed and summarized to elicit the themes/critical success factors from each interview. Lastly the themes/critical success factors of the individual interviews were tabulated, and each theme/factor was weighed by counting the number of respondents who expressed the same or similar themes/factors.

To ensure reliability and validity of the findings from interviews, the interviewees were encouraged to compare the interview findings with documents from the project (monthly status reports, quality gate reports, steering committee minutes etc.). Likewise member checking was done where results from qualitative study were returned to the participants for verification. Also in the entire process of research, an independent ERP expert was involved to review the process and output of the study. The duration of each interview was to the tune of an hour. There was an additional follow up round of interview which used to typically last half an hour where interviewees were presented the outcome of the interview.

To refine the findings of the interviews further, a focus group discussion was organized where the critical success factors elicited from interview were tabled, discussed and finalized.

4   Research Findings

Critical success factors are defined as the limited number of areas in which results, if they are satisfactory, will ensure success [33]. In the context of offshoring of ERP implementations, they can be defined as the factors needed to ensure successful ERP offshoring. The critical success factors have come out well and capture a broad spectrum. Some factors were macro factors like the choice of offshoring partner itself and some factors were micro factors like work & team distribution. The full list of critical success factors that came out prominently as a consequence of in depth interviews and the focus group discussion, are given below.

- Communication & Culture
- Offshoring Partner
- Organization Change Management
- Project Management
- Team Skills
- Work & Team Distribution.

Communication and Culture. Good communication is very important in offshoring. Offshoring has teams at onsite as well as at offshore and communication with clients at onsite happens both in person as well as in the remote mode. In case of remote communication between clients at onsite and offshore teams in India, the communication challenges aggravate. To surmount these challenges, emphasis is given on communication and collaboration infrastructure like telephones, audio conferences, video conferences, instant messengers/chats etc. Further, offshoring location being India meant personnel of offshoring vendors had mostly Indian personnel. Indians have a reasonable fluency in English, but do not know the other European languages like French, German, Spanish, Dutch, Italian etc. Proficiency in vernacular languages is important to succeed in Europe. Further, good cultural understanding was emphasized by many as otherwise errors of context come in and things could be interpreted differently. European client personnel could be seeing a deadline much more rigidly than his corresponding counterpart in the offshoring company. The mannerisms, propriety vary from culture to culture and depending upon the culture the acceptable viewpoints around work life balance, outlook towards work etc. Cultural understanding and sensitivity is required on both the client side as well as the vendor side.

Offshoring Partner. Offshoring is all about working with an offshoring partner and hence the importance of offshoring partner as a critical success factors. The senior management of the offshoring partner should be committed to the offshoring engagement. Some interviewees were of the opinion that to get the right commitment from offshoring partner, it is important to have a CXO connect in the offshoring partner organization. Different offshoring partners have different strengths. So it was paramount that the offshoring partner had strong Europe focus. Most of the Indian offshoring partners have a focus on North America but not so much on Europe. Likewise not all offshoring partners have strong ERP package practices. Most of the offshoring partners have non package strengths which focus on custom code development and maintenance.

Also the partner should have the ability to increase the number of personnel and introduce new ERP skills at short notices. One of the reasons why customers go in for outsourcing is that customers themselves cannot run a full-fledged ERP practice and hence this scalability is an expectation from the offshoring partner. There are two aspects of scalability – onsite and offshore, the former being especially challenging. Onsite scalability is the capability of the offshoring partner to quickly deploy skilled personnel at onsite with the right work visas/work permits. The ability of a vendor to get the right work permits for its personnel is important. Personnel with Indian offshoring partners are mostly Indian passport holders. Indian passport holders need to go through elaborate visa procedures for most of the European countries, unlike personnel from western countries. So lead time involved becomes more. Thus to conclude, the choice of the offshoring partner plays an important role in the success of an offshoring engagement.

Organization Change Management. ERP changes the way businesses are organized. IT offshoring changes the way IT departments are organized. So when ERP and IT offshoring came together, substantial organization change management effort is required to make it a success. Some interviewees stressed that senior management support is required to make change management a success. Not only should the senior management support be there, but this support should be there in a very visible manner. At times, the negative consequences of offshoring can be as serious as retrenchment. If left alone, at the working level, seeing a fellow worker exit or a working relationship getting severed is painful and workers can take steps detrimental to offshoring. Senior management focus should be to re-skill and redeploy rather than outright retrenchment.

Project Management. While project management is a must for any successful project, in case of offshored ERP implementations there are extra project management overheads as work has to be split, sent to offshore, monitored, and delivered from offshore. The accomplishment of these aforementioned activities becomes even more daunting as teams are in different time zones and are geographically disparate. This calls for a dedicated focus on project management to ensure that offshoring activities dovetail into the larger ERP implementation project plan. Since the offshoring work is interwoven between client and offshoring partner, project management has to be a priority item for both the client and offshoring partner organization. In the research, what also came to the fore was that offshoring vendors based in India were more oriented towards PMP framework as compared to Prince2 framework. However in Europe, it is Prince2 methodologies that are more prevalent.

Team Skills. Team skills like business process skills, ERP package skills, requirement elicitation skills were accorded importance by most of the interviewees. Interviewees emphasized on business process skills which were dependent upon the industry of the client organization. The need for offshore to talk business process language came to the fore. Since it was mostly technical work that was getting offshored, the offshore personnel were mostly technical with little business process knowledge, whereas when the requirements were coming from client/onsite, it was from personnel who understood business processes & hence were unfamiliar with technical language. Further even when the vendor personnel had business process knowledge, it had to be grounded in the context of local statutory laws and rules. Also, since the business process are to be mapped on to the ERP package, hence good skills in the ERP product are important. It is important to know the base functionality of the ERP product and also the way ERP product could be configured with minimal customization to meet the customers requirement. Another type of skill that was emphasized was the requirement elicitation skills. Requirement elicitation has to be efficient so that requirements elicited are crisp, detailed and well documented.

Work and Team Distribution. ERP offshoring calls for well thought of decisions around work & team distribution between onsite and offshore. Prudence has to be exercised at the time of deciding what has to be offshored. It was reasoned by interviewees that it is easier to offshore technical (programming) work as compared to functional work. Requirement elicitation is best done onsite whereas the downstream technical work in terms of technical design, coding/configuration, unit testing is best done offshore, before the work again gets pushed to onsite for integration testing, user acceptance testing, cutover and go live activities. Further the right split of personnel between onsite and offshore plays a key role in success of ERP offshoring. Excessive offshoring can make the entire engagement extremely risky. A over staffed onsite can lead to erosion of offshoring benefits. For successful offshoring a healthy but lean presence of personnel is required at onsite, who can co-ordinate and route artifacts between client and the offshore team. Onsite team also provides same time zone response and doubles as a quick response team. So compromising with onsite staffing beyond a certain level is not advisable in the interest of the success of ERP implementation offshoring.

5   Conclusion

The critical success factors elicited adequately represented the areas that need to be focused on for ensuring success in offshoring of ERP implementations. After the semi structured interviews the critical success factors were ten but the focus group discussion helped to consolidate and group these factors into a manageable six factors. These factors ranged from soft issues like communication & culture to hard skills present within the team like ERP skills, business process skills & requirement elicitation skills. Some of the factors were organization level factors like offshoring partner and organization change management. There were also detail oriented factors like work & team distribution. And offshoring of ERP implementations being the quintessential projects they are, project management also came as a factor.

Some of the critical success factors are client specific, some are vendor specific and some are both client and vendor specific. Organization change management is a client specific critical success factor. Offshoring partner is a vendor specific critical success factor. Critical success factors like communication & culture and project management are both client and vendor specific. Team skills, and work & team distribution are predominantly vendor specific but clients can also have a say in these critical success factors.

During the interviews, influencers like infrastructure (connectivity infrastructure etc.), did get mentioned but stopped short of being critical success factors. Experts unanimously felt that given the advancements in infrastructural technologies like VPN lines, dedicated leased lines etc., this was no longer a risk.

Within communication, language came up prominently. Language is one of the primary reasons why countries in Eastern Europe are coming up as offshoring locations and giving Indian offshoring vendors stiff competition. Many of the Indian offshoring vendors have set up offshoring centers in Eastern Europe.

This study has concluded well but there lies scope for future research. The research has potential to be extended along the lines of various industries like banking, manufacturing, utilities, retail etc. There could be industry specific differences or commonalities that would help enriching the understanding. Further the above is a qualitative study and there is room for taking up a downstream quantitative study which can extend the qualitative study undertaken so far.

References

1. Antoine, R.M.B.: The offshore trust: a catalyst for development. J. Financ. Crime **14**(3), 264–278 (2007)
2. Aydin, M.N., Groot, J.D., Hillegersberg, J.V.: Action readiness and mindset for IT offshoring. J. Enterp. Inf. Manage. **23**(3), 326–349 (2010)
3. Baharum, Z., Ngadiman, M.S., Haron, H.: Critical factors to ensure the successful of OS-ERP implementation based on technical requirement point of view. In: Third Asia International Conference on Modelling and Simulation, pp. 419–424. IEEE (2009)
4. Bradley, J.: Management based critical success factors in the implementation of enterprise resource planning systems. Int. J. Acc. Inf. Syst. **9**, 175–200 (2008)
5. Chadee, D., Raman, R.: International outsourcing of information technology services: review and future directions. Int. Mark. Rev. **26**(4/5), 411–438 (2009)
6. Chen, C.C., Law, C.C.H., Yang, S.C.: Managing ERP implementation failure: a project management perspective. IEEE Trans. Eng. Manage. **56**(1), 157–170 (2009)
7. Chou, S.W., Chang, Y.C.: The implementation factors that influence the ERP (enterprise resource planning) benefits. Decis. Support Syst. **46**, 149–157 (2008)
8. Clott, C.: An uncertain future: a preliminary study of offshore outsourcing from the manager's perspective. Manage. Res. News **30**(7), 476–494 (2007)
9. Cooke, D., Gelman, L., Peterson, W.J.: ERP trends - Conference board (2001). www.conferenceboard.ca/documents.asp?rnext=869
10. Davis, B.: Finding lessons of outsourcing in 4 historical tales. Wall Street J. (2004)
11. Davis, G.B., Ein-Dor, P., King, W.R., Torkzadeh, R.: IT offshoring: history, prospects and challenges. J. Assoc. Inf. Syst. **7**(11), 770–795 (2006)
12. Gallagher, K.P., Gallagher, V.C.: An exploratory study of organizing structures for post implementation ERP. In: 43rd Hawaii International Conference on System Sciences. IEEE (2010)
13. Garcia-Sanchez, N., Perez-Bernal, L.E.: Determination of critical success factors in implementing an ERP system: a field study in mexican enterprises. Inf. Technol. Dev. **13**(3), 293–309 (2007)
14. Gioia, R.: ERP survey results point to need for higher implementation success (2002). www.robbinsgioia.com/news_events/012802_erp.aspx
15. Gonzalez, R., Gasco, J., Llopis, J.: Information systems offshore outsourcing - a descriptive analysis. Ind. Manage. Data Syst. **106**(9), 1233–1248 (2006)

16. Gregory, R., Prifling, M., Beck, R.: The role of cultural intelligence for the emergence of negotiated culture in IT offshore outsourcing projects. Inf. Technol. People **22**(3), 223–241 (2009)
17. Guang-hui, C., Chun-qing, L., Yun-xiu, S.: Critical Success factors for ERP life cycle implementation. Int. Fed. Inf. Proc. Res. Pract. Issues Enterp. Inf. Syst. **20**, 553–562 (2006)
18. Hestermann, C., Woods, J.: What ERP is and what the associated terms really mean. Gartner Research, G00170997, 2 (2009)
19. Holland, H., Light, B.: A critical success factors model for ERP implementation. From Trenches IEEE Softw. **16**(3), 30–36 (1999)
20. Hunton, J.E., Barbara, L., Reck, J.L.: Enterprise resource planning systems: comparing firm performance of adopters and nonadopters. Int. J. Acc. Inf. Syst. **4**, 165–184 (2003)
21. Jensen, P.D.O.: A learning perspective on the offshoring of advanced services. J. Int. Manage. **15**, 181–193 (2009)
22. Jing, R., Qiu, X.: A study on critical success factors in ERP systems implementation. In: International Conference on Service Systems and Service Management, pp. 1–6. IEEE (2007)
23. King, W.R.: Issues in IS Offshoring. Inf. Syst. Manage. **25**, 287–289 (2008)
24. Kumar, V.M.N., Suresh, A.V., Prashanth, P.: Analyzing the quality issues in ERP implementation: a case study. In: Second International Conference on Emerging Trends in Engineering and Technology, pp. 759–764. IEEE (2009)
25. Lacity, M.C., Rottman, J.W.: Effect of offshore outsourcing of information technology work on client project management. Strateg. Outsourcing Int. J. **2**(1), 4–26 (2009)
26. Lacity, M.C., Khan, S.A., Willcocks, L.P.: A review of the IT outsourcing literature: insights for practice. J. Strateg. Inf. Syst. **18**, 130–146 (2009)
27. Lampel, J., Bhalla, A.: Embracing realism and recognizing choice in IT offshoring initiatives. Bus. Horiz. **51**, 429–440 (2008)
28. Mirani, R.: Procedural coordination and offshored software tasks: lessons from two case studies. Inf. Manage. **44**, 216–230 (2007)
29. Peng, G.C., Nunes, M.P.: Interrelated barriers and risks affecting ERP post implementation in China. In: 43rd Hawaii International Conference on System Sciences. IEEE (2010)
30. Poston, R., Grabski, S.: Financial impacts of enterprise resource planning implementations. Int. J. Acc. Inf. Syst. **2**, 271–294 (2001)
31. Preston, S.: Lost in migration: offshore does not mean outsourced. Strateg. Leadersh. **32**(6), 32–36 (2004)
32. Rajneesh, C., Dwivedi, R., Sherry, A.M.: Offshoring ERP implementations: critical success factors in swiss perspective. In: 18th Americas Conference on Information Systems, August 2012
33. Rockart, J.: Chief executives define their own data needs. Harvard Bus. Rev. **57**(2), 81–93 (1979)
34. Shao, Z., Feng, Y., Hu, Q., Yang, L.: A conceptual model for studying the influence of charismatic leadership on ERP implementation lifecycle. In: 42nd Hawaii International Conference on System Sciences. IEEE (2009)
35. Skok, W., Legge, M.: Evaluating enterprise resource planning (ERP) systems using an interpretive approach. Knowl. Process Manage. **9**(2), 72–82 (2002)
36. Soliman, K.S.: A framework for global IS outsourcing by application service providers. Bus. Process Manage. **9**(6), 735–744 (2003)
37. Song, Y., Han, J., Cheng, D., Zhang, Y.: An empirical research on the impact of CSFS on adoption of ERP. In: International Conference on Wireless Communications, Networking and Mobile Computing, pp. 6254–6257. IEEE (2007)

38. Stratman, J.K.: Facilitating offshoring with enterprise technologies: reducing operational friction in governance and production of services. J. Oper. Manage. **26**, 275–287 (2008)
39. Tafti, M.H.A.: Risks factors associated with offshore IT outsourcing. Ind. Manage. Data Syst. **105**(5), 549–560 (2005)
40. Tate, W.L., Ellram, L.M.: Offshore outsourcing: a managerial framework. J. Bus. Ind. Mark. **24**(3,4), 256–268 (2009)
41. Tsai, W.H., Lee, P L., Shen, Y.S., Yang, C.C.: The relationship between ERP software selection criterion and ERP success. In: International Conference on Industrial Engineering and Engineering Management, pp. 2222–2226. IEEE (2009)
42. Tsai, W.H., Lin, S.J., Lin, W.R., Liu, J.Y.: The relationship between planning & control risk and ERP project success. In: International Conference on Industrial Engineering and Engineering Management, pp. 1835–1839. IEEE (2009)
43. Tsai, W.H., Shen, Y.S., Lee, P.L., Kuo, L.: An empirical investigation of the impacts of ERP consultant selections and project management on ERP is success assessment. In: International Conference on Industrial Engineering and Engineering Management, pp. 568–572. IEEE (2009)
44. Upadhyay, P., Dan, P.K.: An explorative study to identify the critical success factors for ERP implementation in Indian small and medium scale enterprises. In: International Conference on Information Technology, pp. 295–299. IEEE (2008)
45. Upadhyay, P., Dan, P.K.: ERP in Indian SME's: a post implementation study of the underlying critical success factors. Int. J. Manage. Innov. Syst. **1**(2:E1), 1–10 (2009)
46. Yanhong, Z.: ERP implementation process analysis based on the key success factors. In: International Forum on Information Technology and Applications, pp. 25–27. IEEE (2009)
47. Yasar, F.J., Al-Mudimigh, A., Zairi, M.: ERP implementation critical success factors – the role and impact of business process management. In: IEEE-ICMIT, vol. 1, pp. 122–127 (2000)
48. Youngdahl, W., Ramaswamy, K.: Offshoring knowledge and service work: a conceptual model and research agenda. J. Oper. Manage. **26**, 212–221 (2008)
49. Yuying, Z., Yanan, X.: Evaluation indicator system and weights research of communication effects in ERP implementation project. In: International Forum on Computer Sciences – Technology and Applications, pp. 423–427. IEEE (2009)
50. Zhang, L., Matthew, K.O.L., Zhang, Z., Banerjee, P.: Critical success factors of enterprise resource planning systems implementation success in China. In: 36th Hawaii International Conference on System Sciences. IEEE (2003)

Why Does the System Usage Differ Between Organizational Units? – A Case Study in a Knowledge-Intensive Project Organization

Merja Mattila[✉]

Aalto University School of Business, Helsinki, Finland
merja.mattila@aalto.fi

Abstract. This paper seeks to examine how a case company exploits new staffing procedures and enterprise system (ES) functionalities in order to improve allocation and control of project resources. The paper relies on qualitative data collected through an in-depth case study in a large European high-tech company over a period of one and a half years. In order to understand the system usage in the case company the paper employs institutional theory and Orton and Weick's concept of coupling. By combining the concept of coupling with the elements of system usage - work assignment, user, and system –, the paper explains why system usage differs between organizational units. Findings show how the use of new ES functionalities is influenced by features of organizational unit, features of work assignment, individual characteristics as well as target customer. The paper also recommends selective system use in a knowledge-intensive project organization.

Keywords: Competence catalogues · Enterprise systems · Knowledge-intensive organizations · Coupling · Project management · Staffing

1   Introduction

Companies are seeking new ways to create and capture value. One important way to increase value in the organization is to innovate new business models and concepts. The challenge is to efficiently combine structures and procedures that enhance innovation with tools that support allocation and control of resources. In order to find a balance between these often competing objectives companies may implement integrated matrix organizations, common procedures and new enterprise system (ES) functionalities. By standardizing internal procedures and by mandating enterprise system use in organizational units, a company's management aims to allocate and control resources more efficiently.

In this paper an enterprise system is defined as a software package that "enables the integration of transaction oriented data and business processes throughout an organization" [1]. It includes both the enterprise resource planning (ERP) system functions and all the other applications providing an integrated information system for most functions of a company.

© Springer International Publishing Switzerland 2015
D. Sedera et al. (Eds.): Pre-ICIS 2010-2012, LNBIP 198, pp. 95–110, 2015.
DOI: 10.1007/978-3-319-17587-4_6

In order to shed light on the issues that have an impact on the use of newly implemented ES functionalities, this research adopts the lens of institutional theory and the concept of coupling [2] in the context of a knowledge-intensive project organization. The paper follows the lead of Comstock and Scott [3] and emphasizes that a company consists of subsystems that are combined with each other in different ways. Enterprise system use in these subsystems i.e. organizational units is examined by adopting a commonly used framework for system usage i.e. user, system and task (e.g. [4]). Recognizing the complexity of system usage and that the business value of ES is rarely linked with the features of the ES itself (e.g. [5–7]) this paper leaves the system in the background, and focuses on the user, herein enhanced to cover organizational unit, and the task, herein work assignment. As previous literature recognizes the importance of loose coupling associated with enterprise systems [8] this paper goes deeper into analyzing the coupling of the organizational unit and the work assignment with system use in a knowledge-intensive organization. Based on in-depth case data from different managers, specialists and ES users within a publicly quoted case company, the paper figures out why the use of new ES functionalities differs between organizational units.

The findings show that the features of the organizational unit, the features of the work assignment, individual characteristics and target customer cause the variation in system usage between organizational units. By introducing two concepts - the organizational unit coupling and work assignment coupling, the paper presents how some organizational units and work assignments are tightly coupled with staffing procedures and the use of ES functionalities while other organizational units are loosely or even decoupled with them. Further, as the system usage and new ES functionalities themselves represent the institutionalized procedures of some organizational units and the stabilized procedures of certain customers or industry areas, the findings emphasize the impact of target customer on the system usage.

Given that this research is only a snapshot of the use of new ES functionalities during an organizational transformation, it is important to understand the dynamics of system usage. The theoretical contribution of this study is achieved by combining the concept of coupling with elements of system usage in a knowledge-intensive project organization. It broadens the discussion into the fit of enterprise system functionalities with all elements of system usage. The practical contribution of this paper is to demonstrate why organizational units have different fit with new ES functionalities. It also recommends selective system use regarding those work assignments and organizational units which have poor fit with system use.

This paper is organized as follows. Theoretical underpinnings are presented in Sect. 2. Section 3 introduces the research approach and process. In Sect. 4, the case description is outlined. Section 5 contains the case analysis and the discussion. And finally, Sect. 6 includes the conclusion and implications as well as future directions.

2 Theoretical Underpinnings

In this paper enterprise systems are defined as software packages that "enable the integration of transaction oriented data and business processes throughout an organization"

[1]. An enterprise system includes the enterprise resource planning (ERP) system functions and all the other applications providing an integrated information system for most functions of a company. Enterprise systems allow allocation and coordination of resources across time zones and geographical locations, while keeping the data available and centralized.

Scott [9] defines institutions as "social structures that have attained a high degree of resilience". He suggests that institutional elements (regulative, normative, cultural-cognitive) produce meaning, stability and order to social behavior. These institutional elements move from place to place and time to time with the help of four types of carriers, which are symbolic systems, relational systems, routines, and artifacts [9]. As presented previously [10–13] this paper considers technology, i.e. the enterprise system, as a fourth institutional carrier. While socially constructed by the actions of e.g. designers or users, once developed technology tends "to become reified and institutionalized, losing its connection with the human agents that constructed it or gave it meaning to be part of the objective, structural properties of the organization [11]". The paper emphasizes the duality of enterprise systems by noticing that while enterprise systems are subject to institutional forces and institutional processes that set the rules of rationality, they also represent institutional commitments by constraining the action of users (e.g. [12]). Further, as the development and the use of ES functionalities often emphasize logics of certain organizational units (e.g. [11]), rationalities of other organizational units may be in conflict with ES usage.

In the similar way as an enterprise system is a combination of different modules a company consists of subsystems [14, 15], which vary in their degree of coupling with each other. In this research subsystems consist of organizational units, which may be loosely coupled with the other parts of the company in order to achieve innovation, agility or flexibility. Further, the use of enterprise system may combine differently coupled organizational units together. In order to study how organizational units are coupled with the system usage, this paper adopts the concept of coupling [2, 15, 16]. The concept of coupling defines tightly coupled systems as highly integrated and responsive to each other, while decoupled systems are seen as separate and indifferent to whatever occurs in other parts of the system. Loose coupling includes the presence of both tight coupling and decoupling (e.g. [13]). Because disturbances in one part of a system need not cause disturbances in other parts, loosely coupled organizations are currently seen to survive longer [17]. This paper also recognizes recent literature on coupling in organizations [13, 18–20].

The business value of enterprise systems is rarely linked to the ES technology itself, but rather to how organizational features support the system usage (e.g. [5–7]). By adopting a commonly used framework for the system usage i.e. user, task and system (e.g. [4]) and recognizing the complexity of ES use this paper focuses on the influence of organizational unit and work assignment on system usage. By analyzing organizational unit coupling and work assignment coupling this paper also participates in the discussion of appropriateness of ES in the organizations [8, 13].

3 Method

By adopting a view that reality is socially constructed by humans this paper attempted to understand the enterprise system usage through the meanings that users assigned to it. As ES users translated these meanings according to their own frames of reference, this research employed the interpretive case study approach [21]. The interpretive approach was selected in order to help to make sense of present events and in order to recognize the formation of new patterns in everyday staffing practices. The aim was to be close to the everyday practices and the system use, while keeping enough distance to be able to problematize them [17].

In order to reveal the underlying assumptions, expectations, and knowledge that people had about global staffing process and the use of new enterprise system function-alities in it, we conducted focused interviews in the case company, here named Neon. During the first phase between December 2008 and September 2009 we conducted 12 focused interviews about the company's transformation process, newly implemented matrix organization and the new enterprise system functionalities. In order to achieve a comprehensive understanding about the use of the new ES functionalities in different parts of the organization, 19 additional interviews were conducted between March and August in 2010. The total of 31 interviews covered different interest groups, positions, competence areas and industry fields. One or two researchers conducted face-to-face interviews on interviewees' own experiences and perceptions. The interviews lasted for 40–90 mins, they were recorded on MP3 and later transcribed for subsequent analysis. Furthermore, an extensive review of the company's documents, Intranet and training materials was carried out.

As the research progressed, the research data was analyzed "in order to draw valid meaning to realize when an interview should be conducted to fill in gaps" [22]. The analysis and interpretation of the research data continued throughout the research in order to assure that the findings were grounded in the case data. In order to categorize the data the research data was coded. During the initial coding codes such as Requested competence, Work assignment, Nature of project work, Time frame, Target customer, System, Organizational unit or Individual characteristics of employees emerged from the data (Fig. 1I Initial coding). These emerged codes were joined together into cate-gories (Fig. 1II Coding) such as features of Work assignment (WA), Organizational unit (OU), Individual characteristics (IC), Target customer (TC), and System (SYS). As this research adopted a view that the system usage was more linked with work assignment and user than the features of the enterprise system itself, the system was cut out from the data analysis. Next, these categories were placed in the framework of system usage [4] by linking target customer and individual characteristics with both work assignment and organizational unit (Fig. 1III Placing of categories in the selected theoretical frame-work). Thereafter, organizational unit and work assignment were combined with the concept of coupling (Fig. 1IV Using selected concepts and frameworks as sensitizing device & developing the theory further). Analyzing of research findings was done at the organizational unit level.

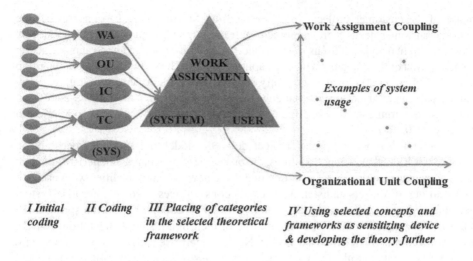

I Initial   *II Coding*   *III Placing of categories*   *IV Using selected concepts and*
coding   *in the selected theoretical*   *frameworks as sensitizing device*
                                framework   *& developing the theory further*

Fig. 1. The data and construct alignment in the empirical data analysis process.

4   Case Description

4.1   Case Company

The case company Neon (a pseudonym) is a large European high-tech company operating in project business. With over 16,000 employees in close to 30 countries it delivered IT, R&D, and consulting services to several customer sectors either locally or globally. At the beginning of 2009 Neon implemented a new matrix organization structure in order to support its new corporate strategy and a global project delivery model. The transformation process was materialized through a transformation program spreading over a three-year period from 2009 to 2011.

Previously the company structure had been based on customer-specific industries, which varied greatly in their size, procedures, operations, and ability and need to benefit from the global network. During the transformation process employees were continuously transferred from industries into competence pools located in service lines. These competence pools were structured according to the employees' competencies on certain technology or work assignments. In the new matrix structure the industries were responsible for sales and customer relationships, and the service lines took care of project or service delivery. While service lines became responsible for delivery, the business responsibility remained at the customer-specific industries.

4.2   Staffing and Enterprise System

As an important part of its new strategy and global project delivery model Neon implemented a new global staffing process in February 2009. This new global staffing process replaced small, industry- or customer-specific teams, which had taken care of every phase of the customer projects. The new staffing function aimed to ensure that the external customer needs were combined with the internal employee competencies by allocating right people to the customer projects and services. It also aimed at maximizing the utilization of the company's human capital globally. The staffing management group consisted of about 50 global and country staffing managers organized first globally by competence areas. Due to e.g. challenges of geographical distances, time zones and language requirements, staffing function was reorganized by delivery countries in January 2010.

In order to support its global project delivery model and staffing process Neon modified its ES with new functionalities, the project resource management (RM) module and competence catalogue (CC). In practice these new ES functionalities were used for both staffing of projects and staffing of continuous services. Neon's enterprise system had mostly been implemented during the years 2004–2009, while in the spring 2010 some organizational units were in the middle of their first ES implementation (Fig. 2). Based on a commercial, US-based product Neon's enterprise system was integrated with local banks, local payroll systems, common invoice system and common reporting and budgeting system [23]. It also had the basic operational functionalities for an expert organization. However, the ongoing organizational transformation process with simultaneous implementation of new procedures and tools set a wide variety of challenges for the organization [24].

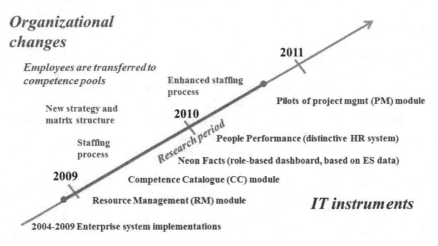

Fig. 2. Timeline of organizational transformation process and new IT instruments

The employees were expected to input and update their competence profiles and administrative assignments into the system on a regular basis. The line managers were responsible for the utilization rate and that the employees' work assignments were updated in the RM module. On a high level the resource searching and matching went as follows. First, a resource requester such as a project manager planned the project resource requirements and assignments. Then a project manager sent a resource request to the global staffing monitor by using the RM module. Next, the global staffing monitor allocated a resource request to a staffing manager in a certain delivery country. In order to find suitable candidates the staffing manager reviewed competence requirements as well as the utilization and assignments of employees by using the CC and the RM modules and his/her personal networks. After matching the requirements and resources the staffing manager offered candidates to the project manager, who made the final decision in cooperation with business units.

If internal candidates were not found, staffing was allowed to use subcontracting, internal competence development or recruiting in collaboration with business units. However, responsibilities between industries and service lines regarding these procedures were unclear. As all the interest groups were eager to acquire the best available resources for their work assignments, for example internal competence development through project work required a lot of negotiations and caused conflicts between different interest groups. Also the role of staffing between industries and service lines was confusing as staffing managers had neither business nor project delivery responsibility.

In conclusion, the business units argued being losing business opportunities all the time due to the unclear staffing process. Further, in spite of the formal staffing process, a lot of staffing seemed to be carried out separately through personal networks. Particularly experienced employees took advantage of their own networks, while inexperienced employees were more dependent on the formal staffing process and new ES functionalities.

4.3 Work Assignments

Work schedules and reservations were typically input into the RM at the beginning of the project, but they were not updated after that. As project work assignments were highly dependent on other work assignments, idle time commonly occurred. However, costs of idle time were handled differently in different organizational units causing conflicts between them. Also some work assignments such as sales work or internal development were not visible in the system. The inaccurate and incomplete reservation data in the system caused misunderstandings and conflicts between the resource seeking industries and the resource offering service lines. Due to unreliable reservation data the system could suggest candidates, who were not available in practice:

> "The problem is that the information is not updated regularly. For example I know that a couple of persons have extremely heavy work load, but according to the RM module their work loads are practically zero. The challenge is that if a person works for sales, there is not necessarily a project in which he/she could be assigned to in order to get his/her work load visible. Another thing is that I have project managers, who are making assignments to a project by themselves. And when they are busy in taking care of many things at the same time, they easily forget to update their own reservations." Head of Service Unit.

4.4 Competencies

As job titles and descriptions varied in different parts of the organization and definition of resource request typically required a lot of technical knowledge of possible competence areas, some users were skeptical about the use of the RM module. Generic competencies (such as project management competencies) serving different businesses were often easier to define into the system than more specific technology competencies. Some businesses had solved this problem by adding their special business competencies into the system. However, defining of competence items into the system was seen frustrating as one interviewee expressed:

> *"It is visible, that Neon is mostly a software development company. Competencies are to a large degree defined into it (competence catalogue) according to software development assignments. The same shows up in our People Performance tool (dedicated tool for HR) too. And our competencies are always very difficult to find from any of the tools used in Neon."* Service Desk Manager.

The employees rated their competence levels by using objective evaluations such as course degrees or certificates or by evaluating them subjectively. Basically the employees were seen willing to take any kind of task that had a fit with their competencies. However, some employees were arguably hiding certain competencies in order to avoid work assignments in certain competence areas. Also employees' eagerness to develop their existing competencies seemed to be impossible to define into the system. These subjective evaluations as well as incomplete competence profiles decreased the trust in the quality of the data.

The competence profiles included an employee's skills and knowledge in a certain competence area. Employee's personal features such as cooperation skills, motivation, drive, behavior or on-the-job experience were not included into the competence catalogue. However, these features were emphasized in project work, where personal relationships between project members and customers were very important. Finding the best possible mix between features of work assignment and personal characteristics of a person required a lot of communication between staffing and line managers. As a result staffing should have known a person so well that it was able to identify those of his/her competencies and shortcomings that had an influence on performing a work assignment.

Transferring employees back and forth between industries and service lines set challenges for maintaining customer or industry specific knowledge. In large competence pools line managers were not always aware of the customer or industry specific competencies of their recently arrived subordinates. Defining of these specific competencies into competence profiles was considered difficult or even impossible.

4.5   Target Customer

The system usage was also influenced by local institutionalized procedures in different parts of the organization. These procedures were related with e.g. their target customers. For example the bidding phase differed between customers. While some customers expected a response to the request for a tender in two months, some expected to get a response in a couple of hours. In addition to differences in time frame, the customers' established procedures regarding interviews of key persons, elaborateness of agreements or willingness to use global delivery centers varied greatly. Most surprising finding was that the use of the RM module varied even inside the staffing function.

5   Case Analysis and Discussion

As demonstrated above the use of staffing process and the new ES functionalities varied greatly between organizational units. In this paper the system use was analyzed by leaving out the ES technology itself and focusing on:

- The features of organizational unit
- The features of work assignment
- Individual characteristics, and
- Target customer

The features of an organizational unit consisted of characteristics which illustrated the unit's dependence on other organizational units. For example some organizational units had very different business model and everyday work practices, they operated in different locations and time zones, and they were forced to use the system. *The features of work assignment* represented the nature of work assignment, i.e. requested skills, competencies and technologies, time frame, or requirements of project work. Respectively *Individual characteristics* consisted of features of requested competence and employee's own attitude towards the system usage. These features included level, evaluation and demand of person's competencies, ego, pride, professionalism, background, or other features such as motivation, cooperation, drive or personal characteristics. *Target customer* included characteristics such as procedures, business environment or specific requirements, i.e. language, confidentiality, customer or industry specific knowledge, which had an influence on the system usage. Individual characteristics and target customer had an impact on system usage throughout both work assignment and organizational unit.

In order to uncover the relationships between these elements a 2-dimensional framework of system usage was created (Fig. 3). In this framework the x-axis represented the nature of unit coupling and y-axis the nature of work assignment coupling. Basically the work assignment coupling was high when the features of work assignment supported the system usage. For example requested skills, competencies and technologies could be defined easily and unequivocally and personal knowing of resource was not necessary. Respectively unit coupling was high when an organizational unit was highly dependent on other organizational units, staffing process and the use of new ES functionalities. These organizational units often represented large competence pools in service lines. Also some industry units, whose former employees were transferred into these competence pools, had high unit coupling. Also established procedures with target customers and individual characteristics impacted both unit and work assignment coupling and the system usage.

In the second phase, the 2-dimensional framework of system use was completed by bringing the concepts of coupling [2] (Orton and Weick 1990) into the context of system usage. The theoretical background of tight and loose coupling as well as decoupling was presented in the theoretical part of this paper. Next, the system usage was analyzed in each of these dimensions by introducing examples of system usage in Neon.

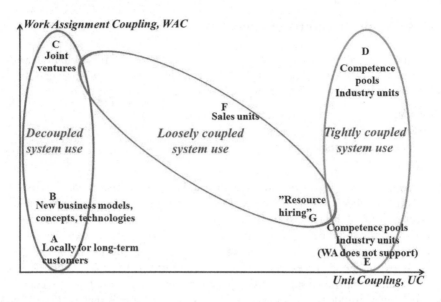

Fig. 3. Coupling of system usage in Neon.

5.1 Decoupled System Usage

First, some organizational units were knowingly disconnected from the system use. These organizational units were typically located in an industry, provided projects and services locally for certain long-term customers or sold their own software products. Naturally, requested competencies and technologies were found within their own organizational units. They had often not adopted a matrix form, but were operating in a hierarchical or in a hybrid form. Customers of these locally operating units were not ready to use the global delivery model often having certain specific requirements such as language or very strict confidentiality requirements as one interviewee narrated:

> "We have long-term relationships with our customers. Customers are willing to know our people and of course we want to know them too. It has been a clear advantage in our deliveries that we know each other and our respective procedures". Project Manager.

Due to the fact that both unit coupling and work assignment coupling of these organizational units were low the system usage was categorized as **Decoupled** (Fig. 3A).

Second, also some other parts of the company seemed to be disunited from the system use. The aim of these parts of the organization was to find new customers by implementing new business models, concepts, services or technologies. The ways to do business with these new customers were not established and the decision making process in e.g. offering or staffing phase was more flexible. The nature of their work assignments differed greatly from the main business in the company. For example these work assignments typically required a lot of work in advance, lasted less than 3 months, sometimes a couple of hours only and were invoiced by hours, not by days. Due to these reasons the resource planning was made at a remarkably detailed level and the use of common staffing procedures as well as the RM module was seen too complicated. As a result these units had implemented their own resource management tool, My Staffing Beta. Typically these units had low unit coupling and from low to medium work assignment coupling (Fig. 3B).

Third, some joint ventures created challenges for common staffing process and the use of the ES functionalities. These organizational units had not adopted common procedures and tools yet, although their staffing needs were high. At the time of the research these units were still decoupled from system usage with low unit coupling and high work assignment coupling (Fig. 3C).

5.2 Tightly Coupled System Usage

On one hand, large competence pools were very dependent on the resource requests they received from other parts of the organization. Typically these units operated in an integrated matrix structure, which required a lot of connections between e.g. different superiors, locations, or time zones. Formal staffing procedures and the ES functionalities seemed to be essential for these units. On the other hand, employees of these large competence pools had been transferred from the industry units. As the industry units had lost their competencies, they were very dependent on the staffing process and the RM as one interviewee narrated:

> "A person, who has people, also has the power. Of course it is more challenging for me now, because previously I used to be self-sufficient, I had project managers, architects, consultants, and all the prioritizing in my own hands. Now I am totally dependent on the staffing process. And in order to get things work, that we really have employees with right competence profiles, staffing has a challenge how it succeeds in allocating and prioritizing existing employees for different assignments. Of course it (staffing) is allowed to use subcontractors, if it doesn't find any in the organization. But it will be challenging, because certain competences such as a project manager are in a key role in a project." Director, Industry Unit

As unit coupling of these organizational units was high, the system usage was categorized as **Tightly coupled.** Typically work assignment coupling was also high, although it varied according to e.g. requested skills, technologies and customer or industry specific competencies (Fig. 3D). As a matter of fact the new ES functionalities were used in these organizational units even if the nature of the work assignment did not exactly support the system usage (Fig. 3E).

5.3 Loosely Coupled System Usage

As illustrated above low organizational unit coupling was the reason for decoupling, while high organizational unit coupling was the reason for tight coupling. **Loosely coupled system usage** (Fig. 3) had features from both of them. The main reasons for loose coupling were the impact of target customer and individual characteristics.

The sales process seemed to be loosely coupled with system use. Although the sales units required information on competencies during the sales process, staffing was rarely requested to map a certain competence area. Obviously unclear boundaries and lack of common procedures inhibited collaboration between the staffing function and the sales units. Also the individual characteristics of the persons involved and the procedures of target customers had an important impact on collaboration. Further, competence areas regarding sales cases seemed sometimes so narrow that the sales person already knew the possible candidates and their availabilities without staffing and the system use. Typically unit coupling of sales units was average, while work assignment coupling varied from low to high (Fig. 3F).

Target customers had often certain established procedures that did not support the use of staffing and the new ES functionalities. For example some organizational units operated in industry fields of high competition, employed new technologies, and provided projects and services to geographically distributed customers. As unit coupling was rather high the work assignment coupling was low (Fig. 3G). In fact staffing activities of these organizational units resembled resource hiring.

Individual characteristics were another reason for loosely coupled system usage. According to some interviewees the definition of competencies into the system was difficult and frustrating. Particularly, top consultants, who were always busy with their work assignments and got them through informal channels in any event, felt inputting and updating of competence profiles useless. In addition, the information regarding competencies was input into two different systems in different formats. In conclusion, the main deficiency seemed to be that information regarding employees' reservations was not created during the project management process, but the reservation data was expected to be input into the system for staffing purposes. There were also some competing views about who should use the system in the first place.

6   Conclusion and Implications

Based on the in-depth case data from different interest groups within the publicly quoted case company, the paper studied why the use of the new staffing procedures and enterprise system functionalities differs between organizational units. By employing the lens of institutional theory and the concept of coupling [2] into the context of system usage [4] and by adopting the view that the business value of the enterprise system is rarely linked with the features of the ES itself (e.g. [5–7]), this paper focused on the effect of organizational unit and work assignment on system usage.

The findings show how organizational units are differently combined with the system usage in Neon. These differences are mainly caused by the features of organizational unit, the features of work assignment, individual characteristics, and target customer. On one hand both resource offering competence pools and resource seeking industry units operating in a matrix structure are highly dependent on common staffing procedures and the use of new ES functionalities. Basically the system is used for staffing all work assignments in these organizational units even if the features of work assignment do not always exactly support the system usage. Typically the features of work assignment support the system usage when requested skills, competencies and technologies are easily and unequivocally definable and knowing of employees personally is not necessary. On the other hand some organizational units are consciously separated and disconnected from the common staffing process and the use of new ES functionalities in Neon. Generally requested competencies and technologies are found in their own organizational units, and their business model and everyday activities differ greatly from the main business in the company. Also some joint ventures are currently disconnected from the system usage. However, due to the high work assignment coupling of these units, it would be beneficial to combine them more tightly with the system usage. Another issue is that due to e.g. organizational boundaries and strategy it may be completely out of the question to combine joint ventures more tightly with the system usage.

Individuals and different interest groups respond in different ways to the newly implemented staffing process and the new enterprise system functionalities. Due to limited interest and time or difficulties in seeing the benefits of the new ways of doing things they are not able to use new functionalities properly. Also their individual characteristics have an impact on system usage through level, evaluation and demand of employees' competencies, other features such as motivation, cooperation, drive and personal characteristics, ego, pride, or professionalism.

Previous ways of staffing are not possible in the new matrix organization, while operative implementation of new procedures and tools is still ongoing. Procedures regarding e.g. project management differ between organizational units being influenced by individuals' and organizational units' own background as well as established procedures of target customers. These established procedures of target customers often include certain specific requirements regarding schedule, language, confidentiality, or customer of industry specific knowledge, which do not support the use of new ES functionalities. Further, some organizational units operating in industry fields of high competition by employing new technologies and by providing projects and services to geographically distributed customers are very willing to adjust their internal procedures according to the customer needs. As a matter of fact target customers mainly define how the business is done in these cases. However, due to the great variation in both unit coupling and work assignment coupling, it would be beneficial to reconsider if it is reasonable to combine certain organizational units, e.g. certain sales units, more tightly with the system usage. Recognizing of all skills and competencies as well as availabilities may in turn create opportunities and new business models in the knowledge-intensive project organization.

6.1 Theoretical Implications

The paper describes how the ES functionalities are locally used in conducting everyday staffing actions by dismantling elements of system usage for organizational unit and work assignment that are studied separately. As expected local staffing practices are connected to many other actions and reproduced in organizational parts gradually becoming translocal. The paper suggests that new elements – organizational unit and target customer – have an important impact on the use of common staffing procedures and new ES modules in a knowledge-intensive project organization and brings them into the framework of system usage. Although the new elements of system usage cannot be generalized to all organizations, they may be useful in analyzing system usage in knowledge-intensive project organizations.

By emphasizing that the use of new enterprise system functionalities should be focused on certain organizational units and work assignments that have the best fit with the system usage, the paper also participates in the discussion of appropriateness of ES in the organizations [13].

6.2 Practical Implications

The implementation of common staffing procedures and ES functionalities is seen as the management's way to improve efficiency of resource allocation and control in the newly implemented matrix organization. By using these procedures and tools Neon aims to transform into a virtual organization in which the required project teams will be staffed virtually.

However, the system usage for integrating competencies, skills and availabilities with work assignments poses challenges. For example finding the best possible mix between the requested competencies, person, and work assignment requires that all relevant requested competencies are defined into the system. While staffing and the use of new ES functionalities requires system usage skills, wide knowledge of requested competencies or technologies as well as networking skills, dedicated users, who would use the system on behalf of the line managers, could be worth considering. Due to the fact that the use of new ES functionalities serve the staffing function more than other organization units, the staffing function should take more responsibility about for example support and training and linking the entire project delivery process with the system usage. Further, the information regarding reservations is not produced during the project management process and the reservation data is often updated manually into the ES. The implementation of a new project management module in due course will probably reduce or even take away this manual work.

While the staffing network offers an unusual way to collaborate across boundaries in order to combine skilled employees into a suitable project team, the prioritizing seemed to be very challenging. This is emphasized when certain top consultants are requested at the same time for many simultaneous projects for different customer projects. Even if the competencies and availabilities of top consultants are more visible in the organization, the staffing decisions require a lot of negotiations between several parties. Further, although finding some sporadic top level competencies seems to be important for interviewees, all important competencies should be developed in order to ensure the company's long-term success. However, the procedures for internal competence development by using staffing and common tools are not yet stabilized in Neon.

In conclusion, this paper recommends reconsidering the system usage regarding those organizational units and work assignments, which have poor fit with the system usage. It also suggests that some organizational units, such as certain sales units or joint ventures, could be more tightly coupled with the system usage. Regardless, it seems to be too simplified to use the system only for simple work assignments, while more complex work assignments are handled with informal, personal networks. In fact, some interviewees are irritated about how even some of the simplest and shortest work assignments are carried out using the system.

6.3 Future Research

As mentioned before the everyday staffing tasks in Neon are carried out by using both formal and informal networks. Future research will go deeper in studying the differences of system usage between employees and employee groups.

In a knowledge-intensive company the professional norms are steering actions. These professional norms are a part of the employees' professional identity. As the data collection at Neon continues the research is expected to raise discussion about internal competence development in a way that enables the company to remain viable. Future research will combine this fundamental managerial problem about human competencies at work with the system usage.

Acknowledgments. Excerpted from UK Academy for Information Systems Conference Proceedings 2011. Used with permission from Association for Information Systems, Atlanta, GA. 404-413-7444; www.aisnet.org. All rights reserved.

This research paper was a part of a longitudinal case study. We would like to thank the company involved for the time and engagement allocated by contact persons and all interviewees.

References

1. Markus, M.L., Axline, S., Petrie, D., Tanis, S.C.: Learning from adopters' experiences with ERP: problems encountered and success achieved. J. Inf. Technol. **15**(4), 245–265 (2000)
2. Orton, J.D., Weick, K.E.: Loosely coupled systems: a reconceptualization. Acad. Manag. Rev. **15**(2), 203–223 (1990)
3. Comstock, D.E., Scott, W.R.: Technology and the structure of subunits: distinguishing individual and workgroup effects. Adm. Sci. Q. **22**(2), 177–202 (1977)
4. Burton-Jones, A., Straub Jr., D.W.: Reconceptualizing system usage: an approach and empirical test. Inf. Syst. Res. **17**(3), 228–246 (2006)
5. Davenport, T.H.: Putting the enterprise into the enterprise system. Harvard Bus. Rev. **76**(4), 121–131 (1998)
6. Peppard, J., Ward, J.: Unlocking sustained business value from IT investments. Calif. Manag. Rev. **48**(1), 52–70 (2005)
7. Zammuto, R.F., Griffith, T.L., Majchrzak, A., Dougherty, D.J., Faraj, S.: Information technology and the changing fabric of organization. Organ. Sci. **18**(5), 749–762 (2007)
8. Berente, N., Yoo, Y., Lyytinen, K.: Alignment or drift? loose coupling over time in NASA's ERP implementation. In: Proceedings of the 29th International Conference on Information Systems (ICIS), Paper 180. AIS Electronic Library (2008)
9. Scott, W.R.: Institutional carriers: reviewing modes of transporting ideas over time and space and considering their consequences. Ind. Corp. Change **12**(4), 879–894 (2003)
10. Barley, S.R.: Technology as an occasion for structuring: evidence from observations of CT scanners and the social order of radiology departments. Adm. Sci. Q. **31**(1), 78–108 (1986)
11. Orlikowski, W.J.: The duality of technology: rethinking the concept of technology in organizations. Organ. Sci. **3**(3), 398–427 (1992)
12. Gosain, S.: Enterprise information systems as objects and carriers of institutional forces: the new iron cage? J. Assoc. Inf. Syst. **5**(4), 151–182 (2004)

13. Berente, N.: Institutional Logics and Loosely Coupled Practices: The Case of NASA's Enterprise Information System Implementation. Case Western Reserve University, U.S.A (2009)
14. Lawrence, P.R., Lorsch, J.W.: Organization and Environment - Managing Differentiation and Integration. Harvard University Press, Boston (1967)
15. Weick, K.E.: Educational organizations as loosely coupled systems. Adm. Sci. Q. **21**(1), 1–19 (1976)
16. March, J.G., Olsen, J.P. (eds.): Ambiguity and Choice in Organizations. Scandinavian University Press, Bergen (1976)
17. Czarniawska, B.: A Theory of Organizing. Edward Elgar Publishing Limited, Cheltenham (2008)
18. Fitz-Gerald, L., Carroll, J.: A good fit? implementing enterprise resource planning systems in loosely coupled organizational systems. In: Proceedings of Pacific Asia Conference on Information Systems (PACIS), Paper 43. AIS Electronic Library (2006)
19. Volkoff, O., Strong, D.M., Elmes, M.B.: Technological embeddedness and organizational change. Organ. Sci. **18**(5), 832–848 (2007)
20. Marabelli, M., Newell, S.: Managing loose coupling in the implementation of large-scale ERP. In: Proceedings of the 18th European Conference on Information Systems (ECIS), Paper 102. AIS Electronic Library (2010)
21. Walsham, G.: Interpreting Information Systems in Organizations. Wiley, New York (1993)
22. Miles, M.B., Huberman, A.M.: Qualitative Data Analysis: An Expanded Sourcebook. Sage, Thousand Oaks (1994)
23. Mattila, M., Nandhakumar, J., Hallikainen, P., Rossi, M.: Reorganizing projects through enterprise system: emerging role of enterprise system in radical organizational change. In: Proceedings of the 43rd Annual Hawaii International Conference on System Sciences (HICSS-43). IEEE Computer Society (2010)
24. Mattila, M., Hallikainen, P., Rossi, M.: Challenges in implementing enterprise system functionalities in a matrix organization. In: Proceedings of the International Conference on Research Challenges in Information Science (RCIS), pp. 579–588. IEEE Computer Society (2010)

An Action Research Study of a Healthcare Enterprise Information System at the Faroe Islands: Towards a Problem-Solving Method for IT Public Value

Bjarne Rerup Schlichter[⊠], Per Svejvig,
and Poul Erik Rostgaard Andersen

School of Business and Social Sciences, Aarhus University,
Bartholins Allé 10, 8000 Aarhus C, Denmark
{brs,psve,ros}@badm.au.dk

Abstract. Obtaining business value from IT is a recurring theme that has diffused into healthcare information systems (HIS) where stakeholders often question the value of IT investments. Having completed the implementation of an integrated HIS, the Faroese Health Service (FHS) has commenced discussions concerning getting value from their IT investment. In order to fulfill this objective an action research project was started in the fall of 2010 consisting of two cycles: (1) setting the stage for benefit realization and; (2) benefit realization in a pilot area. The first cycle has revealed that it is not possible to distinguish between working processes and HIS, that benefit realization in healthcare (a public organization) has a much broader perspective than just financial value and that the reaping of benefits is quite difficult. This paper reports on the first two action cycles. Framed by the theory of Style Composition in action research we suggest a method to identify and realize emergent IT public value in an HIS action research project. The method is presented and discussed, and issues and concerns for further research are presented.

Keywords: Action research · Problem-solving cycle · Healthcare information systems · Benefit realization

1 Introduction

The relationship between information technology (IT) and organizational performance has been a recurring theme in information systems (IS) research [1, 2]. Given the enormous investment in IT, the discussion on how to obtain proper value and payoff has become very important for both public and private organizations. The IT value debate has also diffused into healthcare [3, 4] and is closely related to a more general discussion about measuring the performance of healthcare systems [5, 6].

The general discussion about IT value and the broader discussion about measuring performance in healthcare motivated us to start an action research project in the Faroe Islands. The Faroese Health Service (FHS) has completed the implementation of an integrated Healthcare Information System (HIS) and it is time for them to consider

© Springer International Publishing Switzerland 2015
D. Sedera et al. (Eds.): Pre-ICIS 2010-2012, LNBIP 198, pp. 111–118, 2015.
DOI: 10.1007/978-3-319-17587-4_7

reaping the benefits, which is the subject of this action research project. The problems of implementing (and realizing the benefits from) information systems in the healthcare domain, also known as Electronic Patient Journals (EPJ) or Electronic Medical Records (EMR) [7, 8], are similar to those seen in Enterprise Resource Planning (ERP) implementations [9, p. 3]. The reason is that the natures of HIS and ERP are alike in terms of accumulating data elements and hence coordinating complex processes [10].

Thus the aim of this paper is to present and discuss a method to guide the problem-solving cycle during an emergent IT public value research project in a healthcare setting. The empirical study reported in this paper covers the first two action cycles in the action research project, where we focus on establishing baselines and organizational capacity to achieve the benefit realization of HIS. Due to the emergent and practical nature of the project, an action research approach was chosen. Action research can be used to advance academic knowledge and enlighten professional practice [11].

This paper proceeds as follow. The next section explains the research methodology and setting of the project by showing the three action cycles structuring the research project. This is followed by a detailed description of the activities and observation from Action Cycles 1 and 2. This description, in the form of a table, forms the empirical foundation on which our analysis in Sect. 4 (towards a problem solving method for emergent IT public value) is based. The paper concludes with a discussion of the issues and activities which need to be addressed in case of further research.

2   Introduction

We have undertaken an action research study in the Faroe Islands to fulfill the objective of reaping the benefits from the FHS's implementation of an HIS. Action research involves close cooperation between practitioners and researchers to bring about change. The action research process can be defined as a number of learning cycles consisting of predefined stages. The action research cycle starts with diagnosis, which refers to the joint (practitioner and researcher) identification of problems and their possible underlying causes. Action planning specifies the anticipated actions that may improve or solve the problems and action taking refers to the implementation of those specified actions. Evaluation is the assessment of the intervention, and finally, learning is the reflection on the activities and outcomes [adapted from 12].

The action research project was initiated in the fall of 2010 and came to an end 2014. The project consisted of two action cycles: (1) setting the stage for benefit realization from the HIS and (2) benefit realization in a pilot area; (see Fig. 1).

The Faroe Islands are a self-governing territory within the Kingdom of Denmark with roughly 48,000 inhabitants. The FHS is a small organization compared with healthcare services in other countries and consists of three hospitals and 27 general practitioners (GPs). In 2005, the FHS began the implementation of an integrated HIS covering both the hospitals and GPs. The project faced many problems during its first years, even to the point where discussions concerning halting the project materialized, particularly based on the experiences of high costs (financial as well as personal) and dubious benefit realization [9]. The situation in 2012 was that 530 healthcare professionals are using the HIS, covering all areas of the hospitals and GPs. One of the

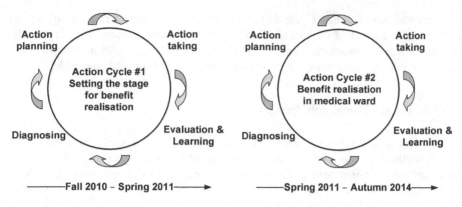

Fig. 1. The two action cycles in the action research project

authors has followed the implementation process and prepared an evaluation report based on DeLone and McLean's [13] success model. The report concludes that more needs to be done if the FHS is to obtain proper value and payoff from its HIS implementation. The users were satisfied with the solution and they derived very good support from it in their clinical work, but no initiatives regarding harvesting the potential benefits had been planned or implemented [14].

One of the main challenges identified during Action Cycle 1 was to establish a method to solve the identified problem of emergent public IT value in a situation where neither a business case nor a formal description of hoped-for benefits guiding the process existed. Senior management wanted to attain more value and a greater payoff from the HIS implementation but had not formulated a specific strategy which could direct benefit realization.

The use of action research has become widely accepted [15] and work has been done to conceptualize the concept to be able to understand and enhance the different elements of action research practice, which is often divided into problem-solving and research cycles [16]. In the present study we collected and applied empiricism about the Methodologies used during the problem-solving cycle during the first two phases of the Foresee project as shown in Fig. 2.

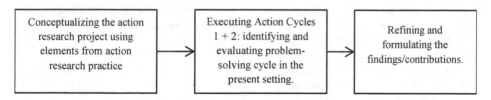

Fig. 2. The research process

As the aim is to contribute to the problem-solving cycle in our case *how to* achieve value from investing in and implementing HIS—the following analysis will go through the action research cycles and show how the different activities led to specific artifacts and hence contributed to the overall research.

Where the aim of Action Cycle #1 (setting the stage for benefit realization) was to understand the context of the project (and hence the area of concern of the research) and identify a pilot project, the aim of Action Cycle #2 was to establish a baseline and execute the pilot to learn more about and structure the problem-solving cycle.

3   The Action Research Process

We have had a high degree of interaction with the FHS [17] and used a variety of research methods in the two action cycles executed ('Setting the stage for benefit realization' and 'Benefit realization in the pilot area'). This is specified in Table 1 below [adapted from 18]:

Table 1. Summary of action research

Action Cycle #1 (Fall 2010–end 2011)	Action Cycle #2 (Spring 2011–2014)
Diagnosing	
HIS was operational for 530 health professionals in fall 2010. However, senior management wanted to achieve more value and payoff from the HIS implementation. FHS has not formulated a specific strategy which could direct benefit realization, so the first part of the action research project was exploratory, aiming to identify potential benefit areas for different stakeholders.	There was an on-going discussion during the first quarter of 2011 in order to define the scope for the pilot area and organize the project. Care for stroke (apoplexy) patients was selected as the pilot area and Action Cycle 2 began in Spring 2011. The diagnostic phase for Action Cycle 2 has thus mainly been a decision process for FHS to determine where to do the pilot.
Action planning	
The planning phase involved activities such as preparing a semi-structured interview guide which was formulated from IS value literature [e.g. 2, 19, 20]. A pilot interview was conducted with the former project manager of the HIS implementation project (November 2010), which brought about several changes to the interview guide such as framing and focusing questions for health professionals. The former project manager also helped us to shape the first cycle for the medical ward at the national hospital because they had the most mature implementation of HIS (operational since 2009). Interviewees were selected and interviews planned.	The planning was done in May 2011. Action Cycle 1 has mainly been driven by the researchers as a research activity, but Action Cycle 2 has to be driven by FHS as an ordinary project in order to succeed. An FHS project manager was appointed. Several workshops and a steering committee meeting were held in May 2011 in order to initiate the project. The main areas covered were: Project Management: Goals, scope, organization, planning, workshop process and risks were discussed [21]. Process modeling: Description of the care for stroke patients using swim lane diagrams [22].

(*Continued*)

Table 1. (*Continued*)

Action Cycle #1 (Fall 2010–end 2011)	Action Cycle #2 (Spring 2011–2014)
Action taking	
Seven interviews with health professionals (doctors, nurses, administrators and a secretary) at management level were conducted in December 2011. We presented a preliminary table with action areas derived from the interviews at a management meeting immediately after the seven interviews were conducted. Two action areas were selected as possible candidates for the benefit realization pilot, i.e., the medical process and patient care for stroke patients.	June 2011: Further process modeling was undertaken and a draft of specification key performance indicators (KPIs) were prepared and linked to the process model. The project was named: "The good stroke care course". September 2011: A questionnaire was completed by 37 health professionals and seven were interviewed. The questionnaire and interviews were about health professionals' views on the stroke care course. This will be used as a baseline. September 2011 to November 2011: The questionnaire and interviews were analyzed. The process model and KPIs were revised. November 2011: The process model and KPIs were again discussed. Two pilot stroke patient interviews were held. All 40 patient records related to stroke in 2011 were reviewed by healthcare professionals, assisted by researchers. February 2012: The configuration of HIS to support the stroke process model and KPIs were discussed. 2013–2014: Ongoing support to the pilot ward and the implementation agency in the ministry to secure progress.
Evaluation & Learning	
Data sources Documents, seven interviews and focus group meeting. *Data analysis* The interviews were taped, transcribed verbatim and coded in NVivo [23]. This resulted in 103 codes of which 38 codes were related to KPIs, such as: medication use and errors, and length of stay at hospital.	*Data sources* Documents, process model with KPIs, questionnaire, nine interviews and a number of workshops, and a review of 40 patient records. *Data analysis* The interviews were transcribed and briefly coded. The questionnaire was analyzed using descriptive statistics. The workshops were the intervention arena to produce the process model and KPIs. A review of 40 patient records was undertaken to establish a baseline for several KPIs. Redoing of reviews of patient records and KPI's due to difficulties to assure a consistent interpretation of content.

All activities were presented and evaluated in sessions with the researchers of the action research project. Two of the important artifacts produced during the problem-solving cycle (a process diagram and a table of Key Process Indicators) are shown in Annex A.

4   Towards a Problem-Solving Method for Emergent IT Public Value

We have proposed a problem-solving method for emergent IT public value based on the experience derived from the two cycles in the AR process. The method should be seen as a conceptual method that will have to be adapted to the situational and contextual circumstances of a given organization [inspired by 24]. The method is shown in Fig. 3.

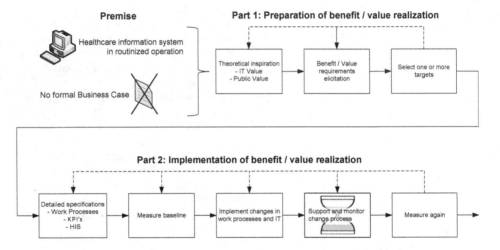

Fig. 3. The problem-solving method for emergent IT public value

Figure 3 shows that the premise for the method is a stabilized and routinized HIS [25] and that no formal business case has been specified [26].

Part 1 deals with the preparation of benefit/value realization. This part starts with consideration of the theoretical underpinnings of IT Value [e.g. 27] and public value [e.g. 28]. This is followed by the elicitation of more specific benefit/value requirements together with the agreed stakeholders. Part 1 ends with a management decision about which benefits/value targets should be selected and possibly the prioritization of the targets (e.g., a pilot area could be selected, as in our case with 'care for stroke patients').

Part 2 is the actual implementation of measures to accomplish the selected targets. This part starts with a detailed discussion about work processes, KPI's and the supporting HIS (see Table 1 for an example of specified KPIs). The next step is to measure the baseline which could be undertaken using surveys, questionnaires, interviews, measurements, etc. This step is followed by a more "traditional IT project", where the agreed changes in work processes and IT are implemented; in our case, with the 'care for stroke patients', this predominantly consists of reports in the HIS system and changed work processes, which could be sufficiently challenging. The changed work processes and the HIS system, now in operation, have to be supported and monitored to ensure that the suggested benefit/value realization is taking place. After six months to one year it is time to measure again and hopefully to measure some improvements.

The dashed lines and arrows in Fig. 2 indicate a highly iterative process in both Parts 1 and 2 which might be repeated many times. The implementation of HIS (or Enterprise Systems more broadly) is a continuous activity and the benefit/value focus is accordingly continuous.

5 Conclusion

The aim of this paper was to identify and specify a method for realizing benefits in the problem-solving phase of an emergent healthcare information systems action research project. The actions taken and their resulting artifacts are documented in Table 1, describing the two action research cycles. The suggested two-staged method (preparation of benefit/value realization and implementation of benefit/value realization) is shown in Fig. 3.

In future research it could be interesting to verify the developed model in other benefit realization projects.

Acknowledgements. The authors will hereby thank staff at the Faroese Ministry of Healthcare and at the wards for their assistance in this project. In addition we will extend our gratitude to reviewers and participants at the pre-ICIS ERP-workshop in Orlando for the valuable feedback on earlier versions of the paper.

References

1. Kohli, R., Grover, V.: Business value of IT: an essay on expanding research directions to keep up with the times. J. Assoc. Inf. Syst. **9**(1), 23–28, 30–34, 36–39 (2008)
2. Melville, N., Kraemer, K., Gurbaxani, V.: Information technology and organizational performance: an integrative model of it business value. MIS Q. **28**(2), 283–322 (2004)
3. Devaraj, S., Kohli, R.: Information technology payoff in the health-care industry: a longitudinal study. J. Manage. Inf. Syst. **16**(4), 41–67 (2000)
4. Friedman, C., Wyatt, J.: Evaluation Methods in Medical Informatics, vol. 19. Springer, New York (1997)
5. Murray, C.J.L., Frenk, J.: Ranking 37th - measuring the performance of the U.S. health care system. N. Eng. J. Med. **362**(2), 98–99 (2011)
6. Reeves, D., et al.: Analysis: how to identify when a performance indicator has run its course. BMJ **340**, c1717 (2011)
7. Chiasson, M.W., Davidson, E.: Pushing the contextual envelope: developing and diffusing IS theory for health information systems research. Inf. Organ. **14**(3), 155–188 (2004)

8. Hough, C.B.H., Chen, J.C.H., Lin, B.: Virtual health/electronic medical record: current status and perspective. Int. J. Healthc. Technol. Manage. **6**(3), 1 (2005)
9. Schlichter, B.R.: Development of trust during large scale system implementation. J. Cases Inf. Technol. **12**(2), 1–17 (2010)
10. Berg, M.: Patient care information systems and health care work: a sociotechnical approach. Int. J. Med. Inform. **55**(2), 87–101 (1999)
11. Van de Ven, A.H.: Engaged Scholarship: A Guide for Organizational and Social Research. Oxford University Press, New York (2007)
12. Myers, M.D.: Qualitative Research in Business & Management. Sage Publications, London (2009)
13. DeLone, W.H., McLean, E.R.: The DeLone and McLean model of information systems success: a ten-year update. J. Manage. Inf. Syst. **19**(4), 9–30 (2003)
14. Andersen, P.E.R., et al.: Effektvurdering af EPJ/THS i det færøske sundhedsvæsen. Aarhus School of Business, Aarhus (2010)
15. Baskerville, R., Myers, M.D.: Special issue on action research in information systems: making is research relevant to practice–foreword. MIS Q. **28**(3), 329–335 (2004)
16. Mathiassen, L., Chiasson, M., Germonprez, M.: Style composition in action research publication. MIS Q. **36**(2), 347–363 (2012)
17. Svejvig, P., Andersen, P.E.R.: Setting the stage for benefit realization of healthcare IS: The voice of health professionals. In: OASIS Pre-ICIS workshop. Shanghai, 2011
18. Lindgren, R., Henfridsson, O.: Design principles for competence management systems: a synthesis of an action research study. Manage. Inf. Syst. Q. **28**(3), 4 (2004)
19. Seddon, P.B., et al.: Dimensions of information systems success. Commun. AIS **2**(3es), 5 (1999)
20. Smith, H., Fingar, P.: Business Process Management: The Third Wave. Meghan-Kiffer Press, Tampa (2003)
21. Larson, E.W., Gray, C.F.: Project Management: The Managerial Process. Irwin/McGraw-Hill Series in Operations and Decision Sciences, 5th edn. (International edition). McGraw-Hill Irwin, Boston (2011)
22. Harmon, P.: Business Process Change: A Guide for Business Managers and BPM and Six Sigma Professionals, 2nd edn. Morgan Kaufmann, Burlington (2007)
23. Bazeley, P.: Qualitative Data Analysis with NVivo. Sage Publications Ltd., London (2007)
24. Melin, U., Söderström, F.: Analyzing best practice and critical success factors in a health information system case – are there any shortcuts to successful it implementation? In: ECIS 2011 Proceedings. p. 175 (2011)
25. Markus, M.L., Tanis, C.: The enterprise systems experience-from adoption to success. In: Zmud, R.W. (ed.) Framing the Domains of IT Research: Glimpsing the Future Through the Past, pp. 173–207. Pinnaflex Educational Resources Inc., Cincinnati (2000)
26. Office of Government Commerce: Managing Successful Projects with PRINCE2. TSO, London (2009)
27. Seddon, P.B., Calvert, C., Yang, S.: A multi-project model of key factors affecting organizational benefits from enterprise systems. MIS Q. **34**(2), 305-A11 (2010)
28. Moore, M.H.: Managing for value: organizational strategy in for-profit, nonprofit, and governmental organizations. Nonprofit Voluntary Sect. Q. **29**(Suppl. 1), 183–208 (2000)

ERP System Procurement
in SMEs – Exploring How SMEs Specificities
Affect ERP Procurement in SMEs

Björn Johansson[1]($\boxtimes$), Romualdas Laurinavičius[2],
and Aidė Venčkauskaitė[3]

[1] Department of Informatics, School of Economics and Management,
Lund University, Lund, Sweden
bjorn.johansson@ics.lu.se
[2] UAB Pralo, Vilnius, Lithuania
romualdaslaur@gmail.com
[3] UAB Informacinės Konsultacijos, Vilnius, Lithuania
avenckauskaite@gmail.com

Abstract. Enterprise resource planning (ERP) systems have originally been developed for large enterprises (LEs). However, market saturation, integration of supply chains and technology improvements have led to small and medium-sized enterprises (SMEs) have started adopting ERP systems. Though there is a focus shift from LEs to SMEs in the ERP market, most academic literature on ERP systems is based on findings from LEs. In addition, while the ERP system adoption life cycle consists of three stages: procurement, implementation and post-implementation, academic discourse has mostly focused on implementation or post-implementation phases, indicating a knowledge gap on ERP system procurement stage, especially regarding procurement of ERP system in SMEs. In this study we explore how ERP system procurement is carried out in SMEs. Based on academic literature a theoretical framework on ERP system procurement in SMEs was built, which then was used as a foundation for the empirical investigation. Based on empirical findings we have identified two contrasting ways for how SMEs carry out ERP system procurement. The main contribution is the identification and the explanation of how SMEs specificities affect an ERP system procurement process in SMEs. One implication from this contribution is that it shows that SMEs are a too broad class of organization to do research on.

Keywords: Adoption · ERPs · SMEs · Procurement

1 Introduction

Enterprise Resource Planning (ERPs) systems have originally been designed for Large Enterprises (LEs), however, as many of these already adopted ERPs, a competitive focus shift from LEs to Small and Medium-sized Enterprises (SMEs) can be seen among ERP vendors [1–3]. A number of reasons have led to this shift, including: market saturation among LEs, integration of supply chains between LEs and SMEs, bigger number of SMEs compared to LEs, and technology developments leading to

© Springer International Publishing Switzerland 2015
D. Sedera et al. (Eds.): Pre-ICIS 2010-2012, LNBIP 198, pp. 119–137, 2015.
DOI: 10.1007/978-3-319-17587-4_8

lower hardware prices and software availability [2, 4]. In the paper we follow the European Commission [5] definition of SMEs, that defines three classes of enterprises: micro – employing up to 9 persons, SMEs, where small have 10 to 49 employees and medium from 50 to 249, and lastly large enterprises (LEs) employing 250 or more employees. According to European Commission [5] SMEs accounted for 99.8 % of all enterprises in EU in 2010. Though ERP system vendors have shifted their orientation towards SMEs, several authors [6–8] agree that most academic findings are based on studies of LEs, thus highlighting a lack of focus on SMEs in ERP system discourse.

An ERP system is a highly complex enterprise system that automates and integrates business processes as well as all business transactions in order to provide information as a unified enterprise view of the business for decision-making [9–11]. Despite that ERPs often are seen as a way to increase strategic and competitive advantage, now they are also considered to be, as Kumar and Van Hillegersberg, [12] state, "the price of entry for running a business".

Taking into consideration significant financial investment that is made, potential risks and benefits of ERP implementation, selection of an appropriate ERP system is considered to be extremely important [13]. While successful selection of an ERP system may lead to overall project success, wrong selection may either cause failure of the project or lower the possible benefits of the system as well as company's competitive advantage [14, 15]. However, as Wei, et al. [14] state, "due to limitations in available resources, the complexity of ERP systems, and the diversity of alternatives", selecting an ERP solution is a time consuming and highly complicated task.

The ERP system adoption life cycle can be described as consisting of three stages: procurement, implementation and post-implementation [16]. Our focus in this research is on the procurement stage (also referred to as pre-implementation or acquisition), which begins when the initial idea of adopting an ERP system receives support from management and ends once an ERP solution is purchased from a chosen vendor [17]. Important to clarify is that in our view this stage take place and is the same independent of how the actual implementation is done. In other words this means that the procurement stage is independent from the implementation decision and if it is to implement "on-site" or if for instance using Software-as-a-Service (SaaS) or any other form of Cloud Computing.

Doing research on ERP procurement in SMEs is interesting for at least two reasons: Firstly, research has focused either on implementation or post-implementation, leaving the procurement phase unexplored [17], Secondly, ERP research with a focus on SMEs is scarce especially in the procurement phase with a focus on SMEs specificities and peculiarities. It can be claimed that a number of obstacles are faced by SMEs when implementing ERP systems due to their specificities and peculiarities. Firstly, SMEs do not possess large amounts of financial resources; therefore ERP system implementation is a relatively large investment [1, 2]. Secondly, SMEs do not have a special team dedicated to handle the implementation and post-implementation work [2]. In addition, SMEs seldom rely on formal business strategies, and often approach IS management in a non-formal way, making decisions not based on formal information and decision models [1]. Lastly, the procurement process most likely involves several parties: the client-user organization, and an external consultancy firm helping the client organization [10]. This results in a process, where ERP system purchase decision is a product of collaborative work between several parties. However, all this is more or less speculations since there is a lack of research reported in this area. For that reason we address the following research question: *How is the procurement phase of ERPs carried out in SMEs?*

The rest of the chapter is organized as follows: The next section shortly positions research on ERPs in SMEs and presents some relevant SME specificities. Following sections discuss the importance of ERP system procurement process and describe procurement frameworks found in literature. The ERP system procurement stages described in literature are also presented. Section 6 describes the research method, followed by a discussion around factors involved in ERP procurement in SMEs. Section 7 then presents an analysis of the two contrasting ways found in the empirical data. The model explaining the relationships between the SME specificities and the procurement process is illustrated with an example from the empirical data, followed by the final section which presents some concluding remarks and some thoughts on future research.

2   ERPs in SMEs

It can be claimed that ERPs were originally developed for large manufacturing organizations [1, 13, 18], in fact, Shehab, et al. [19] claim: "It is a fact that ERP is for big firms". However, market saturation of ERPs among LEs, the pressure from large organizations, and the shift of ERP vendors to smaller organizations, have led to more and more SMEs adopting ERPs [4, 19, 20]. A recent study in Sweden shows that 38 per cent of all companies with more than 10 employees have adopted an ERP [21], which clearly indicate that ERPs are of interest also for SMEs.

A number of authors have indicated that the specificity of SMEs has a strong impact on ERP system adoption by these organizations [1, 2, 4, 22]. The general assumption that the principles of a big business apply to a smaller business in a smaller scale has been investigated by Welsh and White [23] and fundamental differences between LEs and SMEs have been identified. According to Welsh et al. [23], the management of SMEs is characterized by: "severe constraints on financial resources, a lack of trained personnel, and a short-range management perspective imposed by volatile competitive environment".

Raymond [24] has proposed a model, showing four dimensions of organizational specificity that might affect the success of IS implementation in small businesses. Based on Raymond's [24] model, Gable and Stewart [4] illustrate specificities of SMEs that have a significant effect on ERP system adoption. The framework, as shown in Table 1, analyses SMEs in four dimensions, including: organizational, decisional, psycho-sociological and information systems, and lists the factors affecting ERP system adoption specific to SMEs. Below we shortly describe the four dimensions:

Organizational Dimension. As SMEs are commonly arranged in a simple and centralized structure, their management has broad control over ERP related activities. However, simplicity of a structure implies less specialization of functions among employees, thus requiring more generic ERP solutions. In addition, size of SMEs determines that these organizations can hardly control their extra-organizational situation, therefore it can be said they have less influence on the market and less power when negotiating with ERP vendors. Lastly, due to their size, SMEs are resource poor both in terms of financial and human capital, thus only a limited number of individuals can be allocated to system implementation and maintenance and their ERP system choice is often determined by financial constraints.

Decisional Dimension. As SMEs have little influence on the market situation, they need to be highly responsive to changes in their business environment. Therefore, decisions in SMEs are often reactive and short term. In addition, SME decision makers rarely use formal management or decision making strategies. In fact, they base their decisions on less information and rely on personal judgment. For these reasons, SMEs tend to underestimate potential costs or benefits of ERP solution alternatives, thus it is more likely that a chosen system will not be the best fitting among alternatives. The factor "Organizational Maturity" was not mentioned by Gable and Stewart [4], but was noted by Raymond [24], however, we see it as relevant and therefore it is included in the table.

Psycho-Sociological Dimension. The CEOs of SMEs commonly have the highest authority in these organizations, and are often characterized as unwilling to share information or delegate decision making to other employees. A CEO being the only one making ERP implementation related decisions may result in evaluation of alternative ERP solutions lacking critical attitudes from other individuals. In addition, Gable and Stewart [4] have identified that lack of ERP system knowledge and experience among CEOs, may result that CEOs have lower expectations from systems and are less critical when evaluating them.

Information System Dimension. Lack of managerial expertise, IS experience and training could result in that SME managers being unaware of potential benefits that sufficient IS management can deliver to organizations, thus functionality of ISs is underestimated. Usually functionality of SME's ISs is in its early stages of evolution, or serving as a tool for accounting. Furthermore, lack of technical expertise determines low level of system sophistication, therefore mostly transactional and packaged applications are used. Lastly, unawareness of potential benefits that ISs may bring leads to ISs being underutilized by SMEs, having little impact on decisional and organizational effectiveness.

Further on the topic of ERP systems in SMEs has been further discussed by other authors. For instance, Ravarini, et al. [1], which in their study of ERP system acquisitions by SMEs, name a number of SME peculiarities that determine the suitability of an ERP system for the SME:

- Adoption of ERP systems is often imposed by exogenous factors, rather than being a voluntary strategic decision. Therefore, little time is spent rethinking IS alternatives, IS management is approached in a non-formal way;
- SMEs are strictly financially constrained, however require highly customized ERP solutions;
- SMEs seek solutions that do not impose important organizational change.

Table 1. SME specificities affecting ERP system implementation [4]

Dimension	Factors	Description
Organizational	Structure	Simple and centralized
	Resource	Resource poverty
	Extra-organizational situation	Uncontrollable
Decisional	Decision cycle	Short term, reactive
	Decision process	Intuitive and judgmental Less use of information Less use of formal management techniques
	Organizational maturity	Immature
Psycho-sociological	Domination by the CEO	Less sharing of information Less delegation of decision making
	Management ideology	More individualistic
	Psychological climate	More positive attitudes Less expectations of organizational computing
Information systems	IS function	In its earlier stages Less managerial expertise, IS experience and training
	IS sophistication	Emphasis on transactional and packaged applications Less technical expertise
	IS success	Underutilization of organizational IS Little impact on decisional and organizational effectiveness

Morabito, et al. [2] have also noted the financial and human capital constraints faced by SMEs previously mentioned by both Gable and Stewart [4] and Ravarini, et al. [1]. In addition, the authors identified, that SMEs in an attempt to avoid lock-ins in ERP systems, unless absolutely certain about future requirements, hesitate to purchase these systems.

The question is then how these specificities affect ERP system procurement in SMEs.

3 Importance of ERP Procurement Process

In order to survive organizations need to overcome numerous obstacles. Companies are surrounded by a constantly changing business environment, compete with their products, deliveries, price and quality, aiming to bring the best customer satisfaction while remaining flexible and responsive [13]. In order to remain competitive in these dynamic markets organizations adopt ERP systems [12]. ERP systems are business management systems consisting of integrated sets of comprehensive software, which are used to manage and integrate various functions and processes within an enterprise [18, 19].

The established benefits that successful implementation of an ERP system brings to an organization has made ERP systems become widespread among many companies. In fact, implementing an ERP system is defined as "the price of entry for running a business" [12] or as a necessity to remain connected to other enterprises in a network economy [25], because multinational organizations often limit their partners to those using the same ERP software as themselves [19].

The recognized ERP system contribution to the competitive performance of organizations, has resulted that ERP software is currently among the fastest growing segments within information technology (IT) industry [26]. In addition, market research shows that average ERP software costs, project costs and project duration have been decreasing within the last years [27]. ERP software market has matured to level, where more and more generic ERP software is being customized, thus niche markets are creating niche products and niche vendors [28]. These reasons illustrate that ERP software market is maturing, more and more software is being tailored to suit specific needs of organizations, while at the same time ERP software costs are decreasing, thus ERP software is becoming more available.

Faced with the challenges of a global dynamic market, and pressured by other companies, organizations often rush to implement ERP systems [13]. Being exposed to the variety of alternatives of ERP software while disposing limited resources, makes the selection process tedious and complicated [14].

Often organizations base their selection on the conventional financial cost and benefits criteria or other common criteria, which are not tailored to organization's requirements, competitive strengths and business strategies [13, 14]. Having no systematic selection framework results in decisions where a chosen system does not meet the organizational requirements, it conflicts with organizational goals, thus is insufficient to support organization's performance [14].

Organizations often do not realize that selection of an appropriate system is a significant decision. Many times new IT systems are adopted to "mechanize old ways of doing business" or pave the "cow paths", which however, does not address initial deficiencies of organization's performance [29]. Changes imposed by the implementation of an ERP system, are described as: "all-or-nothing proposition with an uncertain result" [29]. A particular system has enterprise-wide implications, requires resource commitment, and implies potential risks as well as benefits related to its implementation [18]. In fact, some describe it to be "a decision on how to shape the organizational business" as ERP systems lock organizational processes and principles in its software [18]. In addition, ERP systems tend to replace majority of organization's legacy systems, therefore implementation of an ERP system is often the largest IT investment in any organization [13]. A wrong choice may have adverse effects on multiple areas of an organization, in worst case may even threaten the existence of an organization [30].

The reasons mentioned above illustrate that selecting and purchasing an appropriate ERP solution significantly impacts both the overall ERP project and the organization, thus highlighting the need for a systematic framework for ERP acquisition.

4   ERP Procurement Frameworks

Since, ERP acquisition is highly complicated and time consuming, various approaches are suggested for conducting and managing the ERP procurement process [14]. One of the methods for selecting an ERP solution was proposed by Ptak [31], suggesting that alternative ERP solutions should be quantitatively compared using a developed weighting of critical system elements, thus providing subjective judgments of the acquisition team. Teltumbde [13] developed a framework where an ERP solution is selected using: the Nominal Group Technique - for development of pre-selection criteria, and adopting the Analytical Hierarchy Process (AHP) for joint evaluation, based on ten system evaluation criteria. The AHP method was also used in a framework developed by Wei, et al. [14], where it served as an evaluation method, judging on criteria representing a system's ability to fulfill its objectives. Wei and Wang [32] suggest using fuzzy set theory to determine system's suitability and rank suitable vendors. Kutlu and Akpinar [33] propose using the fuzzy methodology to distinctively categorize alternative choices.

Other methods for evaluating ERP solution alternatives include: 0-1 programming [34–36], nonlinear programming [37] analytical network processing [36] and the data envelopment approach [38].

It is important to notice that many of these frameworks use sophisticated mathematical calculations, which according to Wei, et al. [14] weaken these methods as they are hard to understand and many of the suggested evaluation attributes are difficult to quantify in real world. In addition, for necessary data to be obtained for the calculations, the models predetermine processes that are carried out during the system procurement. This emphasizes the final system evaluation and the purchase decision, while looks down on other activities of procurement process. For this reason, the models are claimed to lack consideration of different data sources and organization's strategic concerns [14].

A more generic approach is described by Stefanou [16] suggesting an ex-ante system evaluation approach, considering four phases of system life cycle. However, this method mostly focuses on system cost and benefit identification for comparison of alternatives, but does not evaluate a system's suitability or fitness to the organization's needs. Another model is suggested by Verville and Halingten [39], presenting ERP system procurement analyzed from Organizational Buying Behavior field's perspective. The model consists of six stages of the buying process of an ERP system, presenting a high-level overview of the buying principles observed in organizations. Nonetheless, the high-level approach of the model determines that the stages described lack detail and specificity for use in ERP software procurement – the authors claim the model "depicts the principal processes that pertain to the acquisition of packaged software" [39]. However, as it was discussed in previous sections due to their enterprise-wide implications ERP systems are more significant than most packaged software.

To provide a base for the theoretical framework of this study a procurement framework suggested by Poon and Yu [17] was chosen. The authors present four stages of ERP solution procurement process and demonstrate the framework in use in four case organizations. The reasons this framework [17] was chosen are, firstly, the suggested procurement stages are more generic than those suggested by other authors mentioned above: as the framework is not based on a particular mathematical model or a decision making approach, it does not impose procurement steps only necessary for a certain method. Secondly, the suggested procurement stages are general and inclusive of other more detailed stages described by other authors, therefore providing a comprehensive overview of the procurement process. Lastly, while some other frameworks include phases or processes of: business vision [16] and implementation of a chosen system [32], which are out the scope of this study, this framework only illustrates the pre-implementation or procurement phase of ERP system adoption life cycle. The framework, as shown in Fig. 1, consists of four major stages involved in ERP procurement process, including: (1) Formation of the acquisition team, (2) examination of business requirements and constraints, (3) formation of evaluation criteria and (4) evaluation and selection of the best fit.

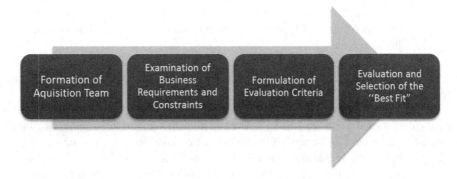

Fig. 1. ERP procurement process [17].

5 Research Framework

The developed research framework, shown in Fig. 2, graphically presents a condensed overview of the literature used in this study. The framework shows the relationship between ERP system procurement process and the specificities of SMEs.

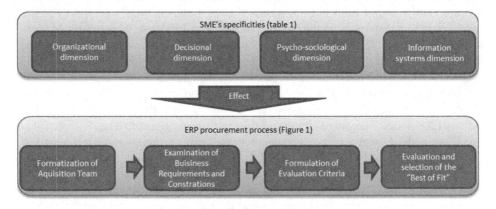

Fig. 2. Research framework.

The stages of ERP procurement process are based on a framework developed by Poon and Yu [17] as it is shown in Fig. 2. The specificities of SMEs shown in the framework present several dimensions of SME peculiarities that might affect ERP system procurement process presented by Gable and Stewart [4] and discussed by other authors [1, 2]. The one-sided arrow 'Effect', shown in Fig. 2, represents that in this study it is investigated how the specificities of SMEs affect the ERP procurement process, but not the opposite effects.

6 Research Method

In order to answer our research question it was necessary to collect empirical data that would include a detailed description of ERP procurement processes in SMEs and explain how SME specificities affect the procurement process. Although, numerous data sources are available, we believe that documents, archival records or similar sources of data are insufficient sources of evidence for our investigation as they are more attributable to the formal bureaucratic environment of large organizations. In contrast, SMEs are characterized as being non-formal, rarely relying on formal decision making or management techniques, and having few authoritative individuals involved in decision making [1, 4]. In addition, being resource poor and having a lower level of IS expertise, SMEs often turn to consulting companies for help in EP selection and implementation [4, 10]. For these reasons, we believe that the most relevant sources of data necessary for our investigation are the individuals representing each of the parties involved in ERP system procurement in SMEs. We believe these individuals are aware of paths and details of the processes they are dealing with, and also possess knowledge about important information that might not be formally stored or documented in the dynamic environment of SMEs.

There are commonly three parties involved in ERP procurement process in SMEs: the buyer-user organization, the external consultancy firm, and the ERP vendor [10]. Therefore, to obtain a thorough and a comprehensive description of ERP system procurement in SMEs we chose to interview representatives of all three parties involved in the procurement process. We argue that the data collected from different parties would provide an objective overview of the procurement process and prevent bias which could likely occur if we would analyze the procurement from a single party's perspective. In addition, collecting data from different parties allowed us to validate findings from one informant with the data from interviews with others, and apply data triangulation, as suggested by Yin [40].

7 Discussing Factors Involved in ERP Procurement in SMES

Analyzing our empirical data, as it is presented in Table 2, we were able to identify two contrasting ways of carrying out ERP system procurement in SMEs: the more formal and the less formal way. However, in academic literature, when describing ERP system procurement, various authors [16, 17] identify or suggest a single way of carrying out this process. In addition, the procurement processes described by various authors

[13, 30] are often similar, include similar stages and follow a similar sequence, and comparing to our findings, resemble the more formal way of carrying out the procurement. The reason for this might be that academic literature describing ERP system procurement is based on findings from LEs, where ERP system procurement, according to one of the interviewed (General Manager in a consultant company), is commonly defined as a project and treated in a formal manner.

Table 2. Comparison of procurement process in empirical data and theory

Empirical data		Theoretical framework	
More Formal	**Less Formal**	**Stage**	**Requirement**
1. Need initiation	1.Need initiation	-	-
2. Acquisition team formation	-	1. Formation of Acquisition Team	Skills and roles of team members
			Diversity in acquisition team
			Assess the need of outside experts
3. Initial requirements definition	-	2. Examination of Business Requirement and Constraints	Determining objectives
4. Marketplace analysis	2.Marketplace analysis	4. Evaluation and Selection of the "Best Fit"	Marketplace analysis
5. Business processes analysis	-	2. Examination of Business Requirement and Constraints	Process mapping or business process reengineering
6. Developing a comprehensive requirement list and evaluation criteria	-	2. Examination of Business Requirement and Constraints	Defining requirements
			Describing constraints
		3. Formulation of Evaluation Criteria	Derivation from objectives and requirements
			Comprehensive and detailed list
			Vendor and system criteria
			Ranking
7. Request For Proposals (RFPs) and demonstrations	3.Meeting vendors and selecting	4. Evaluation and Selection of the "Best Fit"	Contacting vendor
8. Evaluation	-	4. Evaluation and Selection of the "Best Fit"	Selection and decision-making approach
			Authorization of the final choice

First, we have discovered that both more formal and less formal ERP procurement starts with a need initiation step, which is similar to the starting point of ERP acquisition phase as described by Poon and Yu [17]. They argue that procurement begins when the initiated idea of adopting an ERP system receives support from management, while our identified need initiation step defines organization's realization of a certain need and perceiving ERP system as a solution. Although, Poon and Yu [17] do not indicate the need initiation as a separate step, we believe it is necessary to include it as a distinct step of ERP system procurement, as our study shows that in case of SMEs the need for the system may origin either from outside or inside of the organization in that way affecting the path of the process.

Similarly to other authors [17, 39] we have identified the acquisition team formation step in the more formal ERP procurement process. However, in comparison to other studies we have found that team formation is not the first step in acquisition, but follows the need initiation. Also, our empirical data shows that in selection of team members, skills and roles of team members as well as diversity in acquisition team, which were mentioned by Poon and Yu [17], are not so important. In addition, although several informants (one General Manager, and two Consultants) indicate the existence of acquisition team, the actual formation step was not emphasized and not included in the less formal process.

In the more formal ERP procurement process, next step identified, is the initial requirements definition, which is similar to the objectives determination step as discussed by Wci, et al. [14]. As we have found that initial need is formalized into a business case description, similarly Verville and Halingten [39] indicate that it is important to define business problems and opportunities behind this initial rationale to adopt ERPs. On the other hand, we have not found evidence supporting previous studies [17, 32] stating that strategic objectives and goals of the project are determined and structured systematically.

It is also found that marketplace analysis is carried out in both more formal as well as less formal ERP procurement processes. This step resembles marketplace analysis step mentioned by Verville and Halingten [39]. However, while Verville and Halingten [39] emphasize the importance of establishing requirements as well as selection and evaluation criteria before contacting vendors or checking ERP solutions, our study shows that marketplace analysis is carried out after initial requirements formation. In addition, we have found the main information sources and ways used in vendor and system search, which are: asking for positive references from friends, acquaintances and employees, carrying out internet search or directly contacting familiar vendor brands. On contrary to other studies [14, 39], which suggest that a questionnaire is prepared and distributed to listed vendors inviting them to provide information, our empirical data shows that SMEs more rely on marketing demonstrations.

Next step identified in the more formal acquisition process is business processes analysis, which is similar to process mapping, discussed by Teltumbde [13]. However, we have found no evidence that business process re-engineering (BPR) is carried out at the same time as the ERP procurement process, as it is indicated by Wei et al. [32]. In addition, since business process analysis was not emphasized and was mentioned by only two interviewees (the General manager and one Consultant), it could be stated that SMEs tend to follow a more ERP-driven approach, where, according to Poon and Yu [17], explicit process redesign is excluded and organizations follow standard processes as well as "best" practices already incorporated in ERP system.

Regarding the more formal ERP procurement process, it is found that a comprehensive requirement list and evaluation criteria are developed, which has some properties of two stages: examination of business requirements and constraints as well as formulation of evaluation criteria, which are discussed by Poon and Yu [17]. However, we have not found clear separation between requirement list and evaluation criteria formation and our findings show that detailed requirement list comes from the evaluation criteria, when a certain ranking is assigned to each requirement group, which resembles evaluation criteria derivation from requirements as suggested by Wei, et al. [14]. In addition, we have found that evaluation criteria in SMEs has all the same properties mentioned by Poon and Yu [17], which are comprehensive and detailed list, vendor and system criteria as well as ranking.

Also in the more formal acquisition it is found that sending RFPs and performing demonstrations, which resemble the contacting vendor step, mentioned by Teltumbde [13] takes place. In addition, in comparison to other studies [17, 32], same two methods for information requesting are found: vendors are invited to respond RFPs or to make presentations and demonstrations on their ERP solutions. Similarly, in the less formal procurement, the step of meeting vendors and selecting is identified. However, this step only includes demonstrations of the systems, during which selection and evaluation of the systems is carried out based on presented system's capabilities.

In the more formal ERP procurement process, an evaluation step takes place, which has some similarities with evaluation and selection of the "best fit" phase, described by Poon and Yu [17]. Similarly to previous studies [14, 16], our empirical data shows that SMEs, following a more formal acquisition process, choose some kind of methodology for selection and decision-making, where the match between the evaluation criteria and the offered system is evaluated either quantitatively or using expert assessment. However, we have not found any formal authorization of the final choice in SMEs.

Finally, both the more formal and the less formal procurement process finalizes with the step of negotiation and a contract signing, which is similar to the negotiation step as defined by Verville and Halingten [39]. Although, Verville and Halingten [39] state that negotiations are entered when the final choice is made, we have found that in some cases (supported by statements from a Project Implementation Manager) negotiations are entered with several vendors that comply with basic requirements. In such case vendors are informed about their competition score and are allowed to change their proposal terms in order to be selected when the final choice is being made.

8   Analyzing the Two Contrasting Ways

Analyzing how interviewees describe ERP procurement processes we have identified two contrasting ways of conducting procurement: the more formal and the less formal way, shown in Table 2. In addition, we have found that factors depending on their characteristics, presented in Table 1, influence the way SMEs carry out ERP procurement. The influence a factor's characteristic has on the procurement process is identified based on the "cause-and-effect" explanations by our interviewees.

When talking about certain factors our interviewees often used the formulation "if-then", for example one of the Consultants stated:

"If the level of maturity is zero and experience is primary, everything happens relatively elementary <...> If the maturity level is higher or they have some experience or got „burnt", then search is carried out a bit differently."

This example and other findings show that the effect of factor characteristics is either leading organizations towards the more formal or the less formal procurement process. Therefore, based on our empirical data, we have identified, which character-istics of each factor point towards the more formal and, in contrast, the less formal way of conducting procurement. Although, in academic discourse several authors [1, 4] argue that ERP implementation lifecycle and acquisition may be considerably influ-enced by the characteristics of SMEs, it is not discussed how the process of procure-ment is affected by these issues.

In Fig. 3 we present all the factors found that affect an ERP procurement process as well as their characteristics determining whether an organization is likely to carry out ERP procurement in the more formal or the less formal way. However, in some cases interviewees presented only one characteristic of the factors as well as discussed only one side of effect, for instance, that insufficient human resources dedicated to IT lead to the less formal process. For those factors, as shown in Fig. 3, we left one arrow marked with a question mark, because we believe that those effects may exist, but enough empirical evidence supporting them was not found.

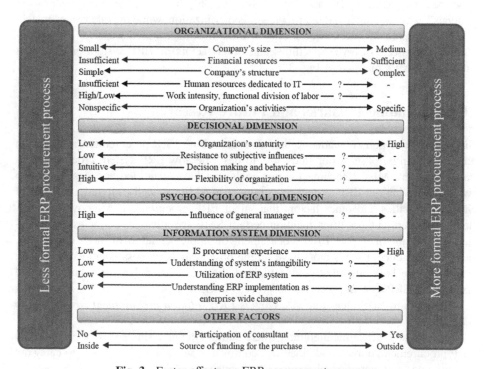

Fig. 3. Factor effects on ERP procurement process

9 Illustrating Discussions

In this section the effect of SME specificities and factors on ERP system procurement in SMEs is illustrated by relating the factors and specificities shown in Fig. 3 to a real life system procurement example presented by one of the interviewees questioned during this study.

Based on interviewee's descriptions, a characteristic for every factor that best defines our informant's organization was chosen, for example, interviewee's organization has 100-120 employees, thus the organization's size is defined as medium sized. Once the characteristics of all factors were defined, Fig. 3 was checked to see which procurement process a certain characteristic is pointing to, and the column "Procurement Type" for each factor was filled. Lastly, the actual procurement process carried out in interviewee's organization was compared, to the one mostly suggested for this type of organization in the column "Procurement type". The comparison of procurement processes is presented in Table 4.

After the analysis of organizational, decisional, psycho-sociological, information system and other factor characteristics in this particular organization, as shown in Table 3, it can be seen that most of the characteristics indicate that ERP system procurement process is likely to be carried out in a more formal way according to Fig. 3. Looking at Table 4, which shows the procurement steps in interviewee's organization and compares them to our identified more formal procurement process, it can be seen, that the procurement process carried out in interviewee's example is very similar to our described more formal ERP acquisition process. Only one step, the "business process analysis", was not conducted in interviewee's organization, while the other steps match.

The example of interviewee's organization illustrates our discussion by demonstrating the effects of SME specifities and other factors on ERP system procurement process in SMEs pictured in Fig. 3.

10 Concluding Remarks and Future Research

Since the major part of academic literature describing ERP procurement is based on LEs, the main purpose of our study was to describe how ERP system procurement is carried out in SMEs. Reaching for our goals, we have identified and described two ways of carrying out ERP system procurement in SMEs as well as found a number of SME specificities and other factors that affect ERP procurement. Moreover, in academic literature authors often mention certain SME specificities, obstacles and peculiarities that might impact ERP procurement or implementation in these companies, however, the effect these factors have on the procurement process is not explained. In our study we have identified and explained the relationship between our identified factors and ERP system procurement process in SMEs.

The main research question was: *How is ERP solution procurement carried out in SMEs?*

In contrast to academic literature, where authors define a single way of carrying out ERP procurement, our study defined two contrasting ways SMEs are likely to carry out procurement: the more formal and the less formal way. While the more formal process resembles the procurement process described in academic literature and presented in our theoretical framework, we have not found the less formal process discussed in academic discourse. We find it surprising that, although, academic literature clearly indicates the obstacles that SMEs encounter during ERP procurement and implementation process, different sequence or steps of the procurement process imposed by the obstacles are not presented. We believe the reason for why the less formal process is not discussed is that existing research is based on findings from LEs, who tend to consider system acquisitions as projects and treat them in a more formal manner.

Table 3. Characteristics of the organization in the procurement example

	Factors	Description of the organization of I5	Characteristic	Procurement type
Organizational	Company's size	100-120 employees	Medium	More formal
	Financial resources	The system procurement was financed by the EU funds	Sufficient	More formal
	Company's structure	Several departments exist in two cities	Complex	More formal
	Human resources dedicated to IT	Project Implementation Manager responsible for IS development and IT department of 7 employees	Sufficient	?
	Work intensity/ functional division of labor	Several departments responsible for different functions exist. Acquisition team for ERP procurement was formed.	- / High	-/?
	Organizations activities	Only few solutions in the world suit organization's activities, combining a study management IS together with an accounting system	Specific	More formal
Decisional	Organization's maturity	-	-	-
	Resistance to subjective influences	The need for ERP system emerged inside of company, when they outgrew the capacity of previous system. Marketplace analysis was conducted using internet search. Systems were evaluated using a predefined method.	High	?
	Decision making and behavior	An Excel table was filled according to the proposals received, then coefficients were calculated and used when selecting system	Rational	?
	Flexibility of organization	-	-	-
Psycho-Sociological	Influence of general manager	Infrastructure manager was a person making the final decision	Low	?

(Continued)

Table 3. (*Continued*)

Information system	IS procurement experience	The company has a procurement experience, as they had previously implemented a similar system	High	More formal
	Understanding of system's intangibility	The company had not only evaluated system's price and technical qualities, but also vendor's reliability and technical support. Procurement was treated as a project.	High	?
	Utilization of ERP system	Organization's IS consists of an accounting and a study management system, which are integrated. System serves the needs of 70 employees working with the core of the system and 3000 students.	High	?
	Understanding ERP system as enterprise-wide change	Working groups consisting of employees from different departments were formed to determine system's requirements	High	?
Other	Participation of consultant	Consultants were employed for the selection project	Yes	More formal
	Source of funding for the purchase	The system procurement was financed by the EU funds	Outside	More formal

Table 4. Comparison of more formal and the sample SME's procurement process

More formal procurement steps	Procurement steps in sample SME
Need initiation	Need initiation
Acquisition team formation	Acquisition team formation
Initial requirements definition	Initial requirements definition
Marketplace analysis	Marketplace analysis issue arises
Business processes analysis	–
Developing a comprehensive requirement list and evaluation criteria	Developing a comprehensive requirement list and evaluation criteria
RFPs and demonstrations	RFPs and demonstrations
Evaluation	Evaluation
Negotiation and signing the contract	Negotiation and signing the contract

The starting point for our study was that the size of organizations is the main source of differences in ERP system procurement process between LEs and SMEs. However, we have found that the category of SMEs is too broad, as differences between procurement processes carried out in SMEs appear. The small companies tend to purchase ERP in the less formal way, while medium sized organizations choose the more formal process. In addition to organization's size, we have also identified a number of other SME specificities and other factors that affect ERP procurement process and determine the way it is carried out.

As mentioned above, the study concludes that there exist two contrasting ERP solution procurement processes carried out in SMEs: the more formal and the less formal way. The main difference between these processes is that the more formal procurement consists of more steps, has a dedicated acquisition team, uses explicit requirements and evaluation criteria, and makes use of rational decision making methods for system evaluation and selection. On the other hand, even those steps, which are similar in both ways, the less formal way are carried out more intuitively, chaotically and primitively, thus we consider the more formal way a more sophisticated way of procurement.

Furthermore, most of our identified ERP solution procurement stages carried out by SMEs were mentioned and described in academic literature. However, we have identified one additional step, the Need Initiation, which we have not found presented before, but it was mentioned by all of our interviewees. The importance of this step is that the need may arise from different sources: either from inside or outside of a company and this determines how much the sequence of the process will be influenced by subjective sources, such as vendors. In addition, our findings show that SMEs are not very familiar with ERP system functionalities and market, thus are not able to develop a comprehensive requirement list and evaluation criteria prior to marketplace analysis. Therefore, differently from academic discourse, our findings show that, in SMEs only some initial requirements are set before carrying out the marketplace analysis, while the detailed requirements are developed only afterwards.

From our empirical data we have identified a number of SME specificities and other factors that affect ERP procurement in SMEs. Our findings support many factors presented in academic literature, however, we have also found a number of factors that are not mentioned in the discourse. Among the key factors determining ERP procurement process, organization's maturity and IS procurement experience were identified. In addition, we have found two, not organization related, factors that also affect ERP system procurement in SMEs and were not mentioned in literature, including: Participation of a Consultant and Source of Funding for the Purchase. However, our main contribution is not identifying the factors but relating the factors to ERP procurement in SMEs and answering the "how" part of the question.

In contrast to academic literature, where SMEs are described providing only one characteristic for a given factor, for example, the financial resources are in general characterized as insufficient, we have found that an SME might have one of the contrasting characteristics of the same factor, for instance, a company might have either a low or a high level of organization's maturity. Depending on these contrasting characteristics of the procuring organization, our identified SME specificities and other factors can have a different effect on ERP system procurement: a factor may either lead organization to carry out the procurement in a more formal way or, in contrary, a less formal way.

Moreover, we have developed a model explaining how SME specificities and other factors affect ERP procurement depending on organization's characteristics. Each factor we have identified should have a two sided effect and contrasting characteristics determining whether an organization is likely to carry out ERP procurement in more or less formal way. However, for some factors we have found only one characteristic and one sided effect, thus further research may be conducted searching for other two-sided effects and finalizing our model.

References

1. Ravarini, A., Tagliavini, M., Pigni, F., Sciuto, D.: A framework for evaluating ERP acquisition within SMEs. In: Proceedings of the AIM International Conference, Montpellier (2000)
2. Morabito, V., Pace, S., Previtali, P.: ERP marketing and Italian SMEs. Eur. Manag. J. 23(5), 590–598 (2005)
3. Van Everdingen, Y., Van Hillegersberg, J., Waarts, E.: ERP adoption by Eurpean midsize companies. Commun. ACM 43(4), 27–31 (2000)
4. Gable, G., Stewart, G.: SAP R/3 implementation issues for small to medium enterprises. In: Proceedings of the 5th Americas Conference on Information Systems (AMCIS), Milwaukee (1999)
5. European Commission: Annual Report on EU SMEs 2010/2011, in Editor (Ed.)^(Eds.): Book Annual Report on EU SMEs 2010/2011 (2011)
6. Haddara, M., Zach, O.: ERP systems in SMEs: a literature review. In: Proceeding of the 44th Hawaii International Conference on System Sciences, Kauai, HI, USA, 4-7 May 2011
7. Loh, T.C., Koh, S.C.L.: Critical elements for a successful enterprise resource planning implementation in small- and medium-sized enterprises. Int. J. Prod. Res. 42(17), 3433–3455 (2004)
8. Muscatello, J.R., Small, M.H., Chen, I.J.: Implementing enterprise resource planning (ERP) systems in small and midsize manufacturing firms. Int. J. Oper. Prod. Manag. 23(8), 850–871 (2003)
9. Umble, E.J., Haft, R.R., Umble, M.M.: Enterprise resource planning: implementation procedures and critical success factors. Eur. J. Oper. Res. 146(2), 241–257 (2003)
10. Andersson, A., Wilson, T.L.: Contracted ERP projects: sequential progress, mutual learning, relationships, control and conflicts. Int. J. Manag. Proj. Bus. 4(3), 458–479 (2011)
11. Baki, B., Cakar, K.: Determining the ERP package-selecting criteria: the case of Turkish manufacturing companies. Bus. Process Manag. J. 11(1), 75–86 (2005)
12. Kumar, K., Van Hillegersberg, J.: ERP experiences and evolution. Commun. ACM 43(4), 22–26 (2000)
13. Teltumbde, A.: A framework for evaluating ERP projects. Int. J. Prod. Res. 38(17), 4507–4520 (2000)
14. Wei, C.C., Chien, C.F., Wang, M.J.J.: An AHP-based approach to ERP system selection. Int. J. Prod. Econ. 96(1), 47–62 (2005)
15. Sen, C.G., Baracli, H., Sen, S.: A literature review and classification of enterprise software selection approaches. Int. J. Inf. Technol. Decis. Making 8(2), 217–238 (2009)
16. Stefanou, C.J.: A framework for the ex-ante evaluation of ERP software. Eur. J. Inf. Syst. 10(4), 204–215 (2001)
17. Poon, P.L., Yu, Y.T.: Investigating ERP systems procurement practice: Hong Kong and Australian experiences. Inf. Softw. Technol. 52(10), 1011–1022 (2010)
18. Kumar, V., Maheshwari, B., Kumar, U.: Enterprise resource planning systems adoption process: a survey of Canadian organizations. Int. J. Prod. Res. 40(3), 509–523 (2002)
19. Shehab, E.M., Sharp, M.W., Supramaniam, L., Spedding, T.A.: Enterprise resource planning: an integrative review. Bus. Process Manag. J. 10(4), 359–386 (2004)
20. Seethamraju, R., Seethamraju, J.: Adoption of ERPs in a medium-sized enterprise - a case study. In: Proceedings of the 19th Australasian Conference on Information Systems (ACIS), Christchurch, 3-5 December 2008
21. Statistics Sweden: ICT usage in enterprises 2012, in Editor (Ed.)^(Eds.): Book ICT usage in enterprises 2012 (2013)

22. Buonanno, G., Faverio, P., Pigni, F., Ravarini, A., Sciuto, D., Tagliavini, M.: Factors affecting ERP system adoption: a comparative analysis between SMEs and large companies. J. Enterp. Inf. Manag. **18**(4), 384–426 (2005)
23. Welsh, J.A., White, J.F.: A small business is not a little big business. Harvard Bus. Rev. **59** (4), 18–32 (1981)
24. Raymond, L.: Information Systems and the specificity of small business. J. Small Bus. **2**(2), 36–42 (1984)
25. Boykin, R.F.: Enterprise resource planning software: a solution to the return material authorization problem. Comput. Ind. **45**(1), 99–108 (2001)
26. Karsak, E.E., Özogul, C.O.: An integrated decision making approach for ERP system selection. Expert Syst. Appl. **36**(1), 660–667 (2009)
27. Panorama Consulting Group: ERP Implementation Project Costs and Durations Down, Business Benefits Up. http://Panorama-Consulting.com/resource-center/2011-erp-report/, Accessed 14 March 2012
28. Jacobs, F.R., Weston, F.C.: Enterprise resource planning (ERP) – a brief history. J. Oper. Manag. **25**(2), 357–363 (2007)
29. Hammer, M.: Reengineering work: don't automate, obliterate. Harvard Bus. Rev. **68**(4), 104–112 (1990)
30. Verville, J., Bernadas, C., Halingten, A.: So you're thinking of buying an ERP? ten critical factors for successful acquisitions. J. Enterp. Inf. Manag. **18**(6), 665–677 (2005)
31. Ptak, C.: ERP: Tools, Techniques, and Applications for Integrating the Supply Chain. St Lucie Press, Boca Raton (2000)
32. Wei, C.C., Wang, M.J.J.: A comprehensive framework for selecting an ERP system. Int. J. Proj. Manag. **22**(2), 161–169 (2004)
33. Kutlu, B., Akpinar, E.: ERP software selection using fuzzy methodology: a case study. J. Appl. Sci. **9**(18), 3378–3384 (2009)
34. Badri, M.A., Davis, D., Davis, D.: A comprehensive 0-1 goal programming model for project selection. Int. J. Proj. Manag. **19**(4), 243–252 (2001)
35. Ziaee, M., Fathian, M., Sadjadi, S.J.: A modular approach to ERP system selection: a case study. Inf. Manag. Comput. Secur. **14**(5), 485–495 (2006)
36. Lee, J.W., Kim, S.H.: Using analytic network process and goal programming for interdependent information system project selection. Comput. Oper. Res. **27**(4), 367–382 (2000)
37. Santhanam, R., Kyparisis, G.J.: A decision model for interdependent information system project selection. Eur. J. Oper. Res. **89**(2), 380–399 (1996)
38. Lall, V., Teyarachakul, S.: Enterprise resource planning (ERP) system selection: a data envelopment analysis (DEA) approach. J. Comput. Inf. Syst. **47**(1), 123–127 (2006)
39. Verville, J., Halingten, A.: A six-stage model of the buying process for ERP software. Ind. Mark. Manag. **32**(7), 585–594 (2003)
40. Yin, R.K.: Case study research: design and methods, 4th edn. Sage, Thousand Oaks (2009)

The VCLL: A Multi-view Computation Independent Modelling Language for MDA-Based Software Development

Dmitri Valeri Panfilenko[1(✉)], Christian Seel[2], and Andreas Martin[1]

[1] DFKI GmbH, Stuhlsatzenhausweg 3, Campus D3.2,
66123 Saarbrücken, Germany
{Dima.Panfilenko,Andreas.Martin}@dfki.de
[2] University of Applied Sciences Landshut, Am Lurzenhof 1,
84036 Landshut, Germany
Christian.Seel@haw-landshut.de

Abstract. We propose the CIM-modelling language "VCLL", which extends BPMN to four integrated modelling views. The designed modelling language allows for creating business processes and its relevant data, business rules and organisational aspects. The VCLL focuses on the development of business applications and provides two entry points into MDA. Our proposed modelling language can be used to describe the behaviour of one application (micro view) or it can be used to orchestrate different applications (macro view). Furthermore the VCLL provides a connection to a pre-CIM-level, which consists of unstructured information and reveals the relation of model elements with their origin in recorded interviews, forms, documents, etc.

Keywords: Model Driven Architecture (MDA) · Computation Independent Modelling (CIM) · Model-to-Model (M2M) transformation · Business Process Modelling Notation (BPMN) · Modelling language definition · Graphical Modelling Framework (GMF)

1 Introduction

Today's business information systems are required to ensure optimal support for the company's business processes. But these business processes are changing frequently because of new products, organisational changes, new markets, changes in governance or laws etc. An example for a change in law is the Sarbanes-Oxley-Act (SOX) [1] and one in governance the Aspen Principles [2]. All of these changes have an impact on the company's business processes and have to be reflected in the business information systems that support them. Software engineering approaches based on classical coding are often too slow to keep up with these fast and frequent changes of business processes and information systems. Therefore, a more expressive and efficient development method is needed.

Such a more expressive and efficient way of programming is the Model Driven Architecture (MDA) [3]. It increases the level of abstraction to a new state. MDA aims at faster software development by usage of model-to-model transformations. These models

© Springer International Publishing Switzerland 2015
D. Sedera et al. (Eds.): Pre-ICIS 2010-2012, LNBIP 198, pp. 138–153, 2015.
DOI: 10.1007/978-3-319-17587-4_9

are classified by the MDA concept into three levels of abstraction, namely the Computation Independent Model (CIM) level, the Platform Independent Model (PIM) level and the Platform Specific Model (PSM) level [3, 4].

But most of the existing MDA-approaches (Mellor et al. 2004 [10]) focus on PIM- and PSM-level and the M2M-transformation between them. The more conceptual CIM-level is often neglected. Hence, a real life software development project does not even start with conceptual modelling on CIM-level, but rather based on even more abstract and unstructured verbal information about the application's domain on the pre-CIM-level [5].

A major reason for neglecting the CIM-level in MDA-approaches is the lack of a modelling language understandable to end users and at the same time transformable into PIMs. Therefore, after the presentation of the research approach in Sect. 2 and related work in Sect. 3, we introduce a CIM modelling language that is designed to ease the creation of CIMs and the transformation of CIMs into PIMs in Sect. 4. We present the meta-model based specification of the VIDE CIM Level Language (VCLL) [6] with Meta Object Facility (MOF) [7]. The categorisation and thorough analysis of the supported business processes follows the description of the tool support in Sect. 5, concluding the paper and making outlook statements in Sect. 6.

2   Research Methodology

Research in the field of information systems has two major research interests: the discovery and explanation of currently existing phenomena and the development of new methods and recommendation of actions for the discovered problems [8]. Corresponding to the division into these two objectives HEVNER et al. [9] identify the empirical approach and the design science approach as the two possible types of research methodologies.

This contribution develops a solution for a known problem in context of the MDA. Therefore it follows the design science paradigm. HEVNER et al. provide seven guidelines for design science research, which determine the necessary parts of this contribution and create a sketch for its structure. The introduction shows the relevance of the research problem (guideline 2). The prototypic implementation of the VCLL in section "tool support" is an artefact (guideline 1) that serves as a proof of concept (guideline 3). As the contribution of the VCLL compared to existing modelling languages is determined by the presented meta-model, the research contribution can be clearly identified (guideline 4). The section "related work" refers to guideline 6, as it presents design as a search process. The research rigor (guideline 5) is addressed by this section and the rigorously structured organisation of this paper. Guideline 7 aims at the communication of the research results, which is addressed by submitting this book chapter for the publication.

3   Related Work

The idea of MDA [3, 10] is the translation of information models via different steps into finally executable code. According to the definition of MDA the process of creating software starts with information models on CIM level and transforms them into models on PIM level. These models on PIM level are enriched and then transformed into PSM which results in executable source code after the last transformation [4]. By a separation of concerns through creating CIMs and PIMs before PSMs you reach a kind of interdependence from platforms, languages and systems. The transformation starts on a highly abstract level and gets more concrete with each step down. ERP systems which support manufacturing processes are a very good example how to use MDA. Domain experts can be much more involved in the software development process to bridge the gap between their requirements and the understanding of them by a software engineer. On the three different levels of MDA different modelling languages are used. Therefore, commonly used modelling languages are regarded.

Event-driven Process Chains (EPC) [11] allow for creating semi-formal process models. This semi-formal notation is essentially a sequence of the successive events signalising the important occurrences in the process and functions dealing with the events and further information. It is suitable for a high level design of application systems or organisational structures, but it is not focused on the transformation into an IT system. The disadvantage of this methodology is that though it gives the business users the understandable idea of a business process and its possible paths, but at the same time there is no place for business rules that are standing for the decisions made at important steps in the process model.

Another modelling concept is UML [12]. It gives the IT specialists one of the most substantial tools for modelling the target application systems in different aspects on the different levels of abstraction. At the same time, it is not that well suitable for business users for involving too much knowledge about the technical aspects of the system under construction. It also doesn't provide the mechanisms of dealing with business rules. Though UML can be combined with the Object Constraint Language (OCL) [13], it is in turn too formalised to be used on the requirements level for which the VCLL tool is providing support.

Probably the most extensively used language for modelling of the business processes is the Object Modelling Group's (OMG) standard Business Process Model and Notation (BPMN) [14]. It can be used on different levels of abstractions, firstly, and can also contain a sufficient amount of technical information, secondly. The technical aspects are needed for the lower level implementation of those processes into the Business Process Execution Language (BPEL) for example [15] (which is a machine readable, textual format without an easy-going way to sketch a process in a graphical way). The disadvantage of BPMN notation in its first version was its limitation to a single view, namely the process view that is not always sufficient for the purposes of modelling the systems. It also did not provide the extended methodology for data and organisation modelling, thus weaving the data and organisation constructs into the process view directly. The second version of the BPMN specification provided meta-models amending the claimed issues and making it a good candidate for extension in the next section.

4   VIDE CIM Level Language

The VCLL aims at the integration of functional specialists into the software development process, especially data intensive business applications, which demands certain requirements to be regarded. The language has to be as simple and as commonly understandable as possible for "non-IT-oriented" business domain experts. Furthermore, the CIM-level language should be able to represent information that allows for creating draft UML models on PIM-level. Finally, larger business processes can result into more than one monolithic application. Therefore, the orchestration of different (sub)-applications should be possible.

4.1   VCLL Meta-Model

In order to create such a modelling language different established languages and notations were explored [8]. For example the Business Process Modelling Notation (BPMN), the Business Process Execution Language (BPEL) [15], and the Event driven Process Chain (EPC) [11] have been analysed. It turned out that each has its advantages and disadvantages that can be viewed in "related work" section. Based on our research [6], BPMN offers the best starting point for creating the VCLL (see Fig. 1).

Thus, the BPMN 2.0 meta-model was used as a basis and enriched by different items, partly inspired by other languages as well as newly created. For example, we introduced the concept of business rules, though on conceptual design level we only needed decision rules and constraint rules [16], as well as the data and role concepts. All of the introduced entities are marked in grey. Moreover, as for the differences to the BPMN 2.0 meta-model, the SequenceFlow entity in the proposed meta-model is connected to the FlowObject through 'target' and 'source' relationships, which constitutes a similar connection in the BPMN 2.0 [14] (cf. pp. 86). The difference to the current proposal is that in the BPMN 2.0 specification there are manifold relationships from the SequenceFlow entity to other entities distinct from FlowObject it should provide the notion of source and target for. Several other examples are also visible through comparison of the BPMN 2.0 and the proposed meta-models. Another intention of the VCLL meta-model is the provision of the general overview of the whole of the meta-model entity groupings (see Sect. 4), which are not that clearly graphically brought into relation with one another in the BPMN 2.0.

Decision business rules are used to describe complex branches of the control flow, e.g. if the decision which activity should be the next to be executed depends on the combination of several splitting decisions. Therefore, decision business rules consist of one or more statements. Each statement consists of business variable values and one activity. If the business variables have the values which are described in the statement the activity, which is referred to in the statement, is executed. One decision business rule can consist of one or more statements. The statements have an "or" relation between each other. Optionally, the last row can be added, which contains the keyword "else" as condition. The action which is assigned to this row is executed if no other condition is true.

Constraint business rules can be annotated to any model element on the CIM level and state constraints from a business point of view. For example, defining that an order process can be started by a phone call is not possible for new customers. Constraint business rules are constructs which are similar to natural language in order to make them easily accessible for business users. However, to avoid the ambiguity of natural language, the parts of constraint business rules are further defined. For this purpose, the

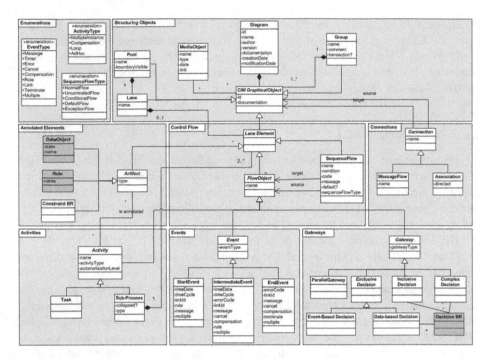

Fig. 1. VCLL meta-model.

use of natural language has to be restricted to the use of standardised statements (Endl [17]). In addition to established approaches like RDF [18] or OWL [19], which both focus on semantic-web-technologies, the approach "Semantics of Business Vocabulary and Business Rules Specification" (SBVR) [20], which is defined by the OMG, proves to be a well-developed concept for describing business rules in an enterprise context.

The people addressed by the SBVR-specification are mainly users from the business domain, who should be enabled to formulate rules in a structured but also easily comprehensible manner. There is also a focus on the necessary transformation of the formulated rules into IT-systems. The SBVR defines specifications for the used vocabulary as well as syntactical rules, to allow a structured documentation of business vocabularies, business facts and business rules. Furthermore, the specification describes a XMI-scheme to share business vocabularies and business rules between organisations and IT-systems. The SBVR is designed to be interpretable in predicate logic with a small extension in modal logic. It also defines demands towards the behaviour of IT-systems regarding their ability to share vocabularies and rules, which complies with the specification [20].

The SBVR-approach uses three perspectives on business rules. The first perspective is derived from the business rules mantra [21] and supports a simplified approximation towards a business rule. This perspective should support the communication with people who are not familiar with the approach, e.g. decision makers. The second perspective is the representation. It contains the specifications of SBVR, which should be used to formulate vocabularies and rules. The third perspective is the meaning. It contains the underlying semantics of the used vocabularies and rules.

4.2   VCLL Architecture

Based on the meta-model shown in Fig. 1, an architecture for the prototype supporting modelling and transforming business processes has been elaborated (see Fig. 2). The most extensively represented process view integrates the other views and consists of eight parts. Structuring objects are the top-level class the model contains. The control flow section introduces lane elements, which are connected to each other by flow objects. The connections section has two further types of connections between objects in a model. The annotated elements part of the meta-model shows model objects that are used to enrich activity objects with relevant information. The activity section tells which elements are representing actions in a model. The events section describes different types of events which tell what kind of triggers could be used in a model. Gateways explain how decisions of different types could be integrated into a VCLL CIM model. The enumerations section is the last section and it gives an overview of the complex types used in three different classes. Data, organisational and business rules views introduce interfaces to three further business process analysis scopes.

In Fig. 2, you can see a simple example of the different views and their interconnection. Inside the data view there are two entities 'opportunity' and 'party', which are connected by a simply expressed association 'is offered to'. Then, there is a business rule defining a branching condition and at least inside the organisational view a role 'sales director'. On top of the picture, the process view shows the business logic as a flow of different functions. After the start event, a function 'Identify opportunity' is executed, doing some work on a data object 'Opportunity', which is imported from the data view. Then, the function 'Create opportunity' follows, which is accomplished by a person who has the role 'Sales director'. After that, at the branch construct, it will be

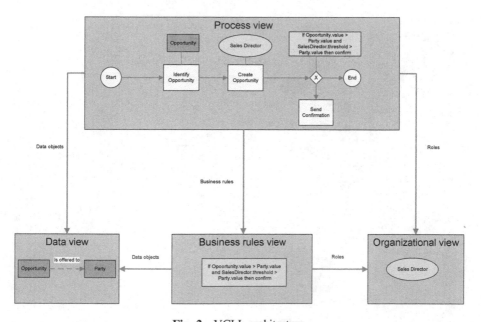

Fig. 2. VCLL architecture.

decided whether to stop the process in case of a negative condition or to go on with the opportunity process and 'Send a confirmation'. The information shown can then be used either focusing on the micro view, i.e. the definition of concrete PIM function or service, or on the macro view, i.e. controlling the call of functions or services by a workflow system. For more information concerning the PIM transformation, see Martin et al. 2008 [22].

Due to the fact that the VCLL is compatible to BPMN 2.0, VCLL models can be used to generate XPDL documents that define the orchestration of different applications. So, VCLL models can be imported by all XPDL compatible workflow management systems. Furthermore, a software tool has been developed that supports the import of unstructured requirements information, the creation of VCLL models and the export into draft UML models on PIM-level or XPDL files [23].

4.3   VCLL Prototype

This section introduces the VCLL supporting modelling tool built on the concepts of VCLL meta-model and architecture (see Fig. 3). The VCLL tool has been implemented with aid of the Eclipse IDE using the Graphical Modeling Framework (GMF)/Eclipse Modeling Framework (EMF) plugins. While the EMF serves for the automated generation of source code based on structured models, the GMF provides a generative component and runtime infrastructure for developing graphical editors based on EMF.

Apart from the modelling capabilities of the process, data, organisational and business rules views, in order to refine the meta-model the object constraint language (OCL) has been used to define the VCLL more soundly. The constraints concern the

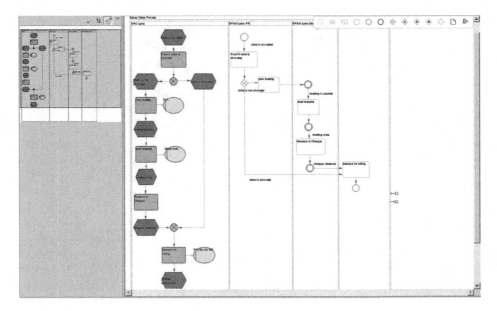

Fig. 3.   VCLL tool.

pool-lane relations of the modelled processes, the event types limitations, sequence flow connections, etc. Moreover, the following model transformation features have been implemented:

1. pre-CIM to VCLL: the conversion of the unstructured models of the pre-CIM level [5]
2. VCLL to PIM: the propagation of the information modelled on the CIM level through VCLL tool to the PIM level in form of XPDL for usage by workflow management tools [22, 24].

The next section will classify and describe the business process types supported by the VCLL tool.

5 Business Process Support by VCLL

5.1 Classification of Business Processes

Business processes can be classified by different criteria. An important criterion for the use and especially the economic benefit of a software support for business processes is their *repetition rate*. The repetition rate as criterion for the classification of business processes is proposed by several authors [25–32]. Despite this criterion being very common, the values that describe the repetition rate differ between different authors. In order to categorise different possible values, we distinguish between three categories of repetition rate: singular, sometimes, frequently. Singular business processes are only executed once. These are business processes which are individual for each customer or are research and development processes which are not standardised. Business processes that are executed sometimes do not occur in the daily business, but occur more than once. An example would be the creation of a balance sheet once a year. The last category contains business processes that occur frequently. These are processes from daily business, which can include variants, but are standardised and documented.

A second criterion for the classification of business processes is their *degree of structure*. The degree of structure as classification criterion is used by several authors, e.g. [25, 28, 29, 31, 33, 34]. The distinction between different degrees of structure is stated differently. BECKER et al. [35] differentiate between ad hoc processes and structures, pre-defined activities but ad hoc processes, and pre-defined processes. By ad hoc processes, they understand business processes that are not structured, planned and documented. Their run-time behaviour is not defined until their execution. The second category consists of planned activities, which can be aggregated to a business process at runtime. The third category consists of planned, managed and standardised business processes, whereas each activity as well as the whole process is known at its build-time. The other references mentioned above describe the first category as hastily formed or unstructured. The second category is not mentioned in all references. The third one is described as structured or formally defined. In order to get an intuitive formulation, the categories are described as unstructured, semi-structured and (fully) structured. Unstructured refers to business processes where the activities and the control flow of the business process are not defined at their build-time. The opposite are structured business processes. Business processes are classified as semi-structured if their activities or their control flow are partly defined at build-time.

The next criterion is the *alignment* of business processes to strategic levels [36, 37]. Traditionally, in economics, three different levels are defined: the strategic, the tactical and the operational level. Strategic business processes serve the purpose of long-time planning and definition of goals. These business processes usually require creativity and are not standardised. In order to realise strategic goals, the strategic business processes are refined into tactical business processes. They usually have a mid-time range. These tactical business processes are refined again into operational business processes. The operational business processes are executed in every-day work. The creation of the business value is done by this type of processes.

The next criterion is the stability or *frequency of changes* of the business processes [28, 38]. Some business processes have to be adapted frequently, e.g. for each project. Other processes are changed rarely and the rest is very stable. The last category, e.g. describes business processes that are predefined by laws, which won't be changed for a long time.

Another attribute of business processes is their *granularity* [34, 39]. They can be modelled in a very detailed manner, so that the activities of the processes can be further refined in a reasonable manner. Compounded business processes have parts that are detailed, but other parts that can be refined by a detailed process. The highest granularity would be aggregated business processes. They are often depicted as value chains. They show the relation and order of groups of process steps, e.g. that the marketing activities are done before the sales activities.

Additionally, several authors classify business processes by the *value they create* [27]. Authors distinguish between business processes of low and of high business value. Business processes that create a low value are mostly administrative and support processes. They are necessary in order to create goods or services but do not create saleable products. Business processes with a high value creation are customer-oriented core processes.

Furthermore, business processes can be classified by their *scope* as intra- or inter-organisational [35, 40]. Intra-organisational business processes take place within one enterprise. All organisational units, hardware and software systems that take part in the processes belong to the same enterprise. Inter-organisational business processes take place between two or more different enterprises. This type of business processes requires interfaces between the application systems that are used in different enterprises. Judicial aspects have to be considered and security aspects have to be taken into account.

In addition, the *usage of persistent data* of a business process can be different [29, 41]. Business processes can just check information or transform a defined input into an output. This type of business processes is very rare. They don't use any persistent data. The second type of business processes uses persistent data but does not create or change it. The larger group of business processes uses, creates and changes persistent data.

A very important criterion for the classification of business processes is the *level of automation* [34, 42]. Three levels are distinguished: manual, semi-manual and automated. Manual business processes are executed by employees without using application systems, e.g. service or consulting processes. Semi-automated business processes are executed by humans, but supported by application systems, e.g. an employee enters the personal data of a customer in an application and the system checks the consistency of data. Automated processes run without human interaction. They are performed completely by application systems, e.g. bookings on bank accounts from one bank to another, which run as batch job every night.

Two other attributes that classify business processes are the *number of process participants* [34] and the *number of parallel instances* [43]. The number of processes participants is classified into two categories: high and low. The *number of parallel instances* can be one, which means there is no parallelism. It can be also be some or many. Some means a small number of instances below ten.

Another attribute of a business processes is data-driven, referring to the data that is involved in the business process. It is the *necessity of using transactions*, which can either be required or not. If it is required the business process has to ensure that it will be completed successfully or comes back to the starting state again, e.g. the transfer of money from one bank account to another has to be done completely and shouldn't stop after withdrawing the money from the first account and before in-payment to the second account.

The attributes for the classification of business processes and their possible values are summarised as morphological box in Table 1.

Table 1. Morphological box for business process classification.

Attribute	Value		
repetition rate	singular	sometimes	frequently
degree of structure	unstructured	semi-structured	structured
alignment	strategic	tactical	operational
frequency of changes	never	sometimes	often
granularity	detailed	compounded	aggregated
value creation	low	high	
process scope	intra-organisational	inter-organisational	
usage of persistent information	none	low	high
level of automation	manual	semi-automated	automated
# of process participants	low	high	
# parallel instances	one	some	many
transaction necessity	required	not required	

5.2   Criteria of Business Processes Supported by VCLL

After criteria for the classification of business processes have been presented, this section classifies the business processes that are supported by VCLL. For this purpose, for each category defined above, the supported business processes are classified.

For the *repetition rate*, VCLL is able to support all types of business processes. But in addition to other software development methodologies, the software development is too expensive for a process which is only executed once in the same way. Therefore, a software development project is only reasonable if there is a trade-off between the resources spent in software development and the benefit the developed software creates. Due to VCLL is aimed particularly at rapid software development, the software development is going to become less expensive and therefore more reasonable for business processes that are only executed sometimes.

Concerning the second criterion, only defined parts of a business process can be implemented. Therefore, structured business processes are supported by VCLL. Semi-structured business processes can be treated with the VCLL methodology in two ways. If the control flow of the business process is completely available then it could be used for the orchestration of VCLL applications based on a workflow management system. Otherwise, the structured and detailed activities can be implemented using the CIM-to-PIM transformation wizard that VCLL offers. Unstructured or ad-hoc business processes are not supported by VCLL, as the logic of the business processes is too vague to create an executable description.

Regarding the strategic *alignment* of business processes, VCLL could support all three levels. But an implementation for the support of creative decisions, which have to be taken in strategic or tactical business processes, are difficult to describe as business processes and to implement in software. Therefore, VCLL supports especially the implementation of everyday business processes with relation to internal or external customers, which are located at the operational level.

Similar to the repetition rate, the *frequency of changes* has an economic impact on the software development process. Business processes, which are unchanged or rarely changed, just need to be implemented once and can stay unchanged. Unfortunately, changing business models, shorter product lifecycles and new competitors in markets increase the need to change business processes and shorten the time in which they remain unchanged. Therefore, the software that supports business processes has to be changed more often as well. As VCLL starts its MDA approach at the CIM level and keeps the relation between CIM and PIM objects, the implementation of changes is relatively fast, because changes in business processes can be propagated to the PIM level. Therefore, VCLL supports frequently changed and unchanged business processes as well. But it's not economically reasonable to implement business processes that are changed faster than it took to implement them.

Regarding the *granularity* of business processes, two types are supported. Detailed business processes, which cannot be further refined from a business perspective, can be transformed into PIM models. Compounded business processes can be used for orchestration. The activities, which can be further refined, are regarded as black boxes and an appropriate application is invoked by the WfMS.

The *value creation* also addresses economic issues. From an implementation point of view, business processes with a low value creation as well as processes with a high value creation can be implemented with VCLL. But the benefit that arises from an implementation of a business processes with a low value creation can be less than the effort for the implementation. Therefore, VCLL especially supports business processes with a high value creation.

The *process scope* that VCLL regards refers to intra-organisational business processes. The modelling languages VCLL uses on CIM and PIM level do not consider special information such as the description of interfaces or mechanisms for information hiding between different enterprises. Because the fact modelling of inter-organisational business processes and software is a field of research on its own [44–46], this kind of models are not in the scope of the project and the methodology being developed.

Concerning the *usage of persistent information*, VCLL is designed to handle persistent data. Most business applications use, create or manipulate data. Therefore, the VCLL has its own data view in order to describe data objects and their usage in the business process. PIM level language elements for data definition and queries on databases have been introduced. Therefore, VCLL can handle all three types of business processes with regard to their usage of persistent data.

The *level of automation* that business processes possess is crucial for their implementability. VCLL supports business processes that are fully automated. They can be described at CIM and PIM level and/or be orchestrated in the sense of the VCLL approach. Semi-automated business processes can be described on the CIM level, because the CIM modelling language also allows the description of activities that are executed manually. However, on the PIM level, manual activities cannot be described. Therefore, in semi-automated business processes, the whole business process is described at the CIM level, but only the automated part is transferred to PIM level. Manual business processes can be described on the CIM level in VCLL, but are not implemented.

Regarding the *number of participants* and *parallel instances* that VCLL can support, a limitation is only given by the target platform on PSM level. If the PSM level supports multiple instances and is able to handle a large number of users, VCLL can be used for this kind of system.

Regarding the last classification criterion, the need of a business process for *transaction support*, VCLL partly supports transactions. For VCLL is based on databases, the transaction concepts of databases can be used. Therefore, a transaction support for data is realised. But transaction support for the process steps itself is only partly possible. The VCLL offers the concept of compensation. This does not allow a roll-back to be done, but defines actions that have to be undertaken in order to undo an activity. As the description of compensations on CIM level are done in the same way as the description of normal business processes they can be implemented at the PIM level as well. Therefore, VCLL offers a full transaction concept for data and compensations for business process activities. An overview of the type of business processes that are supported by VCLL gives the following Table 2:

In general, VCLL supports all types of executable business processes. The only requirement is that the business processes can be described by a set of actions, a control flow between them and data objects the activities are working on. The kind of business

Table 2. Classification of business processes supported by VCLL.

Attribute	Value		
repetition rate	singular	sometimes	frequently
degree of structure	unstructured	semi-structured	structured
alignment	strategic	tactical	operational
frequency of changes	never	sometimes	often
granularity	detailed	compounded	aggregated
value creation	low		high
process scope	intra-organisational		inter-organisational
usage of persistent information	none	low	high
level of automation	manual	semi-automated	automated
# of process participants	low		high
# parallel instances	one	some	many
transaction necessity	required		not required

processes, which are supported optimally, are business processes which just display, create or change data. These actions are typical for administrative processes, such as booking a flight or the administration of a warehouse.

Other domains, such as real-time or embedded systems, are not in the focus of VCLL. Furthermore, VCLL is not designed to depict very complex algorithms, such as those used in artificial intelligence systems, because these kinds of systems require a large number of loops, branches and case differentiation, which are difficult to describe in the control flow of the VCLL.

6   Conclusions and Outlook

The MDA approach is an effective way to create software systems to support business processes. Especially in the world of business information systems with its rapidly changing requirements and large software system traditional software engineering approaches can be too slow. The major problem of MDA is to bridge the gap between business, which is located at MDA's CIM-level and the two technical levels below, namely PIM and PSM. Therefore, a proper CIM-level language is needed. Thus, the meta-model based definition of the VCLL and its four views are presented. The VCLL allows describing business processes, data, organisational structures and business rules in a way that is understandable for business users. Furthermore, to underpin the viability of the VCLL, a VCLL modelling tool based on the Eclipse IDE framework GMF is presented. It supports the creation and linkage of models in all four views of the VCLL and the semi-automated model-to-model transformations from pre-CIM to CIM as well as from CIM to PIM.

Further research is required in the area of structured creation of CIM models, starting with non-formalised and unstructured information, a so-called pre-CIM-level [5]. Additionally OMG's MDA Guide [3] should be enhanced by more elaborated sections for CIM-level modelling and CIM to PIM transformation in order to fill the existing gap in the relation between these levels.

References

1. Sarbanes-Oxley Act of 2002 (2002)
2. Aspen Institute: Aspen Principles and Policy Recommendations. http://www.aspeninstitute. org/policy-work/business-society/corporate-programs/aspen-principles
3. Object Management Group (OMG): MDA Guide Version 1.0. http://www.omg.org/mda/ mda_files/MDA_Guide_Version1-0.pdf
4. Frankel, D.: Model Driven Architecture. Applying MDA to Enterprise Computing. Wiley, New York (2003)
5. Jeary, S., Fouad, A., Phalp, K.: Extending the model driven architecture with a pre-CIM level. In: Proceedings of the 1st International Workshop on Business Support for MDA, co-located with TOOLS EUROPE (2008)
6. Seel, C. Martin, A.: VIDE Deliverable number 7.1: Metamodel and notation of the VIDE process modelling language, requirements concerning process model. http://www.vide-ist. eu/extern/VIDE_D7.1.pdf
7. Object Management Group (OMG): OMG Meta Object Facility (MOF) Core Specification. Version 2.4.2. http://www.omg.org/spec/MOF/ISO/19508/PDF/
8. Seel, C.: Reverse Method Engineering. Methode und Softwareunterstützung zur Konstruktion und Adaption semiformaler Informationsmodellierungstechniken. Logos, Berlin (2010)
9. Hevner, A.R., March, S.T., Park, J., Ram, S.: Design science in information systems research. MIS Q. **28**, 75–105 (2004)
10. Mellor, S.J., Kendall, S., Uhl, A., Weise, D.: MDA Distilled. Principles of Model-Driven Architecture. Addison-Wesley, Boston (2004)
11. Keller, G., Nüttgens, M., Scheer, A.-W.: Semantische Prozeßmodellierung auf der Grundlage "Ereignisgesteuerter Prozeßketten (EPK)". Inst. für Wirtschaftsinformatik Univ., Saarbrücken (1992)
12. Object Management Group (OMG): Unified Modelling Language UML 2.4.1. http://www. omg.org/spec/UML/2.4.1/
13. Object Management Group (OMG): Object Constraint Language. Version 2.0. http://www. omg.org/spec/SBVR/1.0/PDF
14. OMG BPMN 2.0 FTF: Business Process Model and Notation (BPMN), Version 2.0. http:// www.omg.org/spec/BPMN/2.0/PDF

15. OASIS WS-BPEL Technical Committee: Web Services Business Process Execution Language. http://docs.oasis-open.org/wsbpel/2.0/OS/wsbpel-v2.0-OS.pdf
16. Scheer, A.-W.: Geschäftsprozessmanagement und Geschäftsregeln. In: Scheer, A.-W., Werth, D. (eds.) Iwi, Saarbrücken
17. Endl, R.: Regelbasierte Entwicklung betrieblicher Informationssysteme: Gestaltung flexibler Informationssysteme durch explizite Modellierung der Geschäftslogik. Eul, Lohmar (2004)
18. World Wide Web Consortium (W3C): RDF 1.1 XML Syntax. http://www.w3.org/TR/rdf-syntax-grammar/
19. World Wide Web Consortium (W3C): OWL 2 Web Ontology Language Document Overview, 2nd edn. http://www.w3.org/TR/owl2-overview/
20. Object Management Group (OMG): Semantics of Business Vocabulary and Business Rules Specification. http://doc.omg.org/formal/08-01-02.pdf
21. Business Rules Group: The Business Rules Manifesto. http://www.businessrulesgroup.org/brmanifesto.htm
22. Martin, A., Seel, C., Jeary, S., Coles, M., Kanyaru, J., Phalp, K.: Generating software support for industrial business processes. In: Proceedings of the 10th International Conference on The Modern Information Technology in the Innovation Processes of the Industrial Enterprises (2008)
23. Kanyaru, J., Coles, M., Jeary, S., Phalp, K.: Using visualisation to elicit domain information as part of the model driven architecture (MDA) approach. In: Proceedings of the 1st International Workshop on Business Support for MDA, Co-located with TOOLS EUROPE (2008)
24. Panfilenko, D., Seel, C., Martin, A., Loos, P.: The VCLL: a multiview computation independent modeling language for MDA-based software development. In: Pre-ICIS 2010 Workshop on Enterprise Systems Research. International Conference on Information Systems (ICIS-10), Information Technology: Gateway to the Future. Pre-ICIS, St. Louis, Missouri, USA, 12-15 December 2010 (2010)
25. Derszteler, G.: Prozessmanagement auf Basis von Workflow-Systemen. Ein integrierter Ansatz zur Modellierung, Steuerung und Überwachung von Geschäftsprozessen. Eul, Lohmar (2000)
26. Giaglis, G.M.: A taxonomy of business process modelling and information systems modelling techniques. Int. J. Flex. Manuf. Syst. **13**, 209–228 (2001)
27. Leymann, F., Roller, D.: Produktion Workflow. Concepts and Techniques. Prentice Hall, Upper Saddle River (2000)
28. Maurer, G.: Von der Prozeßorientierung zum Workflow Management. Univ. Lehrstuhl f. Allg. BWL u. Wirtschaftsinformatik, Mainz (1996)
29. Picot, A., Reichwald, R.: Bürokommunikation. Leitsätze für d. Anwender. Angewandte Informations-Technik, Hallbergmoos (1987)
30. Rathgeb, M.: Einführung von Workflow-Management-Systemen. In: Hasenkamp, U., Kirn, S., Syring, M. (eds.) CSCW – Computer Supported Cooperative Work Informationssysteme für dezentralisierte Unternehmensstrukuren, pp. 39–66. Addison-Wesley, Bonn, Reading, Mass (1994)
31. Schmidt, G.: Prozessmanagement. Modelle und Methoden. Springer, Heidelberg (2012)
32. Reijers, H.A.: Design and Control of Workflow Processes. Business Process Management for the Service Industry. Springer, New York (2003)
33. van der Aalst, W.M.P.: Formalization and verification of event-driven process chains. Inf. Softw. Technol. **41**, 639–650 (1999)
34. Sheth, A., Georgakopoulos, D., Joosten, S.M.M., Rusinkiewicz, M., Scacchi, W., Wileden, J., Wolf, A.L.: Report from the NSF workshop on workflow and process automation in information systems. SIGSOFT Softw. Eng. Notes **22**, 28–38 (1997)

35. Becker, J., Zur Mühlen, M., Gille, M.: Workflow application architectures: classification and characteristics of workflow-based information systems. In: Fischer, L. (ed.) Workflow Handbook 2002, pp. 39–50. Future Strategies, Lighthouse Point, FL (2002)
36. Heilmann, H.: Workflow management: Integration von Organisation und Informationsverarbeitung. In: HMD, pp. 8–21 (1994)
37. Zhou, Y., Chen, Y.: The methodology for business process optimized design. In: IECON 2003, 29th Annual Conference of the IEEE Industrial Electronics Society (IEEE Cat. No.03CH37468), pp. 1819–1824 (2003)
38. van der Aalst, W., van Hee, K.M.: Workflow Management. Models, Methods, and Systems. MIT Press, Cambridge (2002)
39. Becker, J., Zur Mühlen, M.: Rocks, Stones and Sand – Zur Granularität von Kompo- nenten in Workflowmanagementsystemen. In: IM Die Fachzeitschrift für Information, pp. 57–67 (1999)
40. Hauser, C.: Marktorientierte Bewertung von Unternehmungsprozessen. Eul, Bergisch Gladbach (1996)
41. Kalenborn, A.: Prozessorganisation und Workflow-Management. Organisationstheoretisches Konzept und informationstechnische Umsetzung. Shaker, Aachen (2000)
42. Derungs, M.: Vom Geschäftsprozess zum Workflow. In: Österle, H., Vogler, P. (eds.) Praxis des Workflow-Managements, pp. 123–146. Vieweg+Teubner Verlag, Wiesbaden (1996)
43. Mentzas, G.N.: Coupling object-oriented and workflow modelling in business and information process reengineering. Inf. Knowl. Syst. Manag. 1, 63–87 (1999)
44. Röhricht, J., Schlögel, C.: cBusiness. Erfolgreiche Internetstrategien durch collaborative business am Beispiel mySAP.com. Addison-Wesley, München (2001)
45. Schulz, K., Orlowska, M.E.: Architectural issues for cross-organisational B2B interactions. In: Proceedings of the 21st International Conference on Distributed Computing Systems Workshops (ICDCS 2001 Workshops), 16-19 April 2001, Phoenix, AZ, USA, pp. 79–87 (2001)
46. Schulz, K.: Modelling and Architecting of Cross-Organizational Workflows. Brisbane (2002)

Expert System Applications in E-Learning Environment: Analysis on Current Trends and Future Prospects

Kakoty Sangeeta[1(✉)] and Sarma Shikhar Kr[2]

[1] Distance Education, Assam Down Town University, Guwahati, India
kakoty.sangeeta@gmail.com
[2] Department of IT, Gauhati University, Guwahati, India
sks001@gmail.com

Abstract. Although there are various applications of Expert system in various fields, right from agriculture to the diagnosis of diseases of patients, it has potential for extensive contribution in digital learning. This paper discusses and analyses the present applications of Expert System in e-learning and to see the usefulness and effectiveness of it. The main objective is to focus and highlight the new trends of e-learning system and by integrating Expert System tools with it, how the system will be more effective and beneficial in nature and how the system will work as an Expert E-learning interface. This paper starts with a brief introduction of popular AI technique, the Expert System. This is followed by reviews on some of the recent applications of Expert System in the area of electronic learning. Specific focus has been given to analyse effective integration of Expert tools towards the personalized learning environment. This paper also discusses the application of Expert System for the purpose of learner centric E-learning platform.

Keywords: Expert system · Digital learning · E-learning · Expert E-learning

1 Introduction

E-learning is purely technology-enhanced learning via internet and customized intranets. Because of the technological revolution, the education system has got tremendous changes in the later part of 90s. E-learning, by virtue of its unique, distributed and asynchronous nature, significantly improves the entire educational system. It creates a new dimension of learning that eliminates barrier of time, distance and socioeconomic status. Though E-learning have different prospect in different point of view like from learner side, content repository and management, metadata management and indexing, there is a potential benefits in Adaptive Learning Environments (ALEs). The awareness of ALEs is going high in recent years. To manage all these there is a need of standardizing the whole system, by coordinating emerging technologies and capabilities. Many E-learning standards like SCORM, LOM are available now in market and they are accepted by many academias, institutions, and various Govt. and Non-Govt. organizations. Researchers are also introducing various types of implementable architectures in this field in different periods of time. Most of such standard gives more

© Springer International Publishing Switzerland 2015
D. Sedera et al. (Eds.): Pre-ICIS 2010-2012, LNBIP 198, pp. 154–159, 2015.
DOI: 10.1007/978-3-319-17587-4_10

emphasis on content management of learning procedure by integrating different attractive tools like graphics, animation, videos etc. to make the system more impressive and interactive. The whole learning system will be more interactive and promising if we integrate Expert system (ES) tools to E-learning procedures. One promising application is web security and database security of education system. The ES tools can be used to understand a learner better from their learning history. ES can make the learning system as a decision-maker for E-learners. With ES, the system can act as an expert learning system with more potentiality. Although there are many standards of E-learning in the market, proposals are for standardization of learner profile and content packaging. There is still lack of learner centric E-learning system. The main objective of this paper is to introduce the recent applications of ES in E-learning emphasizing on learner's learning style, learning pattern etc. It also discusses the scope for potential applications and integration of Expert System Technologies to the E Learning scenario in a more effective way. The idea is now to build a "*common reference model*" for a good web-based learning with the capability of commercial or public implementation.

2 Expert System Tool

An expert system is a computer program that works in accordance with human expertise and based on knowledge and reasoning techniques. It can solve problems and can give advice in a specialized domain area. It operates as an interactive system to respond questions, asks for clarification, makes recommendations, and generally aids the decision making process [6]. So, we can say an ES is a decision maker, problem solver, analyzer, and can use as a guide for them who does not have access to expertise. ES provides expert advice and guidance in a wide variety of activities, from computer diagnosis to delicate medical surgery. Instead of simply manipulating data sets, an ES can draw a conclusion which is the main advantage and difference from traditional database programs. It contains both declarative and procedural knowledge. An ES has reasoning capability to arrive at conclusions from stored and supplied facts. A very important kind of ES called Fuzzy ES is used to collect fuzzy membership functions and rules which allow more than one conclusions per rule. Here user has to give his/her confidence also with their inputs. Like the system also give conclusions with confidence level. The basic advantage of using such Expert Systems is that there is no restriction on input data on their limits and the data not necessarily defined clearly in advance. It can give several alternative solutions, either ranked or unranked.

3 Current E-Learning Standards

There are several promising areas of E-learning. Among them content management and web security are main for which several companies have introduced several standards. According to Guild Research report 2006, the e-learning activity "Designing and developing e-learning content" is getting more focus and attention than "Addressing learner requirements and preferences" and for an organization "Improve the quality of e-learning content" got the highest priority than the other objectives. "Extend the global reach of the e-learning content" is the second priority to get the content out beyond the geographical limit [8].

It has been seen in Guild research that e-learner providers are still concentrating to improve the quality of content and few standards are already introduced and accepted by people. One such conceptual model architecture of IEEE is LTSC (Learning Technology Standardization Committee). We can divide the learning standards into five sub standards: metadata, content packaging, learner profile, learner registration and security. For each section already some standards are there and works are still going on to improve it. To support metadata objects like indexing, storage, search, and retrieval of learning, LOM standards of IEEE and Dublin Core Metadata are commonly used standards. For content packaging and communication, the functional model SCORM of ADL is more popular than other standards like IMS Content Packaging Application and IMS Simple Sequencing specification. The most important effort to standardize the learner profile information is the IMS Learner Information package (LIP) specification. There is an initiative for learner registration is the IMS Enterprise Specification [www. imsproject.org]. Sun Microsystems also present a functional model for e-learning. Liu, Siddik and Georgans also proposed one functional model for e-learning to divide the whole learning system into two components: content management system and learning management system [4]. This works advanced than SCORM that defines an interface between each components and subsystem to achieve interoperability.

4 Expert System in E-Learning

The application of ES is rapidly increasing in learning environment to make the system more interactive. One such popular application is the information filtering agent to analyze the learner's web surfing habits and preferences. It filters exactly the information wanted by the learner from unwanted data which saves time and effort of searching from huge amount of data. ES determines what contents to present to the learner. ES can understand learner better and can think better way to make decision. Because of its performance, many decision support systems named as Expert System [3]. AXSYS is an intelligent system for e-learning having visual interface with graphical representations of knowledge [9]. This helps the teaching staff even if they do not have any technical background and arrange the system without any additional technical support. LCDS, The Microsoft Learning Content Development System is an expert system that creates high quality, interactive, online courses. It is a free tool that allows anyone in the Microsoft Learning community to publish e-learning courses. Its recent rank is 7 on the list of best free applications from Microsoft and is available now in seven languages. AAA is an ES of America Accounting Association provides information on Rutgers Accounting web as well as Newsletter, Teaching material and more. EZ-Xpert 3.0 is an end-user development environment with speed and accuracy. It offers a menu-driven, fill-in-the-blank interface with extensive Wizard support and presents an ordered list of tasks that need attention, leading the user through the building of the system. EXSYS Corvid is a decision-making expert system allows non-programmers to easily build interactive Web applications that capture the logic and processes used to solve problems and deliver it online, in stand-alone applications and embedded in other technologies [info@exsys.com]. Marginean and Racovitan, in their research paper, proposed one intelligent E-learning model for the students from the discipline of "Computer Science in economy" to adjust the students with theoretical and practical knowledge and practices [5]. Vostrovsky explained in his paper the utilization of ES in knowledge management and how important ES is to solve problem with consultation of expert [11]. According to Fadzil and Munira ES rules are used in E-learning system in various applications [2]. It can use as a program advising, automated scheduling of classes, making of assignments, plagiarism detection, retaining learners and adapting to their diverse needs and backgrounds, maintenance of property and ensuring security.

5   Prospects of E-Learning Using ES

From the previous sections it is seen that, most of the ES for E-learning are used to manage the contents of SLM. Most of the works are still going on to make the system more attractive and interactive for user. According to Teo and Gay, most E-learning systems are still limited to just being online repositories and lack of personalization learning system [10]. So, one adaptive and assistive learning system for digital learner is very much important in this field. Based on the information about user-access pattern and use behaviour, a designer can improve the site organization and presentation. Adaptive sites can monitor visitor's activity and browsing patterns and learn from them some relevant information. In E-learning environment also an ES can work as a kernel for learner and the learning system. ES can be the expert control system for both learner and the environment that can form an Expert Learning System (ELS).

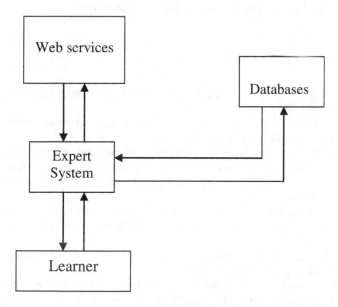

Fig. 1. Block diagram of ELS

Though lots of works going on and already done in content management system, Chen and Chiu argue that yet the E-learning system is lack of appropriate learning content, interaction and sense of participation and the learning problems are often difficult to be detected and solved [1]. They say that an E-learning environment is required to compose learning tools, learning management system, digital content and learning activities. So, this can be the future work to improve the system.

Not much work has been done in self evaluation procedure for learner which can improve by using ES. Evaluation procedure within a time bound is one of the prospective studies. According to Murtaza et al., there are several areas in business decision making and problem solving where ES excels [7].

6 Conclusion

An ES tools can be used to understand a customer better, either as a group or as an individual. ES is such a tool that it enables a computer to give advice concerning an unstructured or semi structured decision that is normally made by a human expert. ES or knowledge based system usually act as a consulting experts in a specific domain areas based on its collection of knowledge. Since e-learning is a promising area of research, and ES is a technology by which one can solve and think a problem better that a human expert, integrating ES with E-learning system is the good suggestion to improve the existing system and make the system more useful and more interactive. A decision support e-learning environment for learners is also possible to work as an Expert E-learner.

In future, the learning solutions and services can be integrated into a new trend which is called mobile learning technology that can help the people who are lack of infrastructure and for the people whose job require to move.

References

1. Chen, S., Chiu, M.: Building an agent-based system for e-learning in digital design. Comput. Aided Des. Appl. 2(1–4), 469–476 (2005)
2. Fadzil, M., Munira, T.A.: Application of Artificial Intelligence in an Open and Distance learning Institution. IEEE Xplore (2008)
3. Hess, J., Chen, W.: Expert system applications in elearning: present and future. In: World Conference on Elearning in Corporate, Government, Health & Higher Education (2005)
4. Liu, X., Saddik, A., Georganas, N.: An implementable architecture of an E-learning system. In: CCGEI, Montreal. IEEE (2003)
5. Marginean, N., Racovitan, D.: Some aspects on adjusting theory with practice using an intelligent Elearning system. Annales Universitatis Apulensis Series Oeconomica 2(10), 5 (2008)
6. Moghrabi, C., Eid, M.: Modelling users through an expert system and a neural network. Comput. Indus. Eng. 35, 583–586 (1998)
7. Murtaza, M., Shah, J., Gupta, V.: Artificial intelligence applications in e-commerce: current trends and future prospects. In: Proceedings of the Academy of Information and Management Sciences, Nashville. Vol. 6, No. 1 (2002)

8. Pulichino, J.: The Learning Guild Research. Future Directions in e-Learning Research Report (2006)
9. Rickett, F.: AXSYS: an intelligent system for e- learning. Kybernetes, **36**(3/4), 476–483 (2007). Emerald Group Publishing Limited Kybernetes
10. Teo, C., Gay, R.: A knowledge-driven model to personalize e-learning. ACM J. Educ. Resour. Comput. **6**(1), 1–15 (2006)
11. Vostrovsky, V.: Expert systems utilization in knowledge management. Agric. Econ. Czech. **52**(10), 451–455 (2006)

Web search

1. http://www.microsoft.com/learning/en/us/training/lcds.aspx
2. www.ez-xpert.com
3. www.exsys.com
4. www.elearningguild.com
5. http://www.imsproject.org

Teaching with Enterprise Systems:
A Three Phased Roadmap

Felix Ter Chian Tan[1][✉] and Darshana Sedera[2]

[1] Information Systems and Technology Management, The UNSW Business School, University of New South Wales, Sydney, NSW, Australia
f.tan@unsw.edu.au
[2] Information Systems Department, Science and Engineering Faculty, Queensland University of Technology, Brisbane, QLD, Australia

Abstract. Educators still face challenges using enterprise systems as a teaching tool despite many universities having approached vendors for resources to enrich their curriculum. Previously, there is relatively little guidance given to educators on how to incorporate enterprise systems into the curriculum. This article describes a three phased – negotiation, knowledge and evaluation – roadmap for teaching with enterprise systems. A roadmap is important to guide educators in addressing the issues associated with the using of enterprise systems in curriculum. Furthermore, the roadmap describes a learn-by-doing approach, to provide a balance of business process and enterprise systems software specific knowledge for students; that the majority of firms seek. Following the roadmap creates the potential for joint creation of teaching and learning value between constituents in a wider eco-system, comprising of educators, vendors, faculties and students.

Keywords: Enterprise systems · Education · Roadmap

1 Introduction

Since the 1990s, many universities and their faculties have endeavoured to incorporate Enterprise Systems (ES) into their curriculum. For more than a decade, ES vendor outreach programs (such as the SAP University Alliance and Microsoft Dynamics Academic Alliance) have sought to provide a platform for universities, professors, software experts and hundreds of thousands of students to share, combine and renew each other's resources to create value in education through new forms of interaction and learning mechanisms [1, 2]. However, educators have been recommended to exercise caution as some universities still struggle not only to realize the potential of ES software as a teaching tool [3] but also to leverage it to teach ES in a meaningful way [4]. As educators in IS technology and management, we continue to be queried frequently about the role of ES and vendor outreach programs, what to teach and how to teach ES in business courses.

Because ES have been able to maintain widespread demand and proliferation in the business landscape over the years, the development of a roadmap to guide educators to enrich their curriculum with vendor resources and to address the industry deficit in skilled

© Springer International Publishing Switzerland 2015
D. Sedera et al. (Eds.): Pre-ICIS 2010-2012, LNBIP 198, pp. 160–173, 2015.
DOI: 10.1007/978-3-319-17587-4_11

graduates is particularly relevant. It has been reported that graduates who pursue ES-intensive coursework command higher starting salaries than those who do not [1, 5]. Given the specific demands for graduates today (and for the foreseeable future), continual adjustments need to be made to ES curricula in order to accommodate relevant courses in a vendor ↔ university ↔ faculty arrangement. The challenge for an ES course is to support the courses that preceded it and vice versa, so that students entering advanced ES courses have adequate knowledge of the content in preceding courses. Incidentally, scholars [6] cautioned educators about the "perennial challenges" (p288) of (and the dangers of not) updating and maintaining the relevance of curricula. She warns of the need for new approaches to developing educational innovations to accelerate the pace of teaching material and curriculum innovation. The literature suggests that the methods of delivery favor certain modular functions of the software [e.g. 7] or favor certain business processes [e.g. 8, 9]. The challenges in delivering a comprehensive and broad education in relevant ES topics include, but are not limited to, student traits (including rote-learning, passive natures and poor self-directed e-learning) [10], pedagogy (or a lack thereof), academic partnerships, and instructional material issues [4].

In this article, we present a step-wise guide to aid new faculties in developing curricula and to encourage discourse among existing faculties on addressing the challenges in using ES in curricula. Our article summarizes how educators work alongside the vendor, other educators and students (who, we propose, are constituents of an ES education eco-system) to create joint value in ES teaching and learning. Building on the work of [4] and [2] we discuss how industry trends influence curriculum redesign, such that academics must not only recognize the wealth of ES capabilities, but also acknowledge the challenges institutions face in mining them. Our guide incorporates software vendor-assisted academic alliances, cloud and open source platforms, and e-learning teaching delivery methods that have been developed in recent times. This article builds on and draws on the authors' experience in the past decade with ES curriculum roll-out across three universities in two states in Australia and therefore we do not claim our conceptualizations are the only pedagogical approach. All the universities participating in this research taught the same ES software (i.e. SAP) and were degree-awarding universities at both undergraduate and postgraduate levels.

While an unspoken divide often exists between research and teaching at universities, we believe that it is timely and necessary to combine current curriculum focusing on ES concepts with new research concepts and teaching tools. The authors have researched and experimented with a variety of pedagogical teaching and learning modes for the purpose of developing appropriate ES curriculum. To this end, we conceptualize three phases – negotiation, knowledge and evaluation – and propose that each phase must sustain a particular set of activities to develop an ES curriculum. The roadmap is meant to be a tentative prescription for educators relating to their own adoption, development, co-creation and quality assessment of ES for teaching. The roadmap can form a concrete checklist and guide that informs educators of opportunities when teaching ES.

2   The State of Enterprise Systems Teaching

In the early 1990s, the emphasis in course development was on theoretical ES-related knowledge including the inherent characteristics of the ES software, such that the contact with ES software in classrooms was minimal. During this time, educators consulted published work in the area and drew on their own or other educators' experiences for teaching materials. In this early stage of ES curriculum deployment, the success of the course depended largely on the altruism of the faculty, its members and the subsequent buy-in of other courses. The demand for institutional resources was higher at the outset, while the educators' ownership of teaching content was low. In this mode, universities and faculties tended to commit considerable time and resources to modifying their undergraduate business and IS curriculum to incorporate ES and attempted to build on these foundations. At the California State University, for example, the success of the ES course relied heavily on the degree of altruism of the faculty as there was no particular incentive for faculty members to emphasize skills training, hence reverting to more orthodox academic elements such as frameworks, analogies, conceptual models, and theories. It was reported in [2] that the general strategy at the California State University was for one faculty member (or sometimes a pair) to develop a course idea and initially offer it as a special topics course. If there was sufficient demand generated for the new course, it would ultimately be added to the official college catalog. This bootstrapping approach thus prescribed starting small and building upon prior achievements. Similarly, at Louisiana State University, it was reported that the success of its ES course was largely due to a combination of an established business curriculum and practitioner interest [2].

Over the next two decades, the proliferation of ES across the business landscape prompted the widespread demand for ES-related skills. Even with belt-tightening by employers, the demand for ES graduates subsequently pushed Louisiana State University to develop a competency center to significantly bring down the costs of curriculum development. Courses included hands-on business process integration and management, strategic ES applications, process planning and control, and business intelligence. Today, the SAP University Alliance, Microsoft Dynamics Academic Alliance and Oracle Academic Initiative are examples of outreach programs that provide university faculty members access to a suite of solutions that can illustrate to students how ES can facilitate the integration of business processes. However, despite the existence of such outreach programs and strong demand from the industry, studies including [11] and [12] have revealed that most IS graduates still do not possess the necessary business process and architectural knowledge of ES packages. Reference [13] identified that ES adopting organizations continue to seek graduates who possess core ES technical knowledge, technology management knowledge and business functional knowledge.

3   The Enterprise Systems Education Roadmap

Figure 1 presents the proposed roadmap for teaching with ES, showing the three phases of negotiation, knowledge and evaluation. Within each phase is the set of activities that must be sustained in order to develop an ES curriculum. Each of the activities is discussed in this section.

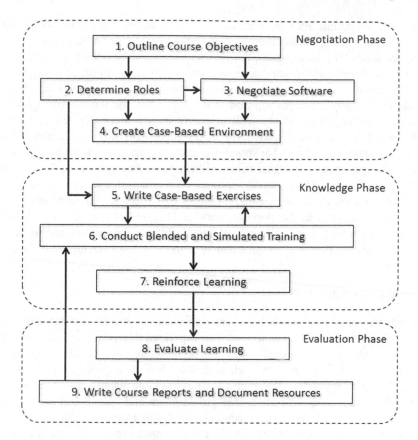

Fig. 1. A roadmap for teaching with ES

3.1   Outline Course Objectives

In the initial phase of negotiating the introduction of an ES course, educators must first outline the specific learning objectives and student learning outcomes, and the relationship of the course to the overall program learning goals and outcomes for all coursework. For example, it might be identified that the aims of the course are to instil an understanding of various ES modules and how they are able to be applied in a business context. For many faculties at a prescribed stage of curriculum development, hands-on experiences with software are often minimal and ES software when implemented may not contain all the information required for all teaching and assessment scenarios; hence, some curricula thrive in the form of spreadsheets or applications. In practice, individual spreadsheets end up acting as central repositories for critical corporate information and are widely regarded as "feral" information systems [14] compared to ES. ES have become the backbone systems for many organizations to integrate back-office applications in goods purchasing, inventory management, finance, and human resource operations; however, ES were not designed for data analysis and decision support [15]. By nature, ES were not originally designed to provide real-time reports to massive numbers of users and these systems possess reporting limitations and involve manual processes [16]. Incidentally, this poses an issue for the often large introductory IS courses in Pacific and Australasian universities in terms of student support and generating reports for assessment purposes. Similarly in the real world, while ES applications are good at capturing and storing data for the day-to-day operations, spreadsheets thrive when dealing with disparate data sources. Regarding curricula content, we found that most foundation courses begin with anecdotal content of how ES have become the critical backbone for many companies' business processes, whereby management and IT organizations alike have become convinced that packaged software (rather than a best-of-breed approach) is a more effective way to satisfy the growing necessities of an increasingly competitive business environment. Subsequently, educators consult the popular work of [17] and [18] to describe how the automation of routine processes in an integrated fashion in the various functional areas such as accounting, inventory control and procurement has become the hallmark of such systems.

3.2   Determine Roles

Merely adopting a notable vendor brand or comprehensive instructional materials is not effective: the course must be enhanced with an experiential learning environment. In ES syllabi, the students should expect to assume an active real-world role in a described case and subsequently be able to work with the ES tools required of that role. For example, students may assume the employee roles in a large manufacturing organization where each student deals with day-to-day procurement and order fulfillment business transactions. Table 1 outlines some examples of roles in a supply chain. To be able to fulfill their roles, students would have to cultivate competence in the role and in the use

Table 1. Examples of roles, titles and related ES utilities in a supply chain [adapted from [19]]

Roles in…	Job Title	Related ES Modules, Functions and Utilities
Financial Management	Finance Manager	General ledger
		Accounts receivables & payables
	Accounts Officer	Consolidation
Sales and Distribution	Sales Manager	Order processing
		Pricing for sales & purchasing
	Inventory Manager	Inventory costing
		Shipment & delivery
Manufacturing	Production Officer	Production orders
		Bill of materials

of the ES tools, through both traditional instructional-centered material and active learning through role-play. This blended learning environment not only provides basic orientation to the ES tools and business roles, it further creates cooperative learning and collaborative work interactions between the students in the later learning phase.

3.3 Negotiate Software

Educators and vendors must work towards an agreement to provide students the opportunity to engage in practical learning experiences that powerfully affirm and complement the member institution's business course curriculum. As the emphasis on the interplay between ES $\leftrightarrow$ workplace knowledge emerged, attention on the adoption of ES software for situated hands-on practice in classrooms grew. Vendors began to make their products available for classroom use. Subsequently, firms like SAP (SAP Education®) now offer 'readymade' software for a variety of ES-related courses that a faculty can implement. Similarly, educators can choose to join an academic alliance offering content and software support from a specific vendor. The impact on institutional resources is high due to the agreement with the software vendor, whilst the educators' ownership of teaching content is high by design. According to recent Gartner research, vendors such as Microsoft, Oracle, SAS, SAP and IBM are leaders – based on the completeness of their vision and ability to execute – in building enterprise-wide platforms on existing applications [in 20]. These leading software vendors distinguish themselves from niche players and challengers in the market by the breadth and depth of their capabilities to support the broad strategies of organizations. That is why the focus of many universities has been on the alignment of ES with strategic organizational frameworks, resulting in internally-funded projects and curricula improvements around ES design and use. The objective has been to motivate students, using a 'recognised vendor brand' ideology. The California State University, Louisiana State University, Worcester Polytechnic Institute and Bentley College (now Bentley University) in the US and Queensland University of Technology in Australia are examples of early alliance members receiving ES support in their curricula design from SAP [2, 6]. US colleges were part of the early SAP University Academic Alliance program which started during the 1996/1997 academic year. In 1997, Louisiana State University became a member of the US program and Queensland University of Technology joined the Australian program. Bentley joined the SAP academic alliance in 1998, and Worcester Polytechnic joined the Oracle program in 2000.

3.4 Create a Support Network

Generally, the members of vendor outreach programs like the SAP and Microsoft academic alliances receive donated software for the classroom, technical support, and access to online training. There has been much enthusiasm for the integration of ICT into higher education and the realization of virtual and electronic learning and teaching environments in recent times [21, 22]. Similarly, we favor an e-learning environment to help students organize their learning and to expose students to pre-determined knowledge and case-oriented problems. Moreover, to create a successful e-learning platform, we rely heavily on back-office administrators and faculty technical helpdesks, to ensure direct and prompt system-related help throughout the sequence of the exercises. In addition, partnerships with vendors introduce business mentors to the programs. Reference [23] highlighted the advantages of having these business support advisors from business incubators, enterprise start-ups and consultancies to enhance the effectiveness of the e-learning tools and the training resource skills required of educators. Through the alliances, ES program coordinators are able to experience first-hand the teaching skills and abilities of real work business advisors to facilitate changes for their small business clients. Furthermore, business mentors act in an advisory capacity during the development of the case-based exercises to supplement the program. These materials are typically designed by faculty with support from alliance mentors and trainers. We suggest that the use of supplementary material and advice generated from academic alliances can enable institutions to be competitive in their educational offerings.

3.5   Write Case-Based Exercises

For the last six years, we have co-developed a number of instructional and learning materials with SAP and Microsoft to immerse students and generate situational awareness of their own 'adopted' roles. Although the teaching case approach has been employed in academic curricula for a long time, a teaching case designed to provide a technical viewpoint using organizational, functional and process viewpoints is atypical in SME and ES curricula. The situated instructional material contains: (1) the steps to complete the procurement and order-fulfillment activities in Microsoft Dynamics but more importantly to extend the current ES syllabi; and (2) the steps to create useful reports for management to add value to the sales process. The philosophy of the instructional material developed is that explanations to the students should be straightforward (less vendor-specific) while emphasizing the learning that can be gained through their analysis of the core sales processes they are completing. The hands-on material provides a worked example [24, 25] to give a systematic demonstration or impart knowledge of how ES are used to solve multiple examples [24] of complex organizational problems including procurement, production planning and order fulfilment (p206). Students also play an important role in co-creating a case-based ES hands-on training schedule. On one hand, a case-based approach is an effective means for higher education to move from more traditional academic to learner-centric pedagogical approaches [26, 27]. However, when set in a more practical context, the challenge (for educators) is to create a business case that: (1) is stimulating enough to invoke discussion and subsequent learning [28]; (2) can demonstrate the practicality of the theoretical teachings; and (3) allows the students to assume a particular role that mimics the real world. Hence, when designing a worked example [24, 25] exercise, the example must allow students to assume role(s) in a case organization, initiate business transactions and experience the business relationships between vendors, clients and customers – given that the educators assume such roles. For this reason, we believe that students play a particularly important role in co-creating a worked example that addresses the identified gaps. In the ES syllabi context, the students are expected to assume an active real-world role in a described case and subsequently are expected to be able to work with the ES tools required of that role. Furthermore, students should perform that role for the duration of the practical program in which they engage in a modular ES (e.g. Microsoft Dynamics NAV).

3.6   Conduct Blended and Simulated Training

In this section, we discuss a blended approach to in-class training that reinforces the textbook theory and principles with ES technical knowledge. Given the proliferation of ES in the current market, it is likely that students and staff are aware of ES concepts. Thus, positioned appropriately within a subject area, ES subjects have shown substantial attraction. Currently, on mature topics of ES, there are trustworthy web and textbook resources in abundance. However, we recommend that a starting university commences with an 'ES lifecycle-wide management' focus and uses an ES to demonstrate fundamental characteristics such as process standardization, best practices, real-time information, multiple-user groups, business processes and complexities in configuration. From a social constructivist viewpoint, and given that students by now are likely to have an understanding of how ES work for specified purposes in an organization, the educator and the learners are equally involved in learning from each other. This interplay, we think, is crucial for constructing a well-structured learning environment (for both the educator and the student), which [29] suggests provides the scaffolding for problem-solving. We think that the benefits are not just for the intended learners. Specifically, through our culture, values and background (as researchers) and including both the subjective and objective learning outcomes as an essential part [30], the interplay between educators, students and tasks shapes the overall learning experience. We have first-hand experience of instances of the benefits provided by such an environment, namely, new publications and repositories, new concepts previously overlooked in the literature, and the potential for new research and analysis of ES topics.

Hence, the emphasis for the faculty becomes building on the adoption of ES software for situated hands-on experiences, in extended and/or simulated environments. For this purpose, educators must actively seek to collaborate through extended activities that promote active teaching and learning. The impact on institutional resources is low, whilst the educators' ownership of the teaching content is high. The running of simulation games is one way to examine the application of practical concepts of ERP in extended activities that promote active teaching and learning. The use of simulation games to enrich ERP programs is gaining popularity, with examples including the so-called muesli supply chain game [9], MURSH-Bikes game [31] and pre/post ERP simulation model game [32]. We comment here on the development of one of these games in the region [see also 33].

The muesli supply chain game (also called ERPsim), designed by HEC Montreal and described in [34, 35], is now used in more than 150 universities worldwide and many Fortune 1000 organizations. Interested universities collaborate and send teams (including a team from the authors' university) to compete with other teams for market share and sales, while at the same time managing the procurement, production, sales and marketing, using SAP. The game involves changing various values and sales parameters within SAP, such as the sale price, in response to the information gleaned from reports such as inventories, market conditions and financials. Each team has an industry mentor from a large logistics firm acting as the supply chain advisor. The game allows students to interact with suppliers, customers and all elements in the supply chain, and teams compete to win the biggest market share by buying raw materials, managing budgets, developing production and distribution schedules, and selling products. They are required to respond to changing variables such as an increase in grain price or a decrease in the foreign exchange rate, with every 25 minutes in the game simulating 30 days in the real world. From our experiences, we find this simulated and collaborative approach to ES education that incorporates a situational case study, business process and software to be useful. Collaborating on a topic of mutual interest with the industry and other academics is also plausible as an extension of the game.

3.7   Reinforce Learning

Typically in our courses, we use a second assignment – and usually a case study assignment – to reinforce the problem-based learning approach (fundamentally between membership and collaborative modes). In this assignment, the students examine a chosen case organization, namely, a real-world organization that has implemented ES, to submit a business report that summarizes the system strategy, implementation sins, critical success factors, business-to-ES fit and extended ES used in the case organization. To complete their assignment, students are encouraged to use a range of resources including published case studies and secondary data such as online articles and other printed media. Often, and with guidance from experienced researchers and educators who implement the case study assignment, the students will develop an understanding of rudimentary theories, their interpretations and the presentation of the case study content [36]. Although studies suggest that using worked examples is an effective instructional strategy to impart the required steps of a complex solution for beginners, [25] suggested that worked examples must be "faded over time" (p203) and replaced with problems for practice. Based on this premise, we use and therefore recommend an assignment to reinforce the students' learning from the laboratory activities. The assignment environment typically describes a problem-based learning approach that originated in the medical field [See 37] where students will adopt the ES to negotiate a series of real-world issues faced by a specified client organization, including inventory, purchasing, logistics and accounting problems. Herein, realistic examples [See 38, p11], feedback and reflection on previous worked example learning processes, and group dynamics are the essential components of problem-solving. During this transition (from worked example to problem-based learning), the educator adapts from the role of instructor to facilitator. As a facilitator, the educator helps students to recognize their role as the vendor, client, inventory manager or account clerk rather than taking the more didactic approach of asking them to solve a complex problem using the ES (e.g. creating a firm planned production order from a sales order). Students, who have by now developed some expertise [25, p.247] with the system, must be and are encouraged to play an active part in generating their own understanding of their role and the problem scenario, and to arrive at their own conclusions. From a constructivist learning perspective [38], this approach encourages students to be active learners, promotes educator-student interchange and is therefore more likely to promote social knowledge construction. Similar to the propositions by Kukla [39] and Savery and Duffy (2001), we believe that through the capture and assessment of deliverables (e.g. the creation of purchase order, goods receipt, picking list) generated from the system, students can compare their version of the truth with that of the educator and fellow learners to get to a new, socially tested version of truth.

3.8 Evaluate Learning

Not surprisingly, feedback should be sought from students and other stakeholders, and continual improvements should be made based on this feedback. However, we do not find a consensual approach to the gathering of student evaluative feedback. According to [40], little research had been conducted on methods to measure the effect of course

Table 2. Selected dimensions and measures for gauging student satisfaction

Measure	Indicators	Sources
System Quality		
Features and functions (SQ5)	SAP ERP includes necessary features and functions	Adapted from [41]
Level of integration (SQ9)	All data within SAP ERP are fully integrated and consistent	Adapted from [41]
Information Quality		
Formatting (IQ4)	Order fulfillment outputs generated from SAP ERP appear readable, clear and well formatted	Adapted from [41]
Conciseness (IQ5)	Order fulfillment outputs generated from SAP ERP are concise (to the point)	Adapted from [41]
Individual Impact		
Learning (II1)	I have learnt much about order fulfillment through SAP	Adapted from [41]
Awareness (II2)	What I completed in SAP ERP has increased my awareness of order fulfillment	Adapted from [41]
System Use		
Frequency (F1)	I spend X number of hours per week on the system completing my tasks	[42]
Exploration level (DP5)	I have explored additional system features in SAP ERP beyond the given specifications	New scale

material on student understanding or students' broader knowledge of business issues. The use of surveys can be considered to: (1) track the students' reactions to the system, tasks and instructions; and (2) evaluate the learning outcomes, at either an early stage or latter stage of the system interaction or both. Toward this end, we recommend a set of measures including ease of use of the system, ease of learning with the system, understandability of reports generated from the system, un-expectancies encountered, adequacy of instructions and so on to canvass the students' reactions to the curricula. Table 2 presents a set of four dimensions and measures that is proposed to represent an overarching measure of student satisfaction.

3.9   Write Course Reports and Document Resources

Individual experiences can be shared by constituents in an ES education eco-system. In the present mode, institutions sign an agreement with an alliance that, in turn, provides content and software. Despite the growth in support structures especially through vendors, current academic institutions and new universities in the SAP academic alliance that are considering teaching ES still face resource constraints. For example, SAP University Competence Centers (UCC) provide access to software through a not-for-profit model. Universities could benefit from UCC curricula by sharing web portals and gaining access to well-tested curricula that is tailor-made for the software access provided by the UCC. Toward this end, faculties can encourage bricolage: by reapplying combinations of existing resources, educators can transform modest resources into contributions that are accessible by the academic community.

This is typical of a bricolage strategy which prescribes a combination and reuse of resources for different applications than those for which they were originally intended or used [43]. Educators in the SAP University Alliance, for instance, share their experiences (through university alliances, competency centers and community sites) to reinforce their own syllabus. For example, several versions of instructional material building on the Global Bikes Inc®, Fitter Snacker® and Fly-a-Kite® datasets have been created, characterizing the re-invention, implementation and testing conducted by the faculties. Encouraging other educators, vendors and students to collaborate via established networks and groups for learning can further establish their curriculum. In order to enhance the co-creation [44, 45] of ES education value, the strategy of developing a relationship with an academic alliance must start with the recognition of the university's infrastructure capabilities and the centrality of processes. Whilst the benefits of joining an academic alliance are evident, the management of the relationship is not so straightforward. The potential for co-creation is evident, given the present state of ES availability and adoption in classrooms. Faculties must understand that co-creation is about the joint creation of value by the vendor and the faculty, not the vendor trying to please the faculty: when managing the co-creation of value, educators highlight the importance of investing in new infrastructure capabilities that are centered on creating markets as a space for potential co-creation experiences. Today, universities have a unique opportunity to develop materials to fit their own contexts and based on the localized scenario. For example, if a particular industry is dominating employment in the location (e.g. mining, automobile, health), universities could develop ES teaching around those industries.

4 Conclusion

This article presents a roadmap for developing a relevant ES course. The roadmap, consisting of ten steps in three overarching phases – negotiation, knowledge and evaluation – offers a more focused effort to curricula design and assessment that reflects current practices in ES education. Our paper provides a checklist and a tentative prescription for educators relating to their own adoption of ES for teaching purposes. More and more faculties are looking to vendor outreach programs to provide access to software and to address the industry deficit for skilled graduates created by the widespread use of ES. However, the successful incorporation of vendor ES and associated materials for classroom use is not straightforward. Our roadmap introduces actionable guidelines to take advantage of hosting services, curriculum support, faculty training and collaboration. We add to the ES education literature on how educators co-create or intend to co-create value within the new ES education eco-system of which they have ultimately become a member (or a constituent). Furthermore, we encourage discussion about our roadmap, particularly in relation to the co-creation of value not only between new faculties and vendors but also between groups of currently participating faculties, and between educators and students through a wider digital network.

References

1. Borquez, A., Connolly, J., Corbitt, G., Mensching, J., Sager, J.: Benefits of academic alliance education: the employer's perspective. In: Editor (ed.): Book Benefits of Academic Alliance Education: The Employer's Perspective (edn.) (2005)
2. Strong, D., Fedorowicz, J., Sager, J., Stewart, G., Watson, E.: Teaching with enterprise systems. Commun. AIS **17**(33), 2–49 (2006)
3. Hawking, P., McCarthy, B., Stein, A.: Second wave ERP education. J. Inf. Syst. Educ. **15**(3), 327–332 (2004)
4. Cameron, B.H.: Enterprise systems education: new directions and challenges for the future. In: Editor (ed.): Book Enterprise Systems Education: New Directions and Challenges for the Future. (edn.), pp. 119–126 (2008)
5. Corbitt, G., Mensching, J.: Integrating SAP R/3 into a college of business curriculum: lessons learned. Inf. Technol. Manag. **1**(4), 247–258 (2000)
6. Markus, M.: Lynne introduction to the 2004 AIS award papers on innovation in information systems education. Commun. Assoc. Inf. Syst. **15**, 16 (2005)
7. Strong, D.M., Johnson, S.A., Mistry, J.J.: Integrating enterprise decision-making modules into undergraduate management and industrial engineering curricula. J. Inf. Syst. Educ. **15**(3), 301 (2004)
8. Draijer, C., Schenk, D.: Best practices of business simulation with SAP R/3. J. Inf. Syst. Educ. **15**(3), 261–265 (2004)
9. Leger, P.-M.: Using a simulation game approach to teach enterprise resource planning concepts. J. Inf. Syst. Educ. **17**(4), 441 (2006)
10. Kember, D.: Misconceptions about the learning approaches, motivation and study practices of asian students. High. Educ. **40**(1), 99–121 (2000)
11. Kim, Y., Hsu, J., Stern, M.: An update on the IS/IT skills gap. J. Inf. Syst. Educ. **17**(4), 395 (2006)

12. Rosemann, M., Maurizio, A.A.: SAP-related education - status quo and experiences. J. Inf. Syst. Educ. **16**(4), 437 (2005)
13. Boyle, T.A., Strong, S.E.: Skill requirements of ERP graduates. J. Inf. Syst. Educ. **17**(4), 403–412 (2006)
14. Houghton, L., Kerr, D.V.: A study into the creation of feral information systems as a response to an ERP implementation within the supply chain of a large government-owned corporation. Int. J. Internet Enterp. Manage. **4**(2), 135–147 (2006)
15. Yen, D.C., Chou, D.C., Chang, J.: A synergic analysis for web-based enterprise resources planning systems. Comput. Stan. Interfaces **24**(4), 337–346 (2002)
16. Oleskow, J., Fertsch, M., Golinska, P., Maruszewska, K., Gómez, J.M., Sonnenschein, M., Müller, M., Welsch, H., Rautenstrauch, C.: Data mining as a suitable tool for efficient supply chain integration - extended abstract information technologies in environmental engineering. In: Allan, R., Förstner, U., Salomons, W. (ed.) Springer, Heidelberg, pp. 321–325 (2007)
17. Markus, L.M., Tanis, C., van Fenema, P.C.: Enterprise resource planning: multisite ERP implementations. Commun. ACM **43**(4), 42–46 (2000)
18. Davenport, T.H.: The future of enterprise system-enabled organizations. Inf. Syst. Front. **2**(2), 163–180 (2000)
19. Hilletofth, P.: Enterprise resource planning systems in higher education. In: Editor (ed.): Book Enterprise Resource Planning Systems in Higher Education Lappeenranta University of Technology, edn., pp. 167–180 (2008)
20. Feiman, J., MacDonald, N.: 2010 Gartner magic quadrant for business intelligence platforms. In: Editor (ed.): Book 2010 Gartner Magic Quadrant for Business Intelligence Platforms Gartner, edn. (2010)
21. Santhanam, R., Sasidharan, S., Webster, J.: Using self-regulatory learning to enhance e-learning-based information technology training. Inf. Syst. Res. **19**(1), 26–47 (2008)
22. Sun, P.-C., Tsai, R.J., Finger, G., Chen, Y.-Y., Yeh, D.: What drives a successful e-learning? An empirical investigation of the critical factors influencing learner satisfaction. Comput. Educ. **50**(4), 1183–1202 (2008)
23. Everall, L., Sanders, R., Hamill, C.: Enhancing business support to SME's through continuous work-based e-learning for business advisory professionals. In: Editor (ed.): Book Enhancing Business Support to SME's Through Continuous Work-Based e-Learning for Business Advisory Professionals (edn.), pp. 346–353 (2008)
24. Atkinson, R.K., Derry, S.J., Renkl, A., Wortham, D.W.: Learning from examples: instructional principles from the worked examples research. Rev. Educ. Res. **70**(2), 181–214 (2000)
25. Clark, R.C., Nguyen, F., Sweller, J.: Efficiency in learning: evidence-based guidelines to manage cognitive load. In: Editor (ed.): Book Efficiency in Learning: Evidence-Based Guidelines to Manage Cognitive Load. Pfeiffer, John Wiley, Inc, edn. (2006)
26. Jacobsen, B.: Assessable case based activities: towards student centred teaching in information systems. In: Editor (ed.): Book Assessable Case Based Activities: Towards Student Centred Teaching in Information Systems (edn.) (2007)
27. Leveson, L.: Encouraging better learning through better teaching: a study of approaches to teaching in accounting. Acc. Educ. **13**, 4 (2004)
28. Hackney, R., McMaster, T., Harris, A.: Using cases as a teaching tool in IS education. J. Inf. Syst. Educ. **14**(3), 229 (2003)
29. Jonassen, D.H.: Instructional design models for well-structured and ill-structured problem-solving learning outcomes. Educ. Tech. Res. Dev. **45**(1), 65–94 (1997)
30. Hmelo-Silver, C.E., Barrows, H.S.: Goals and strategies of a problem-based learning facilitator. Interdisc. J. Prob.-based Learn. **1**, 21–39 (2006)

31. Adelsberger, H.H., Bick, M.H., Kraus, U.F., Pawlowski, J.M.: A simulation game approach for efficient education in enterprise resource planning systems. In: Editor (ed.): Book A Simulation Game Approach for Efficient Education in Enterprise Resource Planning Systems (Information Systems for Production and Operations Management, University of Essen, edn.), pp. 1–7 (1999)

32. Ritchie-Dunham, J., Morrice, D.J., Scott, J., Anderson, E.G.: A strategic supply chain simulation model. In: Editor (ed.): Book A Strategic Supply Chain Simulation Model (edn.) vol. 1262, pp. 1260–1264 (2000)

33. Foster, S., Hopkins, J.: ERP simulation game: establishng engagement, collaboration and learning. In: Editor (ed.): Book ERP Simulation Game: Establishng Engagement, Collaboration and Learning (edn.) (2011). http://aisel.aisnet.org/pacis2011/2062

34. Léger, P.-M.: Using a simulation game approach to teach ERP concepts. In: Editor (ed.): Book Using a Simulation Game Approach to Teach ERP Concepts (HEC Montréal, edn.), pp. 1–15 (2006)

35. Léger, P.-M., Charland, P., Feldstein, H.D., Robert, J., Babin, G., Lyle, D.: Business simulation training in information technology education: guidelines for new approaches in IT training. J. Inf. Technol. Educ. **10**, 37–51 (2011). [1547-9714] yr:2011 vol:10 pg:39

36. Eisenhardt, K.M.: Building theories from case study research. Acad. Manag. Rev. **14**(4), 532–550 (1989)

37. Barrows, H.S.: A taxonomy of problem based learning methods. Med. Educ. **20**, 481–486 (1986)

38. Savery, J.R., Duffy, T.M.: Problem based learning: an instructional model and its constructivist framework. In: Editor (ed.): Book Problem Based Learning: An Instructional Model and its Constructivist Framework (Center for Research on Learning and Technology, edn.), pp. 1–19 (2001)

39. Kukla, A.: Social Constructivism and the Philosophy of Science. Routledge, London (2000)

40. Antonucci, Y.L., Corbitt, G., Stewart, G., Harris, A.L.: Enterprise systems education: where are we? where are we going? J. Inf. Syst. Educ. **15**(3), 227 (2004)

41. Gable, G., Sedera, D., Chan, T.: Re-conceptualizing information systems success: the IS-impact measurement model. J. Assoc. Inf. Syst. **9**(7), 377–408 (2008)

42. Cheung, C.M.K., Limayem, M.: The role of habit and changing nature of the relationship between intention and usage. In: Editor (ed.): Book The Role of Habit and Changing Nature of the Relationship between Intention and Usage (edn.) (2005)

43. Baker, T., Nelson, R.E.: Creating something from nothing: resource construction through entrepreneurial bricolage. Adm. Sci. Q. **50**(3), 329–366 (2005)

44. Prahalad, C.K., Ramaswamy, V.: Co-creation experiences: the next practice in value creation. J. Interact. Mark. **18**(3), 5–14 (2004)

45. Vargo, S.L., Maglio, P.P., Akaka, M.A.: On value and value co-creation: a service systems and service logic perspective. Eur. Manag. J. **26**(3), 145–152 (2008)

Factors Affecting Perceived Satisfaction with a BPM Tool: A Student Perspective

Judy E. Scott[✉] and Jae Hoon Choi

University of Colorado Denver, Denver, USA
{judy.scott,jae.choi}@ucdenver.edu

Abstract. This pedagogical study reports on an innovative collaboration with a business process management (BPM) software vendor. The purpose was to analyze factors affecting students' perceived satisfaction with the vendor's tool. Although BPM software potentially enhances organizations' productivity, user satisfaction is necessary for realization of that goal. Students in teams participated in a process modeling and simulation assignment that required a description of their experience with the BPM tool. Analysis of students' comments using grounded theory resulted in eight propositions and a conceptual model. User knowledge and the quality of the documentation affect perceived ease of use and the skills in report generation that result in user satisfaction. As a result of the student feedback, the vendor may modify the BPM software, which could improve perceived satisfaction and increase productivity in adopting organizations. Suggestions for teaching BPM courses offer implications for educational research.

Keywords: Business process management · Perceived user satisfaction · Simulation

1 Introduction

Business Process Management (BPM) is important to organizations that aspire to efficiency in terms of minimizing costs and the time taken to perform tasks [5, 18, 22]. BPM is also used to improve and monitor business processes associated with regulations and quality [20, 34]. Furthermore, making a process explicit and transparent with BPM prepares the organization for implementing systems and training users [23].

BPM has many alternative definitions. However there is agreement that BPM is (1) a management practice or discipline [1], (2) a general term for the study and improvement of business processes [11, 16, 17], and (3) a set of methods, techniques, tools and technologies to support business process improvement [1, 6]. Nevertheless, there is a lack of a consensus of what BPM really entails [5, 6, 11].

Critical BPM activities and skill sets include process modeling, process analysis, process design, process performance management and process transformation [1, 15, 22, 43]. Process modeling is the set of activities involved in creating diagrams, mapping and models to represent a business process. A process diagram uses simple notation to depict the major elements of a process flow, while a process map is more detailed and

© Springer International Publishing Switzerland 2015
D. Sedera et al. (Eds.): Pre-ICIS 2010-2012, LNBIP 198, pp. 174–189, 2015.
DOI: 10.1007/978-3-319-17587-4_12

may include actors and events. Modeling implies further precision and the use of tools that provide simulation and reporting capabilities.

Process analysis is the first step in establishing a new process or updating an existing process [1]. It is the creation of a common understanding of the current state of the process and its alignment with the business objectives. Techniques used for process analysis include mapping, interviewing, simulations and a study of interactions external to the organization, such as government or industry regulations, market forces and competition. Process design involves the creation of specifications for new and modified business processes. The design takes into account the business context, such as goals and objectives, existing technology and integration with other processes. Process performance management is concerned with metrics, such as time, cost, capacity and quality. The purpose of the metrics is to attribute a value to improving or changing a process. Process transformation is the planned evolution of a business process when the organization uses a clearly defined methodology to monitor and respond to internal and external factors through a strategy of continuous improvement or by initiating needed projects.

Most published BPM research has focused on process modeling [4, 7, 25–30]. Very little BPM research has appeared on process analysis, process performance management, empirical studies and social issues [17]. Furthermore, pedagogical research is needed [3, 10, 11, 40]. This study contributes by attempting to fill gaps in BPM pedagogical research. This research also concerns process analysis and is an empirical study.

The objective of this study is to determine factors affecting students' perceived satisfaction with a BPM tool. The students used the BPM tool for an assignment that included process modeling, process analysis, process design and process performance management. The analysis of students' comments reveals issues with ease of use and documentation. Specifically, students remarked on difficulties with process modeling and simulation report generation. Implications for practice include possible modifications to the BPM tools by the vendor. Implications for educational research include suggestions for offering or improving BPM courses. This is important because practitioners are keen to hire students with knowledge and skills in BPM [8].

The rest of this chapter is organized as follows. The research question is made explicit and a background of published research on BPM and BPM education are presented. Published research on perceived user satisfaction, perceived user satisfaction with BPM, and perceived student satisfaction with BPM software are discussed. In the next sections, the methodology, findings, discussion are presented. The chapter concludes with a summary of the main findings, limitations of the study and implications for research, education and practice.

2   Research Question

The research question for this study is: What are students' perceptions of BPM software? A theoretical understanding of factors that determine satisfaction with BPM software would benefit students and instructors, as well as BPM software vendors, corporate users and organizations adopting BPM.

3   Theoretical Background

In this section, we discuss a background of published research on BPM and BPM education as well as research on perceived user satisfaction, perceived user satisfaction with BPM, and perceived student satisfaction with BPM software.

3.1   BPM Research

Research published on BPM varies from highly technical to behavioral. Searches on the term "BPM" in the AIS eLibrary reveal that organizational-focused BPM research has been limited mostly to conference proceedings. However, there are some recent journal publications exceptions [3, 25–29] and the volume of publications increased markedly in 2010. Nevertheless, there are many gaps to fill and much research remains to be done. Specifically, a literature review in 2009 found little empirical work and not much published on social issues [17].

Publications focus on process modeling, such as user acceptance of process modeling grammars, specifically Business Process Model and Notation (BPMN) [27], and the effects of content presentation format and user characteristics on understanding of process models [25]. Business process modeling success has also been researched [4]. Research on business process design includes studies on workflow and process improvement. Business process transformation research includes studies on business process change [32] and business process reengineering [31].

Despite the plethora of work conducted, there are still issues in relation to BPM that arise and which vary according to perspectives of the stakeholders. From the vendors' perspective, poor understanding of business processes, inadequate training and a lack of BPM standards are major issues [33]. According to educators, issues include a lack of appropriate expertise in the field, lack of resources to develop BPM expertise and difficulty in communicating across multiple stakeholders in the field [5, 6, 11].

3.2   BPM Education Research

Several BPM publications focus on education [3, 5, 8–10, 25, 26, 40]. A descriptive study of a student contest revealed that academic experience and age affected the quality of the business process solution [36]. BPM education did not correlate with the results.

Nevertheless, the need for BPM education has increased with the acceptance of BPM by practitioners, who are keen to hire students with knowledge and skills in business process modeling, simulation and other aspects of BPM [8]. However, appropriate BPM education is not widespread [5, 11].

A BPM education panel at the 2009 European Conference on Information Systems addressed status, challenges and future issues associated with BPM courses and programs [10]. Several tertiary institutions world-wide reported that they teach BPM courses to graduate and undergraduate students. For example, Bentley University and Georgia State University in the USA, Queensland University of Technology in Brisbane

Australia, University of Pretoria in South Africa and University of Vienna in Austria offer state of the art BPM courses [3]. While the two USA programs above are in business schools, the others are in Science and Technology, Engineering and Computer Science respectively. Programs outside of business schools are more likely to be technical and less likely to focus on organizational issues. Challenges in a comparative analysis of the five universities, mentioned above offering BPM courses, include (1) lack of pedagogical resources; (2) positioning BPM courses within the degrees; (3) heavy technology load; (4) minimum course enrollments; (5) limited pedagogical research; and (6) unclear career pathways for students.

Other studies have found there are issues with defining and interpreting the content and boundaries of this emerging field, staying up to date with the dynamic nature of the discipline, developing appropriate teaching resources, and identifying the best teaching practices for preparing graduates for a successful BPM career [6, 11].

Students' satisfaction with using BPM tools is important because their attitude will affect decisions in their careers. If they have a positive attitude then it is more likely they will become BPM evangelists and promote BPM in their workplace. BPM adoption, along with strategic alignment, task technology fit and other critical success factors, has the potential to enhance organizational performance [2, 42].

Perceived User Satisfaction. User information satisfaction (UIS) is one of the five factors of system success [12, 13, 37]. UIS is described as a "perceptual and subjective measure of system success" [38]. Prior research on perceived user satisfaction has focused on systems other than BPM software. For example, determinants of UIS assessed for a general ledger accounting system included relevance, content, accuracy and timeliness of the information produced by the system [38]. Measures of UIS from prior research were used [14, 19, 38]. The researchers also measured satisfaction with the G/L-system features, such as report generation and documentation. Questions were asked on user knowledge, training, ease of use and feature usefulness.

Perceived User Satisfaction with BPM. A research study has been published on user satisfaction with BPM based on the IS success model and the Technology Acceptance Model (TAM) [24]. The findings show that user satisfaction is affected by perceived ease of use (PEOU) and perceived usefulness (PU). PEOU and PU are affected by input and output quality, which are in turn affected by training and support. Although system quality does not directly impact PEOU and PU, it is correlated with input and output quality.

Also, a study on a business process modeling success instrument included UIS [4]. Measures were used for satisfaction with (1) the information conveyed by the process models, and (2) the graphical design of the process models as well as (3) enjoyment using the process models. The measure for "Enjoyment" was adapted from a study on end-user computing satisfaction [14]. However, satisfaction was removed from the final model because of high correlation with "model quality" [4, 39].

Perceived Student Satisfaction with BPM Software. Although some universities and colleges report that students are satisfied with their BPM courses [26], research shows that teaching BPM courses is risky. As mentioned earlier, risks stem from such factors as (1) the lack of pedagogical resources; (2) positioning BPM courses within the degrees; (3) heavy technology load; (4) minimum course enrollments; (5) limited pedagogical research; and (6) unclear career pathways for students [3, 10]. Students are likely to be dissatisfied with inadequate textbooks and other resources and the lack of technology support. Technology support is important for users who lack experience with the tools. As discussed earlier, lack of BPM work experience and prior experience with modeling increase the cognitive load and challenges user understanding [25]. A lower cognitive load will increase PEOU. PEOU was a significant antecedent of satisfaction in a European study [24].

4   Methodology

This section discusses the data collection and data analysis of student comments on using BPM software. Data were collected from graduate students taking a BPM course in a business school at a US university. Most of the students worked full time and took classes at night or online. The course was offered mostly online for several tracks in the Masters programs. Very few students were familiar with BPM software or the concepts of BPM prior to taking the BPM course. However, some students had experience using a drawing tool such as Visio in other courses or at work.

Students worked in teams of three to five individuals on a BPM modeling and simulation assignment, based on an exercise in a BPM book [20]. The teams submitted answers to several questions including instructions to write a paragraph on their experience with the BPM tool. Thirty seven sets of student comments were collected from 2006 to 2012.

The BPM tool used was Ultimus Process Designer. It was chosen to coordinate with a BPM book written by the company founder [20]. The company was founded in 1994 and has over 2,000 customers worldwide. The software has mature features for drawing a process that enables simulating "what if" scenarios based on a set of assumptions. It provides workload and throughput analysis so users can identify bottlenecks and improve the process.

From 2006 to 2010, student teams downloaded the BPM software from a website. When it was no longer available online, the instructor contacted the software vendor for access. Also, for extra credit students could repeat the assignment with another BPM tool.

In 2011, students received login information that enabled them access to a series of three webinars focused on the use of the Ultimus BPM tool. A few weeks later, eight teams accessed the BPM tool remotely using "GoToMyPC". The vendor organized a separate server for each team loaded with the BPM software. This procedure was generous of the vendor since it involved some expense, such as purchase of some of the servers. It also involved vendor time since there were a few instances of the need to reboot the servers. This form of access avoided installation issues, such as crashing computers, since students did not install the software on their own computers. In 2012, three student teams had similar access to the software and training as the teams did in 2011.

The commentary from students was imported into a free-form database for inductive qualitative analysis. The objective was to develop grounded theory [41]. Initial open coding of the data suggested consistent themes, which were reinforced and integrated with the literature review. During axial coding, relationships among sub-categories and themes emerged. Two researchers coded independently and resolved any disagreements by explaining their coding rationale.

Table 1 shows that the BPM course delivery varied over the years from on campus to online or hybrid. GoToMyPC was only used in 2011 and 2012. Over 100 students took the BPM course over the 7 years. However, comments were only required from each team, not each individual. A few teams, such as in 2008, did not provide comments. In 2012, individuals commented.

Table 1. Data collection

Year	Comments	Course Delivery	GoToMyPC
2006	6	Online	No
2007	3	Online	No
2008	1	On campus	No
2009	4	Online	No
2010	6	Online	No
2011	8	Hybrid	Yes
2012	9	Hybrid	Yes
Total	37		

In addition, in 2011 and 2012, students completed a course survey anonymously. One of the questions asked students their opinion on the learning experience of the modeling assignment.

5   Findings

The course survey results showed that 85.7 % students in 2011 and 77.8 % students in 2012 thought the assignment was a "good learning experience" or a "very good learning experience". Only 2 students in each year stated that it was poor or very poor learning experience.

Despite the variation in the BPM courses over the seven years, most of the comments in the assignment coded into consistent themes. The themes that developed from coding the data and from the literature review were (1) documentation, (2) user knowledge, (3) ease of use and (4) report generation. Each theme was coded into sub-categories and summarized in Table 2. Examples of student perception quotes are given for each theme and sub-category for each theme in Table 3.

Table 2. Themes

Themes	Sub-categories
Documentation	Online help
	Search engine
User knowledge	Tool experience
	Tutorial use
Ease of use	User interface
	"GoToMyPC"
	Scenarios
Report generation	Tabular reports
	Graphical reports

The documentation theme has two sub-categories: online help and the search engine. Although some students thought the help file was "well organized and concise", several students complained about the lack of context sensitive help and not enough details provided for them to know what to do with the tool. One student praised the help file as "really helpful because we can search any topic that we want to know." On the other hand, another student thought the search engine was "incoherent."

User knowledge has two sub-categories: tool experience and tutorial use. Almost all the students had not had any experience with a BPM tool. Their knowledge was limited to what they had learned in the course. Several referred to a high learning curve and "unfamiliarity" with the tool. One group declared that the BPM tool was "easy to learn after viewing the 25-minute training video." However, most groups did not comment on the online training that the vendor provided. The vendor provided an activity report which showed logs for the online training. Since only one login was provided for the class including the instructor and teaching assistant, it was not possible to determine which students accessed the training. However, the number of IP addresses on the report was 25 while the number of students in the class was 32. This casts doubt that all students in the class took advantage of the online training webinars. The vendor has offered to issue separate logins for each student next time the course is offered. This would provide data on training at the individual level.

Earlier in the semester the course included content on "swim lanes." Some students commented on the lack of this feature in the BPM tool. For example, students were surprised that the tool "lacked the ability to create standard swim lanes and used 'swim colors' instead" to highlight "various flowbots with a halo of color." Although the

Table 3. Examples of student perceptions

Themes/ Sub-categories	Examples of student perceptions
Documentation/ Online help	"The online help attached to the tool could be more user friendly."
Documentation/ Search engine	"…is really helpful because we can search any topic that we want to know."
User knowledge/ Tool experience	"Granted my unfamiliarity with using a BPM tool may be influencing my opinion on this."
User knowledge/ Tutorial use	"I have to say that the tutorial was not clear, and the help list was not helpful as well. I learned the most from my mistakes and by practice."
Ease of use/User interface	"The Graphical User Interface was quite good for the most part, but it felt cumbersome to make the lines straight and to make them look visually appealing."
Ease of use/"GoTo-MyPC"	"The remote connection did cause problems, as we lost the ability to save our model, as well as the ability to save, load and compare various scenarios."
Ease of use/ Scenarios	"The model and scenario files can become out of sync very easily, which means that a scenario file cannot be loaded with a model file."
Report generation/ Tabular reports	"The modeling allowed us to generate excellent graphical and tabular reports. The tabular reports could then be exported into Microsoft Excel."
Report generation/ Graphical reports	"Having both the tabular and graphical views allowed for two different methods for relaying process metrics."

documentation considered "this was a feature not a defect", students thought it "created confusion and made the diagrams even more difficult to interpret." They would have preferred the tool "allowed the user to switch between swim lanes and swim colors the same way they allowed the user to switch back and forth between standard BPMN glyphs and X glyphs." Another student said "a swim lane could be useful if you wished to print the diagram on a black and white printer, whereas the swim colors would be difficult to distinguish." Furthermore, by not including swim lane functionality, "companies looking to switch vendors for a process modeling tool may not pursue this product."

The ease of use theme has three sub-categories: the user interface, "GoToMyPC" and scenarios. Some students thought the user interface was "well designed and intuitive" and "very much looked like Microsoft Visio." However, others complained that it was "unfriendly" and "cumbersome." The "GoToMyPC" eliminated installation problems but hindered collaboration since only one user from each group could login at a time. Some students found it "very challenging to build and run scenarios" which was a part of the simulation feature of the BPM tool, in which the task resources can be modified. Students had problems saving and reloading scenarios on the remote connected host, and could not compare the reports of two different scenarios.

Finally, the report generation theme has two sub-categories: tabular reports and graphical reports. Several students found that the reporting functions seemed to be "excellent", "rather good," "more than adequate" or "easily readable." However, one student did not think it was "obvious what all the data on the report meant."

In the next section, we discuss relationships among the themes and sub-categories generating eight propositions and a conceptual model.

6   Discussion

In this section, we discuss our findings and integrate the findings with the literature to arrive at a conceptual model and eight propositions. Relationships among constructs in the conceptual model are shown in Fig. 1. Table 4 shows support for the propositions based on the students' comments.

The course survey revealed that most students were satisfied overall with "the learning experience". Nevertheless, some were critical of the BPM software, probably partly due to the stress of time constraints in completing the assignment and worry about grades.

Despite issues with process model satisfaction in prior research [4, 39], and drawing on [38], we propose that user satisfaction with BPM software would be better measured with specific questions on such features as simulation report generation and documentation. Our rationale is that process models are an intermediate outcome while report

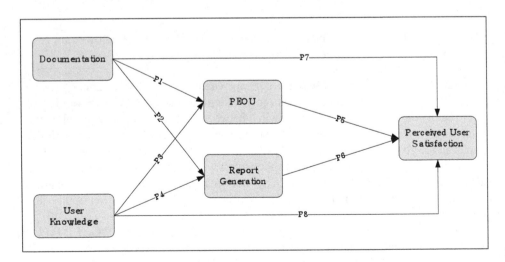

Fig. 1. Conceptual model and propositions

Table 4. Support for propositions

Proposition	Examples of student perceptions
P1: Documentation -> PEOU	"Ultimus help is easy to navigate and thorough with details and explanations. Ultimus is a great tool for users with no modeling experience; the interface is user friendly and easy to learn."
P2: Documentation -> Report generation	"The documentation was pretty sparse ... I found that significant trial-and-error time was required to get anything to work."
P3: User knowledge -> PEOU	"The Process Designer – Support Process online demonstration offered a helpful, brief explanation of creating the process map, and the application soon became easy to use and understand."
P4: User knowledge -> Report generation	"It took some trial and error getting to get the tool to generate reports. I eventually did get the tool to generate the reports."
P5: PEOU -> User satisfaction	"Some of the easier aspects were (1) drag-and-drop features and (2) right clicking into Properties, such as General and Scenario, to update the length of time, sigma, and number of resources."
P6: Report generation -> User satisfaction	"The report generation process was surprisingly quick and the report information was visually clean and easily readable."
P7: Documentation -> User satisfaction	"We also think that the help section is really helpful and well structured. It explains every window, menu, and symbol that are involved in modeling process."
P8: User knowledge -> User satisfaction	"The BPM Modeling software was easy to learn after viewing the 25-minute Process Modeling training video."

generation is a final outcome that facilitates decision making. BPM tool documentation in the form of adequate online help would provide support and encourage the perception that the tool is easy to use [24].

Students who found the documentation adequate (such as the student below) usually thought the BPM tool was easy to use.

"Ultimus help is easy to navigate and thorough with details and explanations. Ultimus is a great tool for users with no modeling experience; the interface is user friendly and easy to learn."

Consequently, the data and prior research lead us to our first proposition:

P1: BPM tool documentation affects perceived ease of use of the BPM tool.

Instructions in the documentation should facilitate report generation [38]. Reports generated by BPM software include simulation reports [1].

The following student's comments showed that documentation affected report generation.

"The documentation was pretty sparse … I found that significant trial-and-error time was required to get anything to work… I was able to get the process model to run and generate a report, but I don't think I had all the properties set correctly, and it was not obvious what all the data on the report meant."

This student perceived that more detailed documentation would have helped report generation. So, the second proposition follows:

P2: BPM tool documentation affects simulation report generation with the BPM tool.

User knowledge is also important [38]. User knowledge is affected by training and prior experience. BPM vendors believe that user training is often inadequate [33]. A recent study found that user understanding of process models depends on BPM work experience, prior experience with modeling and English as a second language [25]. A quantitative study found that training was a statistically significant antecedent of PEOU [24].

The following student appreciated the online training and perceived the software was easy to use.

"The Process Designer – Support Process online demonstration offered a helpful, brief explanation of creating the process map, and the application soon became easy to use and understand."

The student gained the knowledge to understand and use the tool. So, the third proposition follows:

P3: User knowledge affects perceived ease of use of the BPM tool.

Simulation is an important feature in BPM tools [1] and is used to improve processes and for decision support [21, 32, 35]. However, user knowledge is necessary to run simulations and to interpret the results, as illustrated by the following student comment.

"It took some trial and error getting to get the tool to generate reports. I eventually did get the tool to generate the reports."

In this case, the student gained knowledge by trial and error. So, the fourth proposition follows:

P4: User knowledge affects simulation report generation with the BPM tool.

As explained earlier, users with higher PEOU are more satisfied with a technology tool because of the lower cognitive load. PEOU was a significant antecedent of satisfaction in a European study [24].

The following student seems satisfied with the software.

"Some of the easier aspects were (1) drag-and-drop features and (2) right clicking into Properties, such as General and Scenario, to update the length of time, sigma, and number of resources."

This student found some of the features easy to use. So, the fifth proposition follows:

P5: Perceived ease of use of the BPM tool affects perceived user satisfaction.

Generating simulation reports with the BPM tool will promote user satisfaction. The reports provide insights on bottlenecks and alternatives to improve and optimize processes [21, 32, 35]. This is an important goal for using a BPM tool.

The following student was satisfied with the report generation feature of the software.

"The report generation process was surprisingly quick and the report information was visually clean and easily readable."

This student was surprised are how quickly the software generated reports. So, the sixth proposition follows:

P6: BPM tool simulation report generation affects perceived user satisfaction.

As discussed earlier, the BPM tool documentation is a form of support that enhances user satisfaction by providing instructions on how to use the tool.

This student seems to be satisfied with the software partly due to the documentation.

"We also think that the help section is really helpful and well structured. It explains every window, menu, and symbol that are involved in modeling process."

This student's comment shows that documentation contributes to user satisfaction. So, the seventh proposition follows:

P7: BPM tool documentation affects perceived user satisfaction.

User knowledge lowers the cognitive load leading to greater perceived user satisfaction [24].

The following student comment shows that gaining knowledge leads to user satisfaction.

"The BPM Modeling software was easy to learn after viewing the 25-minute Process Modeling training video."

Being easy to learn lowers the cognitive load. So, the eighth proposition follows:

P8: User knowledge affects perceived user satisfaction.

The eight propositions are shown on the conceptual model in Fig. 1 below. In summary, perceived user satisfaction with the BPM tool is affected by the PEOU of the tool, the documentation, the simulation report generation and the user's knowledge. We also expect the PEOU and the report generation to be affected by the documentation and the user's knowledge.

7 Conclusion

Prior BPM research has expressed the need for a focus on process analysis, process performance management, empirical studies and social issues [17] as well as, pedagogical research [3, 10, 11, 40]. This empirical study used an innovative collaboration with a vendor to contribute to pedagogical BPM research. The objective was to determine factors affecting students' perceived satisfaction with a BPM tool. The students used the BPM tool for process modeling, process analysis, process design and process performance management. The analysis of students' comments reveals the importance of documentation and user knowledge on perceived ease of use and simulation report generation. Specifically, dissatisfied students remarked on difficulties with process modeling and simulation report generation. On the other hand, students who found the documentation helpful and who leveraged the training to improve their knowledge of the BPM software commented favorably on PEOU and report generation.

7.1 Limitations

This study has some limitations. First, we cannot generalize the findings to all BPM software since most of the commentary focused on one BPM tool. Second, the graduate students in this study were from one institution. It is not known whether the results would be consistent over other universities or for undergraduate students. Third, the course was delivered predominantly online, although there were on campus meetings in some years. Students taking on campus BPM courses might have different perceptions. Fourth, our results might not apply to corporate users. Users who are not students are likely to be similar in some ways, yet different in other ways. Corporate users who have been exposed to BPM software for some time are likely to have different issues. For example, a published study found PU to be significant and support affected the input and output quality [24]. Another study found that content, accuracy, relevance and timeliness of the information were important to corporate users of a GL system [38]. On the other hand, users who are beginning to learn software might have similar perceptions to the students in our study.

Future research can analyze logs of online training to determine whether the training affects students' perceptions of the BPM tool. Data can also be collected to attempt to triangulate the results. Future research could replicate the study with the GL system described above substituting a BPM system to find out if the results are similar.

7.2 Implications

This study has implications for research. Very little IS research has focused on BPM software despite the important issues that have been identified and the potential for higher organizational productivity. Much more attention has been given to ERP and CRM software. In fact, many researchers and students are not familiar with BPM software. Since BPM software is an example of an IT artifact, focus on this research falls within the IS research domain. Future research can compare BPM software to ERP or other enterprise software to see how issues are the same or different. This study implies that PEOU applies to BPM software similarly to most other software. However, BPM software includes features that are unique. Simulation, for example, can be challenging to users. This explains why PEOU of BPM software is conditional on adequate documentation and user knowledge. The complexity of generating simulation reports and interpreting them in turn affects user satisfaction. These detailed interpretations are more meaningful than studies that vaguely find that technology acceptance depends on PEOU and PU.

Implications for practice include possible modifications to the BPM tools by the vendor. The vendor expressed interest in using the students' feedback for tool improvement. Implications for educational research include potential benefits of further assessment of students' perceptions of tools used in BPM courses. Future BPM courses could expose students to BPM tools that increase their knowledge and skills in simulation as well as modeling. Finally, this study draws attention to BPM education and the advantages of collaboration with practitioners.

References

1. Antonucci, Y.L., Bariff, M., Benedict, T., Champlin, B., Downing, B.D., Franzen, J., Madison, D.J., Lusk, S., Spanyi, A., Treat, M., Zhao, J.L., Raschke, R.L.: Guide to the Business Process Management Body of Knowledge (BPM CBOK ®). Association of Business Process Management Professionals, Chicago (2009)
2. Ariyachandra, T.R., Frolick, M.N.: Critical success factors in business performance management - striving for success. Inf. Syst. Manag. **25**, 113–120 (2008)
3. Bandara, W., Chand, D.R., Chircu, A.M., Hintringer, S., Karagiannis, D., Recker, J., van Rensburg, A., Usoff, C., Welke, R.J.: Business process management education in academia: status challenges, and recommendations. Commun. Assoc. Inf. Syst. **27**(41), 743–776 (2010)
4. Bandara, W., Gable, G., Rosemann, M.: Business processing modeling success: an empirically tested measurement model. In: Proceedings of the 27th International Conference on Information Systems, Milwaukee (2006)
5. Bandara, W., Indulska, M., Chong, S., Sadiq, S.: Major issues in business process management: an expert perspective. In: 15th European Conference on Information Systems, St. Gallen, Switzerland, pp. 1240–1251. (2007a)
6. Bandara, W., Rosemann, M., Davies, I., Tan, C.: A structured approach to determining appropriate content for emerging information systems subjects: an example for BPM curricula design. In: Proceedings of the 18th Australasian Conference on Information Systems, Toowoomba, Australia, pp. 1132–1141 (2007b)
7. Becker, J., Niehaves, B., Thome, I.: How many methods do we need? - a multiple case study exploration into the use of business process modeling methods in industry. In: Proceedings of the 16th Americas Conference on Information Systems, Lima, Peru (2010)
8. Caporale, T., Citak, M., Lehner, J., Oberweis, A., Schoknecht, A., Ullrich, M.: Motivating course concept: using active labs for Bpm education. In: Proceedings of the 21st European Conference on Information Systems, P. 12 (2013)
9. Chircu, A., Grover, V., Majchrzak, A., Rosemann, M.: Business process management and the is field: have we finally arrived or just missed the boat? In: Proceedings of the 31st International Conference on Information Systems, St Louis, MO (2010)
10. Chircu, A.M., Chand, D., Bandara, W.: Business process management education in academia: its status, its challenges and its future. In: Proceedings of the 17th European Conference on Information Systems, Verona, Italy, June 8–10, 2009 (2009)
11. Delavari, H., Bandara, W., Marjanovic, O., Mathiesen, P.: Business process management (BPM) education in australia: a critical review based on content analysis. In: Proceedings of the 21st Australasian Conference on Information Systems, Brisbane, Queensland (2010)
12. DeLone, W.H., McLean, E.R.: Information systems success: the quest for the dependent variable. Inf. Syst. Res. **3**(1), 60–90 (1992)
13. DeLone, W.H., McLean, E.R.: The delone and mclean model of information systems success: a ten-year update. J. Manag. Inf. Syst. **19**(4), 9–30 (2003)
14. Doll, W.J., Torkzadeh, G.: The measurement of end-user computing satisfaction. MIS Q. **12**(2), 259–274 (1988)
15. Dumas, M., Rosa, M.L., Mendling, J., Reijers, H.: Fundamentals of Business Process Management. Springer, Heidelberg (2013)

16. Enzinga, D.J., Horak, T., Chung-Yee, L., Bruner, C.: Business process management: survey and methodology. IEEE Trans. Eng. Manage. **24**(2), 119–128 (1995)
17. Ho, D.T.-Y., Jin, Y., Dwivedi, R.: Business process management: a research overview and analysis. In: Proceedings of the 15th Americas Conference on Information Systems (2009)
18. Hribar, B., Mendling, J.: The correlation of organizational culture and success of BPM adoption. In: Proceedings of the 22nd European Conference on Information Systems (ECIS), June 9–11, 2014, Tel Aviv, Israel (2014)
19. Ives, B., Olson, M.H., Baroudi, J.J.: The measurement of user information satisfaction. Commun. ACM **26**, 785–793 (1983)
20. Khan, R.: Business Process Management: A Practical Guide. Meghan-Kiffer Press, Tampa (2004)
21. Kumar, M., Bhat, J.M.: Discrete event monte-carlo simulation based decision support system for business process management. In: Proceedings of the 16th Americas Conference on Information Systems, Lima, Peru (2010)
22. Malinova, M., Hribar, B., Mendling, J.: A framework for assessing Bpm success. In: Proceedings of the 22nd European Conference on Information Systems (ECIS), June 9–11, 2014, Tel Aviv, Israel (2014)
23. Mathiesen, P., Bandara, W., Watson, J.: The affordances of social technology: a business process management perspective. In: Proceedings of the 34th International Conference on Information Systems, Milan, pp. 1–11 (2013)
24. Poelmans, S., Reijers, H.A.: The deployment of business process management systems: a quantitative analysis of end-users' evaluations. In: Proceedings of the 18th European Conference on Information Systems (2010)
25. Recker, J., Dreiling, A.: The effects of content presentation format and user characteristics on novice developers' understanding of process models. Commun. Assoc. Inf. Syst. **28**(6), 65–84 (2011)
26. Recker, J., Rosemann, M.: Teaching business process modelling: experiences and recommendations. Commun. Assoc. Inf. Syst. **25**(32), 379–394 (2009)
27. Recker, J., Rosemann, M.: A measurement instrument for process modeling research: development test and procedural model. Scand. J. Inf. Syst. **22**(2), 3–30 (2010)
28. Recker, J., Rosemann, M., Green, P., Indulska, M.: Do ontological deficiencies in modeling grammars matter? MIS Q. **35**(1), 57–80 (2011)
29. Recker, J., Rosemann, M., Indulska, M., Green, P.: Business process modeling- a comparative analysis. J. Assoc. Inf. Syst. **10**(4), 333–363 (2009)
30. Reijers, H.A., Recker, J.C., van de Wouw, S.G.: An integrative framework of the factors affecting process model understanding: a learning perspective. In: Proceedings of the 16th Americas Conference on Information Systems: Sustainable IT Collaboration around the Globe, Lima, Peru, August 12–15, 2010
31. Rosemann, M., Bruin, T.D.: Towards a business process management maturity model. In: Proceedings of the 13th European Conference on Information Systems (2005)
32. Rothengatter, D., Katsma, C., Hillegersberg, J.V.: Simulation as a method to support complex organizational transformations in healthcare. In: Proceedings of the 16th Americas Conference on Information Systems, Lima, Peru (2010)
33. Sadiq, S., Indulska, M., Bandara, W., Chong, S.: Major issues in business process management: a vendor perspective. In: Proceedings of the 11th Pacific Asia Conference on Information Systems, pp. 40–47 (2007)
34. Schaefer, T., Fettke, P., Loos, P.: Control patterns - bridging the gap between is controls and Bpm. In: Proceedings of the 21st European Conference on Information Systems, P. 88. (2013)

35. Schiefer, J., Roth, H., Suntinger, M., Schatten, A.: Simulating business process scenarios for event-based systems. In: Proceedings of the 15th European Conference on Information Systems, St. Gallen, Switzerland, pp. 1729–1740 (2007)
36. Schmidt, W.: Relationship between BPM education and business process solutions: results of a student contest. In: Stephanidis, C. (ed.) Universal Access in HCI, Part IV, HCII 2011. LNCS, vol. 6768, pp. 622–631. Springer, Heidelberg (2011)
37. Seddon, P.B.: A respecification and extension of the delone and mclean model of is success. Inf. Syst. Res. **8**(3), 240–253 (1997)
38. Seddon, P.B., Yip, S.K.: An empirical evaluation of user information satisfaction (Uis) measures for use with general ledger account software. J. Inf. Syst. **5**, 75–92 (1992)
39. Sedera, W., Rosemann, M., Gable, G.: Measuring process modeling success. In: Proceedings of the 10th European Conference of Information Systems, Gdansk, Poland, pp. 331–341 (2002)
40. Seethamraju, R.: Business process management - a missing link in business education. In: Proceedings of the 16th Americas Conference on Information Systems, Lima, Peru, pp. 1–9 (2010)
41. Strauss, A.L., Corbin, J.: Basics of Qualitative Data Research: Techniques and Procedures for Developing Grounded Theory. Sage, Thousand Oaks (1998)
42. Trkman, P.: The critical success factors of business process management. Int. J. Inf. Manage. **30**, 125–134 (2010)
43. Weske, M.: Business Process Management: Concepts, Languages. Springer, Architectures (2012)

Business Model Dynamics — Towards a Dynamic Framework of Business Model Components

Julian Krumeich[✉], Dirk Werth, and Peter Loos

Institute for Information Systems (IWi)
at the German Research Center for Artificial Intelligence (DFKI GmbH),
Stuhlsatzenhausweg 3, Campus Bld. D3 2, 66123 Saarbrücken, Germany
{Julian.Krumeich,Dirk.Werth,Peter.Loos}@dfki.de

Abstract. Since the mid-1990s, in the course of the rising commercial use of modern Information and Communication Technologies (ICT) and the transformation of traditional to digital business, the business model concept has prevailed as a promising unit of analysis. To describe business models, they are typically broken down into single business model components. However, there is a lack of knowledge on the dynamics between them, i.e. which dependencies and interdependencies exist between business model components. Hence, a successful transformation and innovation of business models still remain a heavy task without having such knowledge on the internal behavior. Thus, this paper provides a comprehensive analysis of business model literature aiming to discover structural relations between business model components. This was achieved by analyzing numerous individual literature sources. In pursuing this explorative approach, a large number of dependencies and interdependencies could be discovered and mapped onto the unifying Business Model Component Framework, which was developed prior to this study. (This paper is a revised and expanded version of a paper entitled "Interdependencies between Business Model Components— A Literature Analysis," [65] presented at the 19th Americas Conference on Information Systems (AMCIS 2013), Chicago, Illinois, August 15–17, 2013, AIS Electronic Library (AISeL), pp. 1–9.)

Keywords: Business model · Business model components · Literature analysis · Interdependencies · E-business

1 Introduction

1.1 Motivation

The rising commercial use of modern Information and Communication Technologies (ICT) has significantly changed companies' business practices since the mid-nineteen nineties [1, 2]. Competitive situations have to be considered increasingly from a global perspective and far beyond traditional industry borders [3]. Even small Internet start-ups were quickly able to act globally and bring real competition to long-established companies. In addition, ICT function frequently as an enabler for entirely new business activities besides just supporting them. This led to the realization of many innovative

© Springer International Publishing Switzerland 2015
D. Sedera et al. (Eds.): Pre-ICIS 2010-2012, LNBIP 198, pp. 190–215, 2015.
DOI: 10.1007/978-3-319-17587-4_13

business ideas forming the "new digital competitive landscape" [4, 5]. Even though many of these ventures failed, others have significantly changed the business landscape (cf. Facebook, Google and Twitter for some remarkable examples). As a consequence, the question "What business am I in?" could not be easily answered anymore [6].

As an appropriate means to analyze the new competitive landscape, the business model concept has prevailed and has increasingly moved into the interest of research, but also into practical application [7]. The correct alignment of a company's business model is accorded high priority for gaining and maintaining competitive advantages and finally for ensuring business success [8]. Considering the rapidly changing environment enterprises and their business models are facing, a business model that is highly competitive from today's perspective might be outdated in the near future [9]. This observation implies the great importance of innovation and a continuous improvement of business models [10, 11]. In this regard, the "Global CEO Study", which IBM conducts every two years, revealed in its 2006 implementation a share of 30 % of the 765 interviewed CEOs which put an innovation focus on their business model [12]. Especially companies with comparatively fast-growing profit margins exhibit a focus on business model innovation twice as high as their competitors. The subsequent study in 2008 with 1130 respondents yielded similar results [13]. Accordingly, financially outstanding companies employ all basic forms of business model innovation. It was the strong conviction of most interviewed CEOs that products and services are not enough to distinguish between competitors. Consequently, 70 % of the CEOs were in the progress of implementing extensive business model changes. The 2010 study [14] highlighted creative executives as most successful in experimenting with business models and realizing quantum leaps via appropriate innovations. Additionally, a fast and prompt implementation of business model innovations was attributed an increased importance.

1.2 Relevance for Information Systems Research

For a successful implementation and management of business models, dedicated software tools are essential. In this regard, the business model concept needs to be taken into account from an information systems' perspective. The demand for such systems becomes most evident regarding the visualization or even simulation of business models, which are not feasible without software support [15].

Moreover, there are further domains that are interesting for information systems research. For example, the business model concept can be employed for Business/IT Alignment. Here, the concept can function as a mutual means of communication between the business and IT domain [15]. As business models represent the business logic of a company, they can also be utilized during the development of enterprise applications [16]. In this context, business models can be used for requirements engineering by gathering and representing high-level business goals [17].

The shown relevance of the business model concept for information systems research is reflected in many papers published in information systems journals like the European Journal of Information Systems [18–20] or the Communications of the Association for Information Systems [15]. Even though, several research domains have intersection points with the concept, research is mainly conducted in silos [21]. Consequently, knowledge on business models is quite fragmented, which calls for a clarification and synthesizing of the concept to be able to utilize it successfully [20].

1.3   Research Contribution

To describe business models, they are typically broken down into single business model components. While there have been several discussions pointing out dissent on the constituent components of business models since the beginning of business model research [7], recent attempts on developing general business model frameworks, which bundle the proposed components in literature, demonstrate progress in research [22]. Even though consensus is progressively growing, these frameworks typically only allow for a static consideration. Recent analyses criticize the lack of bundled knowledge on business model dynamics, in particular regarding the relations between single business model components, i.e. which dependencies and interdependencies exist between them [7, 23, 24]. Hence, the transformation and innovation of business models still remain a heavy task without having such knowledge on the internal behavior. In order to success-fully innovate and adapt a business model, knowledge about these dynamics must be present and implemented in dedicated software-supported systems.

The need for knowledge on structural dynamic insights on business models apart from static aspects can be illustrated by an intuitive example from the automotive industry. The question "which components does a car consist of" can be answered easily by any car manufacturer: an engine, a braking system, four tires and many more. However, to build a car that stands out from competitors, it is essential to know how these components relate to each other and hence need to be aligned. This means, it is not sufficient to build the strongest motor engine in a motorcar to have the best sports car, it rather depends on the optimal alignment in the sense that e.g. the suspension system as well as the braking system are well-adjusted and aligned to the actual engine performance and customer needs.

Thus, the objective of this paper is to provide a comprehensive analysis of business model literature aiming at discovering and bundling existing, but scattered knowledge, on structural relations between business model components and providing a framework describing the dynamics of business model components. To be more specific, the main research question is: *which dependencies and interdependencies exist between business model components?*

This research gap needs to be closed in order to successfully build business model management systems supporting the innovation process of business models, since having knowledge on the internal dynamics is crucial to preserve the consistency of a business model, i.e. updating all those components that depend on an actually changed component [25, 26]. The addressed research goals by this paper are summarized as follows:

- Provide an overview of existing knowledge on business model dynamics in literature.
- Clarify which are the key components of business models in the sense that they are most influencing other components.

- Elucidate which components are most influenced by other components without having strong impact on other ones.
- Bundle this knowledge and propose a dynamic business model framework describing how business model components are related to each other.

1.4   Applied Research Methodology and Paper Structure

The methodology applied to address the research question is a structured literature analysis. It forms the basis for deriving a structured model of business models dynamics, which stems from examining the chosen literature for (mutual) dependencies of business model components. The process of analyzing literature follows the methodology proposed by [27]. This verified process—entitled "Reconstructing the Giant"—allows for a rigorous study.

Following [27], we first conceptualized the scope of our analysis by defining and relating relevant search terms in order to discover promising literature among the numerous publications on business model research, which have already been published in just a few decades of research [7]. The search includes a combination of the terms "business model", "business engineering", "value modeling", "business model components and relations", "business model dynamics" as well as related ones. The search has been performed (including backward and forward searches) on the literature databases Thomson Reuters Web of Knowledge, EBSCO Business Source Premier and Google Scholar. Afterwards, literature mainly focusing on business model components and their relations between each other, but also literature dealing with business model innovation have been chosen and screened to find further promising literature in provided references. As an initial result, far more than 80 papers could be identified.

In order to consider the most significant ones—in terms of providing insight on the dynamics of business models—the final selection met some criteria. In detail, the literature needed to be

- of high-quality, which was guaranteed by selecting only sources from highly-ranked (e.g. ISI impact factor >1.5) journals (e.g. European Journal of Information Systems or Strategic Management Journal) and conferences;
- highly-considered among scientists which is reflected in the citation frequency on Thomson Reuters Web of Knowledge and Google Scholar.

However, by applying this methodology some of the most current literature might not have been selected, since it does not fulfill the "citation frequency" requirement. To overcome this concern, recent promising, but low-cited papers were manually selected. Furthermore, a small amount of publications from lower-ranked journals and conferences as well as not-ranked textbooks has been chosen—which we had been aware of due to prior studies—since they provide promising insights on the structural relations of business models and thus should be included in a comprehensive analysis. As a result, the selection consists of 35 relevant publications.

In the next step, the existing heterogeneous knowledge on interdependencies between business model components within these publications—e.g. based on business model components with varying names and classifications—has been transferred to the Business Model Component Framework, which was recently proposed by the authors [22]. This framework claims to be general and unifying and will be introduced in detail in the next section. As a result, an explorative derivation of the dynamics in the business model structure is performed based upon relevant literature. Since the literature foundation is partly based on practical examples, the practical impact is to some extend validated as well. Even though these examples stem from different industries and domains, the derived dependencies are still general enough to attest them a general applicability. Hence, they are not restricted to particular cases or industries. In addition, since this paper is the first one explicitly addressing this research gap—previous ones only call for such a research without presenting any result—it also aims at encouraging other scientists to conduct research regarding interdependencies (e.g. in specific domains) based on the general results and insights provided in this paper.

To apply the proposed methodology, the remainder of this paper is organized as follows. Section 2 comprises discussions on business model research regarding current definitions, existing component frameworks and business models as dynamic constructs. Section 3 presents the findings of the underlying literature analysis. Subsequently, Sect. 4 elucidates the study's key results and points out some limitations including the need for further research. Finally, Sect. 5 summarizes the paper and gives an outlook on future business model research.

2   Related Work

In the mid-1990s, new economic and social situations, which had resulted from the development of modern ICT including the Internet, caused a drastic change to the overall competitive situation of companies [2]. Even small Internet start-ups were quickly able to act globally and bring real competition to long-established companies. Hence, this shift in the competitive situation is often referred to as the "new digital competitive landscape" [5]. Consequently, traditional units of analysis—like the Resource-Based View [28] and Market-Based View [29]—had been put into question, which led to the search for a new unit of analysis having the capabilities to depict the digital economy [4]. Eventually, the business model concept has established as the new unit of analysis able to successfully describe the value creation—not only within the digital landscape [30]. As a result, based on business model analyses, it is possible to determine why the competitive position of companies within the digital landscape has decreased and why they were successful at all [31].

2.1   Business Model Definitions

Porter's [32] frequently quoted statement—"The definition of business model is murky at best"— remains intact to the present day. Despite the existence of multitude definitions in literature, no consensus can be attested. To the contrary, there are substantial discussions regarding the existent terminological dissent [20, 33]. This concern can be attributed to several causes of which [34] identified three major ones. In the first place, the term emerged in several scientific disciplines concurrently. Secondly, the concept embodies diverse theories. Thirdly, starting with the "New Economy", business models are a rather new field of research. Reference [21] emphasized this last point as well. They believe that any new and promising concept will be subject to definitional and conceptual discrepancies during its emergent phase.

Induced by the heterogeneous original disciplines, the concept pursues different objectives. Consequently, this leads to diverse definitions (cf. in the following [33]). From an Information Systems perspective, business models are utilized to explain the meaning of e-business as well as the employment of information and communication systems. Another reason for the fuzzy comprehension of the term is the lack of explicit definitions within publications in this area, which implicitly assume a common understanding of the term. The number of such publications is estimated to be more than one third. A reference to previous definitions is also missing in most cases. Reference [33] identified this approach in only 20 % of the considered literature. In order not to follow this approach, this paper adopts a definition which was proposed on the 2011th International Conference on Information System by the authors [7]: *"The business model concept is linked but still distinct to the concept of business strategy. It describes— mainly textual on a highly aggregated level—the business logic of an underlying company by a combination of interdependent offering, market, internal as well as economical business model components in a static and dynamic way beyond the company's borders. Furthermore, it is not limited to a certain type of business or industry and is thus generally applicable and intended for internal as well as external addressees."*

2.2 Business Model Component Framework

Apart from explicit textual definitions, the concept of business models is frequently also defined by its constituent components, which for themselves do not form a whole business model, but only a specific part of it [15, 35]. Besides the term "component" numerous synonyms are used in literature, e.g. elements, dimensions, factors, building blocks, partial models, sub models and parts. Nevertheless, the term "component" is used most frequently and will therefore be adopted in this paper. From a semantically point of view, i.e. apart from terminological differences, no consistent descriptive pattern with dimensions has become prevalent so far [34]. Consequently, no consensus about the constituent components of a business model exists in the current research environment [7, 36]. To have a foundation for the undertaking in this paper, i.e. depicting identified interdependencies between the multitudes of proposed components, the findings have been mapped onto the Business Model Component Framework, which was recently proposed by the authors [22] and which claims to be general and unifying. To provide a common understanding, the components are characterized in the following (for more details on the Business Model Component Framework, its derivation process based on a literature analysis as well as other existing frameworks, it is referred to the original source [22]).

Value Offering Model. Components belonging to the Value Offering Model are strongly connected with each other. As a result, several literature sources put some of them together to a single component. In particular, the Product and Service Offering is often considered as part of the Value Proposition. Nevertheless, since they are strongly linked, but still distinct components, the framework developed in this article breaks down the components as much as possible in order to draw a clear picture on existing business model components.

Value Proposition. The Value Proposition is considered to be the key component of business models. Several literature sources express this central role by recommending to start a business model development based on this component [37, 38]. In this regard, the Value Proposition describes which benefits business models provide their customers—of course, this need not be equal to the benefits customers will actually receive. In addition, the Value Proposition not only expresses the benefits customers will receive, but also the value-adding partners participating in the business model [4].

Product and Service Offering. As mentioned, the Product and Service Offering is closely intertwined with the Value Proposition, since it expresses which product and service offering actually realizes the Value Proposition [8]. The fact that companies can achieve the same Value Proposition by offering different products and services demonstrates the strong linkage of both components (cf. [38] for an illustrative example on its differentiation).

Competitive Advantage. Besides specifying a Value Proposition and its realizing Product and Service Offering, the long-term sustainability, i.e. the Competitive Advantage, of a business model's value offering has to be assured. Hence, this component serves for formulating to what extent a business model is different—from a positive point of view—to competing ones [6] and how its competitive advantage will be maintained [8]. Moreover, strategic growth decisions—as future directions of the business model in contrast to its current operation based on the Value Capturing Model—should be captured within this component, i.e. for instance whether a company should rather continue to grow in its current market or whether it should enter new market places [39].

Competitive Model. In order to identify a business model's competitive advantage and to derive actions how to maintain it, the Competitive Model depicts the competitive environment of a business model [40]. Thus, the Competitive Model reflects competing business models and highlights potential risks for the own business model.

Value Capturing Model. The Value Capturing Model is closely related to the Value Offering Model, since it determines which customer and market segments are being addressed, on which ways and how these relationships are organized.

Customer and Market Segment. In order to successfully implement the Value Offering Model, it must be adapted to its targeted customer and market segments. In this context, customer and market segments can be differentiated by a variety of criteria. The stronger the segmentation, the stronger a business model addresses niche markets instead of mass markets [9]. Modern ICT pave the way towards a goal-oriented and detailed clustering of both customers and markets. However, since they also facilitate a business model's geographic expansion—even for small companies—, differentiating customers and markets is becoming increasingly vital for business model's success [41].

Communication and Distribution Channel. Besides specifying the Customer and Market Segment, choosing appropriate channels to distribute and communicate with them is critical for success [20]. Channels can be distinguished in own and partner channels, both of which can be further differentiated in direct and indirect channels [9]. Modern ICT enable a communicative integration of customers into the value creation process aiming at developing the Value Proposition in accordance to segment or even customer-specific needs [34].

Customer Relationship. Even though Customer Relationship is an essential component for business models, it is only less considered in literature (cf. [41] and the occurrence frequency of 41 %). The importance of (long-lasting) customer relationships results in high costs occurring from one-off transactions. Hence, customer relationships should be formed adequately considering the Customer and Market Segment. This will induce new customers, maintain existing ones and increase their share of wallet. In doing so, the classification of customer relationships can range from self-services to co-creation [9]. The latter one reflects the growing direct involvement of customers into the development and decision-making process for creating the Value Proposition, which can be improved by using modern ICT [41].

Value Creation Model. While the Value Offering Model and Value Capturing Model describe which values are distributed and to whom, the Value Creation Model describes aspects regarding the actual value creation within companies.

Resource Model. To operate a business model, companies need to have certain resources [9] that can be distinguished [8, 42] into tangible, intangible and human resources. All of them can either be created in-house or sourced from external partners [43]. Hence, resources have the characteristics of being tradable and not company-specific [34].

Competence Model. However, resources are not sufficient to create value in terms of the Value Proposition [8, 42]. Thus, it is vital to have abilities enabling the usage of resources as well as their transformation to new combinations of resources which are—according to the concept of core competencies—rare, valuable, costly to imitate and non-substitutable [8, 44]. These abilities are referred to as competencies and contribute significantly to a business model's success. In contrast to resources, competencies are both non-tradable and company-specific.

Activities and Processes. As mentioned, to successfully implement business models, competencies are needed to carry out activities and processes that finally culminate in the provision of the Value Proposition [9, 43]. Hence, companies have to determine how to create the Value Proposition by answering two questions: which are the key activities and processes that have to be done internally and which ones by cooperating partners. In literature, four major types are distinguished [34]: Layer Player, companies covering one specific value creation stage for several value chains; Integrators, companies covering every stage within a value chain; Market Maker, companies mediating between different value adding processes; and Orchestrators, companies covering large parts of the value creation, but outsource specific parts to partners.

Organizational Structure. The component Organizational Structure is used to define a business model's roles and responsibilities [4, 45] for allowing a goal-oriented implementation of the Activities and Processes as well as their underlying Resource Model and Competence Model [8]. In doing so, it is crucial to determine the adaptability of a company's organizational structure in order to react dynamically to changes in its environment [45]. Hence, the Organizational Structure is important and has to be aligned with the overall business model [6].

Cooperation Model. Besides considering the value creation within a company, the network of cooperation outlined by the Cooperation Model has to be addressed in a business model.

Structure and Position. Business models are often enabled by corporative relationships [9], in which external economic parties take over parts of the value creation in order to cooperatively provide the Value Proposition [4]. Consequently, building cooperation networks pursues the goal to optimize a business model and finally its Value Proposition [9, 41]. This is achieved by focusing on activities that can be done with internal resources and core-competencies, while sourcing other parts out to partners. It is of strategic importance to determine whether a business model should focus on many smaller or rather less, but strong cooperation partners (high transaction costs vs. risk of a dominating partner) [39]. Hence, while the Value Creation Model—based on the Resource/Competence Model as well as the Activities and Process component—depicts which resources and processes are internally and externally provided to successfully operate a business model, the Structure and Position component strongly focuses on the external partners providing these aforementioned aspects, how they are interrelated to fulfill the business model's goal as well as which is the focal company's position within this network of partners.

Coordination. In order to successfully operate the Cooperation Model, appropriate communication channels and coordination mechanisms need to be defined as well as rules of the partnerships to be negotiated [4]. In the course of this, it is important not to generate exuberant transaction costs [39]. Coordination concepts can reach from using pure market forces on the basis of individual transactions, to implicit and explicit cooperation agreements, and finally to the establishment of coordination hierarchies or even the fusion of companies [34, 39].

Maturity. Operating a Cooperation Model is accompanied by a certain maturity of its cooperation relationships. Since it is strategically important to determine the maturity, this aspect is concentrated in a separate component. It must therefore be outlined, if the cooperation is established on a strong, long-term basis aiming to increase its efficiency based on the usage of joined standards or on a dynamic basis, but with less risk of being dependent on partners [4, 6, 39].

Financial Model. Financial-based components play a central role in business models because they determine whether a business model is reasonable from an economic point of view.

Funding Model. The Funding Model provides information on the sources from which a company receives capital to operate its business model [40]. In the course of this, the choice of a company's legal form can already have strong impact on its funding possibilities. This is particular important during the start-up phase, since initial operating cash flow might not be sufficient to fully operate the business model.

Revenue Model. The existence of a profit-yielding revenue structure is important for a business model's success, since costs resulting from creating and offering the Value Proposition need to be overcompensated [4]. A poor design or even the lack of a revenue structure was the main reason why many start-ups had failed in the New Economy [46]. Ideally, a network of revenues exists. This should be optimized depending on the targeted market, since this determines whether the price or the volume of the Value Proposition needs a stronger consideration (mass market vs. niche market).

Pricing Model. Additionally, the pricing of the Product and Service Offering is essential for a business model's financial success [8, 35]. In order to gain maximum profits contributing to the sustainability of business models, the pricing must be optimized from two points of views. While the sales volume must not suffer from an unacceptable price, a price arbitrage must not be wasted without resulting in an increase of sales volume [41, 47]. Based on modern ICT, novel and more focused pricing mechanisms can be realized [41].

Cost Model. The Revenue Model and Pricing Model are not the only components which need to be determined to achieve a financially successful business model; the other side of the coin—in form of the Cost Model—does also have to be considered. This component should reveal the major cost-incurring activities of a business model with the overall goal to minimize the costs in achieving the Value Proposition. However, the minimization varies extremely on the Value Proposition's chosen strategy (cf. [9] for cost-driven vs. value driven strategy) [8].

Profit Model. Based on the previous components, a business model's margin structure can be derived that outlines the financial value for its owners. Based on determining a desired profit, the resulting margin, which is needed for each transaction within a business model, can be derived [38].

Distribution Model. Due to the raising number of cooperation relationships in the course of the Digital Economy, the Distribution Model of a business model becomes increasingly important. This component indicates how all investments, costs and revenues are shared among participants in order to assure the sustainable financing of the cooperative value creation [6, 44]. Based on the former mobile service platform i-mode, the importance of a sophisticated Distribution Model is outlined by [48]. Another good example is the one of Apple's Distribution Model, in particular regarding how revenues are shared among Apple and developers of mobile applications [44].

2.3 Interdependencies Between Business Model Components

The fact that business model components have structural relations between each other is undisputed; however, in business model literature these relations have not been explicitly discussed and analyzed resulting in a research gap [7]. From a theoretical perspective, relations between components can exist in the form of dependencies or influences on other components. The case of a component being dependent on another, but also influencing this other component is called interdependency [20, 49], i.e. a mutual dependency [50]. In particular, these (mutual) dependencies highlight the inherent dynamic of business models, which will be outlined in the subsequent subsection. To take up the initial example from the automotive industry, while increasing the engine performance of a car requires increased braking power, the relation between both components cannot be considered as interdependent, since increased braking power does not demand raising engine performance.

Since no fundamental reflection of this pivotal characteristic of business model components has been conducted so far in research [23, 24], this paper outlines the first approach of bundling the implicit knowledge about the internal structure of business models on an abstract level. Several aspects emphasize the importance of knowledge about this structure. Based on the close connections between the components, changes that result from external influencing factors can induce changes of other components [4]. Thus, even small changes can call for various adaptations of other components [34, 35]. These dependencies essentially affect the structure of business models and emphasize the dynamic of the concept [26]. Hence it is important to consider and maintain an equilibrium of the components when updating a business model architecture [20, 23, 51]. Thus, no single component should be regarded or changed in isolation [34, 52, 53]. An equilibrium of this type can be attested if business models are consistent with regard to an internal and external "fit" [54]. An internal fit is satisfied if all business model components are adapted among themselves and reinforce each other [6]. The external fit however gives priority to external influencing factors. Hence, the alignment of business model components is supposed to take place in conformity with the respective environment [54].

2.4 Considering the Dynamic of Business Models

In order to ensure ongoing competitiveness and the success of a company's business model, a continuous adaptation and optimization is required [9, 18, 24]. Primarily two reasons constitute this need for change (cf. in the following [34]). On the one hand business models cannot be optimally implemented from scratch based on a blueprint. On the other hand even an established business model is subject to constant adaptations, which can be traced back to the discovery of unused potentials within companies' resources. This can be understood as the result of a steady increase of knowledge. The necessity for change can as well result from the changing environment whose influences can make the business model wear out over time [35]. Additionally, adaptations that result from internal structural relations and the adherence of a fitting of all components are subsumed under this necessity for change. Therefore a characterization of the different degrees and starting points of adaptations within business models is of particular interest (cf. Fig. 1).

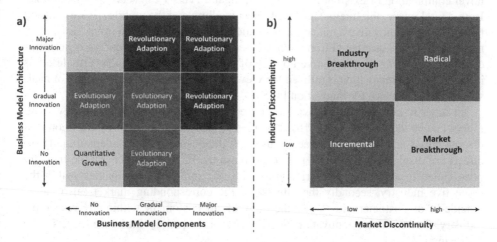

Fig. 1. (a) Degree and kind of business model adaption based on [34]. (b) Degree of innovation of adaption based on [24]

Adapting a business model can induce changes of its components or influence its overall architecture. According to [55] the architecture of a business model can be defined as the interfaces and mutual relationships between the business model components. Thus—depending on the degree of change—three basic adaption schemes can be differentiated (cf. [34] and Fig. 1a). It should be noted that the estimation of the degree of change is performed from the subjective view of the respective company. Consequently, even a revolutionary adaptation of the own business model does not necessarily imply an innovation for the surrounding world [4].

- **Quantitative Growth:** Neither elementary nor architectural adaptations are performed. However, the existing set of component interactions is optimized, e.g. due to a positive sales growth among existing customers [26, 56].
- **Evolutionary Adaption:** This scheme encompasses either a gradual change of the elements or the architecture for both axes are adapted gradually at most. One example is the transfer of a business model into a different industry.
- **Revolutionary Adaption:** A fundamental innovation of at least one axis is performed, while the other one is subject to a gradual change at least. An example from the real business world is Apple's iTunes business model, which revolutionized the music industry. In this case even from an objective external point of view the term "revolution" is adequate for the business model.

The iTunes example also reveals the importance of an objective innovation level that is caused by the adaptation of a business model (cf. Fig. 1b). An innovation in this context does not necessarily require new technical achievements. It might as well consist of a novel combination of existing resources [4]. Again, iTunes can serve as an example. Both digital music, the Internet as distribution medium and the mobile devices existed before Apple's innovative application. This idea of innovation, which is not based upon new technologies, originated from Schumpeter [57]. However, his concept is not sufficient for explaining the innovative novelty of business models [58]. Nevertheless, his interpretation of innovation is utilized for viewing the business model as a unit of analysis as well as a place for innovation [4, 58].

In order to consider the innovation degree from an objective point of view, four ranges can be identified (cf. Fig. 1b). The axes within the figure refer to the amount of discontinuous and innovative effects caused by the business model adaptation. These effects are displayed with regard to two dimensions: First, the effects on the industry (also called inside-out or enterprise view), i.e. the sum of all companies within the respective industry, secondly the effects on the corresponding market (also called outside-in or customer view), i.e. the sum of all customers within the respective industry. The resulting innovation degrees are subsequently introduced (cf. in the following [24]):

- **Incremental Innovation:** Even though the business model is different from the previous one in this case, no discontinuity can be attested for the two dimensions. A business model might for instance be adapted only for a new specific customer segment that was not addressed before.
- **Industry Breakthrough:** In this case a discontinuity within the industry is triggered while the innovation appears rather incremental to the customers. Reference [24] mentions the business model of the newspaper "Metro" whose financing consists only of advertisements without an actual sale price of the paper. This model had huge impact on the newspaper industry, whereas the customers did not experience a big change, since the newspaper's content is not essentially different from other comparable papers.
- **Market Breakthrough:** The discontinuity works vice versa in this case. The low-cost car Nano from the Indian company Tata Motors can serve as an example. From the market perspective, i.e. from the potential customers, a radical shift in the offering was achieved. For the automotive industry however no breakthrough could be identified because the car production has just been trimmed to lower cost by abandoning certain features.
- **Radical Innovation:** In this case a breakthrough for both dimensions arises. Once again iTunes illustrates this case. The music industry and customers experienced a change of market mechanisms.

These remarks emphasize the result of the studies mentioned in the introduction—business models need to undergo a continuous change process to stay successful. It does not matter in the first place whether the innovations are of incremental or radical nature, as long as they suffice to revise the "deterioration" of the business model [35]. This shows that business models are not supposed to be used in a static manner for describing the state of the business logic, but rather serve as a dynamic concept that changes over time. This awareness of dynamic motivates the understanding and analysis of the effects of a change within components on the internal structure of a business model.

3   Dynamics Between Business Model Components

Based on the components of the Business Model Component Framework, the dependencies and interdependencies identified in the selected literature have been mapped on them. This was realized by gradually integrating the relations into the framework and labeling each relation with a corresponding literature source number for verification issues. This allows scholars to easily locate and reuse the findings of this paper for further endeavors building upon this original study.

Figure 2 shows the mapping of the discovered dependencies and interdependencies on the components of the Business Model Component Framework. In the following subsections, most of the relations will be concisely illustrated step-by-step based on the component categories. For clarification purposes, it should be noted that interdependencies are depicted by bidirectional arrows; one-way dependencies are depicted by unidirectional arrows pointing towards the direction of influence. The minus sign (-) indicates no reported relation between both considered components in literature. As mentioned, to provide a link between the theoretical framework and the findings of the literature study, each literature reference for the concerning relation is assign to the arrows. Since most relations are shown in several literature sources, a clustering of the literature sources' numbers to an alphabetical character is performed.

3.1   Analysis on the Value Creation Model

A dependency of the organizational structure on the value proposition can be recognized. A value proposition that includes innovative product and service offerings for instance needs a flexible organizational structure and flexible decision-making processes as a basis [45]. However, not only value propositions that focus innovation require a certain organizational structure, but also value propositions that focus low costs. Reference [34] refers to the company EasyJet as an example. Their organizational structures are intentionally flat to keep costs low. Only this makes the cost-focused value proposition feasible. Hence the configuration of the value proposition determines the structure of the organizational structure to a certain degree.

The opposite direction however has not been found in literature. Even though the organizational structure has a small impact on the value proposition caused by the present dependency, this impact cannot be considered as significant for determining the product and service offering. That is why the figure abandons this dependency. The organizational structure is furthermore in interaction with the resources, competencies and value adding activities. Following up the last example, it becomes clear that a flexible organizational structure that aims at realizing innovative value propositions needs to possess an appropriate research and development department. Such a department is equipped with miscellaneous "roles" which have to be staffed with appropriate

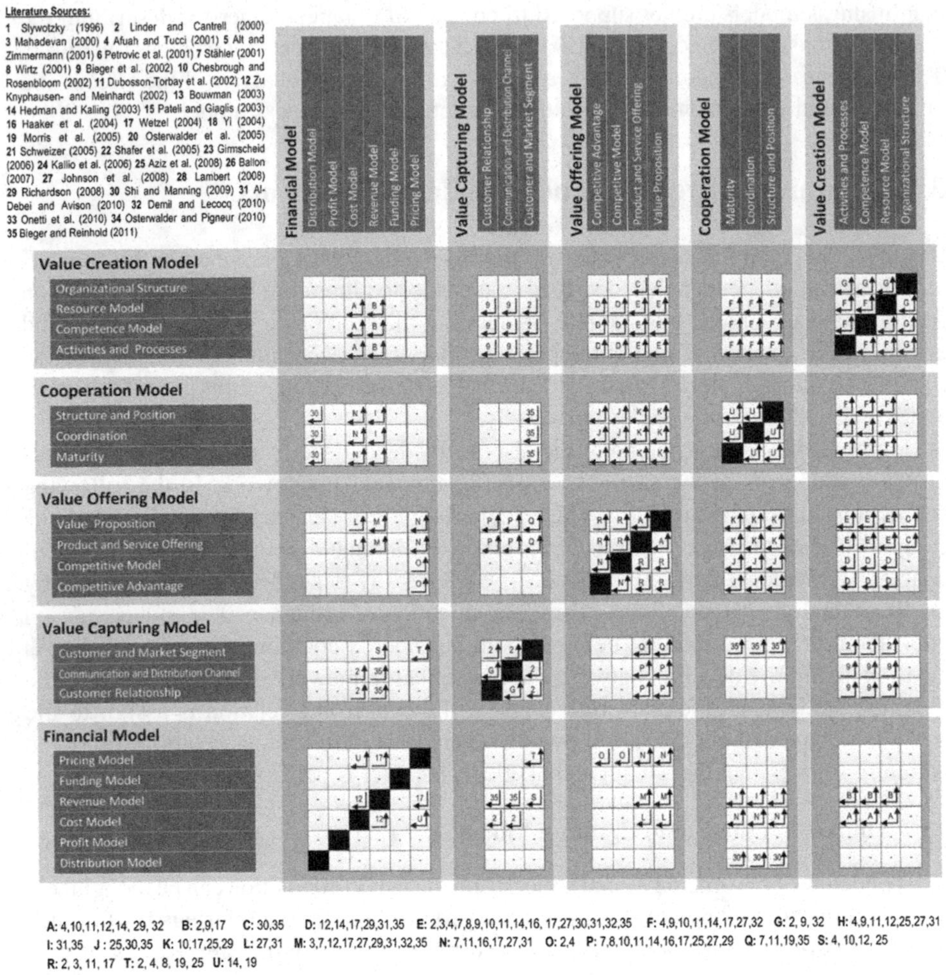
Literature Sources:
1 Slywotzky (1996) 2 Linder and Cantrell (2000) 3 Mahadevan (2000) 4 Afuah and Tucci (2001) 5 Alt and Zimmermann (2001) 6 Petrovic et al. (2001) 7 Stähler (2001) 8 Wirtz (2001) 9 Bieger et al. (2002) 10 Chesbrough and Rosenbloom (2002) 11 Dubosson-Torbay et al. (2002) 12 Zu Knyphausen- and Meinhardt (2002) 13 Bouwman (2003) 14 Hedman and Kalling (2003) 15 Pateli and Giaglis (2003) 16 Haaker et al. (2004) 17 Wetzel (2004) 18 Yi (2004) 19 Morris et al. (2005) 20 Osterwalder et al. (2005) 21 Schweizer (2005) 22 Shafer et al. (2005) 23 Gimscheid (2006) 24 Kallio et al. (2006) 25 Aziz et al. (2008) 26 Ballon (2007) 27 Johnson et al. (2008) 28 Lambert (2008) 29 Richardson (2008) 30 Shi and Manning (2009) 31 Al-Debei and Avison (2010) 32 Demil and Lecocq (2010) 33 Onetti et al. (2010) 34 Osterwalder and Pigneur (2010) 35 Bieger and Reinhold (2011)
Financial Model
Distribution Model
Profit Model
Cost Model
Revenue Model
Funding Model
Pricing Model
Value Capturing Model
Customer Relationship
Communication and Distribution Channel
Customer and Market Segment
Value Offering Model
Competitive Advantage
Competitive Model
Product and Service Offering
Value Proposition
Cooperation Model
Maturity
Coordination
Structure and Position
Value Creation Model
Activities and Processes
Competence Model
Resource Model
Organizational Structure
Value Creation Model
Organizational Structure
Resource Model
Competence Model
Activities and Processes
Cooperation Model
Structure and Position
Coordination
Maturity
Value Offering Model
Value Proposition
Product and Service Offering
Competitive Model
Competitive Advantage
Value Capturing Model
Customer and Market Segment
Communication and Distribution Channel
Customer Relationship
Financial Model
Pricing Model
Funding Model
Revenue Model
Cost Model
Profit Model
Distribution Model
A: 4,10,11,12,14, 29, 32 B: 2,9,17 C: 30,35 D: 12,14,17,29,31,35 E: 2,3,4,7,8,9,10,11,14,16, 17,27,30,31,32,35 F: 4,9,10,11,14,17,27,32 G: 2, 9, 32 H: 4,9,11,12,25,27,31
I: 31,35 J : 25,30,35 K: 10,17,25,29 L: 27,31 M: 3,7,12,17,27,29,31,32,35 N: 7,11,16,17,27,31 O: 2,4 P: 7,8,10,11,14,16,17,25,27,29 Q: 7,11,19,35 S: 4, 10,12, 25
R: 2, 3, 11, 17 T: 2, 4, 8, 19, 25 U: 14, 19

Fig. 2. Dependencies and interdependencies between business model components

actors (i.e. human resources) [35]. Besides this implication of the organizational structure decision on staff requirements, the choice of internal value adding activities also determines the number of roles and departments of the organizational structure [26]. Reference [39] additionally mentions that the organization of a company's core competencies requires a thoughtful design of the organizational structure. On the one hand, the arrangement of the value proposition decides about the required resources resp. competencies as well as the activities for their production and execution. On the other hand, their quality has a significant impact on the design and feasibility of the value proposition. This yields a mutual dependency [18, 38, 45].

Particular core competencies are necessary to realize the choices regarding the design of marketing and distribution channels as well as the customer relationships [39]. The selection of channels and relationships influences the required competencies. The quoted source omits the naming of specific competencies. The question whether an interdependency exists is yet to be evaluated. The literature yielded no remarks in this context. Concerning this question channels and relationships would have to be adapted to the competencies in the first place. Since channels—e.g. pay services—can also be acquired from the cooperation network, a configuration of the channels directly based on the available competencies is not expedient.

The configuration of value activities depends upon the customer and market segment. If a large customer base is addressed, the net product can be maintained at a high level–supposing a corresponding sales and transaction volume [35]. Again the reverse relation has to be reviewed. A company's production limits might affect the size of the addressed customer and market segment to some extent. The arrangement of the supply chain, novel combinations of existing resources and also the creation of new resources can lead to competitive advantages. Thus, the business model is set apart from competitors [10, 18, 20, 50].

An interdependency is exhibited between the supply chain configuration, i.e. the configuration of activities, and the revenue mechanisms [50]. This is manifested by the fact that enterprises endeavor to execute those activities that are linked to high revenue expectations. Reference [35] also mentions this dependency. Beyond that, [39] observes that particular core competencies are required to realize the settlement model. This closes the depend circle and yields an interdependency for the two components. Costs are caused by the procurement and production of resources as well as the transformation process with its value adding activities. Therefore, the cost model is influenced by resources and activities [26, 37, 41]. An optimal implementation of the value adding processes can keep the arising costs at a reasonable level [8]. Vice versa, the concrete implementation of the cost model (e.g. a low-cost strategy) must be reflected within the activities [18, 59]. Therefore, an interdependency between the two components is present.

Resources within a company and especially competencies have an impact on the decision which activities are executed in the company itself and which are outsourced to the cooperation network [37, 39, 41]. Additionally, those activities that can be performed cheaper externally should be outsourced [50]—as long as no risks arise from the external dependency or potential quality decreases [45, 47]. Thus, the selection of a cooperation network, especially of supply companies, depends upon the own resources and competencies or more generally upon the required resources for the value-added process [50]. The applicable resources also depend upon the supply of the cooperation network. If the quality of resources provided by the network decreases, the value-added process is affected [8, 18]. Consequently, an interdependency can be derived.

3.2 Analysis on the Cooperation Model

The cooperation network has indirect, but also direct influence on the value proposition. The indirect relation can be exemplified by the quality of delivered resources that flow into the value proposition during the value adding activities. In contrast to that, providers of complementary goods or involved customers themselves—which can also be subsumed under the cooperation network—have direct impact on the actually realized value proposition, even if those products do not enter the direct value-added process [37, 50]. Additionally, the chosen value proposition influences the cooperation network, because the different actors have to fit in with their value proposition [59]. However, it is yet to be evaluated whether this influence takes places directly or via the components resource model, competence model and activities and processes.

The cooperation network can exhibit a direct impact on the competitive advantage. The quality of general partners or the number of involved customers in the sense of cooperation partners directly determines the competitive advantages of the own company [45, 47]. In contrast to that, competitive advantages can change the own position within the cooperation network [34]. This change could mean that a general partner attends to its own business model because the own business model promises a higher value proposition.

The addressed customer and market segment can influence the cooperation network. This is the case if the business model is targeted to a large customer base. Then—as [34] explains upon the example of budget airlines—a higher negotiating power is present and the own position within the network can be improved [35]. Addressing a smaller audience will usually not yield such advantages.

The cooperation network can exert influence on the revenue model, since revenue mechanisms can become ineffective. This can be because of the cooperation partners' reactions to a company's technical innovations which change the company's position within the network [34]. The chosen revenue model might also affect the cooperation with certain payment partners, though. However, this can happen indirectly via the value proposition—yet, the literature review yielded no direct interaction in this regard. Besides the indirect cost generation of the cooperation network, e.g. when acquiring commodities, direct effects on the cost model can also be assessed. Transaction costs and especially coordination costs arise between the focal company and its cooperation partners [38, 39]. The interaction of both components also becomes clear when considering cost savings via outsourcing. Partners might be able to execute activities more efficiently while the value proposition for the customer stays the same [47]. Decreasing transaction costs encourage the network building process and lead to a higher vertical disintegration [41].

The distribution model also affects the cooperation model. If a change is performed or scheduled herein, like allocating cooperation companies a lower share of profit or revenue, this can lead some actors to switch into a different cooperation network [45].

3.3 Analysis on the Value Offering Model

Communication and distribution channels have an impact on the value proposition; in some cases they enable them in the first place. Reference [4] explains this relation with the example of eBay, but numerous other examples exist. The channels are also important for establishing customer relationships based on a targeted value proposition [41]. The closer the customer relationships are, the better a sense for their needs evolves, which leads to aimed adaptations of the value proposition [41]. On the contrary, the design of the value proposition influences the selection of channels and customer relationships [34, 54]. Especially those value propositions that have customers pay high prices often underlie a long-term customer relationship instead of a transactional relation.

In order to be perceived as intentioned and to generate the promised benefit, the value proposition and its realizing product and service offerings have to be adjusted to the needs of the customers and markets [38, 40, 41, 59]. This is underlined by the observation that existing products can offer a different value proposition to a different customer segment [4]. A change of customer needs has the potential to compromise the value proposition [4]. The value proposition is not only adapted to the customer and market segment, the segment also has to be chosen accordingly to the value proposition [37, 51]. However, the structure of the value proposition does not only have to determine the selection of segments, it can also exert a direct influence on customer and market segments. This is the case if a new offering is highly innovative and triggers a market breakthrough.

The product and service offering has an effect on the price fixings [41]. This relation mainly results from the customers' willingness to pay, which is determined by the desired benefit [38, 50]. A particular pricing model can on the other hand influence the value proposition, which is again exemplified by [4] based on eBay. Their innovative pricing model resulted in a novel value proposition. If the pricing model follows a policy of market penetration, i.e. the prices are always low on a relative basis, a rather low quality of the product and service offering can be expected [54].

The arrangement of the revenue model—like a revenue mixture or a new revenue possibility—can influence the value proposition [4, 59]. In case of an innovative revenue structure even new value propositions can be created [38]. For an example it is referred to pre-paid-models of mobile communications providers. However, the design of the product and service offering also induces a certain revenue mechanism [34, 38, 50]. It is often considered as a rule of the industry which revenue models are used for which products [10]. Apart from that, the product and service offering determines to a high degree which revenues resp. profits are generated. At this point, it is illustrated how architectural business model innovations take place: traditional dependencies, i.e. the rules of an industry or market, are abandoned and new compositions are realized [4].

The value proposition and product and service offering have an impact on the competitive advantages if they provide a technical superiority. Hence, the competitive advantages depend on the value proposition [35, 50]. Furthermore, competitive advantages can results from an adequately customer-focused value proposition as long as it matches the customers' preferences [41]. In this regard, the computer manufacturer Dell serves as a good example. The more robust a value proposition is, i.e. regarding the barriers to entry for potential competitors, the longer competitive advantages can be maintained [60]. Reference [38] points out the value proposition's impact on the cost model, since it incurs costs to realize it. However, this impact is rather indirectly because these costs rather exist based on the usage of resources as well as the implementation of activities. Nevertheless, there incur costs from the product and service offering which are not directly linked to the value creating activities—e.g. costs for guarantees and warranties.

Competitive advantages can be used to obtain higher prices for the corresponding value proposition. This is due to the fact that the underlying product or service offering provide additional value compared to competitors, which result in a higher willingness to pay [8, 35]. Moreover, competitive advantages that result from a very efficient value creation or a market dominance can also be used to offer very competitive prices. However, all of these impacts can result directly based on the value proposition. Hence, a direct impact of the "competitive advantages" on "price model" seems questionable.

3.4 Analysis on the Value Capturing Model

The selection and arrangement of distribution and marketing channels as well as relations to customers depend significantly on the customer and market segment that is actually addressed [35]. The arrangement of customer relations can have impact on the revenue model. In this regard, long-term customer relations often result in increased share-of-wallet; on the other hand, transactional relations can often allow higher overall revenues volumes regardless of specific customers. However, this is accompanied with a lower quality in terms of the product and service offering prices [34]. The arrangement and selection of channels have direct impact on the cost model. As a consequence, an existing business model that is unprofitable in terms of costs, can become very profitable when aligned to new channels, e.g. the Internet, since the cost structure will be noticeably optimized [35].

Obviously, the price model has a direct impact on the customer and market segments [35]. For example, if a market penetration price policy is followed, i.e. the prices are kept very low, a large group of customers is addressed. On the other hand, following a high price policy, only a small selection of customers will be addressed [54]. Accordingly, the price model needs also to be aligned to the chosen customer and market segment, since they only have a specific willingness to pay [8]. The greater the size of a chosen customer segment, the more likely the probability to generate a higher quantity of revenues [8]. Hence, the selection of the customer segment has a direct impact on the revenue model [37]. As a result, according to [10], the rules of the economic and commercial game determine exactly which revenue sources for which market segment can be chosen.

3.5 Analysis on the Financial Model

According to [10], the revenue model is depended on a company's cost structure. As a result, costs that are independent from value creating activities should be compensated by usage-independent revenues. Moreover, the cost model impacts the price model, since a low price strategy for example requires a low cost strategy in general [18]. The opposite relation is stated by [54]; however, it should be pointed out that a low cost strategy does not necessarily imply a low price strategy. The pricing of the product and service offering influences the revenue mechanisms, since customers with a low willingness to pay, are more willingly to make transactional independent payments [50].

4   Discussion and Limitations

4.1   Key Results of the Analysis

The analysis clearly revealed that there is indeed knowledge on the structural relations between business model components in literature; it concurrently confirmed that this knowledge is only hardly applied and described in an explicit manner.

A first key result is that there are several components within same component categories featuring structural coherence. This means that these components basically have the same interdependencies and dependencies with other components. Moreover, they are interpedently linked with each other. For instance, take the components Value Proposition and Product and Service Offering. Both have e.g. a strong bidirectional relation with the Customer and Market segment, i.e. if the value proposition or the offering is changed, this will affect the addressed customer and market segments and vice versa. Furthermore, the value proposition strongly depends upon the product and service offering, but also influences it in order to actually provide the proposition. In addition to these mutual dependencies, their strong connection can also be derived from the fact that they are often proposed as a bundle in literature. This also corresponds to the component analysis of the authors in [22]. In doing so, the offering is frequently considered as part of the value proposition. Structural coherence can also be found in the Value Creation Model, in which the components Resources, Competencies and Activities and Processes have same interdependencies and dependencies. In addition, the three components within the bundle Cooperation Model are also virtually identical with regard to the structural relations to the remaining components. Last but not least, the same applies for the components Communication and Distribution Channel and Customer Relationship in the Value Capturing Model.

Another key finding is especially relevant from a practical perspective, i.e. when creating or adapting a business model. By considering the most influencing and most influenced components (cf. Fig. 3), it can be shown that for example the Value Proposition resp. Product and Service Offering yield the most interdependencies, while not being influenced by other components in an unidirectional way. This underlines the fundamental role of both components, meaning that they have the strongest lever to the business model's success and in the same time can be actively formed for the best alignment. In contrast, the components Competitive Model resp. Competitive Advantage are the most influenced ones; yet, they only do very rarely influence other components unidirectional. This implies that they can hardly defined by executives in a direct way, they are rather a result of the structural coherence and fit of the overall business model, i.e. it is strongly dependent on the dynamics and arrangement of the other components.

Based on the analysis it was also possible to show the dynamics between business model components onto the Business Model Component Framework, resulting in a dynamic framework. While Fig. 3 shows these findings, it combines the structural coherent components (cf. beginning of this subsection) for sake of clarity. To clarify the figure in more detail, it should be noted that interdependencies are shown in red color (resp. dark grey in black and white mode) while one-way dependencies are shown in blue color (resp. light grey). Furthermore, the differentiation is symbolized by the arrow

210   J. Krumeich et al.

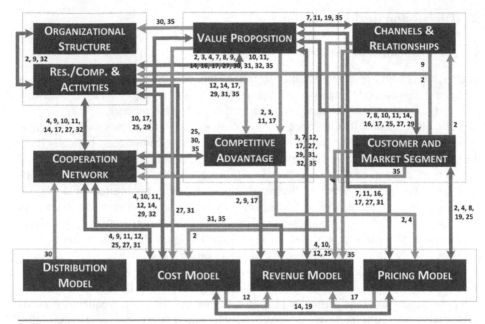

Literature Sources:

1 Slywotzky (1996) 2 Linder and Cantrell (2000) 3 Mahadevan (2000) 4 Afuah and Tucci (2001) 5 Alt and Zimmermann (2001) 6 Petrovic et al. (2001) 7 Stähler (2001) 8 Wirtz (2001) 9 Bieger et al. (2002) 10 Chesbrough and Rosenbloom (2002) 11 Dubosson-Torbay et al. (2002) 12 Zu Knyphausen- and Meinhardt (2002) 13 Bouwman (2003) 14 Hedman and Kalling (2003) 15 Pateli and Giaglis (2003) 16 Haaker et al. (2004) 17 Wetzel (2004) 18 Yip (2004) 19 Morris et al. (2005) 20 Osterwalder et al. (2005) 21 Schweizer (2005) 22 Shafer et al. (2005) 23 Girmscheid (2006) 24 Kallio et al. (2006) 25 Aziz et al. (2008) 26 Ballon (2007) 27 Johnson et al. (2008) 28 Lambert (2008) 29 Richardson (2008) 30 Shi and Manning (2009) 31 Al-Debei and Avison (2010) 32 Demil and Lecocq (2010) 33 Onetti et al. (2010) 34 Osterwalder and Pigneur (2010) 35 Bieger and Reinhold (2011)

Fig. 3. Dynamics between business model components (Color figure online)

heads, which indicate the direction of influence. Again a labeling with a corresponding literature source number allows an easy locating of details about the respective relation.

Further interesting findings are among others the influence of the Communication and Distribution Channels on the Value Proposition. This relation might not be obvious; yet, taking eBay as an example, it shows that with an innovative Distribution Channel (via the Internet), a new Value Proposition for lots of customers can be created. Prior to eBay, only a small market segment had been addressed by auctions. Another unapparent finding is the dependency of the Revenue Model on the Value Proposition. While the opposite dependency is obvious, this dependency becomes clear when taking the pre-paid-models of mobile communication providers as an example that have innovatively created new propositions for entirely new customer segments. Taking the newspaper "Metro" as another example, it can also be shown that business model innovations, like an innovative Revenue Model, do not only influence the Value Proposition, but can also trigger an industry breakthrough. In doing so, traditional industry rules regarding gaining revenues are innovated leading to competitive advantage. Another important finding related to the Value Proposition is that same product and service offerings can provide different propositions when addressing different customer segments. Moreover, a disruptive value proposition may also directly influence the market segment and trigger an industry breakthrough without affecting the actual customers. These few practical examples already demonstrate that the findings are general enough to apply them to different domains; thus, they are not limited to a specific industry or example. In a nutshell, the key findings of the analysis are summarized in the following list:

- Identification of **structural coherent components**
- **Components with the most interdependencies** [number of relations]: Value Proposition/Product and Service Offering [11], Components within the Cooperation Model [9], Resource Model/Competence Model/Activities and Processes [8], Revenue Model [8]
- **Components most influencing other ones** [not including interdependencies]: Customer and Market Segment [9], Communication and Distribution Channel/ Customer Relationship [5]
- **Components most influenced by other ones** [not including interdependencies]: Competitive Model/Competitive Advantage [5], Revenue Model [5], Cost Model [4].

4.2 Limitations of the Study

The aim of this study was to bundle the heterogeneous and implicitly-given knowledge on the internal structure of business models in literature and to present it in an abstract manner. However, it was not in the scope of this study to outline actual recommendations regarding how the internal structure of business models should be changed in order to increase a business model's success. This should be incumbent on subjective decisions made by executives. Nevertheless, based on the knowledge gained through this study, these decisions can be influenced in a positive way, since the obtained insights on the internal structure of business models help to figure out which implication to other components may exist by changing one component. Another limitation of the study is that the discovered dependencies and interdependencies do not claim to be exhaustive. Additionally, since the structural relations were discovered based on a literature analysis, they should also be empirically underpinned, refined and extended in future works. This could be initially achieved by means of expert interviews. In doing so, the findings of this paper can serve other scientist as a broad basis of hypotheses for validation purposes.

5   Summary and Outlook

This paper has provided a comprehensive analysis of business model literature aiming to discover structural relations between business model components. This was achieved by analyzing numerous individual literature sources, which often provide (small-scale) case studies. In pursuing this inductive approach, a large number of dependencies and interdependencies could be discovered and mapped on the Business Model Component Framework, which was recently proposed by the authors [22].

In future work it is of particular importance to research—beyond "simple" relations—so called causal loops within the structural relations of business models. According to [24], causal loop diagrams offer an appropriate way to depict the dynamic of business models. In the course of this, the concept of causal loops originates from the

Systems Dynamics research [61]. A first step towards this direction is done by [62] in the context of abstract e-business models. Causal loops have also been already researched and depicted on an instance level, i.e. based on concrete business models [63, 64].

References

1. Ghaziani, A., Ventresca, M.J.: Keywords and cultural change: frame analysis of business model public talk, 1975–2000. Sociol. Forum **20**, 523–559 (2005)
2. Sampler, J.L.: Redefining industry structure for the information age. Strateg. Manag. J. **19**, 343–355 (1998)
3. Bieger, T., Krys, C.: Einleitung – Die Dynamik von Geschäftsmodellen. In: Bieger, T., zu Knyphausen-Aufseß, D., Krys, C. (eds.) Innovative Geschäftsmodelle, pp. 1–10. Springer, Heidelberg (2011)
4. Stähler, P.: Merkmale von Geschäftsmodellen in der digitalen Ökonomie. Ph.D. thesis. Josef Eul Verlag, Lohmar, Cologne (2001)
5. Bettis, R.A., Hitt, M.A.: The new competitive landscape. Strateg. Manag. J. **16**, 7–19 (1995)
6. Slywotzky, A.J.: Value Migration: How to Think Several Moves Ahead of the Competition. Harvard Business School Press, Boston (1996)
7. Burkhart, T., Krumeich, J., Werth, D., Loos, P.: Analyzing the business model concept - a comprehensive classification of literature. In: Thirty Second International Conference on Information Systems (ICIS 2011), Shanghai, pp. 1–19 (2011)
8. Afuah, A., Tucci, C.L.: Internet Business Models and Strategies: Text and Cases, 2nd edn. McGraw-Hill/Irwin, New York (2003)
9. Osterwalder, A., Pigneur, Y.: Business Model Generation. Wiley, Hoboken (2010)
10. zu Knyphausen-Aufseß, D., Meinhardt, Y.: Revisiting Strategy Ein Ansatz zur Systematisierung von Geschäftsmodellen. In: Bieger, T., Bickhoff, N., Caspers, R., zu Knyphausen-Aufseß, D., Reding, K. (eds.) Zukünftige Geschäftsmodelle – Konzepte und Anwendung in der Netzökonomie, pp. 63–90. Springer, Heidelberg (2002)
11. Heitmann, M., zu Knyphausen-Aufseß, D., Mansel, R., Zaby, A.: Auf der Suche nach Einflussfaktoren auf die Wahl des Geschäftsmodells – Das Beispiel der Biotech-Industrie. In: Bieger, T., zu Knyphausen-Aufseß, D., Krys, C. (eds.) Innovative Geschäftsmodelle, pp. 229–248. Springer, Heidelberg (2011)
12. IBM: Expanding the Innovation Horizon – The Global CEO Study 2006 (2006). http://www-935.ibm.com/services/us/gbs/bus/pdf/ceostudy.pdf
13. IBM: IBM Global CEO Study 2008 – The Enterprise of the Future (2008). https://www-935.ibm.com/services/us/gbs/bus/pdf/gbe03080-usen-ceo-ls.pdf
14. IBM: Capitalizing on Complexity – Insights from the 2010 IBM Global CEO Study (2010). http://www-935.ibm.com/services/us/ceo/ceostudy2010/
15. Osterwalder, A., Pigneur, Y., Tucci, C.: Clarifying business models: origins, present and future of the concept. Commun. Assoc. Inf. Syst. **16**, 1–25 (2005)
16. Gordijn, J., Akkermans, H.: E^3-value: design and evaluation of e-business models. IEEE Intell. Syst. **16**, 11–17 (2001)
17. de Castro, V., Marcos, E.: Towards a service-oriented MDA-based approach to the alignment of business processes with IT systems: from the business model to a Web service composition model. Int. J. Coop. Inf. Syst. **18**, 225–260 (2009)
18. Hedman, J., Kalling, T.: The business model concept: theoretical underpinnings and empirical illustrations. Eur. J. Inf. Syst. **12**, 49–59 (2003)

19. Pateli, A., Giaglis, G.: A research framework for analysing eBusiness models. Eur. J. Inf. Syst. **13**, 302–314 (2004)
20. Al-Debei, M.M., Avison, D.: Developing a unified framework of the business model concept. Eur. J. Inf. Syst. **19**, 359–376 (2010)
21. Zott, C., Amit, R., Massa, L.: The business model: recent developments and future research. J. Manag. **37**, 1019–1042 (2011)
22. Krumeich, J., Burkhart, T., Werth, D., Loos, P.: Towards a component-based description of business models: a state-of-the-art analysis. In: 18th Americas Conference on Information Systems, Seattle, pp. 1–12 (2012)
23. de Reuver, M., Haaker, T.: Designing viable business models for context-aware mobile services. Telematics Inform. **26**, 240–248 (2009)
24. Bucherer, E.: Business Model Innovation – Guidelines for a Structured Approach. Shaker Verlag, Aachen (2010)
25. Shafer, S.M., Smith, H.J., Linder, J.C.: The power of business models. Bus. Horiz. **48**, 199–207 (2005)
26. Demil, B., Lecocq, X.: Business model evolution: in search of dynamic consistency. Long Range Plan. **43**, 227–246 (2010)
27. vom Brocke, J., Simons, A., Niehaves, B., Riemer, K., Plattfaut, R., Cleven, A.: Reconstructing the giant: on the importance of rigour in documenting the literature search process. In: 17th European Conference on Information Systems, pp. 2206–2217 (2009)
28. Wernerfelt, B.: A resource-based view of the firm. Strateg. Manag. J. **5**, 171–180 (1984)
29. Porter, M.E.: Competitive Strategy: Techniques for Analyzing Industries and Competitors. The Free Press, New York (1980)
30. Amit, R., Zott, C.: Value creation in e-business. Strateg. Manag. J. **22**, 493–520 (2001)
31. McGrath, R.G.: Business models: a discovery driven approach. Long Range Plan. **43**, 247–261 (2010)
32. Porter, M.E.: Strategy and the Internet. Harvard Bus. Rev. **79**, 62–78 (2001)
33. Zott, C., Amit, R., Massa, L.: The business model: theoretical roots, recent developments, and future research. IESE Business School Working paper No. 862, Navarra (2010)
34. Bieger, T., Reinhold, S.: Das wertbasierte Geschäftsmodell – Ein aktualisierter Strukturierungsansatz. In: Bieger, T., zu Knyphausen-Aufseß, D., Krys, C. (eds.) Innovative Geschäftsmodelle, pp. 13–70. Springer, Heidelberg (2011)
35. Linder, J., Cantrell, S.: Changing Business Models: Surveying the Landscape. Institute for Strategic Change, Accenture (2000)
36. Onetti, A., Zucchella, A., Jones, M., McDougall-Covin, P.: Internationalization, innovation and entrepreneurship: business models for new technology-based firms. J. Manage. Governance **15**, 1–32 (2010)
37. Chesbrough, H., Rosenbloom, R.: The role of business model in capturing value from innovation: evidence from Xerox Corporation's technology spin-off companies. Ind. Corp. Change **11**, 529–555 (2002)
38. Johnson, M.W., Christensen, C.M., Kagermann, H.: Reinventing your business model. Harvard Bus. Rev. **86**, 57–68 (2008)
39. Bieger, T., Rüegg-Stürm, J., von Rohr, T.: Strukturen und Ansätze einer Gestaltung von Beziehungskonfigurationen – Das Konzept Geschäftsmodell. In: Bieger, T., Bickhoff, N., Caspers, R., zu Knyphausen-Aufseß, D., Reding, K. (eds.) Zukünftige Geschäftsmodelle: Konzepte und Anwendung in der Netzökonomie, pp. 35–62. Springer, Heidelberg (2002)
40. Wirtz, B.W.: Electronic Business, 2nd edn. Betriebswirtschaftlicher Verlag Dr. Th. Gabler GmbH, Wiesbaden (2001)

41. Dubosson-Torbay, M., Osterwalder, A., Pigneur, Y.: eBusiness model design, classification and measurements. Thunderbird Int. Bus. Rev. **44**, 5–23 (2002)
42. Grant, R.M.: Contemporary Strategy Analysis: Text Only, 7th edn. Wiley, Hoboken (2010)
43. Lambert, S.: A conceptual framework for business model research. In: 21st Bled eConference "eCollaboration: Overcoming Boundaries Through Multi-channel Interaction", Bled, Slovenia, pp. 277–289. (2008)
44. Ballon, P.: Business modelling revisited: the configuration of control and value. J. Policy Regul. Strategy Telecommun. Inf. Media **9**, 6–19 (2007)
45. Shi, Y., Manning, T.: Understanding business models and business model risks. J. Private Equity **12**, 49–59 (2009)
46. Alt, R., Zimmermann, H.-D.: Introduction to special section – business models. EM Electron. Markets **11**, 3–9 (2001)
47. Aziz, S., Fitzsimmons, K., Douglas, E.: Clarifying the business model construct. In: AGSE International Entrepreneurship Research Exchange, Melbourne, pp. 795–813 (2008)
48. Lindmark, S., Bohlin, E., Andersson, E.: Japan's mobile Internet success story – facts, myths, lessons and implications. Info **6**, 348–358 (2004)
49. Klang, D., Wallnöfer, M., Hacklin, F.: The anatomy of the business model: a syntactical review and research agenda. In: Druid Summer Conference 2010 on Opening Up Innovation: Strategy, Organization and Technology, London, pp. 1–32 (2010)
50. Wetzel, A.: Geschäftsmodelle für immaterielle Wirtschaftsgüter: Auswirkungen der Digitalisierung – Erweiterung von Geschäftsmodellen durch die neue Institutionenökonomik als ein Ansatz zur Theorie der Unternehmung. Verlag Dr. Kovac, Hamburg (2004)
51. Haaker, T., Bouwman, H., Faber, E.: Customer and network value of mobile services: balancing requirements and strategic interests. In: Proceedings of the 25th International Conference on Informations Systems (ICIS 2004), Association for Information Systems, Washington, pp. 1–14 (2004)
52. Haaker, T., Faber, E., Bouwman, H.: Balancing customer and network value in business models for mobile services. Int. J. Mob. Commun. **4**, 645–661 (2006)
53. Kindström, D.: Towards a service-based business model – key aspects for future competitive advantage. Eur. Manag. J. **28**, 479–490 (2010)
54. Morris, M., Schindehutte, M., Allen, J.: The entrepreneur's business model: toward a unified perspective. J. Bus. Res. **58**, 726–735 (2005)
55. Zollenkop, M.: Geschäftsmodellinnovation: Initiierung eines systematischen Innovationsmanagements für Geschäftsmodelle auf Basis lebenszyklusorientierter Frühaufklärung. Deutscher Universitäts-Verlag, Wiesbaden (2006)
56. Yip, G.S.: Using strategy to change your business model. Bus. Strategy Rev. **15**, 17–24 (2004)
57. Schumpeter, J.: Theorie der wirtschaftlichen Entwicklung, 5th edn. Duncker & Humblot, Berlin (1952)
58. Amit, R., Zott, C.: Value Drivers of e-Commerce Business Models. INSEAD, Fontainebleau (2000)
59. Richardson, J.: The business model: an integrative framework for strategy execution. Strateg. Change **17**, 133–144 (2008)
60. Mahadevan, B.: Business models for internet-based e-commerce: an anatomy. Calif. Manag. Rev. **42**, 55–69 (2000)
61. Forrester, J.W.: Industrial dynamics: a major breakthrough for decision makers. Harvard Bus. Rev. **36**, 37–66 (1958)
62. Kiani, B., Gholamian, M.R., Hamzehei, A., Hosseini, S.H.: Using causal loop diagram to achieve a better understanding of e-business models. Int. J. Electron. Bus. Manage. **7**, 159–167 (2009)

63. Casadesus-Masanell, R., Ricart, J.E.: From strategy to business models and onto tactics. Long Range Plan. **43**, 195–215 (2010)
64. Casadesus-Masanell, R., Ricart, J.E.: Competing through business models. IESE Business School Working paper No. 713, Navarra (2007)
65. Krumeich, J., Burkhart, T., Werth, D., Loos, P.: Interdependencies between business model components—a literature analysis. In: 19th Americas Conference on Information Systems, Chicago, pp. 1–9 (2013)

Challenges and Reflections on Information, Knowledge, and Wisdom Societies and Sociotechnical Systems

Antonio José Balloni[1,2(✉)] and Andrew S. Targowski[3]

[1] Department of Public Policy, The University of North Carolina at Chapel Hill, Chapel Hill, USA
antonio.balloni@cti.gov.br
[2] Center for Information Technology Renato Archer (CTI), São Paulo, Brazil
[3] Western Michigan University, Kalamazoo, USA
andrew.targowski@wmich.edu

Abstract. This paper has been invited to be published by the Springer LNBIP series/2014 and so, it is an improved version from those version accepted for presentation at the Fifth Pre-ICIS workshop on ES Research, St Louis/USA 2010 [1]. The paper considers some challenges and reflections concerned with Information and Knowledge/Wise Societies and Sociotechnical Systems. After a brief and innovative panorama on the information and knowledge/wise societies and sociotechnical system we present the core of this work: challenges and reflections related with our society and systems. For some of these challenges and reflections has been proposed answers such as: treatment of the organization as a living being → synergism & collaborative ecosystem research efforts; a unfair shared leadership, information partnership and a collaborative relationship in the age of knowledge and, a new way of development, which comprises the social, economical, cultural and environmental spheres leading us to a new model of perception and knowledge of the world & present financial crisis; the future... Those questioning are still open to create new insights and interests.

Keywords: Information society · Knowledge society · Wisdom society · Sociotechnical system · Technical system · Social system · Concept · Wisdom · Theory of constraints

1 From the Information and Knowledge Societies to Sociotechnical Systems

A similar contribution of this paper has been published in [2]. The main difference between that publication and this one is: we are now taking into consideration the challenges and reflections on three societies: **information, knowledge and wisdom**. In the

Work partially supported by the State of São Paulo Research Foundation (FAPESP). A.S. Targowski—President Emeritus of the International Society for the Comparative Study of Civilizations (2007–2013).

© Springer International Publishing Switzerland 2015
D. Sedera et al. (Eds.): Pre-ICIS 2010-2012, LNBIP 198, pp. 216–237, 2015.
DOI: 10.1007/978-3-319-17587-4_14

previous publication we have considered only the knowledge society aspects. Therefore the core of this paper has been substantially modified and may be characterized as a completely new and in depth opinion paper.

In the 21 century, Information and Communication Technology (ICT) is redefining the businesses concepts and operations. Customer service, business operations, strategies of products development, marketing and distribution depend very, or sometimes even totally on IST. The ICT and its costs are starting to make integral part of enterprise day-by-day well-being. However, many enterprises still believe that just the simple act of computerizing them, spreading computers and printers throughout departmental units, connecting them in a network and installing applications systems, can fulfill the expected benefits. However, ICT technology, without planning, management and effective action from knowledge/wisdom workers and above all, without considering the sociotechnical systems, does not bring any meaningful and sustainable contribution to the enterprise's well-being [1, 2].

From the Information Society to the Knowledge Society and the Wisdom Society

The Information Wave which follows the Agriculture Wave and Industrial Wave in the 21st century triggers the rise of an information society. It is a society in which the creation, distribution, diffusion, use, integration and manipulation of information is a significant economic, political, and cultural activity. Information society is seen as the successor to industrial society. Closely related concepts are the post-industrial society (Daniel Bell), post-Fordism, post-modern society, knowledge society, Telematics Society, Information Revolution, and network society (Manuel Castells).

The information society applies ICT in its operations, and such technologies as data warehousing and data mining may discover *knowledge* governing a given organization. Since it discovers through computerized processes (data mining) rules that govern a given organization. For example; the best selling products on Mondays at the Wal-Mart stores are baby pampers and beer. This rule leads to two business strategies, if the business is concern, then these two goods should be stored in faraway wings of a store to increase the buy on impulse. If the customer convenience is the guiding strategy, then those two goods should be stored in the same alley. Hence, a store manager is knowledgeable specialist who creates the knowledge society.

The Knowledge Society is one in which knowledge becomes a major creative force, a major component of any human activity. Economic, social, cultural, and all other human activities become dependent on a huge volume of information and knowledge. The knowledge societies are not a new occurrence: a fisherman have long time ago shared the intuitive knowledge of predicting the weather for their community and his knowledge belonged as the social capital of that community.

The knowledge society's economy creates wealth through knowledge-driven understanding of economic activities. People that have the means to partake in this form of society are sometimes called digital citizens.

Example of:

A. Societies that can blossom to knowledge societies:
   1. People from the same field
      - Teachers teaching the same subject
      - Fans of the same musical group
      - Artists with similar interests.
   2. People from different fields
      - Engineers talking to scientists about a scientific issue related to their engineering project
      - Researchers of different fields discussing a common research problem
      - Artists interested in fractals getting in touch with programmers
      - Mystics talking to scientists.
B. Nations that clam that blossom from knowledge societies
   - Finland and United Kingdom which are in the post-industrial societies and develop intellectual properties which sell abroad.

What is New in a Knowledge Society [3]?

With ICT technologies, knowledge societies need not be constrained by geographic proximity, it is de facto a network society, tele-communicationally connected by the Internet. This connection growth in its capacity and declines in terms of its operational cost as it is depicted in Fig. 1.

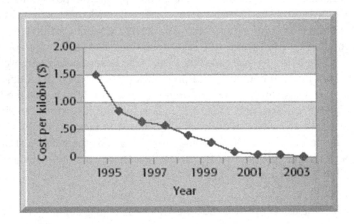

Fig. 1. Internet costs per Kb as published in [1, 2]. Potentially, the Internet has the power to be ubiquitous and this has changed the economics of information. The trends presented by this figure -1995 to 2003- agree with the trends presented by Fig. 2 -1980 to 2010-. However, when it comes to Internet access, the The Global Information Technology Report 2013 presents that 77.3 % of individuals in advanced economies use the Internet, about three times as many as in developing countries (25 %), [4].

Furthermore, ICT technology offers much more possibilities for sharing, archiving and retrieving information/knowledge as it is illustrated in Fig. 2;

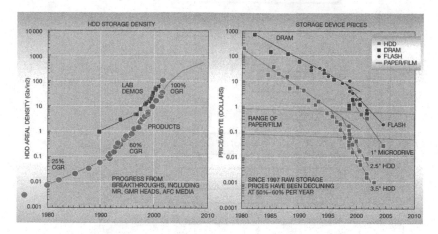

Fig. 2. According to Morris and Truskowski [5], HDD storage density is improving at 100 percent per year and the price of storage is decreasing rapidly and is now significantly cheaper than paper or film. Everything about ourselves could be now stored in any personal computer! However, when it comes to the PC ownership Global Information Technology Report 2013 presents that 77.7 % of individuals in advanced economies have a PC, about three times as many as in developing countries (22.2 %), [4].

It becomes more evident that knowledge has become the most important capital in the present age, and hence the success of any society lies in controlling and making use of it. However, knowledge is not the ultimate virtue of humans. The ultimate virtue of humans is wisdom, and those who are wise create the wisdom society.

The Wisdom Society is a society whose citizens are able to make good judgment and choices. The ICT systems process cognitive units such ones as data, information, concept, knowledge, and wisdom, which support human decision-making in societal activities. Figure 3 illustrates the Semantic Ladder, which illustrates the rise of the Wisdom Society, which is able to make good judgment and choices, [6]. The info-communication process conveys meaning through those five units of cognition:

- *Datum*

A measuring unit of cognition that describes transactions between natural, artificial or other semantic systems. In business, data can measure performance characteristics of production, distribution, transportation, construction, or service. For example, *Dow Jones* index, of say 10,000 points on a Monday of a given month and year, will be the *data* [6].

- *Information*

A comparative unit of cognition that defines a change between the previous and present state of natural, artificial, or semantic systems. Businesses often compare performance characteristics in two or more periods. For example, The fact that on the following

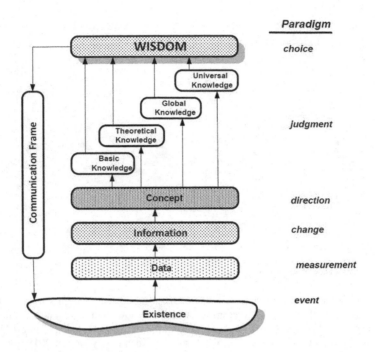

Fig. 3. The Model of Semantic Ladder – The Targowski Model [6]. Man began to evolve from Existence to Cognition, from religion to science: their reasoning was independent and logical, understanding the cause-effect relationship. Figure 3 as published by the author [6].

Tuesday *Dow Jones* was 8,000 points, that is, 20 % less than the day before, will be *information*. This is a rather unpleasant kind of information, which characterizes the *change* of the index by minus 20 %. This information demands that the investor conceptualizes a new solution [6].

- *Concept*

A perceptive unit of cognition that generates thoughts or ideas that creates our intuition and intention – a sense of direction. For example, due to the market strong change, should an investor to sell, to buy, or to hold his/her stocks? So, *Concept* may be about the choice of one of three option-concepts. Because the stocks fell in price and are cheap, a new package of shares can be bought (C1); in other words, having slumped so much, they cannot keep falling; another option (C2) will be the sale of one's stocks in order not to make bigger losses. Finally, the third solution (C3) will be neither selling nor buying stocks. Now, having three concepts/options of a solution, a judgment needs to be made as to which solution is the best [6].

- *Knowledge*

A reasoning unit of cognition that creates awareness based on scientific data (ex.: Census Bureau, research), rules, coherent inferences, laws, established patterns, methods and their systems - is a set of principles, rules and research data which the investor will make use of in the assessment of each of these options - [6]. Knowledge provides a point of reference, a standard for analyzing data, information and concepts. Knowledge can be categorized in many ways. Let's take a look at their four following kinds [6]:

- **Basic Knowledge:** indicates that one should buy shares when they are cheap and sell when they are expensive.
- **Theoretical Knowledge:** might indicate that a decline in the prices of stocks may result from the economy entering a recession.
- **Global Knowledge:** suggests that a war with state X is imminent and this fact will increase the needs for the sake of war.
- **Universal Knowledge:** implies is that when the economy enters a recession, profits from trading stocks dwindle but money can be made on trading bills of exchange (bonds).

Once again elaborating on the previous examples, an investor will apply his/her or adviser's financial knowledge to find out which concept he/she should apply. He/she can also apply remaining kinds of knowledge to evaluate each concept option.

According to Targowski [6], Wisdom is the most essential virtue of man; also, it is the most important intellectual resource, determining the earthly success of the human species. The main components of Wisdom are *good judgment* of the situation in small and big picture, both short- and long-term, local and global, stressing the possible effects on the economy, environment, climate and society, as well as a prudent, tolerant and practical *choice*, not only aware of decision-making strategies but of universal contexts, too; a choice that comes to fruition in effective action, but in the context of the *art of living* since man is no computer they are guided by numerous influences, such as emotions, which can distort the best judgment and choice.

- *Wisdom (W)*

A pragmatic unit of cognition that generates volition -a chosen way of acting and communicating- the most essential virtue of man; also, it is the most important intellectual resource, determining the earthly success of the human species [6]. Wisdom is a process of choosing among available concept options, based on knowledge, practice, morale, or intuition, or on all of them. Concluding our example, the investor has received an assessment of the situation in the four categories of knowledge and now has to make a choice between three options/solutions. Since he would lose by selling the stocks, he rejects the option C1. As war is coming, and stocks might increase in value, he does not buy but, rather, decides to keep his shares and waits. So, they selected the option C3 and time will tell whether this was a good, and hence wise, choice [6].

So, Semantic Ladder -Fig. 3-, which illustrates the rise of the Wisdom Society, explains that wisdom is not knowledge; neither is it information nor data. It is *judgment*, and the *choice* of concepts of thinking and action. Moreover, in order that the concept would be properly formulated, one needs to be well-informed; that is, one has to have verifiable data. In order to make a wise assessment, one needs to have good knowledge: basic, theoretical, global and universal. Not all have such kinds of knowledge, and therefore their judgments are not wise within a range of knowledge a decision making subject has. This is not to say that if one has a wide the range of knowledge at their disposal, one has a guarantee of a wise judgment. There are other factors, such as emotions, intuition, luck or a will to implement a wise action, etc. All is an art of living. The word 'art' used here refers to an intuitive and innovative approach to the known and right principles of judgment and an ability to create new principles and breaking the rules, outdated for the case [6].

Events occur at the existence level that are communicated as data and inserted into the Semantic Ladder of a person, discipline or organization. These data are subsequently processed into information, and information is processed into concepts, which are later evaluated by available knowledge—filter, before one of those concepts will be chosen by decision-maker's wisdom. Then, a *frame* consisted of a message and decision-maker's intentions (very often different than the message's content) is returned as a feed-back to the level of existence.

Examples of the Wisdom Society are as follows:

(A) Business Society: Wall Street brokers who make millions while other suffers financial crisis. Their wisdom is aimed only at their personal gains in short terms. In long terms their personal-oriented wisdom leads to the financial crisis (as it is in 2008–2011).
(B) Costa-Rican politicians who do not maintain the military force and keep their country in peace and prosperity.
(C) Cold war politicians who kept the world in balance, despite of having atomic bomb, which if used could destroy the planet.

Technical Systems versus Sociotechnical Systems
As it is widely know, the implementation of a new technology has been associated with problems often linked to resistance by the work force and failure to achieve the expected benefits [7]. Figure 4 reflects the generic architecture of a socio-technical system.

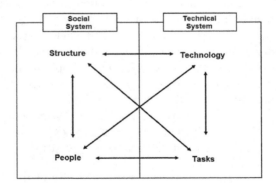

Fig. 4. The Information System (IS) influence access to key resources such as Intellectual Property, Central Competency and Financial Resources: "removes" peoples from their comfort zone and performance management. These key resources could be now in a IS instead in the hands of workers and, this IMPLIES organizational and political resistance. To implement changes, all four components must be changed simultaneously [10].

Hence, a sociotechnical system -Fig. 4 - is composed of the following components:

- *The social system* – it is an livable organization, (Fig. 5) – comprised of the employees (at all levels) and their knowledge, skills, attitudes, values and needs they bring to the work environment as well as the reward system and authority structures that exist in the organization.

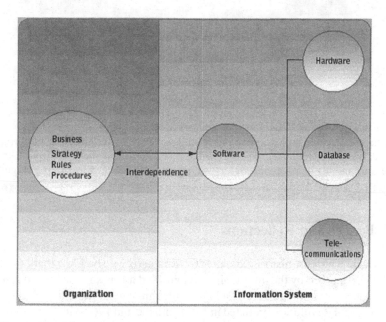

Fig. 5. There is an interdependence between organizations and IS [1, 2, 13, 14].

- *The technical system* – represented here by an information system, (Fig. 5) – comprised of the devices, tools and techniques needed to transform inputs into outputs in a way which enhances the economic performance of the organization.
- The mission of the Sociotechnical Approach is: to secure the fit between technical and social systems. Any organizational system will be able to maximize performance only if the interdependency of these systems is explicitly recognized, and designed for their sustainability.

Therefore, researchers, notably at the Tavistock Institute in London, suggested that it would be needed a fit between the *technical system* (represented by an information system) and the *social system* which together made up an organization [7–13], depicted in Fig. 5.

The fit (or alignment) between the *technical system* and the *social* system is illustrated in Fig. 6:

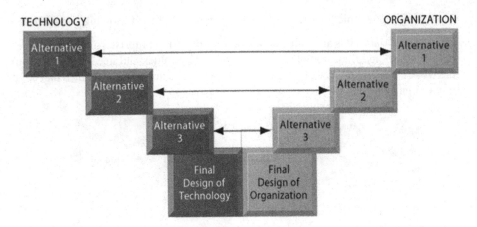

Fig. 6. The sociotechnical perspective on technical and social systems. The performance of a technical system is optimized when both the technology and the organization mutually adjust to one another until a satisfactory fit is obtained [1, 2, 13, 15, 16]. Figure 6 as published by the author [16].

2   Challenges and Reflections

If we go back a little in history (about 150 years ago) we shall see that competitive advantage was marked by the ownership of capital and assets such as natural resources, estates, etc., but today we are experiencing a fourth great revolution, that of knowledge.

The Industrial Revolution (initiated in 1750 until the mid 1960s) in its first movement was marked by the strong development of the production processes. The second moment of that revolution, took place in the 1970s, marked by the expansion of the Japanese industry. The industrial world was overtaken by drastically improved manufacturing processes. Concepts such as Just in Time (JiT), Lean Production, Kanban Card/View, Six Sigma were created and defined quality as being "the differential". Today quality is just a basic requirement of any manufacturing!

In the 1980s and 1990s the third moment of the Industrial Revolution, was marked by a scientific and technological inventions in the West, lead by the Americans' mass applications of computers and their networks. It led to the digital movement via online software and methodologies capable of controlling in detail the management of an organization, and increasing their gains in productivity.

Then from the mid 1990s on, the investment in access to new ICT technologies evolved into a non impeditive factor in face of the vertiginous decrease on their prices. Figure 7 explains how digitalization (as the fourth movement of the Industrial Revolution) enabled organizations to compete at same levels of electronic technologies.

Today, a great movement in the Industrial Revolution is towards appreciation of the intellectual asset, which can be energized inside the organizations. It treats key specialists of an organization as a great competitive differential. Here is the rise of the Age of Knowledge [17].

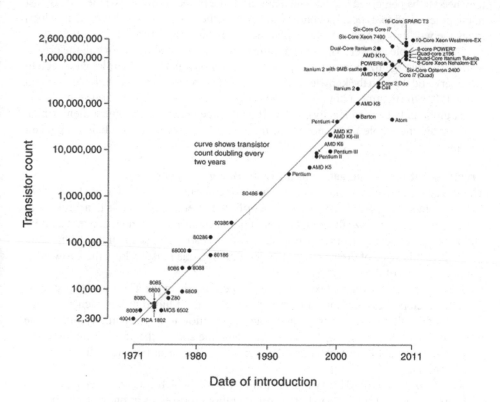

Fig. 7. Packing more transistors into less space has driven dramatic reductions in their cost and in the cost of the product they populate -see Fig. 2-. The investment in access to new technologies evolved into a non impeditive factor in face of the vertiginous decrease on their prices enabling organizations to compete at same levels of electronic technologies. It leads to the fourth movement of the Industrial Revolution. [1, 2, 18, 19].

In the 21st century, technology-oriented specialists want to move our civilization from so called the Information Age to Knowledge Age. At the same time one can observe the emergence of an increasingly globalized and virtualized culture, triggered by the development of fast computers with unlimited storage and application of global tele-communication which both conquer the behavior of humans, developed in the last 6000 years of civilization.

One Can Ask What About the Social-Technical Issues Involving ITC and People? A possible answer to such question could be provided by what is known as Action Network Theory: the emerging issue is linked to the complexity of the real which shall not be able to be reduced since the great relations' network (peer to peer) became evident through the technological development of ICT and the Internet [20, 21].

There is also a vision where the world is seen as an intricate fabric made up of connections, of several types, alternate, combined and juxtaposed, determinant of the structure of the whole [22]. And it is such world, full of connections and relations, that they need to be perceived in a holistic manner, as the properties of the whole are not lost in the practice of analytical reductionism, which rather proper to the mechanism which treats the world as a machine, and explaining it via the explanation of its parts.

Other possible answer to the questioning could be provided by "knowing the organizations". The organizations are composed of complex organisms (**people**) who need to be understood through the knowledge of nature of their relations and within a determined context. It is the treatment of the organization as a *living being*, through a systemic view (think globally but acting locally), that will enable the emergence of phenomena which shall enable the whole to be more than the sum of the parts of such being/organism (organization)!

Treatment of the Organization as a Living Being → Synergism!

There is an opinion that organizations, known as relations' networks, cannot be reduced and "systematized". Also, the focus on **people** is not enough, since it is necessary to connect and contextualize them in the organization's cause. So, connecting and contextualizing the people in the organization's cause may lead to a concept of the differential. To achieve this stage of organizational understanding, one must address the knowledge of the dynamics of the system as whole!

How to theorize such context? An answer, perhaps, is in the Theory of Constraints (TOC), which possesses as one of its pillars the concept of Inherent Simplicity: "a deep understanding that there is always a simple explanation to any seemingly intractable problem. This leads one to use the intuition to find the core of the problem and develop a solution which both solves the immediate problem and doesn't create additional problems along the way" [23, 24].

The utilization of the Theory of Constraints (TOC), which considers the application of the exact science principles to human organizations, possesses as one of its pillars the concept of Inherent Simplicity and, the difficulty, initially, is to believe in such statement. Therefore it is necessary to study the cause-and-effect relations from the system in question in order to discover such Inherent Simplicity.

On the present causality map the technological, psychological, environmental and political elements must be present, demonstrating all inevitable logical links between causes and effects (visible or not). Such logical maps, called "trees" in the TOC (from present reality, from future reality, etc.) help us in obtaining an essential systemic view.

The creator of the TOC, physicist Eliyahu Goldratt, applied the exact science principles to human organizations and demonstrated, amongst other things, that technology is necessary, but not sufficient. The personal factors, especially those linked to individual performance *measurement*, generally exert a very strong influence in any context, which frequently frustrate any initiative for change [25, 26].

But in the end, a simple answer to the previous question (How about the social-technical question involving IT and people?) could lead to the following: the social-technical question involves the people (obvious) and everything surrounding them, including the IT. It is a question of utility, of functionality, of usability for the consumer (if we are to discuss market), for the user (if we are to discuss society). How to demonstrate this?

One of the aspects which are becoming important at everyone's everyday life has to do with the values changes in our society. As well as manual labor was the basis for the Agricultural Wave, and capital and energy were basic at the Industrial Wave, the computer networks and human beings are essential in the Information Wave. Hence, one would like to know, how to deal with the social-technical questions in the Information Wave and its Knowledge Age?

A possible answer can be related to the Facebook phenomenon, with its 500 million users which is a very good example and place to raise the social-technical questions for the Knowledge Age. Its growth 'provoked' other social networks with specific purposes, but every network's dream is to become a *facebook*. Today, organizations participating in such network, not only use 'fakes', but show their face, in order to get closer to their consumers, to provide better service, offer most suitable products, and receive users' suggestions.

Sales teams are being managed with the aid of Google, keeping the team informed of processes and procedures uniformity, distance training, study groups and collaborative works in real time. Furthermore, heads of major organizations communicate with their personnel via blogs (Wordpress, Blogger, and alike). A small detail to be observed, not of little importance, is that "teens of up to The present world financiathe same way the rest of the post-teen humanity faces ID and Individual Taxpayers Registry ID. Are such statements based on facts, and how can we prove this? Can we?

The answer is Yes: by the end of the 2010s blogging, photo- and video-sharing, social networking and on-line gaming had been embraced by half the Internet users worldwide. Some regional patterns seem to emerge: Asian countries are leading the adoption of these, followed by the US and Europe, Fig. 8 [27].

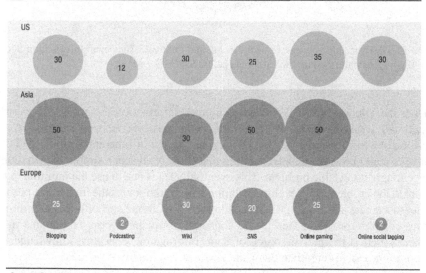

Source: (Pascu, 2008a), estimation based on existing surveys

Fig. 8. Prevailing trend of Internet users in Europe (25 %), USA (30 %) and Asia (50 %). [1, 2, 28].

We are living a unique moment in history, discovering that, despite our way of traditional thinking and living, which is not based on the holistic paradigms and at the same time humans are being in the middle of transition from the industrial to a dehumanized digital economy. At the same time we are moving towards the development of a sense of unity and perception of the whole and, hopefully, towards a sustainable economy? Is the present economic crisis (2008–2010) developing such sense of unity and perception of the whole? Figure 9 shows an representative model for such concern, identifying the 5 moral dimensions of a society across individual, social, and political levels of action [1, 2].

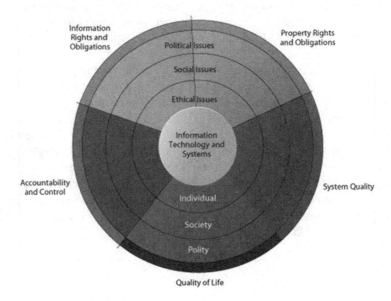

Fig. 9. The Relationship between Ethical, Social, and Political issues in an Information Society [1, 2]. Figure 9 as published by the author [1, 2, 29, 30].

Does the solution for this knowledge-oriented information society go, necessarily, through the social-technical IT questions? One possible answer is: Yes! Again, according to what previously showed about the concept of Inherent Simplicity (TOC), an answer could be: a deep understanding that there is always a simple explanation to any seemingly intractable problem. This eventually leads one to use the intuition to find the core of the problem and develop a solution which both solves the immediate problem and doesn't create additional problems along the way. Some sort of hope in intuitively solving complex problems lies in the constantly growing access of humans to the Internet, which is the global source of data, information, concepts, knowledge, and wisdom if one can differentiate them and know how to interpret them?

The access to the Internet and television by all citizens is becoming essential for the participation in a real time democratic life. See Fig. 10 [27].

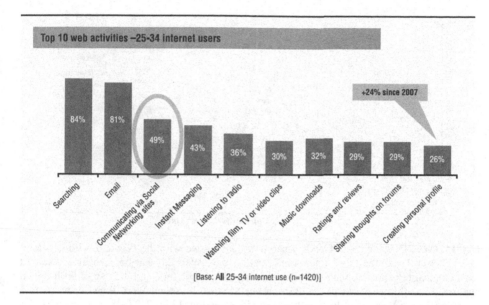

Fig. 10. This survey shows an increase of web activities for 25–34 years old users. It seems that feeding the brain information becomes as natural as feeding the body so as to perform physiological functions. The information, in great volume is available almost always only to a technological elite, instead of favoring inclusion, it reinforces *exclusion* – and the old humanity dilemma repeats itself: lack of food or information as well as their unbalanced or excessive consumption continue to cause the disarrangement and halting of systems to the same extent. [1, 2, 27].

Is it the Onset of a Negative Impact from the Social-Technical Questions?
Maybe not! It could be the opposite: deals with the positive impact from the social-technical questions, now are defined by the Ultimate Consumer. Not withdrawing the importance of TV and other means of mass communication, the consumer market on the Internet estimates the 'value' of products through clicks and, nowadays (**and in the future**), this is what matters. The supplier who relates with such public square is able to estimate the impact of its product analyzing the number of clicks. This kind of measurement is provided in Fig. 11 for the current period [27, 28].

This kind of measurements for the future as estimated in Fig. 12.

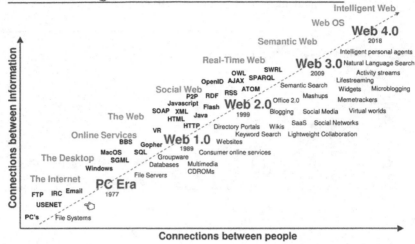

Fig. 11. Web Developments Trends: Everything has started with the Web 1.0, with its statics sites. Web 1.0 was the not-for-profit information age. Web 2.0 can be seen as a result of technological refinements, such as broadband, improved browsers, and the rise of flash-driven application platforms. It has generally been regarded as the social Web. Web 3.0 refers to a supposed third generation of Internet-based services, see Fig. 12 [1, 2, 27, 28].

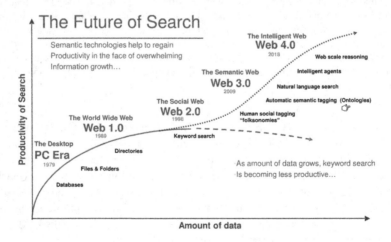

Fig. 12. The measurements of the future searches. Web 3.0 refers to a supposed third generation of Internet-based services. Web 4.0 must predict the management and the intelligent use of all available knowledge in the net with media convergence and a more intuitive search mechanism. Based on previous demands from the Internet users as well in about the study of their behavior in the web, the sites would start to deduce their next intentions… [1, 2, 27–30].

3   The Future of ICT-Driven Societies

For countries in development, such as Brazil, to transform their condition, it is necessary, *NOW*, to advance their *R&D* and local *Collaborative Ecosystem* research efforts.

This R&D and local collaborative ecosystem (*ecosystem refers to a combined components of an ICT-oriented environment*) research efforts must consider the principle of the Systemic View (*thinking globally but acting locally*), and it may be accomplished by the integration among one of these interdependent subjects: ecology, biology, communication, organizations, economy, education, communities, technology, culture and the human being (*human, social, psychological, intellectual and mental ecology: social-technical systems*).

How to Elaborate/Build a New Way of Development, which comprises the Social, Economic, Cultural and Environmental Spheres, and that Leads us to a New Model of Perception and Knowledge/Wisdom of the World – A Good Social-Technical System?

Maybe an answer to such questioning "good social-technical system" is in the following. There is no definitive way to answer this question. Perhaps it will be appropriate to return to the TOC, which was developed by a physicist Eliyahu M. Goldratt, who applied the exact sciences principles to human organizations and demonstrated, amongst other things, that technology is necessary, but not sufficient.

The current strategy to see everything in the world in term of the quest for lower cost and better profit cannot be sustained for a long period. The present world financial crisis (2008–2010) is a symptom of a new Sociotechnical System (or symptom of a gigantic Information System?), which is not, yet, well defined and cannot be explained in terms of the paradigm of the 19th century economy. Today's crisis is the result of a catastrophic failure, primarily in the financial system but also of our economic and political systems; is the result of the reductionist, atomistic thinking that had long dominated humanity's approach to problem-solving [31].

The challenge now is in the application of the systemic thinking - to design a society (regulator) that actually measures and focuses on systemic risks, rather than on the individual parts of the system, system thinking focuses on the performance of a system as a whole [32]. This is in contrast to an approach that breaks systems into parts and focuses on the performance of the individual parts, on the assumption that if each individual part is improved then the sum of the parts will also be better. This assumption often proves wrong in practice. The only profession that believes truly in system thinking is architecture, where the design process starts by asking what sort of building is desired, and then works backwards to focus on what individual parts are required. An architect never starts by saying, "Here are the parts, what can I build from them?

Yet, the present economic model cohabits with the principle of shortage, of centralized production, of hierarchical relations, of private property. The model of the future has its sustentation in the non scarce goods, in collaborative production, in network relationships, in common or collective property and in ascent of the intangible goods.

Is Globalization is at Risk with the 2008–2010 Financial Crisis? The Answer is Yes

The crisis has increased calls for a new "Bretton" to better regulate the global economy. World leaders, however, will be challenged to renovate the IMF (International Monetary Fund, special UN agency that was founded in 1944 to stabilize exchange rates and to facilitate international commerce) and devise a globally transparent and effective set of rules that apply to differing capitalisms and levels of financial institutional development. Failure to construct a new all-embracing architecture could lead countries to seek security through competitive monetary policies and new investment barriers, increasing the potential for market segmentation. Again, it is the sociotechnical concern of IT [33–35].

Concerning Brazil [36], inserted in the world-wide context, the wide scale changes occurring in the environment business has compelled the enterprises to radically modify their organizational structures and productive processes: sociotechnical concerns. The main factors of these changes are: the products' globalization, the wide scale of electronic processes use, the nature of the job (*shifting from industry to the services sector*) and the emergent markets as China, India and Brazil. Therefore, for the Brazilian enterprise, now and in the future, to maintain a sustainable position in the world-wide market, it is vital apply the approaches proposed here.

But, a question remains to be answered: "will management of IT and the emergency of global partnerships allow Brazilian enterprises to compete more effectively in the global marketplace, or will they be undermined by greater global competition in their "home territory"? Indeed, is there such a thing as "home territory"?"

Here it is important to remember what Winston Churchill said [1, 2]: "We shape our buildings; thereafter they shape us." Therefore, *the collaborative work space and sociotechnical environment of tomorrow are being shaped today!* Who is willing to take responsibility for the space shaped in Brazil?

How can we define many of the ethical and social dimensions that arise with connectivity and information privacy (sociotechnical concern), with an unfair shared; leadership, information partnership and a collaborative relationship in this Age of Knowledge/ Wisdom? Can Brazil think that its future is in the Wise Society?

Could we change the 2025 global trend as shown by Fig. 13? [35]. Or, in a best and more positive scenario, how could we make the best use from the Demographic Window of Opportunity we are passing through as shown in Fig. 14?

Finally, it is important to draw the attention to new ways of organizations arising in the past few years and which provoked a reorganization of the social sectors. An important class of such new organizations is the so called Learning Community, promoting Education and the Social Asset with the development of individual qualities at people networks, dynamized by the electronic networks (Fig. 10), leading possibly to new ways of acquaintance and relationship, aiming essentially at the transformation of knowledge, of circumstances, of institutions, of concepts, of the Arts, of the Sciences and values from the human being.

However, the great challenge of the 21st century shall be to change the system of values behind the global economy, so as to make it compatible to the demands of human dignity and to the ecological sustainability in a system where the ITC of information

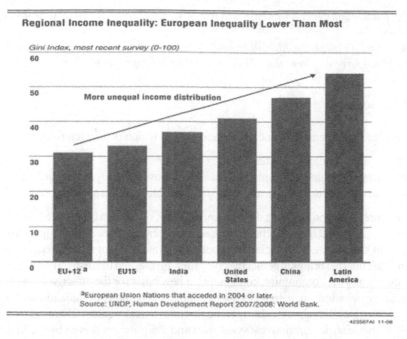

Fig. 13. Income distribution. A Transformed World [1, 2, 35].

THE DEMOGRAPHIC WINDOW OF OPPORTUNITY

According to UN demographers, a country's demographic window of opportunity can be estimated by identifying those years in which the proportion of children (0 to 14 years of age) in the total population is less than 30 percent, and the proportion of seniors (65 years and older) is less than 15 percent.

Country	Median Age, 2010	Median Age, 2030	Demographic Window of Opportunity
Brazil	29	35	2000 to 2030
India	26	32	2015 to 2050
China	35	43	1990 to 2025
Russia	39	44	1950 to 2015
Iran	26	37	2005 to 2040
Japan	45	52	1965 to 1995
Germany	44	49	before 1950 to 1990
United Kingdom	40	42	before 1950 to 1980
United States	37	39	1970 to 2015

Fig. 14. Demographic Window of Opportunity [37].

changes parameters every 24 months and lowering the income inequality, as it is shown in Fig. 13.

Therefore, we must consider all technological possibilities available to us in Brazil, but we do not have to invent the wheel, but, rather to improve bearing.

4   Conclusions

Our world is fundamentally a sociotechnical world, which is characterized by

- Human and technological interactions.
- Human organizations are living systems and should be analyzed accordingly.
- Their interactions drastically affect people relationships in space and time [35].

Therefore, if we consider that the core knowledge is embodied in people's heads (tacit knowledge, [36]), and their abilities to utilize them generate new knowledge, we cannot speak about knowledge/wise society without taking into account these interactions.

Since the Internet brings together the computer, media, and the distributed intelligence of the family and the community, constituting a new basis for the effectiveness of socio-technical organizations then, in this way, beyond the economic, organizational, cultural, and technological dimensions, the specific sociotechnical context characterizes every knowledge/wise society initiatives: synergism and ubiquitously driven by the Internet!

However, management opposition persists, because sociotechnical system by nature enables collaborative decision-making and shared leadership. Management has been reluctant to give up the power and authority they have worked so hard to establish.

Indeed, sociotechnical system challenges the traditional management taboos that of sharing information and knowledge with subordinates on a need to know basis only [36].

The central corner stone of a technocratic bureaucracy is that decision-making is top-down and implementation is bottom up. Amazingly, many postmodern organizational leaders still believe information is best kept in the minds of senior management who have been trained how to use it, make decisions, and implement policy. In this mechanistic model, managers pretend to know and employees pretend to cooperate.

This new emerging scope of the social *modus operendi* is changing our mentality about knowledge and wisdom. The last questions remain to be answered: *Who or what will be driving innovations in this new era? What can be the impact of the sociotechnical system in such innovations process? Or, is the Sociotechnical system is being considered by the political leaders of the emerging knowledge/wise society?*

References

1. Balloni, A., Targowski, A.S.: Challenges and reflections on information, knowledge, and wisdom societies & sociotechnical systems. In: International Conference on Information Systems – ICIS, Saint Louis, USA (2010). http://repositorio.cti.gov.br/repositorio/bitstream/10691/214/1/Paper_JITCAR_ICIS7.pdf. Accessed 15 July 2011
2. Balloni, A.J.: Challenges and reflections on knowledge society & sociotechnical systems. Int. J. Manag. Inf. Technol. - (IJMIT) (2010). http://airccse.org/journal/ijmit/papers/0210ijmit3.pdf. Accessed 27 Oct 2010

3. Sverker, S.N., Vessuri, H.: Knowledge Society vs. Knowledge Economy: Knowledge, Power, and Politic. Palgrave Macmillan Ltd., New York (2007)
4. Bilbao-Osorio, B., Dutta, S., Lanvin, B. (eds.): The Global Information Technology Report 2013: and Jobs in a Hyperconnected, World (2013). http://www3.weforum.org/docs/WEF_GITR_Report_2013.pdf or http://liblog.law.stanford.edu/wp-content/uploads/2013/06/WEF_GITR_Report_2013.pdf. Accessed 22 Mar 2010
5. Morris, R.J.T., Truskowski, B.J.: The evolution of storage systems. http://signallake.com/innovation/morris.pdf or http://www.researchgate.net/publication/224101796_The_evolution_of_storage_systems. Accessed 22 Mar 2010
6. Targowski, A.S.: Harnessing the Power of Wisdom: From Data to Wisdom. Nova Science Publishers, New York (2013). ISBN 978-1626188907
7. Keen, P.G.W.: Information Systems and Organizational Change- Sloan School of Management, MIT (1981). http://itu.dk/~rasesp/davesGuf/p24-keen.pdf. Accessed 22 Mar 2010
8. Leavitt's Diamond An Integrated Approach to Change - Also known as Leavitt's System Mode. http://ugdyk.blogspot.com.br/2013/11/leavitts-diamond-integrated-approach-to.html. Accessed 22 Mar 2010
9. Vincent, M.: Written: Leadership On Point by RLA Associate Meghan. http://blog.richardlevinassociates.com/?p=357. Accessed 22 Mar 2010
10. Kim, M., Sharman, R., Cook-Cottone, C.P., Rao, H.R., Upadhyaya, S.J.: Assessing roles of people, technology and structure in emergency management systems: a public sector perspective (2011). http://www.som.buffalo.edu/isinterface/papers/Assessing_roles_-Oct_storm.pdf. Accessed 22 Mar 2010
11. Bostrom, R.P, Heinen, J.S.: MIS problems and failures: a socio-technical perspective, part II: the application of socio-technical theory. MIS Q. 1(4) (1977). http://www.jstor.org/discover/10.2307/249019?uid=3737664&uid=2129&uid=2&uid=70&uid=4&sid=21103828908083. Accessed 22 Mar 2010
12. Interdependence of Organizations and Information Systems. http://goo.gl/nvJ0SI. Accessed 22 Mar 2010
13. Why Information Systems? Slide8. http://goo.gl/nvJ0SI. Accessed 22 Mar 2010
14. Katz-Haas, R., Lee, Y.W.: Understanding interdependencies between information and organizational processes (Chapter 11). In: Wang, R.Y., Pierce, E.M., Madnick, S.E., Fisher, C.W. (eds.) Information Quality. Advances in Management Information Systems. M.E. Sharpe Inc., New York (2005)
15. Lucas Jr., H.C., Baroudi, J.: The role of information technology in organization design. J. Manage. Inf. Syst. 10(4), 9–23 (1994)
16. Balloni, A.J., Fontes, E.G., Laudon, K.C.: Segurança em Sistemas de Informação: Aspectos Sócio Técnicos. In: Balloni, A.J. (eds.) Por que GESITI? – Segurança, Inovação e Sociedade. Komedi (2007). http://www.cti.gov.br/noticiaseeventos/2006/gesiti/gesiti_2007.htm. Accessed 22 Mar 2010
17. Guevara, A.J.H., Dib, V.C.: The Ager of Knowledge and the growing relevance of human and social capital (2000). http://in3.dem.ist.utl.pt/downloads/cur2000/papers/S26P05.PDF. Accessed 4 Jan 2010
18. Gilheany, S.: Moore's Law and Knowledge Management (2004). http://www.ee.ic.ac.uk/pcheung/teaching/ee4_asic/notes/Lec%201%20Moore%20Law%20and%20Knowledge%20Management.pdf. Accessed 22 Mar 2010
19. Moore's law, From Wikipedia, the free encyclopedia. http://en.wikipedia.org/wiki/Moore%27s_law. Accessed 22 Mar 2010

20. Aidemark, J.: IS planning and socio-technical theory perspectives. Växjö University (2007). http://www.iseing.org/emcis/EMCIS2007/emcis07cd/EMCIS07-PDFs/571.pdf. Accessed 4 Jan 2010
21. What is Actor-Network Theory? http://carbon.ucdenver.edu/~mryder/itc_data/ant_dff.html. Accessed 4 Jan 2010
22. Capra, F.: The Web of Life: A New Scientific Understanding of living Systems. Anchor Books, New York (1996)
23. Goldratt, A.M.: The Theory of Constraints and its Thinking Processes (2009). http://www.goldratt.com/toctpwhitepaper.pdf. Accessed 4 Jan 2010
24. Mabin, V.: Goldratt's "Theory of Constraints" Thinking Processes: A Systems Methodology linking Soft with Hard (1999). http://www.systemdynamics.org/conferences/1999/PAPERS/PARA104.PDF. Accessed 4 Jan 2010
25. McMullen Jr., T.B.: Introduction to the Theory of Constraints (TOC) Management System. The St. Lucie Press, Boca Raton (1998)
26. Mabin, V.J., Balderstone, S.J.: The World of the Theory of Constraints: A Review of the International Literature. The St. Lucie Press, Boca Raton (2000)
27. Ala-Mutka, K., Broster, D., Cachia, R., Centeno, C., Feijóo, C., Haché, A., Kluzer, S., Lindmark, S., Lusoli, W., Misuraca, G., Pascu, C., Punie, Y., Valverde, J.A.: The Impact of Social Computing on the EU Information Society and Economy. In: Punie, Y., Lusoli, W., Centeno, C., Misuraca, G., Broster, D. (eds.) European Commission, Joint Research Centre Institute for Prospective Technological Studies (2009)
28. Spivack, N.: Web Evolution Nova Spivack Twine (2009). http://www.slideshare.net/novaspivack/web-evolution-nova-spivack-twine?from=share_email. Accessed 4 Jan 2010
29. Balloni, A.J., de Souza Bermejo, P.H.: Governance, sociotechnical systems and knowledge society: challenges and reflections. In: Varajão, J.E.Q., Cruz-Cunha, M.M., Putnik, G.D., Trigo, A. (eds.) CENTERIS 2010, Part I. CCIS, vol. 109, pp. 42–51. Springer, Heidelberg (2010). http://repositorio.cti.gov.br/repositorio/bitstream/10691/249/1/2_Centeris-2010-paper_reviewed_final.pdf. Accessed Mar 2014
30. Balloni, A., Bermejo, P.H.S., Holm, J., et al.: Governance, sociotechnical systems and knowledge society: challenges and reflections. In: Enterprise Information Systems, pp. 42–51. Springer, Heidelberg (2012). http://repositorio.cti.gov.br/repositorio/bitstream/10691/215/1/IGI_2010-paper_reviewed_final_IGI_permission.pdf. Accessed Mar 2014
31. Ackoff, R.L.: Redesigning the Future: A Systems Approach to Societal Problems. Wiley, New York (1974)
32. Emery, F.E., Trist, E.: Introduction to volume 1. In: Emery, F.E. (ed.) Systems Thinking, selected readings, vol. 1, 1st edn. Penguin, Harmondsworth (1981)
33. Dooley, M.P., Folkerts-Landau, D., Garber, P.: An Essay on the Revived Bretton Woods System (2003). http://www.nber.org/papers/w9971 or http://www.nber.org/papers/w9971.pdf. Accessed 4 Jan 2010
34. Dammasch, S.: The System of Bretton Woods. A Lesson from History (2006). http://www.ww.uni-magdeburg.de/fwwdeka/student/arbeiten/006.pdf. Accessed 4 Jan 2010
35. Fingar, C.T.: Chairman, National Intelligence Council - Income distribution Global Trends 2025: A Transformed World (2008). http://www.dni.gov/files/documents/Newsroom/Reports%20and%20Pubs/2025_Global_Trends_Final_Report.pdf or http://goo.gl/zywiHN. Accessed 4 Jan 2010
36. Balloni, A.J.: Why GESITI: why management of system and information technology. In: Camarinha-Matos, L.M. (ed.) Virtual Enterprises and Collaborative Networks. CCIS, vol. 149, pp. 291–300. Springer, Boston (2004)

37. Global Trends 2030: Alternative Worlds a publication of the National Intelligence Council, December 2012, NIC 2012-001, ISBN 978-1-929667-21-5. http://www.dni.gov/nic/globaltrends - Facebook.com/odni.nic/ Twitter: @odni_nic or http://info.publicintelligence.net/GlobalTrends2030.pdf or http://publicintelligence.net/global-trends-2030/ or http://goo.gl/u6rNsw. Accessed 4 Mar 2014

The Role of Past Experience with On-Premise on the Confirmation of the Actual System Quality of On-Demand Enterprise Systems

Sebastian Walther[1], Rebekah Eden[2(✉)], Gaurang Phadke[1], and Eymann Torsten[1]

[1] University of Bayreuth, Bayreuth, Germany
{s.walther,gaurang.phadke,torsten.eymann}@uni-bayreuth.de
[2] Information Systems School, Queensland University of Technology, Brisbane, QLD, Australia
rg.eden@qut.edu.au

Abstract. The paper examines the role of past experience with an on-premise enterprise system on the confirmation of the actual performance of a cloud enterprise system. The research model is built on expectation-confirmation theory conceptualizing and interlinking the different elements of system quality which differ strongly between on-premise and on-demand solutions. As the research is exploratory in nature and the sample size is very small, the data is analysed using SmartPLS. Results show that most of the confirmation can be explained through actual performance, whereas past experience with on-premise has no significant effects on confirmation and actual performance.

Keywords: System quality · Expectation-confirmation theory · Cloud enterprise systems · Cloud ERP

1 Introduction

The emergence of cloud computing has dramatically changed the application of Enterprise Resource Planning (ERP) systems within organisations [1]. According to Armbrust et al. [2] cloud computing is "application delivered as services over the Internet and the hardware and systems software in the data centers that provide those services." Historically ERP systems have been utilised by large enterprises to provide an integrated package of applications with the goal of providing a competitive advantage to the adopting organisations [3] with very few small and medium enterprises being able to afford them [1]. However cloud computing has revolutionised ERP systems, and brought about a new phenomenon, cloud ERP. Cloud ERP utilises Software as a Service [4], which allows for the traditional ERP system to be present on the cloud, making it an affordable, easy to implement and flexible software solution. According to research by Gartner Group, in 2009 SaaS (Software as a Service) sales had reached $7.9 billion dollars, with approximately two thirds of the sales attributed to Cloud CRM (Customer Relationship Management) and Cloud ERP systems. It is projected that by 2013 SaaS sales will increase to $14 billion [5].

The research question was triggered by exploratory interviews we conducted with managers of leading on-demand enterprise system providers in 2011, where the

© Springer International Publishing Switzerland 2015
D. Sedera et al. (Eds.): Pre-ICIS 2010-2012, LNBIP 198, pp. 238–246, 2015.
DOI: 10.1007/978-3-319-17587-4_15

interviewees were just able to explain the benefits of cloud solutions when comparing them to existing on-premise enterprise systems. This observation led to the research question explored in this paper: to which degree do cognitions about our past experience with an on-premise information system influence the confirmation process of the cloud offering?

A vast body of literature has explored the antecedents of confirmation, most of them in the context of the predominant frameworks in IS: the expectation-confirmation theory (ECT) [6] and the expectation-confirmation model [7, 8]. However, ECT has also been applied in several marketing-specific contexts to predict repurchase intentions of products or services [9, 10]. Limited work has been conducted into studying the confirmation in the context of SaaS [11, 12], whereas the focus of these studies pertained to the actual performance of the system, as opposed to past experience with previous on-premise use. In other contexts, past experience has been shown to influence expectations and therefore to influence confirmation indirectly [13].

This study explores the research question by comparing the influences of previous on-premise use and the actual on-demand system quality on confirmation in the context of on-demand enterprise systems in the post acceptance phase. To highlight the exploratory character of the study, we used a small sample of top managers, executives and IT personnel, analysing the data using SmartPLS, as PLS is well suited for small sample sizes [14, 15].

The paper is organized as follows. First, the theoretical background is given to outline the theoretical considerations, which are then applied in Sect. 3. Section 4 outlines the methodology including the description of the data gathering procedure, as well as the data analysis method. Finally, the results are presented and discussed.

2   Expectations in IS Research

According to ECT, the process of repurchase manifestation is as follows [6]. Consumers have (pre-purchase) expectations before a service or product is consumed. These expectations are shaped by distinct factors including word of mouth, company image, and past experience [13]. Temporarily shifted, there is an initial consumption, where the perception of the actual performance is shaped. This performance is then rated against the original expectations (confirmation). Based on their extent of confirmation, customers form an attitude (or satisfaction) which then influences behavioural intentions (see Fig. 1).

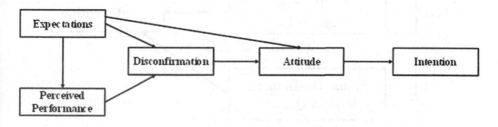

Fig. 1. Expectation-Confirmation Theory [6]

ECM [8] is an integration of ECT and TAM which focuses on post-acceptance variables (but is not limited to it). It modifies the framework in two dimensions. First, pre-purchase expectations are excluded. This is the case as satisfaction and confirmation capture all influences of pre-acceptance variables. Furthermore confirmation is directly defined by and therefore incorporating pre-purchase expectations. Second, perceived usefulness is included to represent post-purchase expectations. This is consistent with ECT's expectation construct, which is defined as belief or sum of beliefs. Perceived usefulness has been demonstrated to consistently influence user intention throughout the process of IS usage.

Recent research on expectancy-confirmation theory has investigated a large variety of factors, such as: trust, perceived privacy risk [16], emotions and habits [17] or perceived ease of use [18], as variables being influenced by confirmation or influencing the repurchase intention directly. Only few studies could be identified capturing prior experience [19], pre-usage beliefs and attitudes [20] or pre-purchase expectations [16] as antecedents of (dis-) confirmation. Therefore our paper makes a theoretical contribution on the "left side" of ECT.

3   Research Model

As our study focuses on the pre-purchase side of the confirmation process, we use ECT as framing. The core mechanism by which past experience with on-premise can influence confirmation can be found in [13], which found empirical evidence that past quality can influence (pre-purchase) expectations, which then directly influence the confirmation process. This is theoretically clear, as confirmation has been defined as a function of pre-purchase expectation minus actual performance. As the study is of exploratory character, we do not measure pre-purchase expectations, but focus on the influence of past experience with on-premise on confirmation. Additionally, to capture the actual performance of the system, we measure SaaS system quality as "perceived performance" of the system (see Fig. 2).

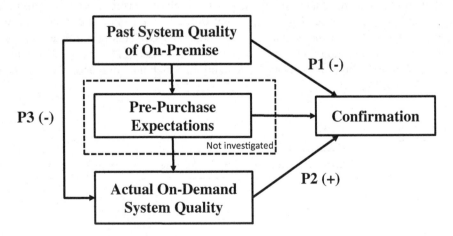

Fig. 2. Research Model

Past experience with on-premise is defined as the perception of the executive in which extent the prior on-premise solution had desirable system characteristics in the dimensions which differ strongly between on-premise and on-demand due to their different underlying infrastructure,[1] whereas confirmation is defined as the user's perception of the congruence between expectation and its actual performance [10]. Theoretical support can be found in ECT, where a good past quality would make it harder to confirm the expectations. This leads to the first proposition:

P1. Executives' perceived past experience with on-premise is negatively associated with their extent of confirmation

Actual on-demand system quality is defined as the desirable characteristics of a system [21, 22][2] in the dimensions which differ strongly between on-premise and on-demand due to their different underlying infrastructure. It is highly important to note, that this does **not** include all system quality dimensions as known from the IS success model. Additionally, it has to be noted that we did not label the construct as SaaS service quality for two reasons. First, it might be confounded with the service quality in the IS success model, which has a distinct meaning (helpdesk). Second, to establish comparability between the constructs past experience and actual performance, we decided to use a more general term like system quality, which includes the SaaS service quality dimensions (except for rapport) and can also be applied in the context of on-premise without confusion. As confirmation is the extent to which (pre-purchase) expectations are verified by actual performance, a higher actual performance (SaaS system quality) should lead to a smaller gap between expectations and performance, resulting in a higher confirmation. This leads to the second proposition:

P2. Executives' perceived actual SaaS system quality is positively associated with their extent of confirmation

Finally, empirical evidence has demonstrated that cognitive beliefs like confirmation and perceived usefulness can be associated similarly to ease of use and perceived usefulness [23]. Theoretical support is found in contrast effect theory, which is a well-known psychological phenomenon, however, has not been applied in IS. Examples of the contrast effect can be found including physiological and visual effects [24]. However, contrast effects can also shape perception [25]. Applied in this context, the human mind would compare the previous experience with the actual experience. Therefore, if the previous experience was good, the new experience will seem to be less good and vice versa, leading to following proposition:

---

[1] We defined 4 dimensions which according to [11] are the characteristics of a cloud offering. However, we do not agree that application is a distinct part of a cloud offering, any software can theoretically be hosted on-premise or on-demand, therefore we do not include the feature dimensions. The same applies to rapport.

[2] Note that we do not define system quality completely congruent to the IS success model, as we explicitly focus on the system quality dimensions which differ between on-premise and on-demand, which excludes things like help desk or application quality.

P3. Executives' perceived actual SaaS system quality is negatively associated with past experience with an on-premise system

4 Methodology

4.1 Data Collection

Empirical data for this survey was collected via an online survey starting mid-September until the end of September. Survey respondents were top managers, line of business managers, IT executives and IT personnel from companies which had a cloud enterprise system implemented. No geographical or industry-specific restrictions were made on the sample. The different hierarchical areas were included to increase the likelihood of detecting the desired cognitive effects and to gain further insights whether distinct hierarchical levels perceive confirmation differently. Additionally, no distinctions were made between the functional area of the cloud enterprise systems (e.g. CRM, HR, Accounting, etc.).

The original sample consisted of 23 cloud enterprise system customers, from which 4 had to be removed due to insufficient fit concerning the target population, leading to a sample of 19 customers. The survey was distributed via several different channels, including social media channels of major cloud enterprise systems providers and direct contacts via E-Mail and business network platforms like LinkedIn and XING. No valid response rates can be extracted, as the distribution was highly heterogeneous to reach a variety of different respondent categories. Additionally, the survey is still in progress, making any respondent rate estimations pure speculation.

Past experience with on-premise and actual system quality were measured formatively, using the SaaS service quality dimensions proposed by [11][3], with the operationalization of the dimensions according to [26][4] on a 7-point Likert scale ranging from strongly disagree to strongly agree. The instrument was developed in a process according to Moore and Benbasat [27], including formative-specific scale development elements [28, 29]. The confirmation construct was measured reflectively according to [8] on a 7-point Likert scale. For the items see Appendix.

4.2 Data Analysis

The reflective measurement instrument showed adequate reliability with all reflective factor loadings above 0.8 above the proposed threshold level of 0.5 [15]. Composite reliability also satisfactory with a level of 0.9 [30]. The average variance extracted (AVE) of 0.75 was above the suggested threshold level of 0.5 [31]. Each formative indicator's weights were assessed using a 1000 bootstrap sample. Only SQ3 was highly

---

[3] The application delivery as part of the service was not included, as we believe that application is not part of a cloud service, as the application itself can either be delivered on-premise or on-demand without any major distinctions. This excludes the dimension features. Additionally, rapport can be seen as part of SaaS-quality, however, in our context, we focus on the quality of the system quality delivered.

[4] Security was newly developed.

significant on a p = 0.01 level. However, this is not surprising, as the number of cases (19) used in the bootstrap is very low. Multicollinearity was accessed using SPSS calculating the variation inflation factors (VIF) with all being significantly below the minimum suggested level of 5 [32].

The structural model was accessed using SmartPLS 2.0 M3 [33] applying the bootstrap algorithm with 1000 sub-samples and 19 cases. Two relationships showed large effect sizes, however, only the relationship between actual on-demand system quality and confirmation showed a weak, but significant relationship. Predictive quality of the model was not assessed in this stage (see Fig. 3).

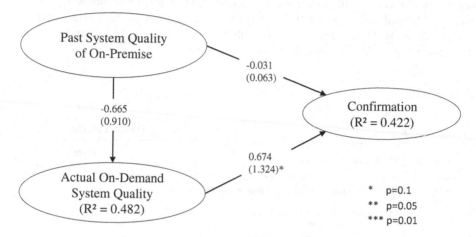

Fig. 3. Results of Path Analysis

5   Discussion, Limitations and Conclusions

The findings are a first initial test on exploring the cognition of past experience with on-premise and its impact on the confirmation of the actual (on-demand) system quality. The results don't show a significant impact of past system quality of on-premise on the connected constructs, however, past system quality of on-premise showed to explain 48 % of the variance in actual on-demand system quality. Future research might therefore find that past system quality significantly affects confirmation indirectly by influencing the actual on-demand system quality. Especially when sample sizes get larger, the significance level of the propositions might rise, and the effect size is already in a decent area. The directions of the effects (negative/positive) were correctly predicted based on theoretical assumptions.

The paper has several limitations which are mainly due to the early stage of research. However, two main limitations can be found within the paper. First, the significance levels of the weights of the formative measures are not significant, making it difficult to interpret the results on a statistical basis, as the results might be biased due to measurement errors. Therefore, to overcome this weakness, the sample size has to be enlarged, or the formative constructs have to be measured differently (e.g. reflective). Secondly, the exclusion as expectations a theoretically developed and empirically proven antecedent of confirmation makes the interpretation of the results difficult. Maybe past experience plays a role when building expectations; however, it might be that expectations do not influence confirmation in this specific context. Deriving answers from this very broad setting is difficult, especially, as the constructs are not significant.

Further research has to theoretically and empirically include the expectations construct to gain results which can be transferred into the existing body of knowledge. Additionally, the sample has to be enlarged to gain more viable results. The portion of variance explained by past experience with on-premise concerning actual performance highlights a direction with which we will further investigate. Other areas of research will have to find out on which antecedents the confirmation of the cloud enterprise systems depends. Many variables might influence confirmation, like attitude towards the software provider or general trust into cloud offerings.

Appendix

ID	Item	Quality Criteria	
Formative Measures		Outer Weights	t-value
Past System Quality of On-Premise (Adapted from Wixom and Todd 2005*)			
PE1	Our previous information system provided information in a timely fashion.	-0.62	0.82
PE2	Our previous information system operated reliably.	-0.86	0.88
PE3	Our previous information system could be flexibly adjusted to new demands or conditions.	1.39	1.27
PE4	Our previous information system was secure.*	0.22	0.45
Actual On-Demand System Quality (Adapted from Wixom and Todd 2005)			
SQ1	Our cloud enterprise system provides information in a timely fashion (response time).	0.03	0.10
SQ2	Our cloud enterprise system operates reliably and stable.	-0.22	0.61
SQ3	Our cloud enterprise system can be flexibly adjusted to new demands or conditions.	1.16	2.81
SQ4	Our cloud enterprise system is secure.*	0.22	0.38
*Newly created.			

Reflective Measures		Outer Loadings	t-value	Composite Reliability	AVE
Confirmation *(Adapted from Bhattacharjee 2001)*				0.90	.75
CO1	My experience with using our cloud enterprise system was better than what I expected.	0.88	4.96		
CO2	The quality of the cloud service provided by our cloud enterprise system was better that what I expected.	0.91	5.44		
CO3	Overall, most of my expectations from introducing my cloud enterprise system were confirmed (reverse coded).	0.82	3.38		

References

1. Raihana, G.F.H.: Cloud ERP - a solution model. Int. J. Comput. Sci. Inf. Technol. Secur. **2**(1), 76–79 (2012)
2. Armbrust, M., et al.: A view of cloud computing. Commun. Assoc. Comput. Mach. **53**(4), 50–58 (2010)
3. Klaus, H., Rosemann, M., Gable, G.G.: What is ERP? Inf. Syst. Front. **2**(2), 141–162 (2000)
4. Monsaas, J.A.: Learning to be a world-class tennis player. In: Bloom, B.S. (ed.) Developing Talent in Young People, pp. 211–269. Ballantine Books, New York (1985)
5. Whiting, R.: The right SaaS pitch for SMBs: the newsweekly for builders of technology solutions. CRN **1294**, 12 (2010)
6. Oliver, R.L.: A cognitive model of the antecedents and consequences of satisfaction decisions. J. Mark. Res. **17**(4), 460–469 (1980)
7. Jerram, C., Treleaven, L., Cecez-Kecmanovie, D.: Knowledge sharing as a km strategy - Panacea or Tyranny. In: Proceedings of the 14th Australasian Conference on Information Systems. Association for Information Systems, Perth (2003)
8. Bhattacherjee, A.: Understanding information systems continuance: an expectation-confirmation model. Manage. Inf. Syst. Quart. **25**(3), 351–370 (2001)
9. Patterson, P.G., Johnson, L.W., Spreng, R.A.: Modeling the determinants of customer satisfaction for business-to-business professional services. J. Acad. Mark. Sci. **25**(1), 4–17 (1997)
10. Spreng, R.A., MacKenzie, S.B., Olshavsky, R.W.: A reexamination of the determinants of consumer satisfaction. J. Mark. **60**(3), 15 (1996)
11. Benlian, A., Kourfaris, M., Hess, T.: Service quality in software-as-a-service: developing the saas-qual measure and examining its role in usage continuance. J. Manage. Inf. Syst. **28**(3), 85–126 (2011)
12. Wang, Y.: The role of SaaS privacy and security compliance for continued SaaS use. In: 7th International Conference on Networked Computing and Advance Information Management (2011)
13. Anderson, E.W., Fornell, C., Rust, R.T.: Customer satisfaction, productivity, and profitability: differences between goods and services. Mark. Sci. **16**(2), 129–145 (1997)
14. Hoyle, R.H. (ed.): Statistical Strategies for Small Sample Research. Sage Publications, Thousand Oaks (1999)
15. Hulland, J.S.: Use of partial least squares (PLS) in strategic management research: a review of four recent studies. Strateg. Manag. J. **20**(2), 195–204 (1999)

16. Park, L., Cho, J., Rao, H.R.: The effect of pre- and post-service performance on consumer evaluation of online retailers. Decis. Support Syst. **52**(2), 415–426 (2012)
17. Lehrer, C., Constantiou, I.D., Hess, T.: Examining the determinants of mobile location-based services' continuance. In: International Conference of Information Systems (2011)
18. Wen, C., Prybutok, V., Chenyan, X.: An integrated model for customer online repurchase intention. J. Comput. Inf. Syst. **52**(1), 14–23 (2011)
19. Yin, G., Cheng, X., Zhu, L.: Understanding continuance Usage of social networking services: a theoretical model and empirical study of the chinese context. In: International Conference of Information Systems (2011)
20. Venkatesh, V., et al.: Extending the two-stage information systems continuance model: incorporating UTAUT predictors and the role of context. Inf. Syst. J. **21**(6), 527–555 (2011)
21. Petter, S., DeLone, W., McLean, E.: Measuring information systems success: models, dimensions, measures, and interrelationships. Eur. J. Inf. Syst. **17**(3), 236–263 (2008)
22. DeLone, W.H., McLean, E.R.: The DeLone and McLean model of information systems success: a ten years update. J. Manage. Inf. Syst. **19**(4), 9–30 (2003)
23. Davis, F.D., Bagozzi, R.P., Warshaw, P.R.: User acceptance of computer technology: a comparison of two theoretical models. Manage. Sci. **33**(8), 982–1003 (1989)
24. Alman, D.H.: Colour-why the world isn't grey. In: Rossotti, H. (ed.) Colour Research & Application 1989, vol. 14, p. 44. Princeton University Press, Princeton (1985)
25. Plous, S.: The Psychology of Judgement and Decision Making. McGraw Hill, New York (1993)
26. Wixom, B.H., Todd, P.A.: A theoretical integration of user satisfaction and technology acceptance. Inf. Syst. Res. **16**(1), 85–102 (2005)
27. Moore, G.C., Benbasat, I.: Development of an instrument to measure the perceptions of adopting an information technology innovation. Inf. Syst. Res. **2**(3), 192–222 (1991)
28. Mackenzie, S.B., Podsakoff, P.M., Podsakoff, N.P.: Construct measurement and validation procedures in MIS and behavioral research: integrating new and existing techniques. Manage. Inf. Syst. Q. **35**(2), 293–334 (2011)
29. Petter, S., Straub, D., Rai, A.: Specifying formative constructs in information systems research. MIS Q. **31**(4), 623–656 (2007)
30. Nunnally, J., Berstein, I.: Pyschometric Theory. McGraw, New York (1994)
31. Fornell, C., Larker, D.F.: Evaluating structural equation models with unobservable variables and measurement error. J. Mark. Res. **18**(1), 39–50 (1981)
32. Hair, J.F.: A Primer on Partial Least Squares Structural Equation Modeling (PLS-SEM). SAGE Publications, Thousand Oaks (2014)
33. Ringle, C., Wende, S., Will, A.: SmartPLS 2.0 (beta), University of Hamburg (2005). http://www.smartpls.de Accessed 28 March 2007

A Benefit Expectation Management Framework for Supply Chain Management Systems

Wenjuan Wang[1]([⊠]) and Felix Ter Chian Tan[2]

[1] Facutly of IT, Shanghai Ocean University, Shanghai, China
wangwj@shou.edu.cn
[2] Australian School of Business, University of New South Wales,
Sydney, Australia
f.tan@unsw.edu.au

Abstract. Organizations invest heavily in Supply Chain Management Systems (SCMS) expecting to receive the benefits claimed by software vendors and implementation partners. Reports suggest a growing dissatisfaction among client organizations due to an increasing gap between expectations and realization of SCMS benefits. This study presents a Benefit Expectation Management Framework for SCMS, based on the Expectation-Confirmation Theory. The expected benefits of SCMS are derived through 41 vendor-reported customer stories and academic papers. The expected benefits are then compared with the benefits realized at a case organization in the fast moving consumer goods industry sector that has implemented SAP Supply Chain Management System seven years ago. The study findings argue for the value of managing client expectations of vendor purported benefits in light of the longer lifecycle and multiple employment cohorts of SCMS. The comparison of benefit expectations and confirmations highlight that, while certain benefits are realized earlier in the lifecycle, other benefits could take almost a decade to realize.

Keywords: Supply chain management · SCM benefits · Case study · Content analysis

1 Introduction

Organizations adopt Supply Chain Management System (SCMS) expecting benefits to the organization and its functions. When implementing a SCMS, organizations typically expect to increase their efficiency and effectiveness of the entire Supply Chain from the acquisition of raw materials to the distribution of finished goods to the retailers/customers [1–4]. Effective supply chains or networks have become increasingly critical for organizations, in order to compete in the global market and networked economy [5].

© Springer International Publishing Switzerland 2015
D. Sedera et al. (Eds.): Pre-ICIS 2010-2012, LNBIP 198, pp. 247–270, 2015.
DOI: 10.1007/978-3-319-17587-4_16

Although there is a rapid growth of SCMS market over the last decade,[1] organizations are facing mounting challenges with in realizing benefits through SCMS. Tarokh and Soroor [8] note that companies face challenges in achieving the planned business goals, and often fail to complete SCMS projects on-time and on-budget, resulting poor end-user satisfaction. Reflecting on findings of ERP studies [9, 10], SCMS benefits are also expected to flow to the organization throughout its lifecycle rather than realizing all-at-once. Therefore, a lifecycle-wide understanding of SCMS benefits and realization and a plan for benefits expectation management are essential for organizations to attain the full potential of SCMS.

This study develops a Benefit Expectation Management Framework for SCMS employing the Expectation-Confirmation Theory (ECT) [11, 12]. Herein we argue that, to the extent the organizations manage their expectations of SCMS benefits effectively, they are able to attain higher levels of benefits yielding and satisfaction. Our Benefit Expectation Management Framework demonstrates the flow of total benefits to the organization using a ten-year SCMS lifecycle since go-live to the expected major upgrade. The framework demonstrates that certain SCMS benefits are attainable at early stages of the lifecycle, while other benefits could take as long as ten years to realize. Furthermore, all SCMS benefits in our framework are categorized according to operational, management and strategic levels. This study takes a similar approach to prior studies [13–15] who applied ECT to investigate general IS, knowledge management systems, and organizational Voice over Internet Protocol systems respectively, examining the variables of 'Expectations', 'Perceived Performance', 'Disconfirmation' and 'Satisfaction' and their relationships in a new context of SCMS.

The paper begins by introducing the theoretical premise of the study. Next, the research design and research methods are introduced. Then, the expectations of SCMS are derived through content analysis. Subsequently, the perceived benefits of SCMS are explored and identified through case study in a large dairy manufacturer. The analysis on the confirmation level of SCMS expectations in the case organization are further conducted based on which an SCMS Benefit Expectation Management Framework is developed. This is followed with a discussion on the key factors affecting the confirmation levels of SCMS expectations. Finally, the theoretical and practical implications of this study and its limitations are summarized.

2 Theoretical Foundation

Expectation-Confirmation Theory (ECT) provides the theoretical lens for this research. ECT has been widely used in the consumer behavior literature to study customer satisfaction, post-purchase behavior and service marketing in general [11, 12, 16] (see Fig. 1). According to ECT, an individual first forms an initial expectation of a specific product/

---

[1] According to Gartner Research Group, the worldwide SCMS market grew 17.6 % in 2007, leading to US$5.9 billion in license and maintenance revenue [6]. AMR Research Group also has a positive expectation of SCMS market to top US$8 billion by 2010. The steady growth of the SCMS market is also evident in the spending for 2008 in Europe, the Middle East and Africa where it is estimated at 11.1 billion Euros [7].

service prior to purchase. Second, the individual accepts and uses that product/service. Following a period of initial consumption, the individual forms perceptions about the performance of the product/service consumed. Third, the individual assesses its perceived performance compared with his/her original expectation and determine the extent to which his/her expectation is confirmed (disconfirmation). Fourth, the individual forms a level of satisfaction, or affect, based on his/her confirmation level and the expectation on which that confirmation was based [11, 12]. Satisfaction is viewed as the key construct in management disciplines for building and retaining a loyal base of long-term consumers [17, 18]. For consumer products/services, the satisfied consumers form a repurchase intention, while dissatisfied users do not continue with subsequent purchases.

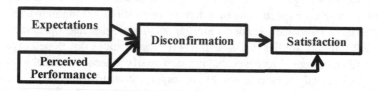

Fig. 1. Constructs of the expectation-confirmation theory

IS researchers have adopted ECT to study IS products/services in settings including online banking [19], e-commerce service [12], computer-based tutorial [20], internet service [21], web portal context [22], net-based customer service systems [23], and application service provider services [24]. Some of these studies assess the implications of expectations and confirmations on user satisfaction [25, 26], while others focus on the continuance of the IS product/service [12, 19]. However, such applications of ECT in the IS discipline have been *limited to simple IS products/services*. More specifically, the analysis of these studies is at the level of the individual end users who make the decision of selecting, using and discontinuing the IS product/service.

Only a handful of IS studies have employed ECT to gauge user expectations and to determine levels of satisfaction. Staples et al. [13] applied ECT to investigate whether the expectations of general IS benefits matched received benefits. Nevo and Chan [14] applied ECT to study the user expectations and satisfaction of knowledge management systems. Nevo and Wade [15] employed the theory to study how to avoid dissatisfaction with organizational IS, taking an organizational Voice over Internet Protocol solution as an example. These three studies identified some unique features of organizational IS which make the application of ECT in this field more complicated than the study of traditional consumer products and services. Insights into applying ECT to study SCMS expectations have been drawn from those studies.

Applying ECT is also motivated by academic research that evidences a growing gap between IS benefits purported by software vendors and the benefits realized by the client organizations [13, 27]. Studies prove that a greater gap between expectations and confirmation is most likely to yield lower levels of satisfaction amongst the client organizations, which ultimately hinder the potential of IS [see 13, 14, 28, 29]. However, unlike traditional consumables where benefit confirmation is immediate, SCMS benefits are realized throughout the lifecycle with some benefits realized several years after the 'go-live' date. Given the time lag of benefits realization and high expectations associated with SCMS, a careful management of benefit expectations is warranted [13]. For example, prior studies [30, 31] found that high expectations may lead to lower levels of user satisfaction, when it is not managed well.[2] From the perspective of the strategic goals, planning and alliances, applying ECT to SCMS can guide the client organization and SCMS vendors to establish long-term partnerships through improved satisfaction of client organizations. Higher-level satisfaction of client organizations will further aid SCMS vendors to attract more clients to adopt their SCMS solutions.

Applying ECT in this context, three theoretical extensions are made. First, the SCMS expectations of the organization are derived through vendor customer success stories, and not through the organization itself. As per suggestions of Nevo and Chan [14], organizations develop expectations of software innovations through customer stories and advertorials of software vendors. Similar methodologies and observations were made in ERP adoption studies [9, 38–40], where organizations developed expectations based on similar sources. Moreover, having past nearly a decade since the implementation, it was deemed unrealistic to get the organization to recall what their initial expectations were. Similarly, having already been exposed to the benefits, retrospective expectations would have introduced biasness of the benefit expectations.

Second, unlike traditional consumer products/services, such as pens, cars, clothes, or e-commerce websites, where the individual develops his/her 'expectations', 'confirms' through consumption experience and develops a level of 'satisfaction', SCMS relate to multiple stakeholders. Moreover, while daily use is often resumed by the operational end users, purchase decisions and decision to upgrade (re-purchase) are often made only by the strategic management. The satisfaction levels of strategic management with SCMS are driven by their own confirmation levels of their expectations, as well as by the satisfaction of other stakeholders in the organization. Therefore, the strategic staff should place emphasis on gathering perceptions from all key stakeholder groups [14]. Consequently, strategic staff can assess the SCMS success and also determine whether SCMS is beneficial to discontinue/continue updating or adopting further modules of the SCMS package.

The third theoretical extension relates to the time lag between expectations, confirmations and satisfaction levels. Unlike day-to-day consumables, full benefits of SCMS take much longer to eventuate. Similar to findings of Ross and Vitale [10] and Shang and Seddon [9] in relation to ERP systems, it is likely that the organization would undergo a 'dip' in performance immediately after the implementation of SCMS, and seem to expect a long-term return on the investment in their SCMS ranging from 10 to 20 years.

Thus, in this study, all constructs are measured at the organizational level. Interviews were conducted with all key-user-groups, designed to understand SCMS benefits at operational, management and strategic levels. Moreover, the organizational benefits

---

[2] Though not suggested in ECT, IS researchers have established strong significant links between user satisfaction and IS success [32–34], organizational effectiveness and performance [35, 36], decision making and efficiency [37], and continued adoption [12, 19].

consisted of both direct and indirect benefits across the whole client organization. Correspondingly, similar to the approach of Nevo and Wade [15], constructs of Disconfirmation and Satisfaction were the aggregate of perceptions of all stakeholder groups. The detailed data sources for each construct measurement are illustrated and fully justified in the following sections.

3   Research Design

The research design entails two main phases: (1) the content analysis phase, to explore the pool of expected benefits of SCMS, and (2) the case study phase, to identify the perceived benefits of SCMS in a large corporation and related factors controlling the confirmation of the expected benefits of SCMS and further impacting client satisfaction. The two main phases of the research involve six sub-steps. As shown in Fig. 2, Step 2 (search for the academic literature) and Step 3 (search for vendor stories) constitute the two data sources of the content analysis phase, while Step 5 (exploratory) and Step 6 (explanatory) are the two main steps of our case study phase, serving as the stages for exploring and interpreting, respectively.

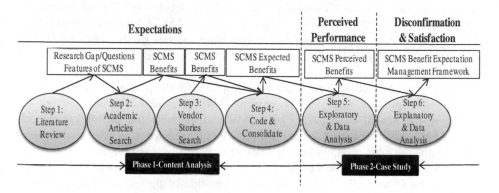

Fig. 2. Research design

The objective of the content analysis is to identify the expectations of SCMS by exploring reports of the potential benefits of SCMS. To achieve this goal, the data sources selected for content analysis had to cover the potential benefits of SCMS through the entire lifecycle, derive the pool of SCMS benefits at a global level, and represent current SCMS use by the top benchmarking corporations. As our research focus is on the post-adoption stage of SCMS use when the system becomes relatively mature, it is difficult to track the pre-expectations of the client organization in practice. This is due to multiple reasons: for example, the staff who were in charge of the system adoption may have left, or the end users may not be the same users who experienced the implementation of the system. Moreover, the method of asking end users and managers to recall what expectations they held before the system can introduce recollection errors [41], and it will be difficult to distinguish expectation and experience. Therefore, we gather the expectations of the client organization on SCMS from secondary resources, in line with extant IS study findings [such as 13–15]. Two data sources were selected for this phase: (1) ScienceDirect database and top-tier IS journals and conferences,[3] and (2) software vendor success stories on top vendor websites. The novelty of the phenomena and the exploratory nature of the research in identifying SCMS benefits justify the inclusion of vendor-reported customer stories as a source of evidence.

Keywords such as "SCM benefits/value/impacts/payoffs", "supply chain management benefits/value/impacts/payoffs" and "supply chain management systems benefits/value/impacts/payoffs" were used to search the titles, abstracts and full text of relevant articles across the ScienceDirect database and top IS journals and conferences. The inclusion of the ScienceDirect database ensured that the search results incorporated SCMS articles from multiple disciplines. A total of 21 key relevant studies (see Appendix 1) were considered to be in the topic domain, with the years of publication spanning from 2000 to 2008. Popular SCMS vendors including SAP, Oracle, JDA software, Ariba and Manhattan Associates [42] were investigated, from which the top two vendors – SAP and Oracle – were selected as the second data source considering their dominant market share and representative SCMS solutions. A total of 20 customer stories were extracted from the SAP and Oracle websites, with 10 cases for each vendor respectively (see Appendix 1). The selected 20 vendor-reported cases covered a variety of modules of SCMS, multiple industries and different countries. All 20 vendor-reported cases relate to large global corporations and their uses of SCMS are at different points in the SCMS lifecycle. Other customer stories were reported on the SAP and Oracle websites but weren't used because the coding results of the 20 cases arrived at theoretical saturation [43].

The case study method is particularly appropriate for the purpose of this study, as our research questions are "how" questions [44] that delve into the process of managing the benefit expectations of SCMS and examine the underlying factors affecting the confirmation of the expectations and their impact on user satisfaction. Specifically, the main objectives of the interviews in this case study are: (1) to explore the received benefits of SCMS by the case organization, and (2) to identify the underlying factors affecting the mechanism of confirmation of the expectations and their impact on satisfaction.

4   Expectations of SCMS

Having identified the 21 studies through literature, each article was carefully read and analyzed for benefit statements. This yielded a total of 150 SCMS benefit statements which were later synthesized to 58 unique benefit statements of SCMS. This synthesis process removed overlapping items to attain mutual exclusivity and parsimony. This inductive approach, following guidelines of Gable, Sedera and Chan [34], attempted to retain the original words as much as possible. To avoid personal bias, two researchers synthesized the SCMS benefit statements separately following agreed guidelines. First,

---

[3] The journals canvassed include: MISQ, ISR, JMIS, I&M, EJIS, ISJ, JAIS, JSIS, JIT, DSS, MS. The conferences include: ICIS, AMCIS.

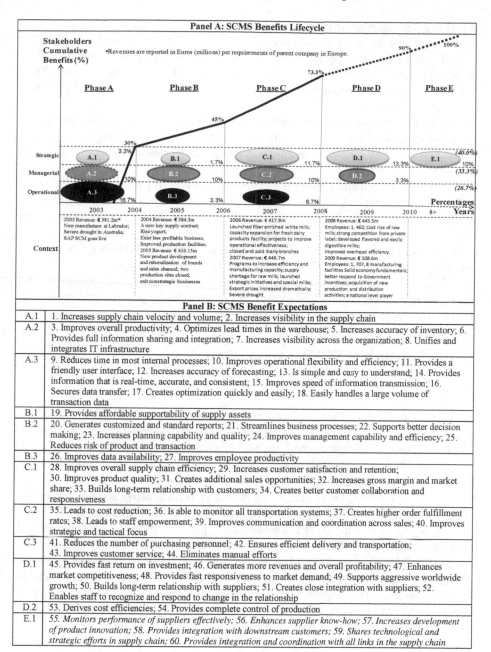

Panel A: SCMS Benefits Lifecycle

Panel B: SCMS Benefit Expectations

A.1	1. Increases supply chain velocity and volume; 2. Increases visibility in the supply chain
A.2	3. Improves overall productivity; 4. Optimizes lead times in the warehouse; 5. Increases accuracy of inventory; 6. Provides full information sharing and integration; 7. Increases visibility across the organization; 8. Unifies and integrates IT infrastructure
A.3	9. Reduces time in most internal processes; 10. Improves operational flexibility and efficiency; 11. Provides a friendly user interface; 12. Increases accuracy of forecasting; 13. Is simple and easy to understand; 14. Provides information that is real-time, accurate, and consistent; 15. Improves speed of information transmission; 16. Secures data transfer; 17. Creates optimization quickly and easily; 18. Easily handles a large volume of transaction data
B.1	19. Provides affordable supportability of supply assets
B.2	20. Generates customized and standard reports; 21. Streamlines business processes; 22. Supports better decision making; 23. Increases planning capability and quality; 24. Improves management capability and efficiency; 25. Reduces risk of product and transaction
B.3	26. Improves data availability; 27. Improves employee productivity
C.1	28. Improves overall supply chain efficiency; 29. Increases customer satisfaction and retention; 30. Improves product quality; 31. Creates additional sales opportunities; 32. Increases gross margin and market share; 33. Builds long-term relationship with customers; 34. Creates better customer collaboration and responsiveness
C.2	35. Leads to cost reduction; 36. Is able to monitor all transportation systems; 37. Creates higher order fulfillment rates; 38. Leads to staff empowerment; 39. Improves communication and coordination across sales; 40. Improves strategic and tactical focus
C.3	41. Reduces the number of purchasing personnel; 42. Ensures efficient delivery and transportation; 43. Improves customer service; 44. Eliminates manual efforts
D.1	45. Provides fast return on investment; 46. Generates more revenues and overall profitability; 47. Enhances market competitiveness; 48. Provides fast responsiveness to market demand; 49. Supports aggressive worldwide growth; 50. Builds long-term relationship with suppliers; 51. Creates close integration with suppliers; 52. Enables staff to recognize and respond to change in the relationship
D.2	53. Derives cost efficiencies; 54. Provides complete control of production
E.1	55. Monitors performance of suppliers effectively; 56. Enhances supplier know-how; 57. Increases development of product innovation; 58. Provides integration with downstream customers; 59. Shares technological and strategic efforts in supply chain; 60. Provides integration and coordination with all links in the supply chain

Fig. 3. The SCMS benefit expectation management framework

the 30 SCMS benefit statements were discussed to form the initial coding scheme. Then two researchers coded the 120 SCMS benefit statements separately. Finally, after all the coding was finished, the two researchers compared results until consensus was attained.

The inter-coder agreement for the analysis of the academic literature was 76.5 %, surpassing the minimum agreement rate of 70 % suggested by Krippendorff [45].

Following a similar process, a total of 179 initial SCMS benefit statements were derived from the 20 customer stories taken from the SAP and Oracle websites. They were then synthesized to 54 unique benefit statements of SCMS, attaining an initial inter-coder agreement of 81.3 %.

Finally, the two data sets (58 benefits from academic papers and 54 from practitioner cases) were consolidated, following the same synthesis process, yielding 60 (sixty) unique benefits of SCMS. The consolidated benefit categories are listed in Panel B of Fig. 3.

The 60 SCMS benefits capture the expectations of SCMS in the organization. In addition, the expectations derived through the content analysis allude to the flow of benefits across the SCMS lifecycle. The benefit statements highlighted pragmatic life-cycle-wide management questions critical to organization. They include: "How long would organizations take to realize most benefits of SCMS?"; "What benefits are realized early in the lifecycle?"; "What benefits are realized much later in the lifecycle?"; and "What stakeholders are responsible in receiving/generating SCMS benefits?" The SCMS Benefit Expectation Management Framework developed herein attempts to provide answers to the aforementioned questions.

5   Confirmation of SCMS Expectations

5.1   Case Context

Three conditions formed the selection of the case organization. First, the use of SCMS in the case organization should at its post-adoption stage, where the system has become stable and relatively mature. Second, the SCMS product employed by the case organization should be from a reputable vendor for comparability. Third, the case organization must be an active user of the SCMS. The case of Company Dairy,[4] a large fast moving consumer goods (FMCG) manufacturer in Australia, is particularly appropriate for our purpose as it has employed the core SCMS product from a top vendor (SAP) for more than seven years. Company Dairy is a leading dairy producer for large supermarkets and other large retail outlets. The FMCG sector is considered a prime example for the applications of SCMS. The specific SCM challenges that FMCG manufacturers face include: (1) highly perishable and shorter shelf-life of products, (2) rapid and unpredictable demand changes, (3) the requirement of specialized storage, (4) unpredictable fluctuations in supply of raw materials due to weather changes, (5) stringent manufacturing and logistical requirements imposed through legislation and standards, (6) seasonality, and (7) a highly demand driven supply chain. With retailers playing the most dominant role in the entire supply chain, the retailer satisfaction is critical for Company Dairy's business. Manufacturers of FMCG, especially in the dairy industry, must maintain a tri-partite balance between three competing factors: customer service, operating overheads, and inventory shelf-life. Attaining the optimal tri-partite balance between these three

---

[4] Name of the company is suppressed to maintain anonymity of the company.

aspects is challenging for all manufacturers, but is especially challenging for dairy producers and in general for the FMCG sector.

The Australian wholesale grocery market provides unusual challenges to dairy product manufacturers. First, due to the vast geographic area, manufacturers must plan their product distribution carefully. This is particularly true with FMCG products. Secondly, the retail grocery market in Australia is dominated (70 %) by two major retailers providing them with tremendous bargaining capability [46]. Thirdly, the deregulation of dairy industry in 2001 [47] led to substantial consolidations and acquisitions leaving only two major dairy producers (Company Dairy is one of the two) [48–50].

Company Dairy implemented SAP SCMS in 2003. After more than seven years in operation, the system is stable and relatively mature. The SAP Advanced Planner and Optimizer (APO) is the main SCMS product adopted by the case company. Initially, Company Dairy only used one module to do part of its business, but it subsequently fully implemented the three modules of SAP APO: Demand Planning, Supply Network Planning, and Production Planning/Detailed Scheduling. The SCM system covers around 95 % of the company's SCM business requirements.

5.2 Data Collection and Analysis

Research access was negotiated and was granted in July 2009. Eight interviews were conducted with the key members of the National Demand and Supply Planning department, Information Technology department, and Logistics and Supply Chain department over a period of 15 months. The duration of interviews ranged from 0.5 h to 2 h, up to 10 h totally. In addition, a series of interactive seminars on SAP SCM in Company Dairy, of approximately 20 h, was delivered by the Supply Planning Manager at the authors' academic institution. Another 2 h interactive seminar on SAP SCM was given by a senior SAP SCM architect, who participated in the adoption and post-support of Company Dairy's SCMS, with a 30 minute follow-up interview. The interviews and seminars were digitally recorded and later transcribed for data analysis. Public presentations of Company Dairy's Chief Procurement Offer were also gathered as the perspective of top management staff. The Chief Procurement Offer plays a key role in representing the company and reporting the performance of its SCMS to public conferences and workshops. Through these steps, we gathered multiple perspectives on SCMS benefits from all levels of stakeholders. Further, short surveys focusing on the timetable of SCMS benefit realizations were sent to the interviewees as complementary data in the second phase of the case study. The SCM experience of the participants ranged from 5 to 15 years.

The interview questions were tailored to the role of the interviewee and were designed to be open-ended and exploratory in nature. Each question was non-leading, and at the same time non-passive to maintain a critical balance between spontaneity and control over the interview [51]. To improve the efficiency and validity of the interviews and seminars, two researchers conducted all the interviews together. One researcher was responsible for asking questions, while the other researcher made notes. While the face-to-face interviews and seminars formed our primary source of data [52], they were supplemented by contact emails, newspaper articles, organizational documents, annual reports, and information from the corporate website. Notes from direct observations of how staff use the system for their work were also used to corroborate the data obtained.

To take advantage of the flexibility that the case study affords, data analysis was performed in tandem with data collection [53]. The emergent concepts in an interview were verified in the following interview until the state of theoretical saturation was reached, which is the point at which it was possible to comprehensively explain the findings of the case study and no additional data could be collected or added to improve the developed framework [51]. The findings from the content analysis formed the initial set of themes through which to analyze the received SCMS benefits by the case organization. In addition, a systematic verification procedure was established to ensure that each finding was supported by at least two sources of data [54]. Data analysis was carried out by recursively iterating between the empirical data, relevant literature and theories, and the emergent concepts and relationships [51].

A multi-level data analysis strategy was employed to analyze the empirical data. Level 1 analysis focused on identifying the received benefits of SCMS in the case organization, and then analyzing the current misalignment between expected and received benefits of the SCMS. The subsequent data analysis levels focused on identifying and examining the underlying factors affecting the level and mechanism of confirmation of SCMS expectations and the corresponding impacts on user satisfaction. Grounded in the case study data, two key factors affecting the confirmation level of SCMS expectations were identified: long timetable and different stakeholder groups. Therefore, Level 2 analysis focused on the timetable of SCMS benefit realization, and Level 3 analysis focused on the classification of SCMS benefits according to each stakeholder group. The ways in which those two key factors affect the confirmation level of SCMS benefit expectations are illustrated and discussed thoroughly in the following sections.

5.3   Expectation Confirmation Through Perceived Benefits of SCMS

Findings of case study data analysis Level 1, Level 2 and Level 3 were integrated and consolidated into a final SCMS Benefit Expectation Management Framework as shown in Fig. 3. This framework clearly shows all the perceived benefits and unperceived benefits by Company Dairy, based on the pool of 60 expected benefits of SCMS. A calculation of the percentage of the difference between the number of perceived benefits and number of expected benefits was employed in this study to assess the level of confirmation of SCMS expectations. This simple and straightforward assessment technique was in line with the means of the "self-assessment" technique proposed by Fearon and Philip [55–57] to measure the alignment between expected and received benefits from Electronic Data Interchange. The level of confirmation of SCMS expectations is also reflected in the SCMS Benefit Expectation Management Framework in Fig. 3.

Overall perceived performance of the SCMS. The participants confirmed the comprehensiveness and completeness of the 60 expected benefits of SCMS (listed in Panel B of Fig. 3). They admitted that no other SCMS benefits could be supplemented. This was confirmed in comments by the Supply Planning Manager, for example, who states: "*All these benefits can cover almost everything*" and the Logistics & Supply Chain Manager who states: *"Yeah, I think you guys have done most of the job, I can't think out other benefits that we expected from this [system]."*

Although some technical limitations still exist, the SCMS is seen as a critical and important tool for the staff to use to perform their job effectively and efficiently. For example, the Supply Planner states: *"I think the system is quite good...APO is more straightforward, like you can see all the calculations. From my point of view, it is perfect"*. The Demand Planning Manager also expresses her satisfaction by stating: *"Oh, yes, definitely the benefits overwhelm the issues...I wouldn't go without the system because now, you have to update the orders, you will put into the data into strategy looking at it or leaving it. This will give you everything for my forecast."*

The SCMS at Company Dairy helps optimize the tri-partite balance between (i) customer service, (ii) operational overheads, and (iii) inventory shelf-life. Good customer service can lead to high customer satisfaction, which can further improve customer loyalty and retention. Through advanced forecasting and planning enabled by the system, the reputation of Company Dairy has improved a lot, and it has been listed as one of the top suppliers of the two dominated retailers. As stated by the National Demand & Supply Planning Manager, *"We strive to get this balance using tools like SAP APO...and it really helps"*. The National Demand & Supply Planning Manager also states that: *"Ok, I think for any company, actually I mean for any FMCG, the biggest advantage will be to optimize satisfaction and customer service...During the last two years, we have been in the top three key suppliers for both Coles and Woolworths; we never sit in the 'warning list' again!"*

The SCMS helps to mediate the tri-partite balance with higher customer service and lower cost in operational overheads and lower stock losses. Company Dairy has achieved this by optimizing the allocation of resources through accurate forecasting and planning. The Production Planner explains how the system leads to cost reduction by controlling the stock level and operational overheads:

> *"With the planning capability of the system, you optimize your warehouse dispatch, you are streamlining you production flow without additional operational overheads...you are not building the stock. You are not making too much. Everything is just supplying adjustment time technology...and there are so much cost effective associated to have the system there. That would be the primary driver behind it...uh, we have definitely realized some, cost savings."*

Confirmation of perceived benefits. The Level 1 analysis of the case study was conducted on the interviews, the short surveys and the contact emails, taking the expected benefits of SCMS (listed in Panel B of Fig. 3) as the coding scheme. The results show that Company Dairy has accumulatively received 54 SCMS benefits of the pool of 60 expected benefits from SCMS in the lifecycle. A large proportion (90 %) of the expected benefits of SCMS has been received by Company Dairy after using the system for seven years. Hence, there is little misalignment between expected benefits and confirmed benefits. Such a high level of confirmation of the expectations of SCMS verifies our approach of taking vendor-reported cases and extant academic literature as the sources of the expected benefits of SCMS. The Production Planner confirms some of the benefits: *"Yes, after solving the initial issues, we achieved the collaboration between all stakeholders in our supply chain [internal]. What we flow over is the logistics side of it, having that visibility in the system, uh, having that visibility into notify the* *requirements in advance...also we can share the information [in the system]."* The Senior IT Business Analyst continues confirming: *"after the system become stable, our forecasting and planning become faster and accurately. We're capable to serve our customer in an effective and efficient manner."*

It is inferred from the undelivered expected benefits[5] and also indicated by the informants that the SCMS in Company Dairy has not realised the function of full integration with its key suppliers and customers. Nevertheless, Company Dairy has an interest in involving its suppliers in its SCMS although this may not happen in the near future due to some limitations. However, the interviewees raised some doubt about further development of the trading partner relationships in the whole supply chain, because many constraints exist. Different system rules among companies make it difficult to form integration of the whole supply chain. Furthermore, full integration is beneficial for the whole supply chain, but it may have negative impacts for an individual company. Each company has their own interests and confidential business information, which makes them reluctant to accept a fully integrated SCMS. For example, full integration may cause the retailers to lose their dominant position in the whole demand-driven supply chain. If they want to change to another supplier, they will spend more money integrating their current systems with the system in a new supplier. The Supply Planning Manager of Company Dairy states:

> *"I think this (integration and coordination of all the links in the supply chain) can be realised later, but not in a short time. Because this will refer what kind of systems you are using, and then what the system interfaces are. The ideal situation is there is a standard SCM system, which all companies are using. All companies are using the same SCM systems, and then the interfaces between different systems are smooth, then every company will use the system, there is no problems ... but now, the interface between systems are horrible, you use yours, and we use ours. Everybody knows that the concept of whole integrations and coordination of supply chain is right, and all of us should go into this direction."*

The SCMS Benefit Expectation Management Framework. By analyzing the confirmed benefits of SCMS and related controlling factors, the SCMS Benefit Expectation Management Framework has been derived inductively as shown in Fig. 3. This framework consolidates the two perspectives of managing SCMS expectations: lengthy lifecycle and multiple stakeholder groups. The two researchers worked together on the development of this framework until full consensus was reached.

The Panel B of Fig. 3 presents the categories of SCMS expectations derived through content analysis. The Panel A of Fig. 3 illustrates a timetable of SCMS benefits and the benefits to different stakeholder groups. The x-axis represents the years from go-live in 2003–2010, with two-year intervals. The y-axis represents the three stakeholder groups: operational, managerial and strategic users [58]. All the percentages in the framework are based on the pool of 60 expected benefits of SCMS (listed in Panel B of Fig. 3).

---

[5] The six undelivered SCMS benefits are: *Monitors performance of suppliers effectively (55), Enhances supplier know-how (56), Increases development of product innovation (57), Provides integration with downstream customers (58), Shares technological and strategic efforts in supply chain (59), and Provides integration and coordination with all links in the supply chain (60)* (listed in Fig. 3).

The cumulative benefits attained across the lifecycle are depicted using a trend line. The percentages on the trend line demonstrate the cumulative benefits according to the five phases. A further analysis is made according to the key stakeholders of SCMS. Grouped at the y-axis, each row demonstrates the percentages of benefits attributed to each key stakeholder group. Furthermore, the bubble and its corresponding notation points to the benefits realized in each phases (e.g. Bubble A.1 denoting benefits to strategic cohort in the first lifecycle phase). The undelivered benefits in Company Dairy are highlighted in italics in bubble E.1. More detailed descriptions, discussion and relevant explanations and justification of how this framework contributes to the application of ECT in the SCMS setting are illustrated in the subsequent section.

6 Discussion and Interpretation

6.1 The Lifecycle of SCMS Benefits

Prior Research in ERP studies has revealed that organizations undergo a dip in organizational performance post the go-live of the system [10]. Similarly, many argue that organizations investing in IT applications realize some benefits immediately, while other benefits take much longer to eventuate [9, 40, 59, 60]. More importantly, many researchers [14, 61] highlight the need for continuous lifecycle management of IS benefits. The SCMS benefits timetable presented in this study is therefore of substantial value to both practice and academia. As stated by the Logistics & Supply Chain Manager in Company Dairy: *"Some benefits from the system [SCMS] emerged earlier, while others take time…it is better to know them to plan well."* In order to develop a benefits timetable, we next decided on the time intervals between each phase. Following Ross and Vitale [10] and Jurison [57], we employed an annualized timetable to capture benefits. From all participating respondents, we sought agreement of the 'first instance of evidence' for each SCMS benefit.

Observations related to the lifecycle of benefits. From the framework developed in this study (Fig. 3), it is evident that Company Dairy has attained almost all the benefits outlined in the expected benefits of SCMS (listed in Panel B of Fig. 3). However, it is clear that the organization did not see all benefits at once or immediately after the go-live date. Company Dairy has taken nearly seven years to attain 90 % of the cumulative benefits, with 10 % of benefits yet to be realized. A number of observations are made from the SCMS benefits timetable:

Early issues – In the early months after implementation of the SCMS (July 2003-early 2004), it was difficult for Company Dairy to see the benefits, and, on the contrary, a lot of issues emerged due to the use of a new system. The IT Business Analysis explains: *"Like we are not expecting anything in the first year, because so many issues, testing the calculations, be familiar with the system, change the process…and the second year needs to have to solve most of these issues…we should be able to start seeing something in two years."*

Short-term benefits – Observing the pattern of benefits realized by the case organization, it is evident that Company Dairy at first managed to realize almost 30 % of the expected SCMS benefits. Through optimizing system capabilities (such as the friendly user interface, easy to understand, real-time, accurate and consistent information, and flexibility and efficiency), the overall productivity and supply chain velocity and volume improved in a relatively very short time (to the end of 2004). The Supply Planning Manager recalls: *"If it was like data mining or something about the system capabilities, it would be very, very short term...once we realized that the system is in good nick,[6] we were confident about getting other benefits."*

No financial or customer satisfaction benefits in the short term – It is interesting to note that Company Dairy neither anticipated nor received any financial or customer satisfaction benefits in the first three years. The IT Business Analyst explains: *"You couldn't talk anything in two years, because you're talking millions and millions of dollars here...we are talking at least five years [for the return on investment]."* The IT Business Analyst confirms the waiting time: *"The first few years were really challenging...we were scrambling to show business benefits and cost saving...but the senior management gave us 2–3 years to prove the value of the system...any large capital investment would take 2–3 years to pay off."*

Five years to reach the primary target – The main target of Company Dairy is to achieve high levels of customer satisfaction and customer service, and these were largely realized around five years after go-live of the system. The Demand Planning Manager confirms: *"After around five years, we achieved great success and our customers put us in their top supplier list. But before that, we often got complaints, or they cancelled their orders."* Using objective company reports, we triangulated the statements of employees on increases in new product lines and experimental products, especially those targeting niche markets (see highlights for 2005–2008 in Panel A of Fig. 3).

Mid-term performance – The mid-term (2005–2007) benefits through the SCMS have made Company Dairy much more agile and flexible. In 2008, Company Dairy faced rapid increases in milk prices in Australia. The Demand Planning Manager explains: *"With the severe drought milk prices hit the roof..., we had standard agreements with retailers and we could not 'pass the buck[7]' to them [retailers]...we then managed to optimize our production and cut-down all possible wastage."* In 2009, the entire dairy industry in Australia faced a challenge of a different sort when one of the leading milk label producers went out of action for several weeks. The Logistics & Supply Chain Manager describes the efficient response of Company Dairy to this crisis: *"We had loads of milk bottles waiting for labels...we ran reports through the system to create batches of dispatches and prioritized them according to our customers."*

Long-term goals – Despite achieving most benefits pertaining to system capabilities within the first year, 7 years from go-live Company Dairy is yet to realize some benefits. The National Demand & Supply Planning Manager outlines future plans:

"We are at the moment checking the continuous improvement whether there is some more benefits for us, like the Global Available to Promise [a module of SAP SCM], and we might try from September to use the details for a specific group of products. No optimization work can be done in SAP SCM at the moment, but there is a plan for the next year...in terms of complete

---

[6] Australian slang for 'working well' or 'in good condition'.

[7] Australian slang for passing the cost of something to the other party.

control of the timing of production, we haven't realized it yet, but there are a few projects to address this issue."

The attaining of some of the currently undelivered benefits in the long run would be possible, such as with all links in supply chain, fully integrating with suppliers and customers, and fully sharing the technological and strategic efforts in the supply chain. The Supply Planning Manager acknowledges the challenge of these tasks, and emphasizes that achieving them will take time:

"This is a difficult thing in Australia... for example, complete integration between suppliers, retailers and suppliers may cause Woolworths [one of the dominant retailers] to lose their dominant positions in the whole supply chain...I think this [full integration and coordination of all the links in the supply chain] will take some time to achieve, not something that we can do in a short time."

Lifecycle to confirm SCMS expectations. As indicated in ECT, consumer satisfaction is formed based on the extent to which his/her expectation is confirmed (disconfirmation) and the expectation on which that confirmation was based [11, 12]. We identified the clients' expectations of SCMS through content analysis, revealed the misalignments between those expectations and the received benefits of SCMS in the client case organization, and identified the timetable of SCMS benefit realization. A lifecycle-wide understanding of SCMS benefits realization was derived as a key controlling factor which will affect the confirmation level of expectations.

As shown in the framework in Fig. 3, it is clear that the confirmation of SCMS benefit expectations depends on time, and the confirmation level will further affect the satisfaction of the SCMS client case organization. Hence, if we neglect the salient factor of time in the mechanism of confirmation, the client satisfaction will be significantly different. For example, when evaluating the performance of SCMS at an early lifecycle phase, the client users may feel dissatisfied, due to the lack of benefits (less expectations are confirmed). However, when evaluating the long term performance of the SCMS, the client users will feel highly satisfied, with most expectations confirmed.

When including the factor of time into both pre-expectations and the post-confirmation stages, satisfaction of the organization will change substantially. When establishing their expectations of the SCMS, clients should remember that confirmation of these expectations will have a long lifecycle, as shown in the different time periods in Fig. 3. Organizations should therefore take a long-term approach in observing full potentials of SCMS. Moreover, the SCMS Benefit Expectation Management Framework will allow organizations to maintain high levels of satisfactions though careful mitigation of confirming expectations based on the lifecycle phase.

Thus, by taking time into consideration, the client organizations can form realistic expectations and perceive a higher confirmation level, increasing the confidence of the client organization on SCMS.

6.2 Benefits Related to Multiple Stakeholder Groups

Our case study collects benefits confirmations at three employment cohorts. Our data collections with Demand Planners, Supply Planners, Production Planners, Demand

Planning Managers, Supply Planning Managers, National Demand & Supply Planning Managers, Logistics & Supply Chain Managers, Senior IT Business Analysts, and Chief Procurement Officers, cover all key stakeholder groups. The data analysis results show that different stakeholder groups have unique perceptions of SCMS benefits with some potential overlap. This is consistent with the findings of the extant IS success/evaluation and IS benefits studies [15, 34, 58].

In both the management science and IS disciplines, the multiple stakeholder perspective is emphasized when conducting organizational research, and the classification of three stakeholder groups, namely, the strategic, management and operational, has reached consensus among those researchers [58, 62]. Seddon et al. [63] argue that when evaluating IS, it is very important to clarify from whose perspective the effectiveness is being judged. Seddon's joint work with Shang [9] proposes a rational method to classify the benefits of enterprise systems according to different stakeholder groups. A similar approach was also taken in a study by Shanks et al. [64], which categorizes the benefits of customer relationship management systems into operational, tactical and strategic levels.

Observations related to multiple stakeholder groups. From the data analysis in the framework in Fig. 3, a number of observations are made in relation to stakeholder groups:

Important for all stakeholder groups – The percentage of benefits relevant to each stakeholder group demonstrates that the SCMS brings substantial benefits to all three stakeholder groups, with 40 %, 33.3 % and 26.7 % of benefits for the strategic, management and operational stakeholders, respectively. This indicates that when evaluating SCMS benefits, perspectives from all stakeholder groups should be taken into account. Different stakeholder groups will benefit from SCMS in different aspects. Hence, only collecting perspectives from one or two particular stakeholder groups can not represent the real perceived performance of the system.

Key benefits to each stakeholder group – Different stakeholder groups have their own key benefit expectations from the SCMS with some overlap. The operational users of the system are more concerned about the system flexibility, efficiency, data availability and reliability. For example, a Production Planner at Company Dairy states: *"Uh, it is user-friendly, it provides the data, provides everything accurate, especially accurate data mining and research numbers, and verifying thing, that was very difficult"*. The Demand Planner also emphasizes system quality, stating that: *"It's very user friendly and it's also very integrity, isn't it?...it's quite easy to say the same screen by integrating the system of person in Melbourne or Brisbane City, to see the same screen, and same information is available for them, much easier to use."*

The management staff emphasize the high quality of the reports and the effective allocation of resources and control in the whole supply chain management process. For example, the Supply Planning Manager states: *"Yes, the biggest thing is the collaboration between all the stakeholders in the supply chain. What we flow over is the logistics side of it. Uh, having that visibility in the system, having that visibility into notify in advance, according to the requirements, also you can share."* The National Demand & Supply Planning Manager confirms this focus, saying that: *"APO was offering more advantages over the R3 system...we have strong forecast accuracy measure and reports now* via *BW [Business Warehouse]...they give me the reports and it works well.*"

Customer satisfaction, market competitiveness and partner relationships, identified as the key targets of Company Dairy, are the keen expectations of both management and strategic staff. The Chief Procurement Officer elaborates: "*Managing post contract supplier and internal relationships enables continuous improvement delivering continued benefits to both organizations.*" The National Demand & Supply Planning Manager states: "*During the last two years, we have been in the top three key suppliers for both Coles and Woolworths.*"

Integration of two perspectives – Observing each phase of the lifecycle, it's evident that the benefits emphasis shifts from operational to strategic along the lifecycle. For example, in Phase A, operational staff receive more benefits than management and strategic cohorts. However, later in the lifecycle (e.g. Phase D & E), strategic benefits outweigh the benefits of operational staff.

Impacts of multiple stakeholders on confirmation of SCMS expectations. The perspective of multiple stakeholders has significant implications for the application of ECT in the SCMS context. When forming expectations of the SCMS, the collection of organizational benefits of SCMS should represent the perceptions of all stakeholder groups. The same mechanism should be employed into the measurements of received SCMS benefits. Correspondingly, the confirmation of the expectations should be bundled with multiple stakeholders. For SCMS, there exists interdependence of the satisfaction among the various stakeholders. The satisfaction of decision makers or the authorized staff is not only driven by their own disconfirmation; it is also influenced by the confirmation level of other stakeholders' expectations in the organization. Satisfaction from any particular stakeholder group can not reflect the true satisfaction of the client organization.

Furthermore, the combination of the two perspectives – long timetable and multiple stakeholders– also has substantial implications. First, it provides insight into how to better manage expectations for each stakeholder group. The operational users can expect to receive SCMS benefits in the short term (within the first three years). It is recommended that a five-year plan is set for management staff to receive most of their expectations of the SCMS. The strategic staff should focus more on the long-term returns on SCMS investment (more than five years). Second, it adds new insights for the conduct of assessments and studies on SCMS benefits, success and evaluation. Organizations should place emphasis on the viewpoints of the operational and management staff when evaluating the benefits and success of SCMS in the short and middle term, while placing more attention on the perspectives of strategic staff when evaluating the performance of the SCMS in the long term.

7 Conclusion

7.1 Limitations and Future Research

This study has several limitations. The study findings are derived through a single case in the FMCG sector. Although researchers have acknowledged that a thorough single case study can be acceptable for qualitative research if the case selected is an interesting case of "typical and legitimate endeavor" [65, 66], a common criticism of the methodology is the problem of generalizability or external validity [52]. While acknowledging the limitations of the single case study, we are confident that our study provides valid and generalizable insights to other SCMS adopters, perhaps more relevance to the FMCG industry. The developed SCMS Benefit Expectation Management Framework was not only grounded in the real case sector but also based on the claims of extant literature and practical reports and further corroborated by the findings of some widely accepted works in the IS and management literature. Therefore, this study conforms to the principles of "analytic generalization" [44]. In future research, multiple case study and follow-up large-scale survey will be designed to broadly generate and validate the developed framework and its relevant discussions so that the boundary conditions of our study can be better defined.

A second limitation may arise from the biases involved in informant recall. Although we designed a good means to avoid recollection bias and difficulties when deriving the expectations of SCMS expectations, the retrospective nature of the collected case study data still existed, including personal interviews, interactive seminars and short surveys. However, given that Company Dairy has used their SCM system for more than seven years, it was not possible to collect the case data from this prior period. Nevertheless, some measures were employed by the researcher to mediate the retrospective bias. One measure was to put emphasis on the viewpoint of staff who joined Company Dairy since the beginning of the SCMS use [67]. Another measure was to adopt a systematic data verification procedure to ensure that all the information used in this study were triangulated by at least two sources of data [54, 66, 67].

There exist substantial potentials of this research to generate more contributions through future research. First, a nonlinear benefit gain perspective will be employed in the next stage to enrich the SCMS benefit expectation framework and yield more interesting results relevant to the SCMS benefit lifecycle. In addition, more detailed analysis will be conducted on the priority for SCMS benefits realization. Furthermore, more theoretical analysis, such as the Resource-Based View of IT business value and contingency theory will be linked with the findings of this study to achieve more theoretical and practical implications.

7.2   Theoretical and Practical Implications

By developing the Benefit Expectation Management Framework for SCMS, this study makes several theoretical and practical contributions. First, this study fills an important gap in the literature. Although there exists well-publicized research on Enterprise Resource Planning system benefits [9, 40] and Customer Relationship Management system benefits [64, 68], there is a dearth of research on studies evaluating SCMS benefits [69]. This is the first try to consolidate and extend extant SCMS benefit studies to develop a comprehensive benefit framework for SCMS. Further, the case study results have shown that there is little misalignment between claimed benefits from the literature and vendor success stories and perceived benefits in the real case. Such a high level of alignment confirms the validity of the SCMS benefits reported by vendors and prior researchers.

Secondly, with a longitudinal study of SCMS benefits in a real case spanning over seven years, this study draws a SCMS benefit lifecycle perspective. This study has operationalized the timetable of SCMS benefits realization across the system lifecycle and identified the relevant contextual information through a real case sector. This is an advanced progress and contributes to the extant IS benefits literature.

Thirdly, this study is believed to be the first to apply ECT to study the expectations of SCMS. Originating in consumer behaviour literature to study individual consumer satisfaction and post-purchase behaviour, ECT has been adopted by IS researchers to study the satisfaction of individual users. This study contributes to the emerging research stream applying ECT to study organizational IS satisfaction [13–15, 70]. More specifically, this study attempts to apply ECT to study SCMS expectations and client satisfaction. By conducting content analysis and case study, this study has operationalized the construct of Expectation, Perceived Performance and Confirmation in the context of SCMS. As with the original ECT model, Satisfaction was treated as a dependent construct of ECT in the SCMS setting and was affected directly by the level of confirmation of SCMS expectations. Furthermore, this study has identified two key factors controlling the level of confirmation of SCMS expectations and exposed the underlying mechanisms affecting the Confirmation construct in the SCMS setting and their mediating impacts on SCMS client satisfaction.

On the other hand, a number of practice implications are expected. First, the framework can aid a client organization to understand return on investment from its SCMS applications, the time-contingent nature of SCMS benefit realization, and the correlation of SCMS benefits to different stakeholder groups. This multifaceted framework can serve as a benchmark for the client organization to better manage its expectations of the SCMS and to monitor the performance of the system. Second, by examining the factors related to the confirmation of client expectations, such a framework can help to enhance the level of client satisfaction, and encourage continued adoption of other SCMS applications. Third, for organizations hesitating to invest in SCMS, this study provides a clear picture of the generation of SCMS benefits, assisting them to make better decisions. Consequently, it may accelerate the development of SCMS products. Finally, it can also aid vendors to better popularize their products, improve client satisfaction, and attract more customers. However, because our study conducted a case study in one organization, the potential for generalization is not strong. We have confidence, however, that the results are applicable for most manufacturing companies in the FMCG industry.

Appendix 1: 20 Vendor-Reported Cases & 21 Academic Articles

20 vendor-reported cases		21 academic articles	
Knorr-Bremse AG	Bartter Enterprises	Vakharia [71]	Liu and Hu [72]
Danisco A/S	Timex Corporation	Frohlich [73]	Kim et al. [74]
DIRECTV	LG Electronics	Sahin and Robinson [75]	Eggert et al. [76]
Robert Bosch LLC	Intersil Corporation	Choy et al. [77]	Zhang and Li [78]
Sappi Fine Paper Europe	Panasonic Factory Solutions Singapore	Subramani [79]	Spekman and Carraway [80]
Lekkerland	Xsigo Systems	Elizabeth et al. [81]	Craighead et al. [1]
Brown-Forman	Koch, Neff & Volckmar GmbH (KNV)	Goutsos and Karacapilidis [82]	Dehning et al. [2]
Telefonica de Espana	YMCA of Metropolitan Los Angeles	McLaren et al. [83]	Kenneth [84]
Siemens Medical	Sealing Devices	Hsu [85]	Kärkkäinen et al. [86]
Borealis	North Tyneside Council	Auramo et al. [87]	Ketikidis et al. [3]
		Auramo et al. [88]	

References

1. Craighead, C.W., et al.: Enabling the benefits of supply chain management systems: an empirical study of electronic data interchange (EDI) in manufacturing. Int. J. Prod. Res. **44**(1), 135–157 (2006)
2. Dehning, B., Vernon, J.R., Robert, W.Z.: The financial performance effects of IT-based supply chain management systems in manufacturing firms. J. Oper. Manage. **25**(4), 806–824 (2007)
3. Ketikidis, P.H., et al.: The use of information systems for logistics and supply chain management in South East Europe: current status and future direction. Omega **36**(4), 592–599 (2008)
4. Laudon, K.C., Laudon, J.P.: Essentials of Management Information Systems. Pearson Education, Inc., Upper Saddle River (2005)

5. Stadtler, H.: Supply chain management - an overview. In: Stadtler, H., Kilger, C. (eds.) Supply Chain Management and Advanced Planning. Springer-Verlag Berlin Heidelberg, Heidelberg (2002)
6. Eschinger, C.: Report Highlight for Dataquest Insight: Supply Chain Management Software Market Share Analysis, Worldwide, 2007. Gartner (2008)
7. Pang, C.: Report Highlight for Dataquest Insight: Business Application Software Market Share Analysis, EMEA, 2007. Gartner (2008)
8. Tarokh, M.J., Soroor, J.: Supply chain management information systems critical failure factors. In: IEEE International Conference on Service Operations and Logistics, and Informatics. Shanghai, China (2006)
9. Shang, S., Seddon, P.B.: Assessing and managing the benefits of enterprise systems: the business manager's perspective. Inf. Syst. J. **12**(4), 271–299 (2002)
10. Ross, J.W., Vitale, M.R.: The ERP revolution: surviving vs thriving. Inf. Syst. Front. **2**(2), 233–241 (2000)
11. Oliver, R.L.: A cognitive model of the antecedents and consequences of satisfaction decisions. JMR J. Mark. (pre-1986) **17**(4), 460–469 (1980)
12. Bhattacherjee, A.: Understanding information systems continuance: an expectation-confirmation model. MIS Q. **25**(3), 351–370 (2001)
13. Staples, D.S., Wong, I., Seddon, P.B.: Having expectations of information systems benefits that match received benefits: does it really matter? Inf. Manag. **40**(2), 115–131 (2002)
14. Nevo, D., Chan, Y.E.: A temporal approach to expectations and desires from knowledge management systems. Decis. Support Syst. **44**, 298–312 (2007)
15. Nevo, D., Wade, M.R.: How to avoid disappointment by design. Commun. ACM **50**(4), 43–48 (2007)
16. Patterson, P.G., Johnson, L.W., Spreng, R.A.: Modeling the determinants of customer satisfaction for business-to-business professional services. Acad. Mark. Sci. J. **25**(1), 4–17 (1997)
17. Decina, P., et al.: Continuation ECT in the management of relapses of major affective episodes. Acta Psychiatr. Scand. **75**(6), 559–562 (2007)
18. Oliver, R.L., Westbrook, R.A.: Profiles of consumer emotions and satisfaction in ownership and usage. J. Consum. Satisf. Dissatisf. Complain. Behav. **6**, 12–27 (1993)
19. Bhattacherjee, A.: An empirical analysis of the antecedents of electronic commerce service continuance. Decis. Support Syst. **32**(2), 201–214 (2001)
20. Bhattacherjee, A., Premkumar, G.: Understanding changes in belief and attitude towards information technology usage: a theoretical model and longitudinal test. MIS Q. **28**(2), 229–254 (2004)
21. Erevelles, S., Srinivasan, S., Rangel, S.: Consumer satisfaction for internet service providers: an analysis of underlying processes. Inf. Technol. Manage. **4**(1), 69–89 (2003)
22. Lin, C.S., Wu, S., Tsai, R.J.: Integrating perceived playfulness into expectation-confirmation model for web portal context. Inf. Manag. **42**(5), 683–693 (2005)
23. Piccoli, G., et al.: Net-based customer service systems: evolution and revolution in website functionalities. Decis. Sci. **35**(3), 423–455 (2004)
24. Susarla, A., Barua, A., Whinston, A.B.: Understanding the service component of application service provision: an empirical analysis of satisfaction with ASP services. MIS Q. **27**(1), 91–123 (2003)
25. Khalifa, M., Liu, V.: The state of research on information system satisfaction. J. Inf. Technol. Theory Appl. **5**(4), 37–49 (2004)
26. Zviran, M., Erlich, Z.: Measuring is user satisfaction: review and implications. Commun. Assoc. Inf. Syst. **12**, 81–103 (2003)

27. Zimmermann, J.: CRM systems still promise more than they deliver. http://www.techrepublic.com/article/crm-systems-still-promise-more-than-they-deliver/5034620

28. Trauth, E.M., Farwell, D.W., Lee, D.: The IS expectation gap: industry expectations versus academic preparation. MIS Q. **17**(3), 293–307 (1993)

29. Aggarwal, R., Rezaee, Z.: Total quality management for bridging the expectations gap in systems development. Int. J. Proj. Manage. **14**(2), 115–120 (1996)

30. Ginzberg, M.J.: Early diagnosis of MIS implementation failure: promising results and unanswered questions. Manage. Sci. **27**(4), 459–478 (1981)

31. Marcolin, B.: The impact of users' expectations on the success of information technology implementation. The University of Western Ontario (1994)

32. DeLone, W.H., McLean, E.R.: The DeLone and McLean model of information systems success: a ten-year update. J. Manage. Inf. Syst. **19**(4), 9–30 (2003)

33. Gelderman, M.: The relation between user satisfaction, usage of information systems and performance. Inf. Manag. **34**(1), 11–18 (1998)

34. Gable, G., Sedera, D., Chan, T.: Re-conceptualizing information system success: the IS-impact measurement model. J. Assoc. Inf. Syst. **9**(7), 377–408 (2008)

35. Gelderman, M.: The relationship between user satisfaction, usage of information systems and performamance. Inf. Manag. **34**(1), 11–18 (1998)

36. Zviran, M., Erlich, Z.: Measuring IS user satisfaction: review and implications. Commun. Assoc. Inf. Syst. **12**, 81–103 (2003)

37. Au, N., Ngai, E.W.T., Cheng, T.C.E.: A critical review of end-user information system satisfaction research and a new research framework. Omega **30**(6), 451–478 (2002)

38. Teltumbde, A.: A framework for evaluating ERP projects. Int. J. Prod. Res. **38**(17), 4507–4520 (2000)

39. Somers, T.M., Nelsonb, K.G.: A taxonomy of players and activities across the ERP project life cycle. Inf. Manag. **41**(3), 257–278 (2004)

40. Seddon, P.B., Calvert, C., Yang, S.: A multi-project model of key factors affecting orgnaizational benefits from enterprise systems. MIS Q. **34**(2), 305–328 (2010)

41. Lawrence, M., Loh, G.: Exploring individual user satisfaction within user-led development. MIS Q. **17**(2), 195–208 (1993)

42. Wailgum, T.: The Top Five Supply Chain Management Vendors. http://www.cio.com/article/391613/Report_The_Top_Five_Supply_Chain_Management_Vendors

43. Strauss, A., Corbin, J.: Basics of Qualitative Research: Techniques and Procedures for Developing Grounded Theory, 2nd edn. Sage, Thousand Oaks (1998)

44. Yin, R.K.: Case Study Research: Design and Methods, vol. 5, 3rd edn. Sage, Thousand Oaks (2003)

45. Krippendorff, K.: Content Analysis: An Introduction to Its Methodology. Sage, Beverly Hills (1980)

46. Carson, V.: Red spot special: Coles up for sale. http://www.smh.com.au/news/business/red-spot-special-coles-up-for-sale/2007/02/23/1171734017312.html

47. DairyAustralia. Deregulation. http://www.dairyaustralia.com.au

48. Doucouliagos, H., Hone, P.: Deregulation and subequilibrium in the Australian dairy processing industry. Econ. Rec. **76**(233), 152–162 (2007)

49. DairyAustralia. Australian Dairy Industry in Focus (2009). http://www.dairyaustralia.com.au/

50. Edwards, G.: The story of deregulation in the dairy industry. Aust. J. Agric. Resour. Econ. **47**(1), 75–98 (2003)

51. Walsham, G.: Interpretive case studies in IS research: nature and method. Eur. J. Inf. Syst. **4**(2), 74–81 (1995)

52. Walsham, G.: Doing interpretive research. Eur. J. Inf. Syst. **15**(3), 320–330 (2006)
53. Eisenhardt, K.M.: Building theories from case study research. Acad. Manag. Rev. **14**(4), 532–550 (1989)
54. Klein, H.K., Myers, M.D.: A set of principles for conducting and evaluating interpretive field studies in information systems. MIS Q. **23**(1), 67–93 (1999)
55. Fearon, C., Philip, G.: Self assessment as a means of measuring strategic and operational benefits from EDI: the development of a conceptual framework. Eur. J. Inf. Syst. **7**, 5–16 (1998)
56. Fearon, C., Philip, G.: An empirical study of the use of EDI in supermarket chains using a new conceptual framework. J. Inf. Technol. **14**(1), 3–21 (1999)
57. Fearon, C., Philip, G.: Measuring success of electronic trading in the insurance industry: operationalising the disconfirmation of expectations paradigm. Behav. Inf. Technol. **27**(6), 483–493 (2008)
58. Sedera, D., Tan, F., Dey, S.: Identifying and evaluating the importance of multiple stakeholders perspective in measuring ES-success. In: 14th European Conference on Information Systems. Gothenburg, Sweden (2006)
59. Jurison, J.: The temporal nature of IS benefits: a longitudinal study. Inf. Manag. **30**, 75–79 (1996)
60. Gattiker, T.F., Goodhue, D.L.: What happens after ERP implementation: understanding the impact of inter-dependence and differentiation on Plant-Leve outcomes. MIS Q. **29**(3), 559–585 (2005)
61. Heinonen, K.: Temporal and spatial e-service value. Int. J. Serv. Ind. Manag. **17**(4), 380–400 (2006)
62. Anthony, R.N.: Planning and Control Systems: A Framework For Analysis. Harvard University, Boston (1965)
63. Seddon, P.B., et al.: Dimensions of information systems success. Commun. AIS **2**(20), 40–55 (1999)
64. Shanks, G., Jagielska, I., Jayaganesh, M.: A framework for understanding customer relationship management systems benefits. Commun. Assoc. Inf. Syst. **25**, 263–287 (2009). Article 26
65. Lee, A.S., Baskerville, R.L.: Generalizing generalizability in information systems research. Inf. Syst. Res. **14**(3), 221–243 (2003)
66. Tan, B., et al.: Evolutionary sensemaking in enterprise applications implementation: insights from a state-owned enterprise in China. In: The 31st International Conference on Information Systems (2010)
67. Pan, S.L., et al.: The dynamics of implementing and managing modularity of organizational routines during capability development: insights from a process model. IEEE Trans. Eng. Manage. **54**(4), 800–813 (2007)
68. Dong, S., Zhu, K.: The business value of CRM systems: a resource-based perspective. In: the 41st Hawaii International Conference on System Sciences (HICSS) Big Island, Hawaii (2008)
69. Wang, W., Sedera, D.: A framework for understanding the benefits of supply chain management systems. In: Pacific Asia Conference on Information Systems, Brisbane, Australia (2011)
70. Lankton, N., McKnight, D.H., Thatcher, J.B.: Incorporating trust-in-technology into expectation disconfirmation theory. J. Strateg. Inf. Syst. **23**(2), 128–145 (2014)
71. Vakharia, A.: J., e-business and supply chain management. Decis. Sci. **33**(4), 495–504 (2002)
72. Liu, J., Zhang, S., Hu, J.: A case study of an inter-enterprise workflow-supported supply chain management system. Inf. Manag. **42**(3), 441–454 (2005)

73. Frohlich, M.T.: E-integration in the supply chain: Barriers and performance. Decis. Sci. **33**(4), 537–556 (2002)
74. Kim, K.K., Umanath, N.S., Kim, B.H.: An assessment of electronic information transfer in B2B supply-channel relationships. J. Manage. Inf. Syst. **22**(3), 293–320 (2005)
75. Sahin, F., Robinson, E.P.: Flow coordination and information sharing in supply chains: review, implications, and directions for future research. Decis. Sci. **33**(4), 505–536 (2002)
76. Eggert, A., Ulaga, W., Schultz, F.: Value creation in the relationship lifecycle: A quasi-longitudinal analysis. Ind. Mark. Manage. **35**(1), 20–27 (2006)
77. Choy, K.L., Lee, W.B., Lo, V.: Design of a case based intelligent supplier relationship management system–the integration of supplier rating system and product coding system. Expert Syst. Appl. **25**(1), 87–100 (2003)
78. Zhang, C., Li, S.: Secure information sharing in internet-based supply chain management systems. J. Comput. Inf. Syst. **46**(4), 18–24 (2006)
79. Subramani, M.: How do suppliers benefit from information technology use in supply chain relationships? MIS Q. **28**, 45–73 (2004)
80. Spekman, R.E., Carraway, R.: Making the transition to collaborative buyer-seller relationships: an emerging framework. Ind. Mark. Manage. **35**(1), 10–19 (2006)
81. Elizabeth, A.W., David, K.H., Mike, J.: Information systems development within supply chain management. Int. J. Inf. Manage. **24**(5), 375–385 (2004)
82. Goutsos, S., Karacapilidis, N.: Enhanced supply chain management for e-business transactions. Int. J. Prod. Econ. **89**(2), 141–152 (2004)
83. McLaren, T., Head, M., Yuan, Y.: Supply chain management information systems capabilities. An exploratory study of electronics manufacturers. Inf. Syst. eBusiness Manage, **2**(2–3), 207–222 (2004)
84. Kenneth, J.: Focused logistics - sense and respond logistics: a transformative autonomic supply chain management system. Logist. Spectr. **41**(3), 21–27 (2007)
85. Hsu, L.-L.: SCM system effects on performance for interaction between suppliers and buyers. Ind. Manage. Data Syst. **105**(7), 857–875 (2005)
86. Kärkkäinen, M., et al.: Roles of interfirm information systems in supply chain management. Int. J. Phys. Distrib. Logist. Manage. **37**(4), 264 (2007)
87. Auramo, J., Inkiläinen, A Kauremaa, J.: The roles of information technology in supply chain management. In: 17th annual NOFOMA Conference. Copenhagen Business School, Copenhagen, Denmark (2005)
88. Auramo, J., Kauremaa, J., Tanskanen, K.: Benefits of IT in supply chain management: an explorative study of progressive companies. Int. J. Phys. Distrib. Logist. Manage. **35**(2), 82–100 (2005)

Trends and Future Research in Enterprise Systems

Norbert Gronau[✉]

CER - Center for Enterprise Research, Potsdam University, August-Bebel-Str. 89,
14482 Potsdam, Germany
ngronau@lswi.de

Abstract. Different streams of influence affect the development, sales and use of enterprise systems in public and private organizations. This contribution highlights some of these influences covering the markets for enterprise systems, the used and needed technology and the usage in enterprises. Questions for further research stemming from this description are derived.

Keywords: ERP · Enterprise Resource Planning · Enterprise system · Market · Technology · Usability · Benefit · Business process

1 Introduction

The acronym ERP stands for Enterprise Resource Planning. Shankararaman and Lum [1] use the term ERP system as a synonym for Enterprise Systems (ES) which can be found frequently in US literature [2].

Robey et al. [3] defines an ERP system as an integrated, cross-functional systems that contain selectable software modules which address a wide range of operations within a firm, such as finance, accounting, human resources, sales, manufacturing and distribution. Another common definition is that an ERP system (1) should be capable of managing at least three resources such as personnel, materials, capacity, finance or information needed during the execution of the business processes and (2) data should be managed in an integrated way and (3) covering functions from various business areas [2].

There are many possible and often used viewpoints on enterprise systems. The obviously most often addressed perspectives in IS research are implementation and user acceptance. This contribution won't add to this kind of work. Instead it aims at more seldom experienced viewpoints where it hopes to find future research topics and from that also a contribution to solve problems in practice. These perspectives are the market perspective, the technology perspective and the enterprise perspective.

2 The Market Perspective

It is not very easy to observe relevant markets for enterprise systems due to missing information about relevant facts. For instance, if the market share of a certain vendor is

© Springer International Publishing Switzerland 2015
D. Sedera et al. (Eds.): Pre-ICIS 2010-2012, LNBIP 198, pp. 271–280, 2015.
DOI: 10.1007/978-3-319-17587-4_17

needed in a certain local market (e.g. Oracle ERP sales in Central Europe) only ballpark figures exists like rankings of software companies or given figures from analysts. It is not revealed whether their market share estimation is based on the number of licenses sold or the amount of money collected. Both figures can lead to wrong estimations about the market. Neither revenues nor user figures tell the whole story. In my point of view only counting companies is valid. One company uses typically one or more enterprise systems after deciding to do so. That decision is the relevant market aspect to observe (from science) and to influence (from ERP vendor's sales processes).

In this section the observed market shares of some internationally known ERP vendors are discussed as a result of the need to grow stemming form their business models. As a way to grow the sales process is described and frequently occurring hurdles identified.

2.1 Business Models

Business models propel the market, because they generate the fuel for ES vendors to invent new solutions, to adopt new technologies and to introduce new products.

In empirical literature, various imprecise definitions of business models can be found. One example is Pinson [4], who defines a business model as a method of doing business so that revenue is generated and the company is sustained. Another typical example from empirical literature can be found in Englen [5], who does not define the term business model itself. The identification of current and future customers as well the needs of customers (by qualitatively interviewing them) is part of the business model. Later, attractive pricing (going beyond a low price), providing reliability, and good value and service in case the customer needs assistance might also be attributed to the business model.

Timmers [6] defines a business model as the architecture for the product, information and service flows, including a description of the various business actors and their roles. Additionally, potential benefits for the various business actors and the sources of revenue constitute a business model [7]. Figure 1 gives an overview over ERP vendors business models [8].

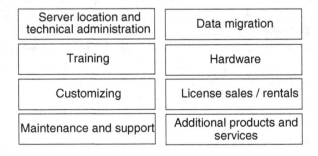

Fig. 1. Software vendor's business model [8]

Support fees sponsor the existing operation of the software company but they are in most cases not high enough to finance innovation. So buying other software vendors allows access to further support fees but does not allow sustainable growth. Sustainable growth is only possible with new customers. Therefore we suggest that market success is not only measurable by market share but also by growth, precisely by new customers generated by a certain ERP vendor.

We observe at the Center for Enterprise research since 2007 the central european ERP market [9] which is a saturated ES market. Although constantly new vendors try to conquer the European - especially the German market - most of them fail. Specially there is no vendor from the United States who is successful on the European market (MS Dynamics NAV and AX are products developed and supported from Denmark, only marketed by Microsoft Corp., USA).

2.2 Market Shares

Most numbers of market shares are wrong, because they measure the amount of money that a single ES vendor collects, but not the number of customers he was able to get. One ES means one decision. Our observed market share only covers ES projects that were reported in journals or on web pages. Figure 2 shows the Top Ten ERP vendors in Germany, covering 1340 projects from 2007 to 2013.

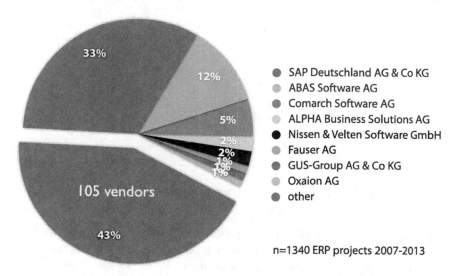

Fig. 2. Observed ERP market shares in Germany (source: CER)

It has to be stated that the number Six on the German market has an observed market share of less than 1 %. The market leader is "other". The US vendors Oracle and Microsoft are within this group. Also relevant for future research on software business models is that with the exception of SAP (and perhaps Comarch in Europe) no other German top vendor is known outside of Germany. Possibly the German market alone generates a steady stream of revenues for a sustainable existence of an ERP vendor. It has to be mentioned that for German software vendors huge potential markets lie outside the German-speaking regions that are not addressed nowadays.

2.3 Sales Process

What are possible reasons why the worldwide software giants Oracle and Microsoft don't succeed in Germany? One possible answer might be that Oracle is lazy in ERP sales, because as the most important database supplier in Germany it gets revenues from other software products than ERP. Interviews of the author of this contribution with leading European Oracle representatives cover this assumption. Microsoft Corp. itself does not sell directly to mid-size customers, but uses business partners that do nearly no marketing. Therefore their projects never show up in the web or the trade journals and their market share cannot be observed.

But for an observation of the market not only the static market share is relevant but also growth, which describes market dynamics. Figure 3 shows the net gain in new ERP customers on the German market for Oracle, Microsoft and SAP. While SAP was able to more than double its new customer numbers, and Microsoft Business Partners at least were able to publish more successful projects in the second observed period, Oracle shows severe problems to get a foot on the German ERP market.

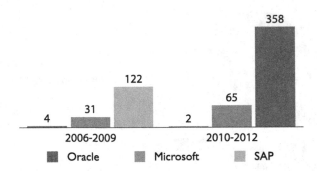

Fig. 3. Net new customers in two time periods (source: CER)

How can this be, all the while Oracles application run successfully all over the world? That points (beside other aspects) to the sales process and mistakes that can be made trying to sell a new ERP system to a potential customer. Figure 4 shows the sales process identified by Center for Enterprise Research at Potsdam University and possible mistakes that happen frequently during ERP sales processes. It has to be stated that these mistakes are in no way tied to just one ERP vendor.

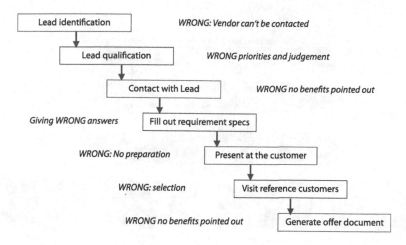

Fig. 4. Sales process and possible mistakes that effect sales success

3 Technology Perspective

The technology perspective covers not only ERP systems but in the same manner all kinds of enterprise systems. Following a very basic layered architecture there are at least three layers of interest with new developments that affect enterprise systems development and organizational integration. These layers are the data layer, application layer and the user interface layer.

3.1 Master Data Management

Master data lives even longer than Enterprise systems itself. As an example one may imagine an ES where the company name's maximal length is 38 characters. That is a hint that the underlying data model stems from a very old master data model that never was adjusted to fulfill today's needs.

Challenges in master data management comprise not only application landscapes but also organizational aspects.

Application landscapes. When master data is spread over multiple application systems normally different terminologies and field definitions are used. The data quality has to be maintained to assure consistency over different applications. Also dependencies between different applications might be found that cannot discovered easily. Examples might be:

- *"When the customer number starts with 77 then payment in advance is mandatory".*
- *"Delivery date 9.9.2099 means that the supplier has not yet provided a valid delivery date".*
- *"The contact person from the last order can be found in the 3rd line of the customer's address".*

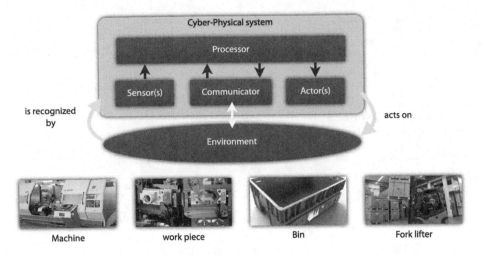

Fig. 5. Principal structure of a cyber-physical system [10]

Although these artifacts can easily be avoided with modern enterprise systems they can be found in most organizations nowadays due to the fact that sometimes very old applications are used beside newer ones and that the life span of an enterprise system can be more than 20 years. Data models can have an even longer life span.

Sometimes the IT administration has to guarantee the operation of an old system with an outdated architecture because the old application provides relevant functionality that is not easy to replace - often due to the specialized nature of the functionality.

After all, also the storage of master data itself may be spread over multiple applications, what can lead to data inconsistency.

Organizational challenges. Beside the above mentioned technical issues also organizational problems occur frequently. In the organization it might be not recognized that maintaining master data is important for the quality and speed of information processing. Often the departments just using ES functionality do not know enough about other departments needs for a high quality of their entered data. Most often there is no defined and controlled master data process so that nobody in the organization has a responsibility for the quality of master data.

3.2   Cyber-Physical Systems

Cyber-physical systems (CPS) include software-intensive systems with processors, sensors and actors to interact with the real world. The sensors capture physical data, store data and plan to co-operate with the real world based on that data and information. CPS are wirelessly and globally connected to other application systems through the internet and therefore able to use globally provided data and services. Control of CPS is also possible using multi-modal human-computer interfaces (voice and gestures) [10] (Fig. 5).

The huge rise in data volume that comes together with CPS is surely relevant for Enterprise systems. While a typical customer order has 50 kByte, which can be stored in the ERP system easily, that customer order will now generate 100 manufacturing orders, of which each will generate at least 10 work tasks that are traced by CPS at least every 10 s. That data handling alone leads to a data volume of more than one GB per single customer order.

In sharp contrast to that development the traditional approach of integrating new data sources in the enterprise system has been the complete incorporation of the data and its structure in the storage area. This approach is highly criticized because the complexity of the integrated system is so high that understanding its internal structure is nearly impossible. When now CPS are to be integrated into the application landscape it cannot be done by completely integrating their data into the common storage. Instead new architectural principles have to be incorporated in the organization that can combine peer-to-peer approaches from CPS with centralized master data management coming from traditional ERP systems.

Another aspect not covered in detail in this contribution is the need for content analyses of the CPS data to find out whether there is useful information in it. In manufacturing this search for information in CPS data can be named "Analytic Manufacturing" [11, 12].

4   The Enterprise Perspective

The enterprise perspective is the most interesting, because most of the market and technology perspectives are depicted in it as well. The term enterprise again also includes public organizations.

4.1   Usability

While for Operating systems like Apples OS X and Microsofts Windows numerous investigations about usability exist there is a lack of specially designed tools and methods to detect flaws in enterprise systems usability and to point out which effort these usability flaws have on quality and efficiency of the business processes modeled in the enterprise system.

A recent study from Potsdam University stated that even with experienced users up to 50 % of efficiency of the business processes is compromised by inadequate usability [13]. Although there can be training against usability flaws the menacing influence on process quality remains.

4.2   Adaptation

Adaptation is one of the most pressing issues concerning enterprise systems due to the long life span of enterprise systems and the frequent changes in their environment, manifesting in changes of products, customers, suppliers, markets, processes and organizational structures. These changes typically take place in a short time frame and often due to pressure from the competition. Sometimes it is not easy or not fast enough to

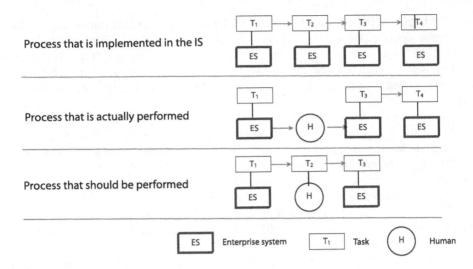

Fig. 6. Different processes that can be found in enterprises

adapt the enterprise system to these changes and additional systems or manual work-arounds are developed and implemented that heavily influence quality and efficiency of business processes [14].

In the context of IT systems adaptability means a change in the system to accommodate a change in its environment. More specifically, adaptation of an IT system is caused by change from an old environment to a new environment. It results in a new state of the system that ideally meets the needs of its new environment. Adaptability allows the system to recognize the need for changes and to respond itself with suited alternatives [15].

4.3   Fit Between Enterprise System and Processes

The purpose of enterprise systems is to model business processes into a consistent set of tasks and data to achieve a certain result that has a value for a customer. Therefore it is important to observe the differences between implemented, intended and actually used processes (Fig. 6).

There are different problems associated to business processes and enterprise systems that can be illustrated using the processes depicted in Fig. 6. Originally, when implementing the enterprise system, the first process in Fig. 6 was intended to use: all tasks are performed by functions of the enterprise system. Due to causes unknown to us the actual performed process includes a manual task, omitting one function of the enterprise system. This might occur after organizational changes that could not implemented into the enterprise system due to lacking time, knowledge or adaptability of the system. Additionally perhaps during the introduction of the enterprise system no process optimization took place. So the ideal process would look like the third depicted process.

Nowadays no method or tool is available to identify the fits nor to come up with possible solutions to it.

5 Conclusion and Further Work

Purpose of this contribution was to identify and describe new research questions for the enterprise systems research and practice community. These questions are at least:

- How can be determined which business models fit for which kind of product and market?
- Is there any systematic way to help software vendors to improve their sales process?
- How can foreign vendors come to the understanding of local markets necessary to be successful?
- What is necessary to cope successfully with master data, both from technical and organizational perspectives?
- Which IS architectures are able to cope with flooding data from cyber-physical systems?
- Which analytic methods, skills and organizational settings will help us to benefit of the incredible amount of data from cyber-physical systems?
- How can be measured that better usability improves business process quality?
- How enterprise systems, also existing systems, can become more adaptive?
- How can the fit between intended, implemented and performed processes be gauged?

Let me add a tenth question that points directly to every IS researcher. This questions asks, whether IS research in its current state will be helpful to answer the questions mentioned above. That to answer will be the task of the near future.

References

1. Shankararaman, V., Lum, E.K., Dale, S.: Integrating enterprise system's 3rd wave into IS curriculum. In: AMCIS 2012 Proceedings (2012), Paper 9. http://aisel.aisnet.org/amcis2012/proceedings/EnterpriseSystems/9
2. Gronau, N.: Enterprise Resource Planning: Architecture, Functions and Management of ERP Systems. Munich, Oldenbourg, 2nd ed. (2010)
3. Robey, D., Ross, J.W., Boudreau, M.-C.: Learning to implement enterprise systems: an exploratory study of the dialectics of change. J. Manage. Inform. Syst. **19**(1), 17–46 (2002)
4. Pinson, L.: Anatomy of a Business Plan: The Step-by-Step Guide to Building a Business and Securing Your Company's Future. aka associates, Tustin (2008)
5. Englen, P.: Business model review. Ind. Eng. **41**(7), 18 (2009)
6. Timmers, P.: Business Models for Electronic Markets. Electron. Mark. **8**(2), 3–8 (1998)
7. Brockmann, C.: An approach to design the business model of an ERP vendor. Ph.D. thesis, University of Potsdam (2014)
8. Brockmann, C., Gronau, N.: Business models of ERP system providers. In: Proceedings of the 15th Americas Conference on Information Systems, AMCIS. San Francisco, USA (2009)
9. Gronau, N.: Enterprise systems knowledge: a new way to detect changes in the ERP market in Central Europe. In: AMCIS 2009 Proceedings (2009), Paper 203. http://aisel.aisnet.org/amcis2009/203
10. Veigt, M.: Development of a cyber-physical logistics system (in German). Ind. Manage. **29**(1), 15–18 (2013)
11. Gronau, N.: Analytic manufacturing (in German). Prod. Manage. **17**(5), 19–21 (2012)

12. Konrad, B., Lieber, D., Deuse, J.: Striving for zero defect production. Intelligent manufacturing control through data mining in continuous rolling mill Processes. In: Windt, K. (ed.) Robust Manufacturing Control, pp. 215–229. Springer, Heidelberg (2013)
13. Fohrholz, C.: Usability of enterprise systems - lack of controllability mostly threat learnability. In: PRE-ICIS Workshop on Enterprise Systems Research in MIS, Orlando (FL), 15 December 2012
14. Katja, A., Norbert, G.: Adaptability concepts for enterprise resource planning systems - a component framework. In: AMCIS 2005 Proceedings (2005), Paper 150. http://aisel.aisnet.org/amcis2005/150
15. Andresen, K., Gronau, N.: An approach to increase adaptability in ERP systems. In: Khosrow-Pour, M. (ed.) (Hrsg.) Managing Modern Organizations with Information Technology: Proceedings of the 2005 Information Resources Management Association International Conference, pp 883–885. Idea Group Publishing, San Diego, CA, USA, (2005)

Author Index

Printed in the United States
By Bookmasters